A Common Law for the Age of Statutes

The Oliver Wendell Holmes Lectures are delivered annually at the Harvard Law School under a fund established out of a legacy to the Law School from Justice Holmes.

Guido Calabresi was the Holmes Lecturer in March 1977.

A Common Law
for the Age of Statutes

GUIDO CALABRESI

Harvard University Press

Cambridge, Massachusetts, and London, England

1982

Library of Congress Cataloging in Publication Data

Calabresi, Guido, 1932-
    A common law for the age of statutes.

    (The Oliver Wendell Holmes lectures)
    Bibliography: p.
    Includes index.
    1. Statutes—United States.   2. Common law—United States.
I. Title. II. Series.
KF425.C34   348.73   81-6747
ISBN 0-674-14604-2   347.308   AACR2

To Bianca, Nina, and Massimo

Acknowledgments

An invitation to give the Oliver Wendell Holmes Lectures at the Harvard University Law School in 1977 caused me to address in a systematic way the issues dealt with in this book. I am particularly grateful to Dean Albert M. Sacks and to the late Richard R. Baxter, Chairman of the Lecture Committee of the Harvard Law School, for their warm understanding, hospitality, and support.

As I started work on the lectures, and more and more as I turned them into a book, I came to realize how much this work owes to my teachers — in the classroom and out of it. More than anything else I have written, it stems from their wisdom and insights. I cannot mention them all, but I will list a few whose stamp on these pages is unmistakable: Alexander M. Bickel, Charles L. Black, Jr., Grant Gilmore, Albert M. Sacks, Harry Wellington, whom I thank too for his always generous friendship and support as Dean of the Yale Law School, and of course Justice Hugo Lafayette Black. They shaped the view of law this book mirrors, and the more than twenty years that have passed since any of them has formally taught me have in no way lessened their influence.

I cannot begin to list those of my friends and colleagues who have at various times read parts of this book and made valuable suggestions. I thank them all and know that they will recognize their contributions and accept my gratitude.

The staff of the Yale Law Library, and especially Arthur A. Charpentier, Librarian and Associate Dean, have been of great help, as have Becky Vasco and Gill Dougherty, my secretaries in Cambridge. I have in so many things I have written thanked Susan

Lucibelli, my secretary at the Yale Law School, that there would seem little left to say. Her patience, dedication, speed, and cheerfulness are always a wonder.

At different times as this book was being written, I visited the European University Institute in Florence at the invitation of Professor Mauro Cappelletti. I should like to thank him for his hospitality, as well as the Faculty of Law of the University of Cambridge, where I have spent this academic year so happily.

The help of my students has been indispensable. I am particularly grateful to my proofreaders, Judith Lachman, Felix Lopez, and Christopher F. D. Ryder, and to my research assistants: David De Wolfe and Kevin Olson; Vincent Wellman, who was a loyal and able assistant for more years than anyone else; and Gail Geddis and Jeffrey Crockett, who started on the book at a particularly difficult time and whose work, then and during my year away from Yale, has been truly extraordinary in both quality and amount.

Finally I thank Anne, my wife, my wisest critic and dearest friend.

G.C.

Cambridge, England
June 1981

Contents

A Common Law for the Age of Statutes

I

Choking on Statutes

The last fifty to eighty years have seen a fundamental change in American law. In this time we have gone from a legal system dominated by the common law, divined by courts, to one in which statutes, enacted by legislatures, have become the primary source of law.[1] The consequences of this "orgy of statute making," in Grant Gilmore's felicitous phrase,[2] are just beginning to be recognized. The change itself and its effect on our whole legal-political system have not been systematically treated.

In this book I will argue that many disparate current legal-political phenomena are reactions to this fundamental change and to the problems it has created. These phenomena include events as diverse as: the increasing tendency of courts to find that constitutions, and especially notions of equal protection, require the invalidation of statutes; the development of "passive-virtue" theories, associated especially with Alexander Bickel, which would enable courts to force legislatures to take a second look at constitutionally doubtful statutes; the development of theories and practices of judicial interpretation of statutes which would make even the proverbial Jesuit blush if they were viewed as attempts to discern any kind of legislative intent; the delegation of substantial authority in lawmaking to administrative agencies; the pressure for sunset laws, which would automatically repeal statutes or regulations after a fixed number of years; and the insistent suggestions for radical reform of our legislatures or even of our whole system of checks and balances.

The "statutorification" of American law is not the only reason for these varied proposals and events. Each one has independent reasons that might explain it. Nevertheless, I believe that as a group they cannot be adequately explained except as a series of *ad hoc* reactions to the deeper change in American law. More specifically, they are reactions to the feeling that, because a statute is hard to revise once it is passed, laws are governing us that would not and could not be enacted today, and that *some* of these laws not only could not be reenacted but also do not fit, are in some sense inconsistent with, our whole legal landscape.

The combination of lack of fit and lack of current legislative support I will call the problem of legal obsolescence. Later, I will discuss the relationship between these two primary components of obsolescence.[3] For now it is enough to note that the reform proposals and judicial actions which have arisen as reactions to the problem of legal obsolescence can readily be shown to be inadequate and unsatisfactory as means of dealing with the problems.[4]

There is an alternate way of dealing with the problem of legal obsolescence: granting to courts the authority to determine whether a statute is obsolete, whether in one way or another it should be consciously reviewed. At times this doctrine would approach granting to courts the authority to treat statutes as if they were no more and no less than part of the common law.[5] At other times it would be used to enable courts to encourage, or even to induce, legislative reconsideration of the statute. Employing a variety of techniques, the courts might begin a "common law" process of renovation in the obsolete law, update the statute directly by replacing it with new rules (derived either from the common law or from statutory sources), or do no more than create a situation in which conscious legislative reconsideration of the law was made likely.[6] The object in all cases would be to permit courts to keep anachronistic laws from governing us without thereby requiring them to do tasks for which they are not suited, or denying to the legislatures the decisive word in the making of constitutionally valid laws.[7]

As stated, this proposal may appear to be radical. It is, instead, far more conservative of traditional American legal-political values than the alternatives so far suggested. What we are dealing with is the slow adaptation of our whole legal-political system to a major change: the preponderance of statutory law. I will be discussing how our legal system has tried by various devices to fit this fundamental change into a traditional legal-political mold, a mold that maintains checks and balances without accepting obsolete legal rules. This attempt has already caused important shifts in the actual relationships between courts and legislatures. My aim in this book is to begin consideration of whether the attempt to fit the fundamental change into a traditional mold is best served by continuing as we have, devising *ad hoc* solutions, or whether instead we would do better if we recognized outright the changes that have occurred and tried to control them by developing a new doctrine.

The integration of a major change into a legal-political system is an immensely complicated phenomenon. Consequently I do not propose here to develop fully the doctrine I have described or to do more than outline the limits and techniques appropriate to its use. The precise form of those limits and techniques, and even whether the doctrine should be adopted openly, can only be determined over time and by many people. This is especially true because the limits and techniques appropriate to the judicial power granted by the doctrine will vary widely with the type of rule and field of law involved.[8] Though I wish to propose a useful step in the integration into our law of the fundamental change that has already occurred in our legal system, my book represents no more than a start in the development of an appropriate doctrine to deal with that change.

Continuity and Change: The Common Law Tradition

Continuity and change are essential attributes of a legal system. Although abrupt or frequent changes are often not desirable, laws must change to meet the needs of changing times and, in democratic systems, the demands of changing majorities or, perhaps more accurately, of changing coalitions of minorities.[9] If legal-political institutions are too responsive to change, however, temporary and unstable majorities are apt quickly to impose their will. New laws are passed only to be followed by quick reversal at the next election, leading to uncertainty and to the defeat of legitimate expectations. Abrupt changes, moreover, can create deep ruptures in society, ruptures that slower, more organic change would avoid.

Different legal-political systems have balanced the need for continuity and change in different ways, some giving more weight to one, some to the other. In the nineteenth century the United States is said to have developed a unique solution to meeting the two requirements.[10] The principal instruments of this system were the common law courts, for most law was court-made.[11] Legislatures did, of course, possess the ultimate authority, subject to constitutional requirements, to make law; however, that authority was exercised sparingly, by modern standards, and in largely revisionary capacity. In such a world, the law could normally be updated without dramatic breaks through common law adjudication and revision of precedents. Change occurred because the doctrine of *stare decisis* was adhered to in a relatively loose fashion and precedents were not, even nominally, ultimately binding.[12] The changes that did occur tended to be piecemeal and incremental, organic if one wishes, as courts sought to discover and only incidentally to make the ever-changing law.

The system, despite its reliance on judges whose relation to the electorate was at best problematical, could at bottom be called democratic because the requirements of the legal process, of "principled" decision making, tended to limit the scope of judicial authority. The incremental nature of common law adjudication meant that no single judge could ultimately change the law, and a series of judges could only do so over time and in response to changed events or to changed attitudes in the people. Just as important, the system could be called democratic because popularly elected legislatures were able to reverse judicial actions when these were sufficiently at war with legislative desires, with what I will call "majoritarian" demands.[13] Legislatures, in a sense, had the last say.

Such legislative revisions had to overcome many obstacles, for the American tradition was anything but sympathetic to easy majoritarianism. Checks and balances of all sorts — bicameral legislatures, federalism, executive authority, and frequently even then, legislative committees — put a heavy burden on those who would revise the common law.[14] After passage, a legislative action had to undergo the ordeal of "strict interpretation" if it was in derogation of the common law.[15] Also, of course, the courts had early asserted their authority to declare a statute unconstitutional and hence invalid.[16] The constitutional weapon, however, was sparingly used because, unlike the others, it denied to the legislatures, to the government's most direct representatives of the people, their last say.[17]

The obstacles I have described were not accidental. Easy

legislative reversal of court decisions would have yielded change but might have damaged continuity, a solution not to America's taste. Yet once the legislature did act in a constitutional fashion, with sufficient clarity to overcome strict interpretation, its actions were final and virtually untouchable by later courts.[18] Nor was there a pressing need for judicial interference. Statutes were rare enough so that, even when they became middle-aged and no longer desirable,[19] they would not greatly inconvenience the polity. In time they would become completely obsolete, and ignored. Even before then they could, unless revised by the legislature, continue to govern as minor anachronisms or small inconveniences—the price paid for the maintenance of a democratic system that gave both change and continuity and that, to do so, seemed to require that legislative actions be taken as final.

The Current Dilemma

This legal world has totally changed. The peculiarly American way of achieving continuity and change has fallen apart for reasons that are too long and complex to be discussed in detail now.[20] In part they have to do with the perceived need for laws that are either more structured or more immediate than could be afforded by judicial decisions. The slow, unsystematic, and organic quality of common law change made it clearly unsuitable to many legal demands of the welfare state. At the same time, the speed with which perceived economic crises have followed upon economic crises has brought forth legislative responses even in areas where the common law might have been capable of making the necessary adjustments. Be that as it may, starting with the Progressive Era but with increasing rapidity since the New Deal, we have become a nation governed by written laws.

Moreover, unlike earlier codifications of law, which were so general that common law courts could continue to act pretty much as they always had, the new breed of statutes were specific, detailed, and "well drafted."[21] Again, unlike the codes, which were compilations of the common law, the new statutes were frequently meant to be the primary source of law.[22] Courts, limited to honest interpretations of these statutes and committed to legislative supremacy, soon enough began to give them the authority they claimed for themselves.

When these laws were new and functional, so that they represented in a sense the majority and its needs, the change presented few fundamental problems. Soon, however, these laws, like all laws, became middle-aged. They no longer served current needs or represented current majorities. Changed circumstances, or newer statutory and common law developments, rendered some statutes inconsistent with a new social or legal topography. Others were oddities when passed (in the throes of a crisis or, perhaps, in an experimental spirit that started no new trend in the law). Still others became increasingly inconsistent with new constitutional developments without, for all that, actually becoming unconstitutional. Despite this inconsistency with the legal landscape, however, such statutes remained effective and continued to govern important areas of social concern, because getting a statute enacted is much easier than getting it revised.[23] They remained effective, even though some of them at least could not have been reenacted and thus could be said to lack current majoritarian support; checks and balances still worked, and interests served by these outdated laws could successfully block their amendment or repeal.[24]

All this led to a peculiar dilemma for the common law courts. America's view of law is still founded on the traditional paradigm I have just described. Judges have been taught to honor legislative supremacy and to leave untouched all constitutionally valid statutes, but they have also been trained to think of the law as functional, as responsive to current needs and current majorities, and as abhorring discriminations, special treatments, and inconsistencies not required by current majorities. They have been taught, and have come to believe, that they have a crucial role to play in keeping the law functional and that the persistence of outdated rules is, to some extent, their responsibility. The common law judicial-legislative balance permitted them to honor legislative supremacy and keep the law functional.[25] Today doing both no longer seems possible.

Faced with this dilemma, it is little wonder that the least willful of judges have responded to their task with open aversion, but have enforced time-worn interpretations of even more time-worn laws.[26] Other judges have acted more aggressively and have used the Constitution or farfetched interpretations to make obsolete laws functional.[27] Not surprisingly, as more judges have taken this road, concern has increased.[28] I would argue that much of the current criticism of judicial activism, and of our judicial system generally, can be traced to the rather desperate responses of our courts to a multitude of obsolete statutes in the face of the manifest incapacity of legislatures to keep those statutes up to date.[29]

Responses and Problems

The remainder of this book will be concerned with actual and proposed responses to the dilemma of "statutorification." I will first look at what the courts have done to deal with the problem, including: the increased use of constitutional adjudication as a device to update the law; the attempt to avoid constitutional adjudication and yet achieve similar results by relying on what Bickel termed the passive virtues; and the development of a whole theory and practice of interpretation designed to circumvent what Robert Keeton has called the legislative "deep freeze."[30]

In all these, and in their shortcomings, will be seen the seeds of a new approach, but before I discuss that approach I shall consider various nonjudicial attempts to avoid legal petrification. The first is the New Deal "solution," the delegation to administrative agencies of the authority to update a law or a whole area of law. The second involves legislative solutions — such as sunset laws — that do not entail major reforms of the legislature itself or of its relations to other bodies, but are designed to help existing legislatures overcome inertia. Their object is to avoid statutory middle age either by continuous rejuvenation or sudden death. The final nonjudicial attempts to which I will turn involve major structural reforms. These reforms range from the most ambitious attempts to make our legal-political system responsive to change to no less wishful attempts to recapture the "golden age" of the nineteenth-century common law.

Since none of these approaches is satisfactory, I'll return to the courts and propose a new relationship between courts and statutes, a relationship that would enable us to retain the legislative initiative in lawmaking, characteristic of the twentieth century, while restoring to courts their common law function of seeing to it that the law is kept up to date.[31] The precursors, both explicit and implicit, of this proposal will be examined, and the conclusion will be reached that we are already doing, badly and in hidden ways, much of what this "radical" doctrine allows. Indeed, an open use of the proposal may well prove to be less dangerous — less prone to unrestrained judicial activism — than today's use of complex subterfuges.

II

The Flight to the Constitution
and to Equal Protection Clauses

There are obviously many reasons why American courts have in recent years engaged in an enormous amount of constitutional adjudication. Only some of these are related to the problem I am discussing. It would be foolish to attribute the proliferation of constitutional decisions dealing with rights of blacks, for example, to the existence of laws that were once majoritarian but that are so no longer. Yet along with these decisions are others that sound surprisingly as if they arise from judicial frustration with laws that do not fit the current legal landscape and which the courts believe could not be currently enacted.

Leaving aside the most obvious example of legislative inertia, reapportionment, since that involves problems all its own,[1] one finds no lack of constitutional decisions of the sort I have in mind. There is little doubt, for instance, that by the time the Supreme Court declared the Connecticut statute prohibiting the sale and use of birth control devices void, that statute had become a legislative anachronism.[2] It could not be repealed and yet it would never be reenacted. It was inconsistent with practice, common law, and other Connecticut statutes.[3] Yet the *constitutional* basis for its invalidity was tenuous, to say the least, especially at the time the decision was made.[4] Penumbras of constitutional prohibitions and rights to privacy were much mentioned, but these concepts had not been, and were not soon to be, applied by the Court in principled fashion in other closely related cases.[5] They could well have been, of course, but the fact that they were not suggests that the Court was not really applying them in the birth control case. In the end, the case was its own justification. The law *was* dead, in both a majoritarian and a consistency sense, even though it retained some sting and the Court did everyone — including the Connecticut legislature — a service by interring it.

Another example is more interesting because at least one member of the Court was quite self-conscious about his role as judicial updater and because the constitutional doctrine used to invalidate the law, the notion of equal protection of laws, has a particular significance for the problem at hand .[6] The case involved the rights of widowers to obtain social security benefits equivalent to those granted widows in the face of a statute that explicitly differentiated between them. The Social Security Act provided that widows of men who had contributed to the social security system were automatically eligible to receive survivor's benefits, while widowers of women who had contributed to the system were not eligible unless they proved that they were dependent on the deceased spouse when she died. The court split three ways, holding that the law as it stood violated the concept of equal protection, made applicable to the federal government by the Due Process Clause.

Four justices found an equal protection violation because the statute discriminated against working women. They emphasized that contributions to social security "earned" less protection for women than men, although their opinion also noted that the only conceivable justification for the statute was "based simply on an 'archaic and overbroad' generalization."[7] A second group of four justices would have approved the statute, arguing that it merely redressed the disadvantages of women in our society and that the statute could not be viewed as a discrimination against working women. They would have held that the statute represented an administratively convenient legislative decision to grant a special benefit to widows and was, therefore, valid even if in some sense it was discriminatory against men.[8]

The telling opinion, written by Justice John Paul Stevens, agreed with the dissenters that the statute should be viewed as a discrimination against men, not women. But Justice Stevens held that the justifications for the statute offered by its defenders could not withstand analysis. He asserted that "this discrimination against a group of males is merely the accidental byproduct of a traditional way of thinking about females" and that due process requires that a law discriminating on the basis of sex be justified by something more than such a stereotype.[9] He also observed in a footnote that if Congress passed the same legislation with a clearer statement of purpose he might well agree with the dissenters and vote to uphold it.[10]

Justice Stevens' crucial point, which was also hinted at in the plurality opinion, appeared to be that the statute was probably out of phase with current thinking about sexual equality and probably remained in force only because of legislative inertia.[11] In light of the deep constitutional changes since the statute's passage, changes that cast increasing doubt on any gender-based discrimination, the Court could require Congress to reconsider, and take current responsibility for, this law if it was to remain in force. As if to justify Justice Stevens' judgment about inertia, Congress in recent modifications of the Social Security Act, designed to increase the system's financial stability, has made no serious attempt to overturn the Court's decision and reenact the cost-saving discrimination on "acceptable" grounds.[12]

The use of the Constitution to eliminate anachronistic laws has certainly not been limited to the federal courts.[13] Indeed, the most enthusiastic user of constitutional adjudication for these purposes has probably been the California Supreme Court. That court's technique in some recent cases is worth noting. Faced with the time-honored, but also time-worn, common law distinction between a landowner's liability to guests and to business visitors, the California court in traditional common law fashion moved to abolish the difference. In what has become a much followed and praised opinion it said that the distinction made no sense under modern conditions.[14] Thereafter, however, the court faced an analogous distinction, created by the legislature, that severely limited the liability of car owners to guests who were passengers in their cars. The court found that such a limitation, based on a distinction no longer found in the common law, violated California's equal protection requirements. It held that guests in cars should be treated just as other guests and invalidated the statute.[15]

In this case the court misjudged the legislature, which reenacted that part of the guest statute not directly affected by the decision.[16] But constitutional principles are constitutional principles, so the

California court, after some false starts, found the new law void.[17] Because the court had resorted to a constitutional weapon in the first guest statute case, its decision to replace a legislative rule with one of its own devising could not be reversed by the legislature. In the end, the court was driven to the point of implying that "the courts should not countenance legislative interference with a universal system of liability for negligence."[18]

There are several lessons to be learned from all of this. The first, and most important, is that judicial use of constitutional adjudication to replace obsolete laws does not return us to the traditional judicial-legislative balance. Once the courts have modified or invalidated a statute on constitutional grounds, they have done much more than act in an area of legislative inertia. If the courts' aim is only to update in an area of inertia and if they are wrong in their judgment that a statute which does not fit the legal fabric no longer has majoritarian support, their use of constitutional adjudication makes legislative correction of their mistake impossible. The consequence of a wrong guess is not merely legislative revision, as in common law adjudication; a wrong guess will entail either a constitutional amendment or the dominance of judge-made law. In the Connecticut birth control case the court was, in retrospect, correct. The law it struck down was an anachronism held in place solely by inertia.[19] In the California guest statute case, on the other hand, another anachronistic and "uncommonly silly law"[20] was desired by the people's representatives and their wishes were ultimately blocked.

I readily agree that there are instances when such a result is proper and desirable. Indeed, the social security case involving issues of discrimination based on sex may be just such an instance.[21] That is, I believe in judicial review and in constitutional adjudication. It is precisely because I think the courts do, and should, have the power to be antimajoritarian (in this sense of the word) in a limited number of situations involving constitutionally mandated rights that I worry about the use of that power by courts to further a totally different function. Few things will destroy judicial review, and weaken those rights we want to have protected by the Constitution, more effectively than its use to overcome legislative inertia in areas involving bad law, perhaps, but no real constitutional issue. Even correct results in cases of this sort, where the Constitution is used to invalidate a law that was only held in place by inertia and was inconsistent with other prevailing legal principles, will tend to spawn highly vulnerable constitutional doctrines and hence may weaken the "core" rights that need to be protected by our constitutions.[22] The inevitable errors — decisions, like that in the guest statute case, where courts believe they are dealing with an anachronism but where it turns out that, anachronistic or not, the law is consistent with current legislative sentiment — cannot help but raise the specter of judicial, nondemocratic domination and cast doubt on judicial review even in areas where it is most appropriate and useful.

The second lesson is related to the first. It may be argued that such updating through constitutional adjudication is not undesirable in jurisdictions, like California, where constitutional amendments are relatively easy and involve direct majoritarianism through, for example, referenda. Certainly, it is hard to argue that the defect in constitutional adjudication in such states is that it, unlike traditional common law updating, deprives the "people" of the last word. But the position that where procedures for amending constitutions are relatively easy courts can use constitutional adjudication to modify or eliminate anachronistic laws, as well as to uphold constitutional rights, is simplistic and wrong.

The statement by a supreme court of a jurisdiction that a law is unconstitutional is and should be more than an invitation to amend the constitution.[23] Indeed, the easier the procedure for amendment, the more must the judicial decrees of unconstitutionality put to the people the seriousness of what an amendment means. Only in this way can constitutional rights be protected from temporary majorities. The use of constitutional adjudication when the object is precisely to see if an old or seemingly anachronistic law still commands popular support cheapens, indeed destroys, the crucial moral force that underlies and protects true constitutional decisions.

I do not wish to exaggerate. Of course, a constitutional decision is not the end of the process of lawmaking, and amendments and revisions of constitutional decisions are proper and frequently desirable.[24] But that is far from saying that amendments should be undertaken lightly or simply because the court was "wrong." Use of constitutional adjudication, even when it seems almost to invite a legislative response, as it was by Justice Stevens in the social security case, but particularly when used in jurisdictions where formal barriers to constitutional amendments are small, would inevitably lead to amendments merely to correct minor judicial errors. Indeed, if it did not, we would be right back to the problem of judicial domination in ordinary lawmaking.

The third lesson is a more technical one and has to do with the use by courts of equal protection clauses to invalidate anachronistic laws. The recent increase in equal protection adjudication has been much noted by courts and commentators.[25] As with the rush to the Constitution generally, only part of this increase is related to the problem of statutory obsolescence. Yet that part is by no means insignificant. To understand why equal protection clauses are used by courts seeking to update statutes, we must consider for a moment the traditional method used by courts to update the common law.

The most powerful engine of change in the common law was, strangely enough, the great "principle" that like cases should be treated alike. Courts acting on that principle could change law, indeed make law, without arrogating to themselves undue power because they always seemed to apply past precedents or principles in new ways to situations *made* new by the world around them.[26] Sometimes, of course, this was in fact the case—because of technological or social change an old rule would begin to treat some litigants unlike other similar litigants. The courts responded, in one way or another, to treat both classes of litigants alike. At other times, however, the change was self-imposed. What is a like case always involves a judgment as to the level of generality to use in assessing similarity. By moving to treat cases alike on successively different levels of generality, common law courts could slowly adjust the law to fit new social policies, and could still claim that all they were doing was treating like cases alike. As I said earlier, since such changes usually required the concurrence of many judges over a long time, and since the legislatures could reverse such judicial decisions when the courts' policy judgments were wrong, such an allocation of accretional lawmaking authority could not ultimately be criticized as undemocratic. (That it has been, rather foolishly, so criticized is neither here nor there.)

I have argued that in recent years courts have found themselves facing statutes they deemed anachronistic, or inconsistent with current legal principles, in precisely the same sense that in the past they had faced some common law rules they deemed anachronistic or inconsistent. That is, they sometimes see like cases being treated differently because social or technological change has made previously even-handed statutes biased. At other times they see statutes that, though still even-handed, seem to be out of phase with current social policies as reflected in more recent statutes and common law decisions. Finally, they see statutes that represent a long-past, constitutionally valid legislative decision to favor one group over another; to treat one group unlike other groups. Such inconsistent treatment would be perfectly appropriate if it represented a current legislative will; however, it must seem suspect when it does not reflect any current or recent majoritarian decision.[27]

In all such instances the courts are of course barred from their traditional common law weapon because they are dealing with statutes. Some courts, as we shall see, have found new weapons in sophisticated uses of passive virtues or have expanded the old weapon of interpretation. Others, instead, have looked to their most traditional and powerful weapon against statutes: constitutional adjudication. Is it any wonder that when they looked to the constitutions they fell eagerly on the equal protection clauses, the constitutional provisions that are most similar in verbal thrust to the great common law principle that like cases shall be treated alike? Such clauses appear to speak to the same problems, and can be used in the same way, as the great common law principle, for both the clauses and the principle attend to the problem of providing equal treatment to those who are equal. Indeed, by varying the level of generality at which it applies "equality," a court can say that equal protection is being denied in much the same way that it traditionally could say that like cases were not being treated alike.[28]

That such a use of equal protection is miscast, and weakens its effectiveness for the constitutional tasks for which it is appropriate, is not for the moment germane, although it is closely related to my argument earlier in this chapter about why constitutional adjudication is a bad way to reform anachronistic laws.[29] My point here is simply that both the flourishing of equal protection adjudication and the particular form that some of that adjudication has taken are directly linked to the courts' perceived need to find a substitute for the common law principle of "like cases alike," a substitute that would empower them to deal with obsolete or wrongheaded statutes left in force by politically checked and balanced legislatures.

Analogously, it may be no accident that the heyday of substantive due process as a means of dealing with statutes that were out of step with judicial views of social policy came at the turn of the century and in the decades immediately following, after the technique of reading strictly statutes in derogation of the common law had fallen into disuse — in part because of the devastating criticism by scholars of its abuse.[30] The courts could get away with using a constitutional blunderbuss in the pre–1930 years against much economic regulation, since the legislatures that passed such laws often represented only temporary majorities, out of power by the time the court invalidated the laws. In such circumstances the effect of destructive strict interpretation or of constitutional invalidity was, in practice, the same. It was only in the New Deal that the due process technique, which the Supreme Court had come to use, nearly proved disastrous. The legislature that had passed the new economic regulation was in power to stay, and the difference between second-look doctrines (like strict interpretation) and holdings of unconstitutionality became crucial. Since the New Deal Congress could not simply reenact statutes the Court had struck down, a confrontation seemed inevitable. Fortunately, the Court reversed itself. This celebrated "switch in time" converted the earlier constitutional decisions into second-look doctrines, and resolved the conflict.

I note all this not to indicate that the behavior of the Supreme Court before the New Deal would be proper under the proposal we will later consider; far from it. This bit of historical speculation is intended only to suggest that courts have long been inclined to turn to the stronger artillery of the Constitution when they are precluded from employing weaker, subconstitutional, means of dealing with statutes they deem out of phase. That the weaker means permit a legislature to overrule a court's decision while the constitutional approach does not, is all too readily lost in the shuffle.

The Passive Virtues

The dangers of constitutional adjudication, when what really was sought was legislative reconsideration, led innovative scholars (primarily Alexander Bickel and Harry Wellington) to develop theories that would allow courts to nullify some statutes and yet give the legislatures another chance, a second look.[1] Sophisticated courts had of course used such approaches before.[2] They responded to the theories with alacrity and even expanded them, applying them to situations broader than those the originators of the theories seemed to have in mind.[3] Nevertheless, perhaps because Bickel was a constitutional lawyer, and a great one, the theories have developed in ways that make them only partly successful in dealing with the problem of statutory obsolescence, a problem that is frequently (what used to be called) one of private law. Moreover, even in the areas for which the theories were designed, they have been effectively criticized as entailing dangerous subterfuges.[4]

Bickel's theories, right from the beginning, seemed to have three quite different aims. All reflected concern with important problems which, though distinct, could plausibly be attacked by the same set of judicial devices. Lumping together these aims has not been helpful.

The first object was to allow courts to leave in force laws they were not prepared to strike down as unconstitutional, without thereby legitimating or strengthening those laws by explicitly holding them constitutional.[5] The laws involved might be moving toward unconstitutionality (as our notions of basic rights changed) and yet not be invalid, or they might be clearly valid and still be at war with the generality of our laws. By allowing the courts to *fail* to act, Bickel hoped to avoid making the repeal of such laws more difficult. If courts, moreover, eschewed a clear holding of validity, the Constitution could more easily continue to grow, and a time might come when these anachronistic laws could be struck down. The courts could in this way avoid a rush to the Constitution and yet avoid support of rules that did not "fit" the legal system. This first object was, I think, the source of the term "passive virtues," for such abstention did indeed make a virtue of inaction. It is obviously linked to the theme of this book, but it is, of all Bickel's aims, the least directly germane.

The same reluctance to have courts prematurely reach ultimate constitutional issues, together with the same desire to induce legislatures to do away with laws that were inconsistent with our general set of legal principles, led imperceptibly to Bickel's second object. This aim entailed action by the courts. If legislatures, executives, and administrators wished to skate close to the constitutional line, and if they wished courts, perhaps through inaction, to let them do so, they should be made to do so openly and face the consequences before the people. Only when these (rather generously viewed) majoritarian bodies deemed it essential to assert the need for restrictions on near-constitutional guarantees should courts be made to employ inaction to let the restriction stand. Only, moreover, when the assertion was clear and unmistakable should courts be forced to decide the ultimate constitutional validity of such a restriction when no device allowing judicial passivity or inaction was available. However, in situations where the governmental body either slid into a possible constitutional violation or intentionally masked from the people what the effects of their actions on near-constitutional rights would be, the courts were justified in requiring a second look, that is in using a temporizing device to strike the action down and in deferring a final decision until the legislature or executive clearly asserted the need for the action.[6]

This was the meaning, Bickel asserted, of disparate doctrines like delegation of powers, void for vagueness, and maybe even of desuetude in its narrow sense of requiring some kind of prior notice to be given before a long-ignored criminal law was resurrected and used against a defendant.[7] Such a view of these doctrines is, I believe, both correct and uncontroversial, especially when "delegation" or "vagueness," if left unchallenged, served to insulate the majoritarian body from facing and taking responsibility before the people. Some questions might be raised whether such an approach would tend to lead courts to avoid constitutional adjudication, even when the state action would have been manifestly void however openly it had been undertaken; but these would be mainly issues of application. The notion that, at the very least, the majoritarian bodies should be made to speak to their constituents in open and candid ways, before actions involving the penumbra of constitutional rights are upheld, seems to have been widely accepted. Indeed, Canada has made a closely related procedure a formal part of its constitutional system.[8]

There was, however, a third and quite different aim in Bickel's passive virtues, an aim closely linked to the problem of legislative obsolescence. Bickel (and in this regard Wellington) viewed both judicial inaction, which allowed anachronistic laws to stand in force but unlegitimated, and doctrines like delegation of powers, vagueness, desuetude, and even rather farfetched uses of "lacks of jurisdiction," as ways of promoting a broader colloquy between the courts and the legislatures. Did the legislature really mean to impose on the federal courts a task which, if constitutionally valid, was unsuitable for courts, they asked in their justly celebrated *Lincoln Mills* article?[9] Should not the courts refuse to perform that task (if they could avoid it by a jurisdictional trick) and, in effect, send the statute back to the legislature for a second look? There was, again, in all this much talk of the need for openness in sending such a law back for a second reading. Yet the jurisdictional device used had a meaning of its own and would not have been used—abused, some would say—had it not been a handy way to make the legislature rethink the issue.

It is a very small step from all this to the notion that analogous—active and passive—devices should be used to induce the legislature to reconsider statutes that are out of date, out of phase, or ill adapted to the legal topography. Failure to uphold a statute frequently meant failure to take cases and hence failure to interpret the statute so as to lessen its anachronistic character. The unlegitimated law would, therefore, remain in force but its stark contrast to the rest of the legal system would ask, as it were, for legislative reconsideration.[10] Desuetude, obviously if in a quite new sense, but also vagueness, delegation of powers, and a Wellingtonian modern version of the old doctrine of strict interpretation of statutes in derogation of the common law readily lent themselves to a temporary nullification of statutes, which at the same time permitted legislatures a second look.[11]

Moreover, where the old statutes did raise constitutional doubts, Bickel's other justification for a second look seemed directly in point. For in those cases the object of the second look was to force majoritarian bodies like legislatures to face the issues and state openly whether or not they intended to abridge what, over time, had become near-constitutional guarantees. When the passage of time made old statutes become constitutionally doubtful, the direct "delegation of power" rationale for temporary nullification applied, and Bickel's last two objects merged. In all these ways, Bickel and Wellington suggested that courts could at times actively force and, at other times, through purposive inaction induce legislative reconsideration of statutes which were not necessarily unconstitutional but which were sufficiently close to the constitutional line to warrant frequent, sunsetlike review.[12]

Even when limited to semiconstitutional adjudication, however, the passive virtues are subject to abuse. This was elegantly demonstrated by Gerald Gunther.[13] Vagueness, delegation of authority, desuetude, yes, even "interpretation of statutes," are doctrines and notions that have a meaning and function of their own. Vagueness and desuetude, for example, are designed to require that actors be warned of the possible consequences of their actions before they act. Interpretation is linked to legislative intent, which at times requires that statutes be read broadly rather than be left unread to emphasize their out-of-datedness.[14] When such doctrines and notions are used not to achieve these tasks but rather to require or induce legislatures to take a second look, they are altered and become incapable of achieving their original functions. "A vital court task," said Gunther, "is the interpretation of legislation . . . free from ulterior purposes [and] Constitutional problems . . . this will be impaired if the Court seeks *spurious* intents to promote a court/legislative colloquy." Inevitably, he continued, such an approach "endangers Constitutional principles." Gunther was worried about such false use of doctrines, even in paraconstitutional cases. His worry that this would lead to a "virulent variety of free-wheeling interventionism" and involve the courts in dangerous subterfuges would necessarily multiply if the passive virtues came to be used to nullify or to induce reconsideration of *all* anachronistic statutes.[15]

Frequently, statutes cannot plausibly be viewed as constitutionally doubtful even though they no longer fit the legal topography. Statutes that, were they common law rulings, would be deemed obsolete and overruled may present no serious constitutional issue whatsoever. Unless the passive virtues can be applied to nullify or induce reconsideration of such statutes, the approach is in the end of little help in solving the problem of legal petrification. But to apply the doctrines to statutes wholly free from constitutional doubt deprives them of their only meaningful limitation and makes the passive virtues very, very active indeed. The danger of destruction or bastardization of valid doctrines, noted by Gunther, becomes magnified, of course. But perhaps more important, the very fact that "tricks" are being used makes it hard to develop any notions that would limit courts to nullification or reform only when it is appropriate and in ways that are appropriate. The danger of lying about the applicability of doctrines is not only that these doctrines lose *their* meaning; it is also that new and appropriate doctrines are not developed.

It is hard, without abusing important doctrines, to find any plausible constitutional infirmity in workmen's compensation laws, rendered trivial by inflation,[16] or in statutory charitable immunity and contributory negligence rules or in guest statutes, even though their common law equivalents are being abandoned right and left. One could, of course, claim that they violate some penumbra of the Equal Protection Clause and hence must be reconsidered by the legislature. But what does even a suggestion that equal protection might apply to such situations do to equal protection *doctrine?* What does it imply for those socioeconomic distinctions that can appropriately be made in the law and are based on current legislative judgments? The implication that statutes must, under pain of equal protection invalidity, be consistent with each other and make no policy discriminations is totally unacceptable, as both Wellington and Ronald Dworkin have pointed out.[17]

The same point can be made about use of vagueness and delegation of power as devices to strike down such laws. Some vagueness is immensely useful if a statute is to be updated by courts in traditional ways, and delegation of authority to administrative agencies was the paradigmatic New Deal response to the danger of legal petrification. To undercut those valid if often unsuccessful attempts, by twisting the doctrines in order to strike down laws that are of no constitutional moment merely because updating has not occurred, would be rank folly.

New Versions To Cope with Legal Petrification

This problem could, of course, be mitigated by developing new doctrines or resurrecting old ones whose thrust is primarily toward laws that do not fit in the legal topography—laws that have become constitutionally doubtful precisely because they are out of phase.[18] In fact, this is the turn Bickel's passive virtues have taken in the hands of scholars like Harry Wellington and judges like Jon Newman.[19] Such an approach would minimize the danger of corruption of doctrines that have functions independent of the desire to update and would therefore seem to escape Gunther's criticism.

The three attempts I shall mention are modern (and probably technically incorrect) versions of desuetude, *cessante ratione legis, cessat et ipsa lex,* and strict interpretation of statutes in derogation of the common law. The first of these was suggested by Bickel in writing about the Connecticut birth control law.[20] The aim was to go beyond the requirement (trivial, from a second-look standpoint) that notice be given before an unused law could be enforced, and to demand instead that such a law be reenacted. Desuetude in Bickel's view could be required if the old law was constitutionally doubtful (or called into question major organic principles, such as the allocation of powers as in *Lincoln Mills*)[21] and if the old law had actually fallen into disuse.

Leaving aside for the moment the requirement of a semiconstitutional link, it is easy to see that this transformation of desuetude is too limited to deal with our problem. Many old laws that are out of phase and would not be reenacted are still enforced. Moreover, many are not penal laws and their continued, if anachronistic, vitality depends on the fact that litigants find them advantageous in their own specific situations. That statutory charitable immunities or contributory negligence rules continue to be used says little about whether, were they penal laws, they would have been allowed to fall into desuetude. No lawyer will fail to invoke them when they serve the client's interest in a civil suit.

Yet even as to penal laws the desuetude approach is insufficient, for prosecutors are frequently reluctant to let old laws fall into disuse when their original reasons for being have faded. It was in just such a situation that Judge Jon Newman resurrected and applied in a novel way the old common law maxim of *cessante ratione legis, cessat et ipsa lex.*[22] The case involved an old Connecticut statute barring abortions. The express object of the statute when passed had been, Newman found, to protect the health of pregnant women. He also found that such an object was not valid today and was not being urged by anyone as a ground for retention of the statute. Newman recognized that there might be modern grounds on the basis of which a legislature might enact such a statute — such as belief that a fetus was a human life and deserved protection from the moment of conception (the Supreme Court had not yet spoken on the issue). He also conceded that most statutes no longer supported by their original rationales should not be invalidated. However, he held that where the statute, whatever its basis, raises severe constitutional doubts, and where it can no longer be supported on the grounds for which it was passed, the courts are justified in nullifying the law and forcing a legislative reconsideration.

The attempt was stunning and, if successful, might even have avoided the highly charged legislative-judicial hasslings that have followed the Supreme Court's constitutional invalidation of anti-abortion laws.[23] It did not work, as we shall see, in part because its constitutional basis led even as sophisticated a judge as Newman to misperceive his role when the issue of staying the effect of his judgment was to be decided. As a result, what might have been a useful judicial-legislative interchange did not take place. In this sense, the case stands as an example of how the Bickelian, constitutional background of such attempts may impede the desired colloquy.[24]

Even if it had worked, however, we would have been left with the nagging feeling that legislative reconsideration could be induced in some important areas of law (the penumbra of the constitution is obviously important), while other areas, less individually crucial but potentially much more meaningful to more people on an everyday basis (because much more pervasive), would remain hopelessly obsolete and beyond reform. Ironically, these would be precisely the areas where without the inapplicable Newmanesque approach no court could act, even though the rationale of the laws had long since ceased to support them. In the abortion cases, for better or worse, the Constitution itself was in the end made available for nullification. In these other areas, unless some other doctrine unrelated to the Constitution were available, no legislative reconsideration could be pressed.[25]

Yet what would we say of a rule which said that *any* statute can be nullified by a court if its original basis has ceased to apply? I, for one, would say that it goes much too far, and occasionally not far enough. By focusing on nullification it ignores the fact that frequently what is appropriate to such a statute would not be nullification but a legislative reconsideration of the issues at stake. Hence it would delay the development of judicial techniques that would induce such legislative review. Simplistic doctrines lead inevitably to simplistic and too limited techniques.[26] More important, even the failure of old rationales may *not* make a statute obsolete or anachronistic. New rationales which make the statute fit the legal topography may have arisen. Conversely, there are also statutes that remain in force, whose original bases can still plausibly be said to apply, which are nevertheless sufficiently out of tune with the total law (common and statutory) to be deemed anachronistic. Such statutes may remain in effect because of legislative inertia and might, in some instances, be appropriate objects of a nonconstitutional forced legislative reconsideration or of a judicially mandated sunsetting.[27] Again, the failure to focus directly on the underlying problem leads to false limits or no limits.

Cessante ratione legis, cessat et ipsa lex—if applied to all statutes—yields potential invalidity where it should not and fails to where it should. When the doctrine is limited to statutes that raise constitutional issues, the dangers of abuse through overapplication are certainly reduced, but its utility is greatly diminished, even in those cases to which it can be applied. In other words, constitutional doubts may be one ground for a judicial reworking of statutes (short of constitutional invalidity), but such doubts are far from the only ground. And the use of constitutional rhetoric may be misleading or even, as we shall see, harmful to a legislative-judicial colloquy.

Harry Wellington's approach to the problem is broader even than Judge Newman's.[28] His notion, outlined in a series of articles, is based on a consistency requirement that would look beyond the existence of single bits of data (such as the persistency of a statute's original rationale). The approach looks to a legal topography that includes both statutes and common law. A statute inconsistent with that topography would become anachronistic. Age of a statute, desuetude in its application, erosion of its original rationale, all these might help make a statute out of step, but no one of them would be needed, and other phenomena, such as developments in statutory or common law or in scholarly writings, might serve as well. The concept and approach — I have taken Wellington somewhat further than he probably cares to go, but not too much, I think — is much like that used by courts at common law to see whether a precedent is still valid. The only addition is that of statutes as objects in the legal topography (and this, since Landis' celebrated article, is both unavoidable and manifestly correct).[29] Wellington's approach is also, and here lies the snare, much like the concept and approach supposedly used by courts in the nineteenth century to justify the strict interpretation of statutes in derogation of the common law — a concept greatly abused and much criticized.[30]

That fact, and what I can only call a loss of nerve, causes Wellington to restrict the applicability of his highly promising approach. When a statute is out of step, in the sense described, *and* when such a statute raises constitutional or semiconstitutional doubts, then the courts are justified in demanding a clear statement of legislative intent, and in interpreting strictly, as did the nineteenth-century courts. Alternatively, if a gimmick, such as vagueness or a jurisdictional defect, can be found (invented is more apt), then the courts may even fail to enforce such a statute or nullify it and send it back for legislative reconsideration. The naked doctrine may have seemed too open-ended and so Wellington hemmed it in with limits, taken eclectically from here and there, which are not especially suited to the problems at hand and which, therefore, do both too much and too little.[31]

I have already argued that a link to constitutional infirmity, though a possible ground for nullification of statutes, is neither a necessary nor a sufficient ground. And I will soon argue that casting constitutional doubts can hinder as well as help the desired judicial-legislative colloquy. Similarly, I have noted that the availability of gimmicks like stretched interpretations, jurisdictional tricks, or "virtuous" doctrines (passive or active) is also neither a necessary nor a sufficient justification for invalidating or inducing a reconsideration of anachronistic laws. And, as Gunther has argued, the use of such subterfuges is dangerous. That, I think, deals with most of Wellington's suggested limits/techniques. The one that remains is his resurrection of the doctrine of strict interpretation of statutes in order to induce reconsideration of anachronistic laws.

In its nineteenth-century version the doctrine of strict interpretation of statutes in derogation of the common law proved subject to substantial abuse, as courts strove to misread and obfuscate offending statutes. Yet I do not wish to focus on the abuse to which any strict-interpretation doctrine is subject. For that abuse is part and parcel of the other (Guntherian) criticisms that can be made of all of Wellington's limits/techniques. Rather, I would like to center on the fact that strict interpretation, though subject to abuse, does not go far enough in restoring a common law–legislative balance, or in permitting courts to deal effectively with legislative anachronisms without precluding a majoritarian last word.

Many anachronistic statutes are clear as clear can be. The art of statutory drafting, as Gilmore has pointed out, has made this increasingly the case and increasingly the problem.[32] Moreover, why should the fact that the original legislature acted clearly or muddily make any difference to whether an anachronistic statute should be enforced, nullified, or reconsidered by the new legislature?[33] It is as irrelevant as whether in the interim a clear and authoritative interpretation of the statute had been obtained from a court.[34] It is, indeed, as irrelevant as the existence or not of jurisdictional gimmicks or passive virtues that might be employed in courts to avoid enforcement of the law.

In the end, all these are subject to the same defect. They are all devices that are being applied to justify a court's nullifying or forcing reconsideration of a statute in situations where, but for the fact that the law is anachronistic, they would not be used. As such, they both corrupt themselves and would leave untouched statutes that ought to be just as vulnerable but as to which no trick is available. And, like all subterfuges, they impede us from asking the basic question: Should courts be allowed to force legislative reconsideration of anachronistic statutes or even to nullify such statutes without thereby precluding subsequent legislative reconsideration? If so, what limitations on this power, and what techniques in its use, will serve to make such reconsideration most effective and least dangerous?

Answers to these questions must be deferred to much later in this book. We have not, after all, considered possible nonjudicial solutions to the problem of legal petrification. We have not even considered the most common judicial device: interpretation. But before we leave the passive virtues, there remains one further issue to be discussed — the fact that the rhetoric of "constitutional dubiety" required by the passive virtues may also hinder the desired legislative reconsideration, the colloquy between the court and the "representatives of the people."

The Problems of Constitutional Rhetoric

To Bickel and Wellington the issue is a straightforward one. Judicial expressions of constitutional doubts force legislatures to think twice before they act. In their *Lincoln Mills* article they say, "The point after all is to ask Congress for sober reconsideration, leaving to Congress the last word. To raise constitutional doubts is to inhibit future legislative action."[35] But is this always the case? Consider for a moment the legislative response to the Supreme Court's assertions that the constitutionality of capital punishment laws was uncertain at best.

In the *Furman* case and its companions, the Supreme Court invalidated essentially all capital punishment statutes then in effect.[36] At the same time, severe doubt was cast on the ultimate constitutionality of such laws. Some death penalty laws might just be valid, but they would have to be very tightly written the Court seemed to say, and even then it was anything but a sure thing. Surely in that situation, it would seem, the Court was trying hard "to ask . . . for sober reconsideration [and] to inhibit future legislative action."[37] At least one member of the *Furman* majority, Justice Stewart, implied as much in a later opinion.[38] A spate of new death laws followed. And the Court, impressed by the fact that capital punishment was not the anachronism they had hoped it was, upheld a fair number of these new laws. Indeed, the reenactment of such laws was relied on by the Court in its finding of constitutionality.[39] Can one, however, truly say that legislatures viewed the issue soberly?

In Connecticut, capital punishment was reinstated by one vote.[40]

It seems fairly likely that one or more favorable votes were cast by opponents of the death penalty, because such votes were helpful in the particular situation of Connecticut politics of that moment. Such Burkean antiheroes, if they in fact voted against their conscience, could readily have justified their vote on the grounds that it did not matter since, after all, the Supreme Court had made it pretty clear that such a law was unconstitutional anyway![41] Rather than inhibiting legislative action, the constitutional rhetoric had created an atmosphere in which legislators could have it both ways. They could satisfy some constituents by voting for capital punishment and yet explain their votes, to themselves and to their anti-death law constituents, on the plausible grounds that the law would never be applied. Only scholars, naive in the ways of majoritarian politics, would have expected otherwise. Only judges, equally naive in those ways and influenced by such scholars, would give such reenactments (meaningful though they may in fact have been) face-value effect.

Yet what was the Supreme Court to do once such laws were reenacted? To ignore the reenactments, or to explain them as legislative game playing, buck passing to the courts, would have been at least as incorrect as accepting the reenactments as manifest signs of legislative desires. The Court, in other words, was caught in a trap of its own making. If only constitutionally doubtful laws can be nullified as anachronistic, then constitutional rhetoric is unavoidable; and equally unavoidable is the fact that legislative reactions will be shaped but not necessarily inhibited by that rhetoric. It is not farfetched to suppose that some of the time a court-legislative colloquy would yield better information were the courts empowered to nullify or demand legislative reconsideration without raising constitutional doubts.

Judge Newman's abortion decision shows another aspect, a converse aspect in some ways, of the effects of a requirement of a constitutional link before a putatively anachronistic law is nullified or reformed. In that case the Connecticut antiabortion statute was invalidated because its original basis—protection of health—was no longer rational, and that fact was held sufficient to raise constitutional doubts.[42] Other possible grounds for reenactment were mentioned by Newman, and while some doubts were expressed as to what legislatures might and might not be permitted to do in the abortion area, these doubts were inevitably the tentative ones of a federal district court dealing with a subject on which the Supreme Court had not yet spoken. As guides to channel legislative reenactment, they were not very helpful.

More important, immediately after Newman's opinion was issued, the question was raised as to whether the judgment should be stayed, pending appeal. Viewing his decision as a constitutional one, involving a constitutional right of plaintiffs to have an abortion in Connecticut in the face of a statute that was void, Newman refused to grant a stay. This left Connecticut without any statute to control abortions at a time when the legislature was sitting with a strongly antiabortion governor. The decision invalidating the prior statute, moreover, gave grounds on which a new statute might be enacted, and it gave little indication that a broad statute was less likely to remain valid than a careful, narrow one that balanced various points of view extant in the state. Passage of a broad statute might in addition be taken as a signal from the people to the Supreme Court—which, as I said, had not yet spoken—of the strength of antiabortion feeling. It is little wonder that the legislature immediately passed a new antiabortion law, broader than the one invalidated, and set the stage for the constitutional confrontation that soon followed.

One may well ask what might have happened had Judge Newman been able to view nullification not necessarily as a constitutional or semiconstitutional action.[43] If he had been able to ask himself what steps would most further a legislative-judicial colloquy, would he have acted as he did on the stay? I think not. I do not mean that in such nonconstitutional cases the plaintiffs' rights are irrelevant. Only that they seem less pressing when they are not immediately based on constitutional rhetoric. In the actual Connecticut situation, legal abortions were readily available in New York, a few miles away, and the actual plaintiffs had already had abortions. Staying the invalidity judgment, which nullified a hundred-year-old statute, would have had little immediate effect on those who sought abortions in Connecticut. It would instead have had an enormous effect in avoiding offense to an important and politically active group and staying an immediate legislative response.

As a result, the "sober reconsideration" would have been less hurried. Connecticut legislators would have had time to learn that the views of the citizenry—albeit predominantly Catholic—were far more complex than might have been suspected in Hartford. Polls taken soon after suggested that some antiabortion law was supported but that strong support existed only for laws which contained many exceptions of a sort that might even have yielded constitutional validity. While this legislative-popular interchange was taking place, moreover, the Connecticut case would have gone to the Supreme Court. That Court, again if conscious of its role in promoting colloquy, could have spoken with more sublety than it did in the capital punishment cases and yet with no less constitutional force. It could have upheld Judge Newman's ratio, and, in dicta, it could have given powerful indications (consistent with what became its ultimate constitutional decision) that some narrow antiabortion statutes might well be upheld while broader ones were bound to fail.[44]

It is not hard to conceive of a legislative response, in those circumstances, which would have been far more circumspect than what ensued. Indeed, one can conceive of a series of differing responses in different states, each faced with analogous judgments, which would have sufficed to meet the Court's still inchoate constitutional imperatives and yet, because legislative and because based on different views on abortion in different jurisdictions, not be as subject to attack as the actual Supreme Court decision has been.[45] Rather than the distinctions based on capacity to pay with which we have been left, we might have seen differences which, though limited by constitutional imperatives, were based on the circumstances in which different American populations deemed abortion appropriate and those in which they did not. This might not have pleased those on either side of the issue who know the truth, but then neither does the current situation, and it would have had distinct advantages over the current situation from a majoritarian standpoint.

I have used two recent, and very doubtful, examples intentionally. It is quite possible that any legislative-judicial colloquy in either of these situations discussed would have been unfruitful. And surely one cannot be certain that the colloquy would have been more useful had it been structured in the ways I suggested.[46] In the end, however, that is not my point. The fact is that the legislative-judicial interchanges that occurred in both cases were *shaped* by the fact that the courts felt compelled to use constitutional rhetoric and constitutional precedents on stays. Had a broader, more open arsenal been at their disposal, they might have chosen other ways to elicit legislative responses: "sober reconsiderations" always; "inhibited ones" perhaps, if the constitutional merits warranted. Unless one believes that rationally structured colloquy is less likely to prosper than colloquy dictated by outside factors, one must conclude that the colloquies that ensued were less open and useful than they might have been. And one must put the blame for that precisely on the fact that the judicial interventions had been linked, by scholars, to constitutional rhetoric. If this is the case when that rhetoric is at least plausible — both the abortion and death cases did, rightly or wrongly, turn out to involve near or actual constitutional rights — it is much more likely to be the case when the constitutional rhetoric is entirely fabricated in order to make subject to reconsideration a law whose only defect is that it is wildly anachronistic. For then the rhetoric is entirely misleading and is bound to misinform the legislative response.

Interpretation

Constitutional adjudication and use of the passive virtues, though not unusual reactions to anachronistic laws, are not the most common judicial responses. The traditional judicial weapon in dealing with statutes has always been interpretation of what the written law means. Just as the increasing prevalence of statutes gave a new impetus and even a new (equal protection) form to constitutional adjudication, so interpretation has been totally recast in the twentieth century to increase its capacity to deal with statutorification of the American legal system. This great achievement can be credited in large part to Henry Hart and the Harvard legal-process school.[1] The development of functional interpretation has been brought further, probably beyond what the devotees of that school would like, by courts and, among scholars, by Robert Keeton and Harry Wellington.[2]

The advantages of interpretation as a way of coping with anachronistic laws are manifest. First, unlike constitutional adjudication and passive-virtue doctrines, interpretation of statutes involves an almost unavoidable judicial task. Words do not interpret themselves. And, long before a medieval court in Bologna held that a statute forbidding the shedding of blood on the streets was designed to control brawls and duels, and was not meant to apply to a doctor who was bleeding a patient, courts have been the instrument selected to explain what legislative words mean. Second, interpretation both invites legislative reconsideration and permits that reconsideration to be shaped by constitutional rhetoric or to be free from it as seems appropriate. When a court says to a legislature:

"You (or your predecessor) meant X," it almost invites the legislature to answer: "We did not." If, instead, the court wishes to say: "You probably meant X, for Y would be unconstitutional or constitutionally doubtful," it can do so, and that signal is also not lost on the legislature. Finally, the scope of interpretation can be, as Hart and Sacks and Keeton have argued, exceedingly broad, for frequently no one interpretation is manifestly right.[3] The very structure of our checked and balanced system ensures that there are often differing readings that can be given to a law, since vagueness in crucial statutory terms or in legislative history will frequently be a prerequisite to obtaining approval from all the groups that could block enactment. Given this fact, the choice among such readings can "honestly" be made to further other appropriate functions of the law as determined by courts guided by traditional principles of adjudication. Among these, obviously, are avoidance of constitutional problems and the forcing of "majoritarian" bodies to face up to whether they really want to limit the penumbra of constitutional guarantees. But an equally plausible function of interpretation, as Keeton and many recent court decisions have demonstrated, is the updating of laws, the avoidance of the "legislative deep freeze."[4]

At the federal level, an important series of examples of interpretation used to update is provided by the Supreme Court decisions that permitted virtually any case arising under the Federal Employers Liability Act and the Jones Act to get to a jury on allegations of negligence. The FELA cases are of particular interest to me because they started me thinking about statutory obsolescence and judicial responses to it.[5] Later I learned that the Jones Act cases (the maritime equivalents of the FELA–tort law cases) were the source of Grant Gilmore's brilliant treatment of the problem.[6] It is surely no accident that the jurist who has been most noticeably troubled by such obsolescence is Robert Keeton, a tort scholar intimately acquainted with all those cases.

At the time the FELA and Jones Act were passed, most employees were covered by what seemed to be adequate workmen's compensation laws. A series of complex, peculiar, and doubtful constitutional decisions made analogous coverage of railroad and maritime employees difficult.[7] Congress was troubled by this and passed laws to limit traditional common law defenses that might have been applied to bar suits by such injured plaintiffs. Full comparative negligence—then almost unknown in the United States—was introduced; and subsequent amendment excluded assumption of risk as a defense. In effect, any negligence on the part of the defendant was made a ground for recovery. Those laws put injured rail employees and seamen in a better position with respect to possible recovery for injuries than the ordinary, common law, tort plaintiff of that time. A series of judicial interpretations soon followed, and the statutes took a full "interpreted" form.[8]

But time passed and conditions changed, and with them so did the common law of torts. All sorts of traditional defenses to tort suits—such as contributory negligence and assumption of risk—were narrowed or even destroyed by courts and juries. New categories of "ultrahazardous activities" were defined and made subject to liability without fault. Plaintiffs who did not stand a chance to recover at common law when the FELA and Jones Act were passed got sizable settlements without having to go to court. Judicial updating of the common law of torts had occurred in a nineteenth-century way, and the field was transformed.[9]

Where did this leave the "beneficiaries" of the FELA and Jones Act? If the Court stayed with what substantively had been intended by the members of those congresses that passed and amended those laws, or adhered to the language they used, these plaintiffs would have been frozen at pre-1940 levels. Any advantage such employees had been given over the common law plaintiff would have been eaten up by the growth in the common law. In time, under a static view of these laws, it would not have been hard to imagine common law plaintiffs as better off than the railroad and maritime employees whom Congress (should we say it?) had intended to favor. The same would have been true if the Court had looked to its own interpretations of these statutes.

Only by ignoring legislative language and legislative intent, and its own prior interpretations, could the Court keep these statutes up to date.[10] Only by some extraordinarily forced readings, which various lower courts resisted furiously,[11] could the Court make these statutes achieve a dynamic, relational intent. For only through such readings could rail and maritime employees be left better off than the ordinary common law victim[12] (a result of which the congresses that passed and amended these laws might or might not have approved). The Court followed this approach and read the statutes as allowing virtually all cases to get to a jury, assuming correctly that juries would act in a common law fashion — and update the laws — in their verdicts.[13]

One may well ask why Congress did not revise the laws and save the Court the trouble. But the reasons, grounded in the complex interplay of interest group politics, are of no special significance. Legislative inertia, absent Court action, was a fact of life in this area. Indeed, the principal judicial opponent of the Court's forced readings, Justice Frankfurter, explicitly justified a narrow, harsh interpretation of those laws on the ground that such a reading would break the log jam of interests and force the legislative hand. Rather than updating the laws to yield easier tort recoveries, he hoped to push the legislatures into enacting — by now clearly constitutional — workmen's compensation laws.[14]

In other words, the great judicial debate was not over whether the Court should live with the outdated laws, but rather over which technique of interpretation would best serve the object of updating and what the updated law should look like. Justice Frankfurter opted for what may be termed judicial blackmail. Justice Black, relying on juries, chose misreading. As we shall see, both techniques, deprived of pejoratives (which properly attach to them when they are applied in interpretation but which would be out of place in a doctrine permitting open judicial updating or nullification), are part of the arsenal that courts could use in applying the doctrine I shall propose later.

A thoughtful choice among Black's rewriting approach, Frankfurter's legislative-reconsideration approach, or other devices should depend on the nature of the statute to be updated, the expectations of the parties involved, the way in which the statute has come to be anachronistic, how the legal topography has changed, and, especially, what needs to be done technically to update a statute and make it fit the legal fabric.[15] To make the statutes conform to a workmen's compensation model required legislative action. Hence Frankfurter opted for a narrow interpretation that tended to force the legislative hand, even though this would leave individual plaintiffs uncompensated pending legislative action and perhaps violate the legislature's desire to favor these victims. To make the statutes conform to a model dominated by the general run of common law tort actions — but with these plaintiffs more favored than others — only required that all cases go to juries. And this was the interpretation Black chose, even though it ignored earlier sound readings by the court of the statutory language. Either Black's or Frankfurter's approach might in theory be right, depending on whether the dominant legal landscape in this area was workmen's compensation or the common law tort suit. But both in practice did violence to legislative intent or language, that is, to the core of honest interpretation. What was manifestly not preferable, therefore, was to put the Court in the position of having to choose among these and other approaches in the guise of interpretation. But more on that soon enough.

The other example of stretched interpretation I should like to pose also arises in a tort context. This one, however, involves a state statute. During the Depression Wisconsin became one of the first states to limit the common law doctrine of contributory negligence. A statute was passed allowing injured plaintiffs to recover so long as their negligence was less than that of the defendant. Damages were to be reduced in proportion to the plaintiff's negligence. No damages were recoverable, however, unless the defendant was more negligent than the plaintiff.[16] For many years this statute remained in force and created relatively little excitement. Its basic pro-defendant bias was noted and at times criticized, but that bias was itself a reflection of the then existing common law bias in analogous situations.[17] After all, the common law doctrine of contributory negligence, which the statute replaced, supposedly barred recovery for all plaintiffs whose negligence, however small in relation to the defendant's, contributed to the harm.

Recently the legal topography has changed dramatically. Following years of erosion by juries and courts, almost unanimous criticism by scholars, and, perhaps most important, the rise of alternative, no-fault systems for dealing with injuries, the common law doctrine of contributory negligence has been abandoned in a large number of jurisdictions.[18] In some states the change has been legislative. (The old rule seemed so harsh, and the no-fault alternatives so beckoning, that legislative inertia was overcome.) In others the common law rule was abandoned (despite its hoariness) by common law courts, which typically replaced the old rule with some form of full comparative negligence — in which damages are allocated in proportion to the relative negligence (or responsibility) of the parties, regardless of which is more negligent than the other.[19]

Wisconsin faced a different situation. It did not have a rule so outrageous that even legislative inertia would break before it. The prevailing rule, nevertheless, did seem to the Wisconsin Supreme Court to be out of phase with the developing legal topography.[20] In deciding what was consistent with current thinking, the court may have relied primarily on traditional common law sources (practical erosion of the old rule, pressure for dramatic change like no-fault, and severe doctrinal criticisms of contributory negligence). Most likely it also considered the force of statutory change in other jurisdictions. In any event, the court deemed the Wisconsin rule to be ripe for reexamination. But the Wisconsin legislature, though faced with reform proposals year in and year out, had failed to act; and the Wisconsin court, like it or not, faced a statute and not a common law rule of its own making.

Amazingly, and perhaps amusingly, this did not daunt it. In *Vincent v. Pabst Brewing Co.*, the court considered the continued validity of the Wisconsin partial comparative negligence law. Three justices held that since a statute was involved they could not act. Four justices asserted the power to construe the statute in a way that would allow them to alter its effect completely; but three of these agreed not to do so immediately, since the legislature was again considering revision of the statute. Three of these four "activist" justices made it clear that, in the absence of legislative action, they would move to full comparative negligence. The fourth refused to say how he would vote should a judicial reconsideration become necessary. In this way, the Wisconsin legislature was informed (blackmailed if you will) that failure to revise the law would lead to a judicial revision, but it was also left in the dark as to what that revision would do. The crucial seventh vote made it impossible for any interest to take comfort in legislative inertia and to rely on inaction to serve its ends.[21] Needless to say, the Wisconsin legislature acted almost immediately and modified the preexisting law, though nowhere near as much as the court probably expected.[22]

How did the court find the power to revise the Wisconsin law in the face of a clearly written statute? The chief justice explained why the court could act, in a separate opinion ending ironically with a dutiful bow to Frankfurter, the advocate of judicial restraint.[23] The 1931 statute, he explained, gave to some common law plaintiffs — those who were less than 50 percent negligent — a new right of recovery. It did not affect the rights of plaintiffs who were more negligent one way or the other. These continued to be barred, he went on, not because of the statute but because the common law of contributory negligence (untouched by the statute) barred them. That common law doctrine was judge-made and hence subject to judicial modification. He understood that the other justices preferred to wait and see if the legislature would act forthwith. He would not have waited, but that was a matter of detail: if the legislature failed to act, nothing prevented the court from abandoning the underlying common law of contributory negligence and permitting recovery by the previously barred plaintiffs. Any other result, he asserted, would mean that "the death of the common law [was] near at hand."[24]

What can one say about such a decision? It worked, and induced the legislature to enact a statute that was presumably attuned to its current desires. It worked better than a judicial finding that the old Wisconsin statute was unconstitutional (on the ground, let us say, that the old statute gave a catastrophically significant effect to a minimal difference in plaintiff negligence, and thereby deprived the 50 percent negligent plaintiff of the protection of the laws equal to that given the 49 percent negligent plaintiff). Such a finding—apart from what it and analogous decisions would do to equal protection doctrine—would have effectively barred the Wisconsin legislature from enacting the new, and still remarkably limited, comparative negligence law that it did pass.[25] But can one say that the decision of the Wisconsin court was honest, that it interpreted the 1931 statute correctly?

Justice Harlan, in a celebrated maritime law case,[26] did something much like what the Wisconsin court did in *Vincent v. Pabst*. In that case, however, congressional action may well have left a gap to be governed by common law. And removal of the gap did not entail the willful ignoring of legislative intent, though the Supreme Court through Justice Harlan certainly chose to construe that intent in the light of the changed legal topography.

Can the same be said for *Vincent v. Pabst*? The question can be argued, but if we are concerned with original intent, the answer is probably no.[27] "Interpretation" is not a meaningless or infinitely expandable word. Yet should the court in *Pabst* have sat and assumed that it could not act, that it could not do what other courts in other states were doing, simply because a Wisconsin legislature some fifty years before had spoken on the subject? The court's decision did not deprive the legislature of its last say; far from it, it invited, even forced, a reconsideration.

What harm did it then do? The harm, if any, must lie in the fact that the court abused interpretation, and that such abuse is undesirable and dangerous. As in the FELA and Jones Act cases criticism is appropriate only because of the doctrine used or abused, not because of the result obtained.

We are all so much a product of the legal-process school that we tend to forget Hart's and Sack's teaching that words do have meanings, that legislatures sometimes do intend some things or at least fail to intend others, and that the very fact that sometimes there is uncertainty — and uncertainty may appropriately be resolved to serve such functions as updating — ought to keep us from creating false uncertainty where it does not exist.[28] An honest recognition that sometimes interpretation is appropriately shaped by ends other than the desire to conform to legislative intent is very different from a sly refusal to follow such an intent even though it can be discerned. Discretion to interpret broadly and functionally entails restraint, if we are to remain honest. But restraint unfortunately deprives interpretation of the capacity to deal adequately with the problem of obsolete laws.[29] The limits of honest interpretation are too constricting, whereas the scope and dangers of unlimited interpretation are too broad.[30] All that Gunther said in criticizing Bickel can be applied here in spades.[31]

So let us consider some examples of rules that, were they common law, would seem anachronistic and, because they are statutory, present serious problems. Let us at the same time think about whether interpretation, as willful as that employed in the FELA-Jones Act cases or in *Pabst,* would suffice to update such laws. Let us finally imagine what meaning would be left to words like "interpretation" or "construction" were they to be read broadly enough to deal with such problems.

Many states in the nineteenth century faced the problem that the common law neither gave damages to the estate of a tort victim who died before judgment nor permitted persons (usually close relatives) injured as a result of the victim's death to recover their own damages. As a result, some states passed survivor statutes allowing the decedent's estate to recover damages; others passed wrongful death acts for the benefit of the damaged relatives. Some damages, such as the lost increase in the net worth of the decedent, could be awarded under either statute. They could appear as lost earnings to the decedent or as lost inheritance to the relatives. Many items of damages, however, such as pain and suffering to the decedent before death and loss of companionship by near relatives, could only be recovered under one of the statutes. Nevertheless, many states passed only one of these statutes in the nineteenth century. It is hard to know why. Perhaps it was because even that expansion seemed a significant innovation at the time; or it may have been because some of the items of damages, excluded when only one statute existed, were items disfavored by the common law of the time. Whatever the reasons, the common law has changed. But in most states the statutes still govern the field, and some states are now facing the fact that items of damages that would be currently recoverable by a victim or by a near relative of a victim, if he or she remained alive, are not recoverable under the single statute on the books of their jurisdiction.[32]

Can this be dealt with by interpretation? Perhaps it can, if one is willing to expand on the game played by the Wisconsin court. Damages of a limited type, it could be said, were granted to a limited category of plaintiffs; what barred other damages and other plaintiffs was the preexisting and modifiable common law. And there we are.

Could a court, by interpretation, have dealt with the more crucial anachronism that many states limited damages for wrongful death to a fixed sum? In 1966, fifteen states maintained some kind of general limit upon recovery—normally $25,000 to $30,000. These limits, some of which had been low when enacted, had often been rendered even harsher by inflation.[33] It might have been possible for a court to say that the fixed sum was a "privilege" the statute permitted and that what barred greater recoveries was not the statute, but the preexisting common law. Such a reading, however, would have accomplished too much. It would have solved the inflation problem but only by converting statutory recoveries, which were intentionally limited by the legislature, into unlimited ordinary tort law recoveries in a situation (death) where legislatures may have reasonably felt that since actual damages had no economically definable limit, some control, even an arbitrary one, was necessary. One may believe that such a legislative judgment was wrong. One may even decide that today such a judgment would never be made. But could a court honestly have interpreted wrongful death statutes to excise the dollar limits?

This particular problem has been remedied by legislatures. The recent increased inflation made the remaining limits so arbitrary and gruesome in their application that, as of 1980, no state maintains a general dollar limit on wrongful death recovery.[34] Nevertheless they lasted long enough to justify our asking whether courts could, by interpretation and especially by expanding upon the move of the Supreme Court in the FELA and Jones Act cases, have acted to correct the dollar limits. One would have to argue that the object of the limits was relational, that it was to allow recoveries but to limit them to a proportion of what could be received in a nondeath case. Just as inflation caused ordinary tort judgments to grow, so should the limits placed on death-damage judgments. The courts would, by this judicially mandated indexing system, be fulfilling legislative intent by altering the numbers clearly set out in the statute. (Analogous readings could theoretically have been used to update workmen's compensation recovery schedules, which, owing to inflation, converted such statutes into charters for the pauperization of workers.)[35]

Changes in the legal landscape have made other elements of wrongful death statutes obsolete. In many states, relatives of wrongful death victims are barred from recovering damages from a negligent party if their deceased relative would be barred from recovering his own damages. Imputed negligence of this sort, which prevents a blameless party from recovering, has been roundly condemned by commentators and is rapidly on the decline in the common law.[36] As a result in many states, while the parent of a contributorily negligent child, who is injured but survives, can recover for grief and medical expenses from a negligent defendant, the same parent could not recover anything from the same defendant if the child died. Conceivably, a court could escape even from this dilemma (although the death statutes contain an explicit provision limiting the death action to those cases where the decedent — not the parent — could have recovered damages had he lived) by claiming to effect some form of relational legislative intent. Under this strained argument, to keep recovery under wrongful death statutes in the same relationship to recoveries under the common law — which, when the statutes were originally passed, frequently imputed the negligence of an injured party to his or her close relatives but no longer does so—the court should follow the changed common law and ignore the clear language of statutes.[37]

If, however, one is prepared to expand the *Pabst* and FELA rulings in these ways in order to accomplish what still might be termed legislative intent, are we left with any meaningful limit on unrestrained judicial activism? The language of a statute would no longer serve as a limit, while a statute's purpose to replace or preempt the common law would only prevent change in the legal rule by the common law courts if it were explicitly stated. And no other limits would have been created, since nominally no new doctrine in need of new limits would be employed. Under such readings of interpretation would courts be barred from doing anything they wished with a statute?

The troublesome answer is yes—but not what one would especially wish to bar. Consider, for example, the situation that might arise in Wisconsin some fifty years after the *Pabst* case and after the statute that followed. That statute was manifestly designed to bar a number of plaintiffs from tort recoveries. In the face of the court demand for a reconsideration of the old comparative negligence statute, the legislature excluded recovery by plaintiffs significantly more negligent than defendants. But suppose that in those fifty years tort law changed still further and no jurisdiction was left with anything but full comparative negligence. Suppose further that in passing other laws dealing with other types of damages, the Wisconsin legislatures consistently made full comparative negligence the rule in those statutes. Suppose, finally, that all these other statutes came through one set of legislative committees, whereas any law modifying the statute passed after *Pabst* would have to go through a different committee and that all attempts at reform had stalled in that committee. Would it be wrong for a court to treat the *Pabst* statute as anachronistic, and once again to force a legislative reconsideration of full comparative negligence? Surely the fact that the *Pabst* court had forced a reconsideration at a time when Wisconsin was not yet ready for full comparative negligence should not freeze the law at that stage indefinitely. Yet neither the *Pabst* nor the FELA tricks, however expanded, would permit it to do so, since the history of the stature would convince even Chief Justice Hallows that preemption was intended.

One can generalize from this and say that interpretation and construction would, if widely expanded, present no limits to the updating of statutes that gave a right to a limited number of parties beyond that afforded by common law. Such statutes could be subject to court nullification even if they were not anachronistic. On the other hand, this broader view of interpretation and construction would be of no help in updating laws that were intended to restrict the common law rights of parties. And this view would preclude such updating even if the statute limiting such rights was totally and hopelessly out of phase.

The point, simply put, is this: the *Pabst* gambit, which effectively destroyed the 1931 statute and did so at a time when (in retrospect) that statute was not really anachronistic, would not have served to permit the court to bar recoveries by plaintiffs less than 50 percent negligent, if tort law and Wisconsin statutes had moved in the opposite directions and rendered the 1931 statute obsolete because it was too favorable to plaintiffs! For the same reason the *Pabst* device would not have helped the California court to force a legislative reconsideration of the state's guest statutes, however out of phase these seemed to be. The constitutional blunderbuss would have still remained the only way.[38]

In other words, interpretation can only incidentally be employed to serve the aims of creating an appropriate twentieth-century equivalent of the judicial-legislative balance we have come to associate with the nineteenth century. No matter how "functionally" courts approach it, as long as it is tied to a search for original legislative intent, interpretation is bound to give courts too much scope in reworking some statutes and, at the same time, to leave courts powerless before other statutory anachronisms. More important, the successful use and occasional abuse of interpretation to cope with obsolete statutes are bound to impede consideration of which limits are appropriate in furthering a modern legislative-judicial colloquy. The tools of interpretation would be covertly employed for ends about which the interpreting courts were silent, and that silence would make evaluation of those ends well nigh impossible.[39]

It is, of course, no answer to say that *all* limits imposed by the words "interpretation" and "construction" could be abandoned, and new ones be designed precisely to achieve the function of coping with statutory petrification, without depriving the legislature of its last word. Even if one assumed, contrary to fact, that this would have no effect on these many situations when the issue of updating is not present, when the proper function for the court is to find out and apply what the legislators wanted, "free from ulterior purposes,"[40] all that would be done would be to create a new doctrine, much like the one I shall propose, and to keep the old language either as a meaningless shell or as a meaningful subterfuge. If one is prepared to face the problem of appropriately defining a modern judicial role in the updating of the largely statutory law, what does one gain by insisting on the fiction that one is "interpreting"? Perhaps, as we shall see, one does gain something, but it is far from clear how much.

In any event, that (like all the most subtle arguments in favor of legal fictions and subterfuges) will not be discussed until later. Before we get to that, we must first consider nonjudicial responses to the problem of statutory obsolescence and then see what an open and candid judicial response to the statutorification of American law might look like.

V

The New Deal Response: Administrative Agencies

The statutorification of American Law can in one sense be dated from the New Deal. Although the process had long since begun and was to continue long after, the particular needs of the Great Depression, the desire to fashion a democratic welfare state in response to the influences of European fascism and Russian communism, and the frustrating slowness of the courts in accepting change, all made legislative lawmaking seem the appropriate solution.[1] Long-term problems were often ignored in the crisis atmosphere of the time and, understandably, little explicit thought was given to what would happen when the New Deal laws became outworn. An underlying belief in the efficacy of relatively simple majoritarian movements operating through the presidency and the legislature (Congress in this case) was, as it had been at other times in our history, momentarily dominant.[2] And perhaps together with that dominance was the feeling that the checks and balances of the past would in time wither away, leaving room for a responsive legislature and president to keep the laws current.[3]

Yet it would be unfair to conclude that no serious thought was being given to the problems with which I am dealing. It was, after all, at that time that Landis wrote his magnificent article on the effect of statutes on the common law. And if that article saw the statutorification of American law as requiring that courts take into account the gravitational pull of statutes in doing their traditional job of updating the common law, it also seemed to envisage the gravitational pull of the common law and of other statutes as requiring judicial renovation of timeworn written laws.[4]

More important, this period saw the proliferation of government bureaus and of independent administrative agencies, and the full development of the latter into an integral part of a governmental structure. Along with the growth of the independent agencies came a whole body of theory to explain their role, function, and significance.[5] Let us pass over the fact that the theory was often simplistic, no less when it led to a Panglossian view of what such agencies could accomplish to benefit mankind than when it suggested a catastrophic view of their effect on human liberties and on democracy generally.[6]

This book is certainly not the place to plunge into the thickets that most discussions of administrative law seem to generate. Nevertheless, an unmistakable function of both the dependent and independent agencies, as conceived in the New Deal, was to give specificity to broad legislative mandates. Thus a not infrequent assumption during the New Deal was that generalized agreement on the appropriate ends of legislation usually existed. The problem was with finding the facts to define the means by which these ends could be achieved. Neither courts nor legislatures were good at finding the facts, at giving the specificity, which would permit achievement of the agreed ends. Agencies instead could do just that job.

Again the notion of easy agreement on ends seems simplistic today, as does the view that any such agreement could readily be discerned from legislative language or history.[7] But this does not alter the fact that agencies were given broad powers to apply laws to the facts of the day and to give specificity to the goals the legislation sought to further. And that involved keeping the legislative mandate attuned to changing times no less than to changing facts.[8] The power to issue regulations and to make prospective rulings could clearly be used, and indeed has been, to renovate statutes before they get out of date.[9]

Without going further into the topic, I would conclude that as a single solution to statutory obsolescence the independent administrative agency and the government bureau have been a dismal disappointment. This is far from saying that no role can be played by such agencies in updating laws. Indeed I shall later suggest just such a role, which would make use of agencies, in conjunction with courts and legislatures, to renovate the law.[10] But I do suggest that it is no accident that many of those most concerned with the petrification of laws and with the tendency of such laws to serve interests that are no longer majoritarian have focused on the administrative agency and the government bureaucracy as the major culprits.[11] Moreover, even if the administrative agencies could be made to overcome their own tendency toward inertia, it would be far from clear whether the changes they would make and the way they would make them would be preferable to the renovation that could be accomplished through a modern version of what I have called the nineteenth-century legislative-judicial colloquy.[12]

There are two problems with administrative agencies as renovators of laws, and they apply both to independent agencies and to dependent ones. The first is that they fail to renovate frequently enough. The second is that when they seem to renovate they do not do it in ways that seem fully legitimate. They are not so majoritarian as we assume legislatures to be, and they are not so conscious of the demands of consistency and principle in lawmaking as we have traditionally asked our courts to be.[13]

Why majoritarianism and consistency should define legitimacy in lawmaking is, of course, no small question. I will not even begin to treat it here, though I will deal with it to some extent later when I discuss what I mean by the legal "fabric," "landscape," and "topography," and how this common law concept ties in to legislative majoritarianism.[14] For now it is enough to assert that traditionally our lawmaking institutions gained their legitimacy by laying claim either to a majoritarian base or to a special capacity for carrying out a principled search for consistencies in the legal fabric.[15]

Why Agencies Fail To Update

The first problem — that agencies fail to update laws — is the one on which reformers, such as Ralph Nader, and scholars, such as Theodore Lowi, have focused.[16] One should be careful not to overstate the point. Agencies differ greatly, from each other and at different times in their lives. Some have been quite aggressive in trying to update the statutes under which they work.[17] Still, as a whole, one can understand why people like Nader and Lowi have been disappointed with agency performance.

It seems to be a fact of bureaucratic life that interests vest around the structure of administrative agencies at least as much as they do around legislatures. The pressure of such interests, moreover, seems to make almost impossible any reconsideration of how the law that created an agency and the regulations issued by the agency fit the changing times.

Frequently an agency will be created to deal with a problem, auto safety, let us say, to pick a relatively new and hence unpetrified area. The original legislative mandate and, often, the original set of regulations are upsetting to those who are regulated. The regulations change the old rules and they are costly. Once the new rules are in place, however, and the difficult problems of transition to the new climate have been overcome, the rules become barriers to innovation, and to entry into the field. Slowly the requirements of specific types of seatbelts, bumpers, and so on, shift from being costly charges imposed on manufacturers to being hurdles for innovators who believe they have developed a better, cheaper way of achieving the same degree of safety.[18]

Why then doesn't the agency change the rules? In the first place, the old rules did achieve a degree of safety, and innovation is almost always risky. Suppose the new device fails — what happens to the bureaucrats who urged the innovation? They are pilloried for failing to protect the public. No analogous risk exists when the same bureaucrats fail to allow the innovation. The cost to the public of sticking with the old is rarely clearly shown and is even more rarely attributable to the glacial slowness in any individual bureaucrat's willingness to countenance change. Because an error that stems from a decision in favor of innovation can be catastrophic to the decision maker, one would expect that most decisions will be against change.[19] And that is exactly what students of the administrative agencies have suggested happens.[20]

When one adds to this inherent bias against renovation three other factors, it is easy to see why agencies fail. The first is obviously the direct pressures on the agency from those who benefit from the old rules. That agencies become captives of those they are supposed to regulate is old hat, perhaps simplistic. Such captivity is said to be due to the fact that often those who make up the agency come from, or ultimately go to work for, those whom they regulate.[21] But both these statements, though probably true enough, miss part of the dynamics of the captivity and tend to link it to "evil people" rather than to deeper structural reasons. Those who are regulated not only benefit from the existence of old rules (because they exclude new-comers) but on the whole believe in them. They grew up under them and readily accept that compliance with old regulations is com-pliance with the public interest.[22] They are also able — almost by hypothesis because they are so well established in the field — to mobilize money and expert knowledge in support of their position. Against this the innovator has few weapons. Since the regulator, like the regulated, will also have grown up believing that compliance with the past regulation is the public interest, the likely result is eas-ily forecast without resort to speculations about evil people.

The second factor that militates against change through adminis-trative agencies is perhaps even more germane to our basic problem. The changes with which I am concerned deal with statutes that are becoming out of date. The power to update, let us say, has been im-plicitly delegated to an agency or bureau, though updating could also be achieved through legislative action. The need for administra-tive renovation exists, then, precisely because the legislature is not acting. One must, in evaluating the chances for administrative reno-vation, consider why the legislature has not acted.

There are, of course, many possibilities, but only one need be mentioned here. A frequent cause for legislative inertia in the face of a needed majoritarian change is the presence of powerfully placed individual legislators who oppose change. Whether they oppose it on the highest policy grounds or on the lowest corrupt ones is of no mat-ter. What does matter is that they have the keys to the legislative freezer. But the very fact that they are so placed almost always means that they are also powerfully placed in relation to the agency from which any nonlegislative renovation would have to come. The same legislative committee that must approve a change in the statute frequently oversees and determines the budget of the agency or bu-reau that could also renew the statute. It would be naive to assume that a congressman powerful enough to block action in the legisla-ture could not do likewise by a phone call to a bureaucrat, especially to one who already has many reasons for doubting the wisdom of a change. Indeed, even a legislator who is not powerful enough in committee to bar change may be able to feign enough power to daunt the agency, and then return to Congress and suggest that action, if any, should be appropriately taken by the agency because of its greater technical knowledge.[23]

Let me emphasize again that such behavior may be induced by the highest of motives as well as by the lowest. This "bias" against change is by no means all bad, for we may wish the scales to be tilted in a conservative direction. None of that, however, matters to the discussion here. For if the question we are asking is whether administrative agencies can effectively circumvent the legislative deep freeze and renew out-of-date laws, the answer is clearly that they have great difficulty in doing so.

The final factor that militates against successful agency updating of statutes is closely linked to the question of legitimacy of change. Often the statute that created the agency, or the law the particular bureau enforces, has become anachronistic because *it* has become inconsistent with broader legal developments — either constitutional or developed in other statutes. It is too much to expect bureaucrats whose job it is to apply a law to undermine that law, consistent within itself, because it has become out of phase with other laws outside their jurisdiction.[24]

My discussion has focused on "safety" regulations and the obsolescence of the laws that mandate them, whereas many administrative and regulatory agencies deal with quite different things. Yet I would suggest that the same kind of empirical data and the same general analysis apply to the likelihood of change coming from most agencies. It clearly applies to agencies whose initial function was to protect new competitors (say trucks) from old giants (railroads) or disadvantaged labor unions from dominant management. But the same inertia can be seen throughout the regulatory landscape. The details of the analysis change, but the reasons why the regulators are likely to stick pretty close to the original rules and political compromises remain much the same.

Perhaps I am looking at administrative agencies in too static a way. Perhaps I am subject to a criticism analogous to what Joseph Schumpeter leveled at those who worried too much about the existence of monopolies.[25] Over time, he argued, monopolies get swept away by great innovations and so their static inefficiencies do not matter. One could make the same argument for administrative agencies and regulations. Every so often, this argument would run, there is a gust of populist reform. Muckrakers of one age will be followed by Naderites and consumerists of another. These gusts come when administrative agencies enter middle age and, when they hit, they tilt the scales of risk in the administrative structure in favor of change. Suddenly the administrator who fails to update is called a scoundrel, a docile and perhaps corrupt captive of the "interests." And with this populist windstorm, the position continues, comes fresh air into the administrative structure.[26]

We may well question the accuracy of such a description, however. How much change have such reform movements actually achieved in old laws and old agencies? How often, instead, have they been diverted into the creation of different (and soon to age) laws and other agencies dealing with other problems? How much have they really changed the risks that condition the bureaucrat's willingness to innovate? All in all, whatever their other achievements, they have done very little in the field of renovation; the wind is strong, many seeds are scattered, but few dead trees are blown over.

Let us nonetheless assume that such movements do bring major changes in the agency structure. Would that suggest that this solution to the problem of legislative aging is a desirable one, or that it achieves a desirable modern version of an older balance? I think not. The old balance was not one that required or sought rapid changes. Continuity and change were what the legislative-judicial balance was designed to afford. Indeed, skepticism of too rapid change was responsible for precisely those checks and balances that are at the root of the problem of legislative obsolescence. A system like the hypothesized one, involving as it does long periods of glacial freeze and occasional quick thaws, is wholly different from the balanced change that the American tradition seems to have chosen. Surely, if we had wanted rapid change, bodies other than regulatory agencies, more representative ones for example, could have been designed to achieve that change. And if we feared it in legislatures, why should we fear it less because it comes only occasionally and in response to movements that may or may not be majoritarian?

Perhaps all this discussion is superfluous because the picture of administrative agencies that achieve a balance made up alternately of periods of stability and of flux may be a fantasy. But even if it were real or, more plausibly, if one could act to make it real, it seems very doubtful that it would achieve the continuity-change balance that this polity sought and probably still seeks.

Comparative Legitimacy of Change

As stated earlier, I have a more fundamental problem with the independent administrative agency and even with the bureaucracy as solutions to the problem of aging laws. My problem would persist even if such agencies could be made to respond in a continuous fashion to the need for change. It involves what can be called the legitimacy of changes achieved through such agencies. I am not, of course, arguing the constitutional validity of administrative delegation. When I say legitimacy I do not mean to talk about a formal legal concept. What I have in mind is a question of comparative institutional capacity to deal with anachronistic laws.

Traditionally, lawmaking institutions in our legal system justify their authority either because, like the executive and the legislature, they are said to understand and represent the demands of the shifting minorities that make up a majority of the governed or because, like courts, they are believed to be particularly qualified to discern underlying principles to which the governed are attached.[27] I will not now discuss why these are thought to be capacities essential to lawmakers, for that crucial question must be treated later when I consider whether the proposal for a judicial role in the updating of laws is legitimate within our traditional scheme of government.[28] For the moment, I shall take for granted that the object of lawmaking is to tend toward consistency of treatment as defined by broad and evolving legal principles, while, at the same time, to permit those preferential treatments demanded by the changing coalitions of minorities that form our ever changing majorities (so long, of course, as these preferences do not violate constitutional principles).

In the context of administrative agencies and government bureaucracy, the question therefore becomes: Can these agencies sufficiently discern shifts in majoritarian demands to make them reliable updaters of those preferential treatments that our legal system must have? Alternatively, can they discern and apply the underlying principles of law, the legal fabric, topography, or landscape,[29] so that they can further the object of consistent treatment in an evolving law?

Harder questions are far to find. I shall not attempt to answer them fully anywhere in this book. What I shall do is to try to compare the institutional capacities of administrative agencies with those that courts and legislatures can bring to these tasks. In this way I hope to indicate why agencies cannot legitimately solve the problem of legislative obsolescence — why, in other words, there is an important common law, judicial, function in the updating of outworn laws. This function requires courts to make use of the particular skills that administrative agencies have, but it cannot rely only on those skills.

Since the legislature retains the right to step in and impose its will by reversing administrative or judicial attempts to update laws, I am not concerned with questions of where the ultimate lawmaking power ought to be. Rather, I am focusing on which institutions are most suited to act in the areas of legislative inertia; to define the starting points from which the legislature will act; and to affect or even set legislative agenda by raising issues that call for legislative response. Because, however, starting points affect end points, and sometimes themselves become end points, the starting points must also reflect either an underlying consistency with legal principles or majoritarian preferences. As a result, capacity to discern these remains crucial.

Administrative agencies undoubtedly have some skills relevant to defining appropriate starting points.[30] They have at their disposal highly qualified staffs and can make use of experts to provide the complex technical data that may be necessary to deciding whether a rule does further consistent treatment of majoritarian preferences. They can issue detailed and prospective regulations, and hence give legislatures a starting point from which to react without thereby adversely affecting legitimate expectations. They are in some sense accountable to majoritarian bodies (legislative and executive), and so have some capacity to discern what shifts in treatment may be needed to respond to current desires.[31] They have, moreover, the kind of detailed knowledge of the particular statute they administer, which can lead them fairly readily to see if some parts of the law have been rendered anachronistic by technological, legal, or even ideological changes. They can if they will, in other words, find and cure inconsistencies that develop within the area they are mandated to oversee. But agencies also lack capacities fundamental to the task of updating law in general, and they lack them precisely because of the very skills they do have.

The mere existence of technical staff, highly concerned with what are often immediate issues, makes it hard to fit a problem in historical context, in a full legal topography. Political accountability leads almost inevitably to an overblown faith in one's capacity to know what the majority wants, and hence to a tendency to emphasize this aspect of lawmaking to the detriment of consistency.[32] In addition, political accountability can readily be made into a justification for agency action which furthers what the commissioner or bureaucrat believes to be right, regardless of majoritarian desires or the legal fabric. The accountable bureaucrat comes to view himself or herself as a person picked to do what he or she thinks best, until fired, rather than as a delegate of those who are so chosen or as a servant of dominant legal principles.[33] Yet the reasons elected legislators and executives are permitted to do what they think best apply to the bureaucrat, to the "independent" commissioner, and to agency staff only in an indirect and attenuated fashion.[34]

Accountability, however, if it fails to make the commissioner or bureaucrat a representative of the majority, tends to make service of principle extraordinarily difficult. For the existence of a staff makes even the independent agency peculiarly subject to financial pressures from individual legislators or members of the executive. Strange to say, an elected court is more independent, less subject to the force and whim of particular legislators and executives, than even regulators on long-term appointments. The capacity of the latter to act depends too much on their staff and budgets not being cut — in other words, on legislative or executive good will.[35] Even an elected court can perform its tasks free from such pressures during its term of office.

Moreover, the existence of staff and the capacity to make detailed and prospective regulations mean that an agency can, more readily than a court, go beyond identifying those laws that are out of date and pressing the legislature to reconsider them. It means that agencies can attempt to work out full and detailed solutions to the problems the out-of-date statutes addressed. But though this is certainly a technical advantage, it leads to substantial danger if, as I have suggested, the agencies are not fully sensitive to majoritarian wishes and are not constrained by the demands of principles. It is, after all, one thing to allow a nonlegislative body to say on its own: "this law doesn't fit," or "it no longer seems to meet majoritarian demands," or even "*I* don't like it, and the legislature should reconsider it." It is quite another to permit such a body to present the legislature with its own version of a totally new statute from which the legislature can dissent.[36]

Finally, accountability, existence of a technical staff, and responsibility to administer a particular statute or set of laws combine to make it very unlikely that agencies will see inconsistencies that have arisen between "their" statutes and the general body of the law or even majoritarian desire outside the statutory area assigned to them.[37] The agency and its staff are picked because of their knowledge of one area. The statute that authorized the agency typically charges it to focus on a particular dimension of the legal landscape and not on the whole. And those legislators who are most influential in overseeing the agency or bureau and its budget are also those who have made their careers on committees primarily concerned with the problems of that same area. It is inevitable that independent agencies and even dependent bureaucrats will lack the general sense of what the polity wants.

The net effect of all this is that agency action to update laws—when it takes place at all—tends to serve what the staff and commissioners believe to be right for society; or what powerful figures in the legislature or the executive want or think the majority wants; or fairly obvious, dramatic modifications in popular sentiments with respect to parts of the statute being administered; or even, occasionally, the need to keep the specific statutory scheme reasonably coherent within itself in the face of technological or ideological changes. But only rarely will such action serve to keep a statute coherent or consistent with the general body of laws and principles that make up the whole of the changing legal landscape.

We may, of course, question whether such principles exist at all and whether, if they do exist, they are so encompassing that they avoid all discretion on the part of those who seek to further them, as Ronald Dworkin argues; or whether instead they are—as seems more plausible to me—softer and less fully directive, as Harry Wellington suggests; whether, in other words, they guide or compel.[38] We may question whether courts seek and follow such principles, or whether they too try primarily to discern the will of the majority or to follow their own sense of right and wrong. We may, finally, question whether in a modern society such principles should legitimately guide lawmaking, or even guide the setting of the starting points to which legislatures must react.[39] But, as I said, the very attributes and qualities that can make administrative agencies useful delegates of majoritarian bodies, and indispensable adjuncts to institutions that are suited to find and apply general legal principles, make it very difficult for the agencies themselves to do the jobs of updating that require a sense of what those principles are.

Does this matter? Let us admit that the sense of the legal landscape, and of the interplay of history and legislative words and scholarly comment, that is needed to discern and apply principles of law cannot readily be transferred to administrative agencies. Does this mean that they cannot be relied on to update laws? Not necessarily; it will only mean this if administrative agencies and dependent bureaucrats fail to justify themselves in the other way we have traditionally justified lawmaking institutions, that is, if they fail adequately to represent and reflect existing majorities.

I said earlier that there is nothing wrong with inconsistent, unprincipled, or preferential treatment—within the bounds of constitutional requirements. Most lawmaking involves just such preferences, and these must be respected as long as they represent the wishes of current majorities or coalitions of minorities or even the past compromises among groups that retain current majoritarian support. It is for this reason that government by directly majoritarian bodies, or by representative bodies unhampered by checks and balances, does not present pressing problems of obsolescence. Such bodies "know" the distinctions that are currently desired, the differences that still matter to people, and respond to them without a self-conscious search into the whole legal-political landscape. (America's past rejection of government by an unchecked majoritarian body is not grounded on a perception that it would be unable to reflect current differences, but rather on the notion that, unchecked, such a system would respond too radically to temporary majorities or desires.)[40]

When a legislature does act and its actions result in statutes, it is fair enough to assume that, at least for a time, the differences, preferences, and inconsistencies it ordained are desired by the governed and are legitimate.[41] Nor need that status be given only to legislative actions. The same majoritarian basis explains why a series of juries can also be used to update laws, without much self-conscious concern for consistency. No single jury can be viewed as representative, but a series of randomly selected ones can sense when rules and distinctions no longer reflect the popular will.[42] The uses of juries to update laws is of course common in America, precisely because juries are effective only as a result of a whole series of separate decisions and hence avoid the perceived dangers of direct, unchecked majoritarianism.

The point, then, is not whether institutions unconstrained by principle can properly update laws; obviously legislatures can, if they but will. Nor is it whether only legislatures can be permitted to do the job; we have traditionally employed juries to do it as well. It is, rather, whether administrative agencies are sufficiently responsive to the electorate so that we can trust *their* sense of what preferences and distinctions are appropriate, to serve at least as the starting point for legislative reaction.

There is little to suggest that they can. The relationship of the independent agency to the majoritarian bodies that oversee it gives us no reason to assume that it has the unselfconscious sense of how a distinction is viewed in the polity at large which we attribute to a legislature, or to the executive as a whole, or to a series of juries. It responds to the majoritarian bodies, but mainly to parts of them and in ways that cannot reflect the mixture of pressures and views we associate with the governed.

The dependent agency or bureau, because dependent on the executive, which can be assumed to have the same sense of the polity, may do better — at least if it can be made dependent on the whole and not just on a small part of the executive body. But then we would be likely to keep it from acting freely, for it could do so without any of the safeguards with which we hem in the executive and the legislature. To allow the truly dependent agency to act to update our laws would, in fact, be to cut through our checks and balances by allowing a majoritarian but unrestrained executive to enforce its views of the popular will as the base from which all other checked bodies would have to move.[43]

Thus administrative agencies fall between two stools as updaters of law. If they were freed from the factors that bind them, they could make rapid changes in our laws, unconstrained by principles or desires for consistency, and do so with great technical capacity. But they would still not do that job so well as an unchecked legislature or executive, which have the representative base essential for such political changes and to which we have been unwilling to give this kind of unchecked power in the past. Nor can agencies do the job of identifying those laws that are anachronistic. For this job requires a sense of the whole legal topography, a subservience to doctrine, and a political independence that courts have and that agencies necessarily lack.

All this does not mean that agencies do not have an important role to play in the updating of laws, both on their own and in conjunction with other institutions. There are ways and techniques (some of which have already been used) through which courts and administrative agencies can overcome their own incapacities and employ each other's skills in the task of bringing about an updating of statutes.[44] Moreover, the very way in which agencies fall between two stools suggests that they would be very good at initiating the process of change when what is involved is the curing of inconsistencies that have developed within the scope of a statute. Similarly, when political or ideological changes have made a part of the statutory scheme suspect, it may be appropriate for agencies to adapt the scheme without requiring a complete review of the law, especially when such political changes are apt to be only temporary.[45]

In addition, agencies do perform many jobs without which our statutory system would become dated far more rapidly than it does. If, for example, the legislature tells the office of a state insurance commissioner to see to it that certain minimal deductions be offered with insurance policies and that these be kept up to date despite inflation, it is easy enough for the administrative agency to perform the task. It would be much harder for courts to do it, especially if the updating requires technical, highly complex, and controversial findings. A court may be able to decide that the task is not being done without being easily able to do it; and yet such tasks are crucial in avoiding an extraordinary amount of statutory obsolescence.

There remain, however, other updating jobs that require either a direct sense of majoritarian wishes or a broad insight into how the law in question fits within the whole legal system. For these, administrative agencies are not especially well-suited. And it would be no answer to give them the skills and responsibilities we attribute to courts, for to do so would hamper them in the crucial technical and political tasks described in the last two paragraphs. To the extent that we favor rapid change in such areas, we are likely to assign such jobs to directly popular or relatively unchecked representative institutions. To the extent that we are fearful of abrupt change, we are likely to look to courts as those bodies most suited to tell us that updating is necessary.

VI

Legislative Responses

The most obvious response to the problems caused by the aging of statutes would seem to be freeing up of the legislatures so that they would find it as easy to revise laws as they do to pass them. Nevertheless, and perhaps surprisingly, there has been relatively little pressure to make the fundamental structural reforms that such a move would require. In the next chapter I shall discuss the reasons for this. Here I am concerned with more limited changes in the legislative process, changes that accept statutorification, retain the basic structure of checks and balances, and yet make easier the revision and updating of laws.

Sunset Laws

The most significant of these changes is the move to limit the time for which statutes and regulations are in force. Some statutes recently passed have had expiration dates written into them.[1] But that is still an occasional phenomenon. What seems instead to be a more general response is the advocacy of sunset laws. The intellectual history of sunset laws is extraordinarily distinguished. The actual achievements and prospects are meager, though it may still be too early to tell.

The American progenitor of sunset laws was no less a titan than Thomas Jefferson, who argued that all statutes and all constitutions should last no longer than nineteen years.[2] The object of Jefferson's proposal was simply to ease change. Continuity was not a value he particularly cherished except as statutes and constitutions might be reenacted because of consistent majoritarian wishes. Rationalist that he was, he may have believed that such a continuity was likely. And that of course is the rub; not many share (or even then shared) to the full his rationalist faith. If all statutes and constitutions were to be reexamined *de novo* every so often, a totally new balance in lawmaking would be established quite unlike the one to which we have grown accustomed. Instead of a system designed to achieve continuity and change in a modern, statutory world, we would have a system that gives us change and little continuity. The traditional American reluctance to be at the mercy of a single, perhaps temporary, majority together with our equally conservative approach to law, which I call our "retentionist bias,"[3] not only doomed Jefferson's proposal when he suggested it but continues to make true sunset systems unlikely.

More recently, Justice Hugo Black appeared to be a proponent of a form of sunset laws.[4] But the difference between his position and the original Jeffersonian view is notable. To Black, statutes were to die, but the Constitution was not. The fundamental charter afforded sufficient continuity and all else could, with little risk, be readily majoritarian. Yet few Americans would be so radical with respect to nonconstitutional policies as Black was willing to be; and just as few are so ferociously attached to the principles he saw as embedded in the Constitution itself. The simple constitutional-statutory balance between continuity and change that Justice Black furthered throughout his career was certainly not the balance we have come to view as the traditional American one. More important, it seems unacceptably simple, dangerous even, to most Americans today.

Because of this widespread reluctance to reconsider "everything" now and then, the recent revival of interest in sunset laws has had a still more limited scope. As proposed by Theodore Lowi and as presented in various legislatures, the main thrust of the sunset movement has been primarily toward regulatory statutes and agencies.[5] (This emphasis is further evidence of the failure of the agencies as full-scale updaters of laws and an ironic twist on the great hopes of the New Deal theorists for such agencies.) The basic object of sunsetting remains the same, however. If the burden can be placed on those who wish to retain an agency or a regulation rather than on those who wish to modify or destroy it, the argument goes, then legislative inertia will no longer serve the dead hand of the past.

Analogous arguments can be made to support the suggestion that all tax deductions be void if not reenacted every so many years.[6]

In its recent form and focus on regulatory obsolescence, sunsetting has sought to make a broader balance between continuity and change than Justice Black's, though still a simple, mechanical one. Some laws, regulatory ones, should be subject to full reexamination and rapid change, while others should retain inertial force for continuity. Since even this compromise would leave the regulatory process subject to an aberrant legislature and a temporary majority, typical sunset laws "time" the death of regulatory statutes so that only a certain fraction of them fall in any one year. Thus no single legislature can totally redo the administrative-regulatory structure in its own image or in response to a short-lived popular majority.[7]

Unfortunately, even these compromises are simplistic. For sunset does not guarantee either that a current majority will rule or that only anachronistic laws will fail to be reenacted. It only deprives a past majority of the benefit of inertia and gives it to those who object to the laws. Since regulatory laws age at different rates and in different ways, a system that invalidates such laws with clockwork regularity gives a tremendous weapon to those who oppose regulation itself; the force of inertia shifts to their side.

If sunset laws achieved their formal object, then many laws, enacted when popular pressure could be mobilized in their favor, would fall by the wayside at the next or next but one sunset, even though they were in no sense out of date or anachronistic. (Some chance event, a catastrophic accident let us say, enabled the majority to be heard, but time would dull the capacity for outrage and make it hard for the still existing majority to be effective five or ten years later.)[8] Checks and balances would ensure that those who lost when the majority could be heard would have a second chance as soon as that majority fell silent. And this second chance would not be linked to any general desire to treat like cases alike, to broad principles or consistencies in the law, but to a mechanical doctrine linked solely to time.

To avoid this danger, legislatures would have to find a way to prevent the reenactment of laws subject to sunset from being blocked in committee. From this it would be but a short step to a legislative procedure that would treat the periodic reexamination or reenactment as a mere form. In other words, sunsetting would defeat itself. If the procedure worked it would almost certainly go too far, and we would be right back where we started, with obsolete laws being automatically reenacted under a special procedure, much as today some fiscal statutes, which could give an occasion for reconsideration of the programs they fund, are treated so as to make any substantive review unlikely.[9]

The point is, in the end, quite simple. Time does not serve as a good indicator of age either in all statutes generally or in regulatory ones in particular. It does not distinguish sufficiently between those in need of reconsideration because they have become anachronistic and those which are in no sense anachronistic. Treating all statutes as immune from reconsideration (unless the inertia exerted by our system of checks and balances can be overcome) is unsatisfactory. But it is more unsatisfactory to force a reconsideration of all statutes, or even of all statutes of a certain category, at periodic intervals and thereby create an all-pervasive reverse inertia. Such a reconsideration either would not be effective because too time-consuming or would serve as the occasion for the employment of inertia to block the reenactment of what frequently would still be majoritarian laws. It is little wonder, then, that sunset laws have been disappointing in those jurisdictions that have tried them. Only trivial regulations, which, one may guess, would have been repealed even without the complex sunset structure, have in fact been abolished.[10]

But can we find a more sophisticated form of sunset? Can we develop a way of sorting out those laws that are in need of reworking or legislative reconsideration without requiring the legislature to rethink a whole area of the law? Can we limit sunsetting to those statutes that no longer fit the legal fabric? Herein lies the real challenge that the sunset movement must face. But it is a challenge I fear cannot be met. It is not the category of law which determines whether a statute is anachronistic, nor is it necessarily the statute's age. As a result, nonjudgmental modes of defining what should be reworked are likely to fail.

If that is the case, the question becomes: What institution or body can be entrusted with the job of determining which laws and rules need renovation or reconsideration? If that job is assigned to an ordinary committee of the legislatute, there will be little renewal for the same reasons that keep existing committees from suggesting renewal on their own. (The same interplay of interests will have the same effect.) If, instead, the job is given to administrative agencies empowered to regulate the area, we are right back to the problems discussed in the last chapter, including the lack of legitimacy and capacity of such agencies to discern what laws *are* out of phase.

We could, of course, create a separate executive and legislative review commission, and give it the task of reviewing statutes to see whether they should be subject to sunset, considering both the apparent majoritarian support for the statute and the fit of the statute in the general topography. To the extent that such a commission was permitted to act primarily on the basis of its view of what a current majority desires, it would, like the President under the Cutler-Johnson proposal, become a dominant, almost unchecked force for cutting through our checks and balances.[11] And one can question whether that would be desirable, even if the commission's majoritarian basis were stronger than, at first blush, one would assume.[12] To the extent, instead, that it was concerned with the fit of the statute, the commission would be exercising a judicial role outside the normal judicial system.[13] Such a delegation of authority to make a principled "judicial" determination to a body outside the regular court system would be more in keeping with the European tradition than with our own.

The Continental tradition has been that as new judicial functions are discerned, they are assigned to bodies outside the normal judicial system. These bodies inevitably act like courts, since they perform judicial tasks, but they remain separate from the ordinary court system. Thus in Europe there are the Conseil d'Etat, the Constitutional Court, and the Court of Cassation, all supreme in their sphere but separate. The American tradition has been to force all of these judicial, and many semijudicial, bodies into one channel that leads ultimately to the supreme court of the relevant jurisdiction. This has been the tendency for courts of claims, for administrative determinations, and for both private and public law. Commissions reviewing statutes on a principled basis would, therefore, probably follow this same pattern and for the same reason: the job and functions they would be performing would be judicial ones, and in the end whatever we called them, they would become courts.[14]

Need we go that far? Could not the task of judgmental sunsetting be performed by advisory law reform commissions?[15] These bodies, composed of retired and current legislators, judges, attorneys, and legal scholars could be asked systematically to study laws that are out of date and to recommend changes to the legislature. This would of course significantly alter their traditional role. As originally envisioned by Cardozo, in a justly celebrated article that took some thirteen years to bear fruit, law review commissions were to concentrate on changing those outworn common law rules that the courts of the time were reluctant to cast away.[16] On the whole they have stayed true to this initial charge. They have tended to deal primarily with private substantive common law and have limited their recommendations for changes in statutes to technical as opposed to policy questions.[17] Thus they have sought legislative review of common law rules that remained in force mainly because the rule was rarely litigated or because the rule could only be replaced by something more detailed than a court could fashion.[18] Occasionally they have urged legislative changes designed to achieve better implementation of clearly accepted legislative purposes. But they have steered clear of making controversial suggestions with respect to statutes, even when these statutes no longer fit the legal topography.

This limited focus of the commissions in the past is no accident and makes it unlikely that they could ever perform differently now. They are not elected or responsive to an elected body; neither can they claim that their subservience to principle and precedent gives them the legitimacy traditionally accorded to judicial actions. For these reasons they have been given no authority to do more than recommend changes. And nothing can destroy the force of such recommendations as to have them systematically ignored. Yet this is almost inevitably the fate awaiting a recommendation for reconsideration of an ill-fitting law that is supported by a powerfully placed legislative minority or even just by the desire on the part of legislators to avoid a fuss. Can anyone, for example, imagine that a stand taken by a law reform commission against the Connecticut statute prohibiting birth control devices[19] would have led to a legislative reconsideration of that law, even though it was almost universally recognized to be anachronistic?

No, authority is needed to enforce judgmental sunsetting, to bring about legislative reconsideration of outworn laws. And if we are reluctant to give that authority to the executive or to courts,[20] we would, properly, be loath to give it to retired worthies, however worthy. Why, moreover, given a lack of authority to make changes, would parties aggrieved by timeworn laws make their complaints known to such commissions? Those who could benefit from prospective relief would, as they do now, lobby legislatures directly. Those who realize that a timeworn law has injured them only after the harm has occurred, would not go to such a commission because it could not help them retroactively. Such people go to courts precisely because courts can give *ex post* relief. And this power, which makes courts keenly aware of the existence of legal anachronisms no one else sees, would never be appropriately given to law reform commissions,[21] unless of course we converted them into real courts.

In summary, the proper placement of the burden of inertia is too complex a job to be done mechanically. For that reason automatic sunsetting fails. Either inertia must be destroyed, through abolition of checks and balances, or inertia must be assigned judgmentally. If it is to be destroyed, we will trust no one — not law reform commissions, not administrative agencies, not even dependent bureaucrats — except an unchecked majoritarian legislature, president, or referendum. If, true to our traditions of checks and balances, we are afraid of such unchecked majoritarian rule, we are bound to assign inertia judiciously, that is, judicially. If inertia cannot be abolished or be assigned mechanically, it is best assigned by a body that can determine how the particular law in question fits in the full sweep of the law and is limited, checked as it were, by that finding. Such a task requires an examination of the whole modern common law fabric, made up of statutes and common law principles. And such an examination is really no more than a modern version of the task traditionally assigned to the common law courts.

Indexing

Before we consider how courts could exercise the power to allocate inertia or discuss approaches that would make any allocation of inertia unnecessary with respect to statutes, we should take a few moments to examine what can be done, beyond limited and mechanical sunsetting, to keep laws from becoming obsolete. In other words, before we turn to broader solutions, we should see if more might be done to limit the areas in which broader solutions are needed. In particular, we should look at some devices available to legislatures which, if employed, might make fewer laws so quickly anachronistic.

One example may suffice to suggest both the remedy and its limits: indexing. Many statutes have become anachronistic because they use figures and sums rendered ridiculous by inflation. It is easy to find dramatic examples of laws designed to help a particular group which, over time and because of inflation, have become the major obstacle that group must overcome.[22] Here, at least, one might see a simple solution to obsolescence. Here no hidden fountain of youth must be found in order to keep laws from middle age, for a drink from one's own faucet will do as well. Legislatures only need to provide an escalator clause that links the set sum to a cost-of-living index, and a major source of anachronism will be destroyed. If, moreover, no single cost-of-living index is thought to be sophisticated enough for a particular statute, then the duty to keep the figure constant in real (rather than money) terms could be effectively delegated to an administrative agency.

Why then have legislatures been so reluctant to adopt this solution, which would surely reduce the problem without requiring major structural changes or even radical reworkings of judicial-legislative balances? There are, of course, instances where indexing has been adopted.[23] There may even be instances where analogous "technical" updatings have been mandated or delegated in areas requiring factual findings more complex than those needed for indexing.[24] Still indexing, simple or complex, is relatively unusual.

One reason is that often the legislature intends a set sum (to stay with a simple indexing example) to go out of date. That is, the sum was not intended to be constant in real rather than money terms. A set money amount may have been no more than a necessary payoff to a powerful group, adopted in order to get a broader statute passed. Or it may have been a recognition that a new law entailed significant transitional problems and that some of the burden of the change should be cushioned. In such situations the legislature may have bet on inflation, and time, to reduce and ultimately destroy the payoff or to let the cushion shrink as the transition period is overcome. Ironically, a set sum that is destroyed by external changes may be a far more effective device *for* change than any sunset or reconsideration requirement written into the law.

Why not recognize that set sums have two opposite functions — one requiring indexing to provide for updating; the other making the lack of indexing the very technique by which updating operates?

Why does not this analysis suggest a yet greater legislative capacity for keeping laws in phase than was at first indicated? The problem is that no sharp line between the two situations is realistic. There is rarely a clear legislative intent to keep money figures real in some cases and to provide a self-destroying payoff or transition in others. In most situations some legislators want one result, some want the other, and some would rather not say what they want. And the law can be passed only because the underlying ambiguity is not resolved.

But why don't legislatures index in those cases where no ambiguity exists and the object is to keep money terms real? Sometimes they do. Yet even here legislatures are likely to be reluctant to adopt across-the-board indexing. If indexing were required to indicate a legislative desire to provide a constant sum in real terms, that would unmistakably suggest that when a figure in a statute is not tied to an index, the figure is designed to self-destruct and to provide only temporary relief. Such an obvious statement would make it far more difficult for the legislature to achieve compromise through ambiguity and would impede the enactment of laws.

Today, when a statute provides for a set sum, one doesn't know for sure if the legislative object is to give transitional relief, ever reduced by inflation, or permanent support. One can cite what may well be examples of each in enacted laws with precisely the same form.[25] These examples are of great use to legislators and to the whole legal-political system, in permitting ambiguous results and compromises, where neither "clear" position would find sufficient support. Thus figures, though nominally clear, perform a function analogous to that performed by ambiguous language. And the requirement or habit that figures be made truly clear in their intent would be as destructive as would any requirement of nonambiguity in language, were that to be imposed on legislatures across the board.

Reluctantly, one is forced to the conclusion that mechanical devices are not effective ways of avoiding obsolescence. As with ambiguous language, a form of judgment is needed if one is to parse what the function of outdated figures is. Yet, in contrast to the judgment required when ambiguous language is used, interpretation is an inappropriate word to describe the process.[26] One may find on examination that no single purpose existed, but would courts then be correct in interpreting, in using the ambiguity as a justification for furthering other, nonlegislative goals?[27] Even in this seemingly simple area, highly complex judgments are called for if legislative desires, majoritarian needs, and the demands of continuity and change are to be met in a system that never stands still technologically or sociologically. In the end, we still face the same three basic possibilities: (1) reliance on relatively unchecked majoritarian institutions to update laws; (2) abandonment of twentieth-century statutorification and return to the supposed nineteenth-century golden age; or (3) development of a contemporary legislative-judicial balance that accepts statutorification and works within it.

VII

Structural Responses

Structural reform designed to deal with obsolete statutes can approach the problem from two diametrically opposite directions. The first approach accepts the move to a statutory state and seeks to mold the structure and philosophy of our government to fit that state. Legislative inertia is attacked directly by changing our legislatures and the structure of our whole governmental system so that revision and updating of timeworn laws becomes at least as easy as the passing of new ones.

The second approach accepts as given our structure of government and its philosophy, and makes no attempt to abolish the obstacles which that structure and philosophy have put in the way of legislative action. It seeks, instead, a return to the pure golden age of the common law, before the orgy of statute making,[1] and assumes that, if we could stop passing so many statutes, the traditional relationship between courts and legislatures would still be effective today. The obvious correlative of this approach is to increase the obstacles to legislative and executive lawmaking. If the first approach seeks to make revision as easy as enactment, the second tries to make enactment as unlikely as revision.

Neither approach has found much explicit contemporary support, although wistful scholars can be found in both camps. The first camp applauds those European parliamentary systems that, nominally at least, make legislative updating easy.[2] Occasionally, it goes further and supports direct majoritarianism through initiative and referendum.[3] The second camp expresses its nostalgia by emphasizing the past glories of the common law.[4] But both groups of reformers miss what, for better or worse, are facts of current American political life, facts that explain why neither finds much support.

I do not wish to dwell on either structural approach in this book because the difficult intellectual issues arise in between. Under the first approach, judicial power to evolve and create the common law would be anachronistic.[5] Under the second, the problem of statutory obsolescence would not exist. Under either, the most difficult issues of the relation between court and legislature would be avoided.[6] These problems, the core of this book, exist *because* neither structural reform seems likely.

Responsive Legislatures and Direct Majoritarianism

The nominal advantages of direct responsiveness to popular majoritarian desires are manifest and have frequently been analyzed. Similarly, the dangers of such direct responses, say through initiative and referendum, form a commonplace part of the literature.[7] The argument that America should abandon many of the obstacles that impede even representative majoritarianism is also not new and was, especially in the thirties and forties, frequently made. The specific obstacles that are most noxious, and most readily dispensable, have varied from time to time: federalism; separation of the legislature from the executive; bicameralism; legislative committees; non-ideological, nonnational political parties; geographical pluralitarianism rather than proportional representation; and even the written constitution. The particular choice of villain has depended on the political issues of the time and the particular reform proposals and ideology of the critic.[8]

What many of these criticisms miss or choose to ignore, of course, is that all of the institutions mentioned are guilty, and that their obstruction of a momentary popular will was in most cases either intentionally assigned or is the product of long-term constitutional growth. This fact by no means makes such obstructive institutions desirable — direct representative majoritarianism may well be a better system than the one we have — but it does help to explain why the pleas of such critics so often go unheeded.

Take, for example, a recent villain: the power of legislative committees to obstruct lawmaking and reform.[9] Such committees are clearly a source of inertia and often bottle up laws and reforms that the full legislature would pass. Moreover, the arguments are unconvincing that such committees are needed for other reasons, and that their capacity to block the legislative will is an unfortunate but inevitable side effect of these other functions. Thus it is sometimes said that legislative committees and their expert staffs are needed to develop the complex laws, and the often even more complex revisions of laws, which a technologically and sociologically complicated society requires. But surely such staff functions, technical analysis, and even legislative drafting can be well enough handled by the executive. And though committees might also have staffs that could provide alternative proposals to those of the executive, when the executive itself has specific legislative aims, a vote in the full Congress on those proposals could be mandated. One could go further and imagine allowing Congress a vote "in principle" on a proposal, if a relatively small group of congressmen petitioned for it, to be followed by an assignment of the drafting of a detailed statute to carry out the proposal, either to a legislative committee or to an executive department (as determined by the vote in principle). Such a detailed draft would not, in this view, be allowed to die in committee but would have to return to the floor.

One could, of course, go on and on. My object, however, is not to cook fully some half-baked suggestions. It is to present them raw, precisely to indicate that their rejection would not stem from mere technical problems. Like most proposals to do away with checks and balances, they fail for the more fundamental reason that all such changes would reallocate power and make law revision too easy, in ways that have never found acceptance in the United States. Thus the first suggestion would be attacked because of the greatly increased power it would give to the executive; the vote in principle might be objectionable because, in practice, many absurd or noxious laws have also been bottled up in committees. In some such cases, Congress would have been bound to pass them if they had reached the floor, especially on a vote in principle, even though passage was against the best judgment of the congressmen themselves. That is, a majority wanted the laws to be killed in committee whatever the congressmen felt they had to say or vote in public.[10]

I am not saying that the benefits of bottling up are worth their costs — far from it. I am simply saying that the technical arguments for having powerful legislative committees reflect deeper structural notions, about what the allocation of power in a democracy like ours should be, and fears of what it would be if the obstacles created in the past were eliminated.

Modifying the role of legislative committees is a minor change. The doubts and misgivings about the reallocations of power are much greater when we consider modifications in the older checks and balances (federalism, executive-legislative separation, and so forth). Yet these are the very checks and balances that would have to be abolished in order to accomplish the kind of responsive majoritarianism which could do away with the problem of statutory obsolescence.

Obsolescence in legal rules exists when laws do not reflect the views of a current majority on what preferences in treatment are warranted by present conditions. The obvious solution is to make laws respond to the requirements of these majorities.[11] If, however, we are afraid to make laws so responsive, then all approaches that seek to focus directly on the current majoritarian basis of a law are in some sense misdirected. They either do not go far enough to solve the problem, or they are blocked by the fact that the cure is deemed worse than the illness. This is not to say that such deep reforms are undesirable. It is only to assert that to most people the unknowns of such reforms are too great; if forced to the choice, they prefer structural conservatism, even if that means living with timeworn laws.

For all these reasons, speculation on what fundamental modifications would be needed to achieve a politically optimal system seems out of place in this book. I am willing to take as given our tradition of legislative inertia in law revision, and our desire for continuity and change rather than quick responsiveness. In that sense this book is deeply conservative. I do not pretend to propose what might be the best solution written on a clean slate, but only to suggest the implications of the changes that have largely unselfconsciously occurred in the last fifty to seventy years and consider what needs to be done, in the light of those changes, to establish a modern version of the old accepted balance between lawmaking and law revision.

The Golden Age and the Reason for Statutes

Deep fears and deeper attachments keep us from making the structural reforms that would make law revision relatively easy. Do analogous concerns keep us from a return to the high days of the common law?

Obsolete laws do not really exist, the devotees of the common law would say, when legal rules respond in a changing, accretional, and continuous way to the underlying principles of the people. Although courts and juries are best suited to discern such principles, the manner in which they do so, and the way in which such notions arise, tend to make the resulting legal rules majoritarian in a basic if not immediate sense. The principles themselves permit only those discriminations and preferences that have come to be accepted by the people over time. And past preferences and discriminations that are no longer wanted, like past compromises among powerful groups, will wither away as many different courts and juries seek to discern the constantly rewoven fabric of the law. A given rule may not fit at any specific moment, but the pressure to change the rule to make it conform to the underlying notions of the "law" is there, and will soon enough win out.[12]

Why, then, don't we try to turn back the clock and make courts the primary agents of lawmaking and law reform, leaving to legislatures the crucial, but limited, function of revising the common law when courts have strayed too far from the deep majoritarian intent or when a crisis requires immediate change?[13] In fact, contemplation of this reactionary reform is even more fatuous than contemplation of a quick change to a "responsible parliamentary system" of government.

The orgy of statute making has not occurred by chance, even if its total effect has been to an extraordinary degree unintended and unselfconscious. It has not, moreover, been limited to our legal system. It is replicated in European parliamentary systems in which special statutes have to a large extent overwhelmed the great nineteenth-century codes.[14] Such a worldwide movement cannot be blithely ignored. It stems from very real requirements of majorities, requirements strong enough to overcome the inertia that all these legal systems developed to protect their traditional modes of lawmaking. These requirements find their roots in technological and sociopolitical changes that made slow, accretional, lawmaking unsatisfactory, even if it responded to legal principles of the particular society. These changes cannot be wished away by anyone who wants to be at all realistic. I need not rehearse all of these requirements but mentioning a few may be useful, and the easiest way of doing this is to look at types of statutes we have passed and to consider what they were intended to do.

The first group of statutes are those so detailed and technical, specific in establishing rights, requirements, and procedures, that it is unthinkable for courts to try to establish them in a common law fashion.[15] Tax laws have always seemed to be of this sort. But in fact they are only an old example of a far broader category encompassing all those laws that regulate the taking and distributing of moneys by the state. In other words, tax laws are in this regard paradigmatic of all the laws of the welfare component of the welfare state. A return to a common law approach to lawmaking would, at the least, entail an abandonment of this social-democratic view of society. To say that such an abandonment is unlikely is obviously to understate. Whether correct or not, whether based on ideological responses to technological change or on independent philosophical movements, our country's commitment to the welfare state remains overwhelming and with it comes a necessary commitment to legislative lawmaking.[16]

The second group of statutes are those designed to yield uniformity in a large nation. These laws are more linked to the speed of technological change than to ideological movements. The common law had a substantial degree of uniformity. Major conflicts in areas like torts or contracts were avoided primarily because the fundamental allocation of rights was about the same in most of our various jurisdictions.[17] The nice questions of conflicts of laws arose in those limited areas (frequently statutory) in which some states had set out on their own, away from the common law fabric.[18] As technological demands made such deviations from the common law more frequent, however, potential conflicts became much greater. At the same time, the "shrinking" of America as a result of technological change made conflicts all the more dangerous. A difference in California and Minnesota law became nearly as significant as a difference between Minnesota and South Dakota. The slow engine of common law change seemed ill adapted to the needs of uniformity. Balancing one's precedents against a slight change in a neighboring state and a greater one in a distant jurisdiction might have been fine in a world in which rail traffic and telephones were new, but it was troublesome even in the 1920s let alone in the jet age. Uniform statute making at that time seemed, and still seems, a sensible response.[19]

The needs of uniformity were magnified by a third, broader ground for statute making. Even apart from the requirements of uniformity with other states, statutes often seemed needed because the common law was changing too slowly to deal adequately with rapid changes in society, even in traditionally common law fields. Moreover, when the common law did change rapidly to meet crises, it often created uncertainties that only statutes could resolve.

Some of the slowness and tentativeness in common law change may have been due to the dominance in the late nineteenth and early twentieth centuries of legal formalism, which, it is said, reduced the willingness and capacity of courts to perform their traditional role as reshapers of the common law.[20] Were that the only cause of the common law's lack of responsiveness to societal change, one could believe that, given today's courts, this ground for statute making might no longer exist.[21] But such a position is simplistic because it does not take into account the fact that common law change — totally apart from formalism — partly depends for its legitimacy on a willingness of courts to make law incrementally and tentatively.[22] As a result slowness, and uncertainty too, are almost inevitable parts of the common law process.

A court may be able to say that an old rule no longer fits the legal fabric and must be overruled, but how often can it say with sufficient certainty that a new rule is the one the legal topography requires? If it cannot, and if it is unwilling to go outside the boundaries of principled decision making and either impose its own will or guess at what a majority wants,[23] the common law court faces a dilemma. It can fail to change the old rule — and leave standing an outworn but certain law. Or, it can overrule the old rule, begin the process of reaching toward a new one, and thereby create an undesirable and potentially intolerable uncertainty.[24] Either way, a statutory response to the crisis seems likely.[25]

Such statutory responses are, of course, quite desirable for a time, and the court, if it acts in a way designed to bring them about, fulfills its role of inducing the reconsideration and updating of dated laws. The problem with which my book is directly concerned arises later, when the statute itself becomes dated. At this stage, however, it is enough to point out that the reason the statute was passed in the first place may well have been a good one, stemming from an appropriate judicial-legislative colloquy. It follows that the desire to return to a time of few statutes in order to avoid statutory obsolescence is misguided.

We may wonder why this same problem did not arise earlier, in the nineteenth century. The answer, I think, lies in the fact that major technological change has occurred faster in this century and has dated common law rules more rapidly; the new rules required by this kind of change have frequently been ones that were technically hard for courts to fashion, entailed the expenditure of public funds, or were in areas where the costs of uncertainty were intolerably high. The development of credit cards[26] and of complex and dangerous machines designed for broad consumer use[27] are but two recent examples of areas that gave rise to a statutory response because the common law was not quick enough to adapt.[28] Statutes concerning medical malpractice and product liability, on the other hand, have been justified because a too rapid common law updating created intolerable instability and uncertainty.[29]

There is always the danger, however, that such statutes will try to do more than make up for the common law's incapacity to provide certainty. Not infrequently such crisis rules reflect the desires of a declining majority, which stands to lose from the emerging common law and wishes to freeze the law before the trend can be fully realized in both courts and legislatures.[30] *Ad hoc* statutes like these are likely to pose quickly and dramatically the problem of statutory obsolescence. Yet at the time they are passed, even these crisis responses often seem preferable to remaining with a clearly outworn common law rule or to living with the chaos created by a judicial undermining of that rule.[31]

Not all of our recent statutes were the result of real crises. Sometimes the old allocation of entitlements made good sense. Nor were all of the crises so pressing that common law methods could not have adequately made the needed changes. But enough of them were real, so that even in the doubtful cases the argument for legislative intervention was plausible and inertia could be overcome.

Moreover, each statutory response to a crisis in one jurisdiction immediately created a uniformity problem — and a kind of secondary crisis — in the others. The old conflicts-of-laws problems often arose in areas where a state had by statute abandoned some common law underpinnings. As states did this with greater frequency to meet crises, lack of uniformity became an ever greater problem. And so both neighboring and distant jurisdictions were prompted to adapt to the change more quickly than they perhaps would have deemed necessary on the basis of their own underlying crisis in entitlements. Once again, since common law courts were reluctant to adopt another jurisdiction's statute in full,[32] the obvious way to avoid conflicts problems was through the enactment of a statute.[33]

As with the welfare state, one may decry the technological changes that have created the crises and the uniformity grounds for statutes, but it is unrealistic to believe that one can turn the clock back and avoid the need for such statutes.

The fourth group of statutes I shall mention are those in which complex conflicts among important, organized interest groups have been resolved or temporarily compromised by legislative intervention. Labor law immediately comes to mind as an example of this kind of legislation. I am not especially knowledgeable in this area of law, and it may be that the underlying conflicts were ones that only detailed and all-encompassing charters could resolve or abate. If so, and if the rise of more structured interest groups has made conflicts like those between labor and management more frequent in this century, still a fourth solid ground for statutorification would exist.

It is also said that all societal conflicts that are deep, and deeply political, can only be resolved by a majoritarian body regardless of whether or not they involve highly structured institutions.[34] But I must say that my own background in common law subjects makes me somewhat skeptical. There certainly were interest-group conflicts at common law as pressing, deep, and seemingly intractable as those existing among interest groups today.[35] And yet the common law courts managed to work out solutions and even temporary compromises in these areas. Of course the solutions they acheived were not necessarily right (but I would be just as reluctant about some recent legislative compromises), nor did all of them ultimately prevail. Some, in fact, were reversed or altered by legislatures that exercised their typically nineteenth-century revisionary role.[36] Nonetheless, the fact of interest-group conflict was not in itself a reason in the last century for statutory intervention, and the methods that permitted courts to solve or stay fights between ranching and farming interests (through developments in tort law) would not necessarily have failed in coping with more modern conflicts among interests.[37]

Once one puts such deep conflicts in the context of the first three sets of reasons for statutorification, however, the likelihood that common law methods will adequately resolve them diminishes greatly. Thus, if resolution of a dispute is eased by government intervention through payments, taxes, or detailed regulations, common law resolution becomes much less likely. Why, after all, should the compromise forgo one of its possible elements? Surely a solution should not be delayed or made more difficult simply to avoid enactment of yet another law when so many have already been passed. Similarly, if a compromise in one jurisdiction creates conflict with a previously established arrangement in another, then the pressure in the second jurisdiction for a speedy statutory reform to reestablish uniformity becomes enormous. Why put up with the costs of living with conflicts in laws if a statutory solution will ultimately be forthcoming; why not pass a national compromise to begin with? If, finally, occasions requiring compromises occur more frequently, because technological changes create new interest groups or alter their status, why (at least when the change has been sufficiently dramatic to overcome even legislative inertia) wait for the common law to adapt to it?

All these sensible enough grounds for *choosing* to enact statutes become mandatory under the current nominal set of rules which requires that courts leave statutes alone. Once a compromise has been enacted, a common law court cannot achieve a new one without infringing on the legislative prerogative. The move to statutorification thus becomes irreversible once the first statutory step is taken.[38] Indeed, it seems irreversible even if the only further compromises that can be made are judicial. It becomes irreversible despite the fact that the old compromise is kept in place by nothing but legislative inertia, unless one changes the rules and permits courts to force the modification of statutes.

The final set of laws are criminal laws. Traditionally these have been largely statutory because in our system criminality has required a degree of foreknowledge, and hence of forewarning, that common law methods seemed to preclude.[39] When criminal and fiscal laws comprised the bulk of statutes, we could readily let them be primarily statutory areas in the midst of a court-made common law. Foreknowledge and forewarning remain valid reasons; that is, they remain as much a part of our society's basic view of what ought to constitute punishable behavior. One may wonder, however, whether the traditional incapacity of courts to give that forewarning and foreknowledge is equally fixed.

Were criminal laws a principal source of the obsolescence problem, I would argue that it would not be impossible to reduce the amount of statutorification and still retain the foreknowledge and forewarning appropriate to criminal penalties. Such laws are not, however, the major source of our problems, so we need not bother wondering if in this area we could turn back to an earlier approach to lawmaking (in the one area, ironically, where the approach was not dominant in the nineteenth century); to do so would not make that much of a difference. Yet, when we discuss the possibility of a new judicial-legislative balance, we may keep in mind that the balance need not be limited to those areas encompassed by what we think of as the traditional balance. It might also cope with areas, such as criminal law, which were basically outside the old solution.

I have avoided listing all areas in which statutes have been or have become dominant. My object has been to suggest that the statutorification of American law has, on the whole, occurred for good reasons, that is, reasons that respond to the demands of the polity, whether or not those demands are good in some ultimate or ideological sense. That being the case, it seems to me self-evident that a return to the nineteenth-century methods of lawmaking will not occur. It follows that any attempt to create new obstacles to statutory enactment in order to slow down statutorification would fail and be misguided to boot.

The very fact that statutorification has occurred at an increasing pace, despite the formidable obstacles our system already puts in its way, is the best argument against thinking we can reverse the trend. The statutes that have been passed had to overcome a very substantial degree of inertia to get on the books. We can now say, with Grant Gilmore, that it is easier to pass a statute than to revise it.[40] But the same checks and balances apply to both passage and revision. Since they were overcome when the statutes were passed, it should be clear that the reasons for the statutorification of American law are powerful, deeply grounded, and for the foreseeable future unlikely to change.

If, then, an abolition of the checks and balances is extremely unlikely and a return to a common law world is unthinkable, what are
we to do? We can live with aging statutes and rely on time to render
them totally irrelevant, or rely on the manifest injustice of a few of
them to cause legislatures occasionally to overcome inertia and
revise them. We can live with and expand the generally unsatisfactory set of judicial and nonjudicial solutions canvassed in the earlier
chapters. Or we can self-consciously set out to consider whether new
techniques or doctrines can be made available to help us intelligently
to assign the burden of inertia. We can see if courts can be used,
through techniques analogous to those they employed in making
common law, to determine where the burden of inertia ought to lie,
to force the legislative agenda. We can ask the question of whether
the burden of inertia is best placed on those who would alter the
determinations of old legislatures and majorities, or whether it can,
through the courts, be assigned in a more self-consciously ra-
tionalistic fashion.

VIII

A New Approach:
Antecedents and Roots

Most of the problems with judicial responses to the statutorification of American law and to the growing obsolescence of statutes have stemmed from one of three facts: (1) doctrines that had other uses were being corrupted to allow courts to achieve judicial updating; (2) the doctrines, even when twisted to allow updating, failed to achieve it in important areas where it was needed and, even when they did allow updating, often updated in less effective ways than might have been accomplished but for the inappropriate doctrinal basis; (3) even where laws were being updated successfully through corruption of other doctrines, no sense of limits appropriate to the updating function was readily discernible, and no attempts to work out sensible limits seemed to be taking place. All three problems are different aspects of the same thing: courts have been using a pickax and calling it a case knife.[1]

The difficulties all arise, in other words, because neither courts nor scholars have faced the questions of when judicial action to induce the updating of statutes is desirable and what form and limits should be imposed on that function. Only if these questions are approached can one then reconsider whether such judicial action should take place at all (or whether we prefer to live with an inertial burden allocated by time and past legislatures)[2] and whether, if judicial updating is desirable, it is nevertheless best achieved indirectly, by subterfuges and by stretching other doctrines, or openly and candidly.

A Hypothetical Doctrine

I will start out by suggesting what at first sounds like a new approach, but which in fact is not much different from what courts have been doing for years through various subterfuges. Then I will consider the antecedents and roots of this approach in the American legal tradition. In the remainder of the book, I will begin to define the limits and techniques appropriate to this new approach. That definition will be only the start of what must elsewhere be a long and complex discussion. My object throughout is to examine the possibility of defining a modern version of what can be described as the traditional legislative-judicial balance, on the assumption that the aim of such a balance is the thoughtful allocation of the burden of inertia in a system of checks and balances which seeks both continuity and change.

To state the approach in summary form is easy; to outline, let alone fill out, its workings is far more difficult. So I will state the approach as a hypothesis. Let us suppose that common law courts have the power to treat statutes in precisely the same way that they treat the common law. They can (without resort to constitutions or passive virtues or strained interpretations) alter a written law or some part of it in the same way (and with the same reluctance) in which they can modify or abandon a common law doctrine or even a whole complex set of interrelated doctrines. They can use this power either to make changes themselves or, by threatening to use the power, to induce legislatures to act. Let us not, for the moment, concern ourselves with the question of whether this authority has been given explicitly to the courts by the legislatures or has been asserted independently by the courts themselves, in a common law way. ("We have, in fact, been doing this indirectly, it is time we said what we were doing and, so to speak, gave a name and a legitimacy to what has simply grown to be the law.")[3]

How should such a power be used? Should all or only some kinds of statutes be subject to it? Should many courts or only the highest courts of a jurisdiction be permitted to exercise it? When should courts using this power act on their own, and when should they instead use the power to press legislatures or administrative agencies into acting? Are there differences in the proper employment of this power and in the proper employment of the traditional judicial authority to update common law rules? Would employment of this power increase, diminish, or leave essentially unchanged the current level of "judicial activism"? These are the specific questions that immediately spring to mind once the approach is stated, even in hypothetical form. I shall return to them in the next chapters, but first it is well to look to the antecedents and roots of such an approach.

The Pomeroy Question and the Restaters

The approach that sounds quite radical when stated baldly has some eminently respectable parents. My genealogical tracing carries me no further back than the Pomeroy question and the California code. In 1872, when California adopted the Field Code as its civil code, that enactment presented a novel problem for the California courts. The legislation purported to codify the common law and the courts had to decide how to deal with this fact. In a series of articles John Norton Pomeroy articulated what he characterized as the "true method" of interpreting the code: it should be treated like the common law and be permitted to grow under the tutelage of the courts as if no codification had occurred. "Except in the comparatively few instances where the language is so clear and unequivocal as to leave no doubt of an intention to depart from, alter or abrogate the common-law rule concerning the subject matter, the courts should avowedly adopt and follow without deviation the uniform principle of interpreting all the definitions, statements of doctrines and rules contained in the code in complete conformity with the common-law definitions, doctrines and rules, and as to all the subordinate effects resulting from this interpretation."[4] (It may well be that there are older suggestions of this sort but, in the absence of any substantial statutorification, they would seem relatively unlikely.[5]) It is significant that, together with the first major attempts at codification in the American context, there also came this realization that codes would, given checks and balances, fall out of date.[6]

Pomeroy's suggested answer was relatively easy to carry out in the context of codification of the common law because of the nature of the nineteenth-century codes.[7] They were on the whole collections of the common law. They often spoke in general terms and so left room for much court intervention and interstitial lawmaking under traditional doctrines. They represented solutions to problems that had been dealt with by the courts for centuries. And they would require the same behavior from courts in code states as that expected from courts in noncode states. In other words, none of the difficult technical problems or any of the serious problems of limitation seemed especially pressing in the issue Pomeroy raised.[8]

Yet the importance of the suggested solution should not be underestimated. For a judicial authority to alter, rather than simply interpret, statutory law was being claimed. That sufficed to make the question problematic.[9] It is not clear to me that the Pomeroy question was ever formally answered at a theoretical or doctrinal level. As a practical matter, it is easy in retrospect to see that courts in code states have treated their codes much like courts in common law states have treated their common law rules and doctrines. In a sense, the common law nature of the codes and the generality of their rules made the practical answer to the Pomeroy question both simple and inevitable, and the doctrinal answer superfluous.

The next assertion of the judicial power over statutes was, if anything, more self-conscious, and it came from those pillars of the legal edifice who were the proponents of the first restatements. The reasons for the birth of the restatement movement are many and need not be rehearsed here.[10] Some of those reasons, however, sound like the reasons that have underlain the amazing growth of statutes over the last fifty years. More to our immediate point is the fact that the restaters, in wanting the law to be collected and described, also wanted (and often succeeded in getting) restatements of law that would be far more specific than those made in either the American or the great European codes. General clauses and loose codes were antithetical to the basic aims of the movement.[11]

As the restaters began to work, the inevitable question arose: What should the authority of the restatements be? The more ambitious believed that the aims of the movement could only be achieved if the restatements were enacted into law in each jurisdiction. But enactment of detailed provisions immediately signaled the danger of legal obsolescence to these lawyers, judges, and scholars, who were, after all, highly knowledgeable in the ways of American lawmaking.[12]

The solution proposed by those who persisted in the desire to have the restatements enacted into law was precisely the one I have given in hypothetical terms. The restatements should have a force of law equivalent to that given a longstanding judicial precedent of the jurisdiction. They should be treated, in other words, with no more or less deference than would be given to a common law rule or set of doctrines.[13]

As we know, the decision was made not to press for enactment of the restatements. The reasons were many, and it is not even clear that fear of legal petrification played a role in shaping the form that the restatements finally took.[14] Again, that is not of any great significance for us today. What does matter is the fact that the restaters foresaw what the effect of wholesale and detailed statutes would be in a system like ours and, conservative though they were, came up with the very same kind of solution we must now consider.

Since the restatements were first proposed, our law has become far more statutorified than would have been the case had the restatements been enacted into law. But because this came about unselfconsciously rather than by design, what seemed to the restaters to be a necessary question — the danger of statutory obsolescence — has not been faced. That in facing it today we return to consider their suggested solution seems neither surprising nor especially radical.

Landis and the Equity of Statutes

The third ancestor is rather different. It is the scholar who first pointed out the crucial consequences for the common law of the increasing weight of statutes in the United States. I am, of course, thinking of James M. Landis. In a powerful article Dean Landis, writing in the 1930s, both saw and analyzed the effect on the common law of New Deal statute-making, then just beginning.[15] He was concerned primarily with the appropriate effect of statutes on common law rules, rather than of the effect of the common law on statutes. And yet his argument implicitly, and at one point explicitly, gives more than vague support for the approach I described here.

The traditional view that statutes live apart from the common law, Landis argued, cannot survive in a world in which statutes are so common a form of lawmaking. The notion that common law rules develop on their own, subject to the gravitational pull (to paraphrase Ronald Dworkin)[16] of other judicial decisions and perhaps of technological or of socioeconomic changes, but immune from any legislative influences, makes no sense. Like judicial decisions, statutes may be particular and exert little or no gravitational pull, or they may represent a basic change in attitude toward law and toward entitlements generally. These last represent a major development in those principles that must guide the common law courts in their lawmaking. A whole course of statutes, like a set of judicial decisions, is likely to have a greater gravitational pull than an odd statute or an odd decision here and there. But, in the end, the common law must include statutes as a fundamental part of its fabric. To treat like cases alike, Landis concluded, courts must revise out-of-date precedents and adjust them to this broader, now in part statutory, common law.

His focus and principal object, as I said, was to encourage courts to be willing to look beyond common law precedents in revising their own out-of-date rules. Yet in the middle of his piece he casually describes an instance in which courts were needed to help update *statutes* that no longer fit the gravitational field he has described.[17] The step is inevitable. If statutes are to be made an integral part of the new common law fabric, if statutes are to become ever more common, and if the fundamental role of common law courts is to keep like cases being treated alike, it is no wonder that in his piece the courts almost came to be treated as having the same type of common law authority over statutes as they did over their own old doctrines.

When Landis wrote, the orgy of statute making had just begun, and his concern appropriately was centered on old taboos that limited the fun, rather than on what would happen after the orgy. So it is not surprising that his suggestion of a common law power over statutes was mentioned only in passing, and that the point of his article was to deal with the courts as updaters of the common law. In that respect he certainly achieved his aim. It would be most unusual for court or commentator today to ignore the gravitational pull of newly enacted statutes in deciding whether an old precedent has continued life.[18] But the full impact of Landis' writing, as well as his passing example, are equally valid as precursors of a more fundamental change. If there is a fabric of the law that defines, justifies, and delimits judicial lawmaking, if statutes are a part of this total fabric of the law, and if courts are to perform their role of treating like cases alike, why should they fail to exercise common law powers over statutes?[19]

The Harvard Legal Process School

The last set of ancestors I will mention is perhaps an unwilling one. But once a child is born, parentage is a responsibility that cannot easily be shirked. The unwilling parents are, I would suggest, Henry Hart and his successors in the so-called Harvard legal process school.[20] Their role as precursors is in a sense ambiguous since they never asserted the kind of authority for courts I am describing here. And yet they did two things that, it seems to me, make consideration of such authority inevitable. They asked what the proper role of interpretation was, and concluded that often it could not be a simple application of the will of past legislatures;[21] and they presented this conclusion in the context of powerful arguments for honesty and candor.[22]

There is no point in rehearsing the many subtle and elegant points made by various proponents of this approach. In a deep sense we are all followers of Henry Hart and know the moves almost by instinct. The main line is, however, worth restating in simple and hence almost caricaturelike terms. Legislative intent—if we are to be honest with ourselves—rarely exists in any unambiguous way. Words, though they have meanings, do not have self-evident meanings. Thus the meaning to be given to words by courts and the legislative intent to be enforced by courts must (literally, for it cannot be otherwise) serve other functions—functions that reflect realistically the institutional capacities of courts and legislatures. Again, if we are to be honest, these other functions should be spelled out and recognized as appropriate bases for interpretation. That this radical (in its time and in its baldness) statement was neither radical nor surprising was demonstrated by showing what courts actually did, and by pointing to those "rules" of interpretation upon which courts unsystematically relied from time to time.[23] One of the functions of interpretation was, of course, maintaining the fabric of the law; in other words, keeping statutes up to date.[24]

From this source came many things: Bickel's passive virtues,[25] Frankfurter's attacks on Black's "dishonest literalism,"[26] and even the more recent judicial and scholarly attempts to use both passive virtues and interpretation in aggressive ways to cope with the problem of statutory obsolescence.[27] The problem that Henry Hart left us with, however, was what a court should do when a statute *is* obsolete and the words, legislative intent, and past interpretations of the law are too clear to permit updating.

Here Hart and many of his followers part ways. Most of those who learned his lessons at one point or another began to shade the candor he preached in order to achieve the judicial functions he advocated. It is a small step from "words are not self-interpreting and legislative intents are obscure at best" to "words and legislative intents can be ignored because they are meaningless apart from other functions, such as updating." A small step, I say, and one made smaller because no clear lines can be drawn, but one that nonetheless abandons honesty; the assertion it makes is not true. Hart and Sacks, in their great unpublished work on the legal process, are quite clear in their own minds that words and legislative intent, properly analyzed, do limit interpretations.[28] Not for them either Bickel's[29] or Keeton's[30] ways out of the dilemma; for honest interpretation does not permit all, or even most, out-of-date laws to be brought into line.

Does it permit enough? Here even the closest followers of Hart slip into subterfuge. Wellington explicitly,[31] and Sacks implicitly, seems to suggest that enough can be done without straining honest interpretation. Yet the behavior of courts, not to mention the arguments of Bickel and Keeton, can only be read as suggesting a different conclusion. And how, except by chance, could it be otherwise? Once again, candor compels the asking of the questions. Why should the ambiguity of words and of initial legislative intent have more than a purely casual connection with the position a statute has in the current fabric of the law? And why should those limits (imposed on the updating of outworn laws), which would follow from an honest adherence to the limited meaning that words and legislative intent do have, be at all appropriate? Why would they not frequently be too restrictive and, at other times, be inappropriately broad? The connection between the limits imposed and the functions to be performed is, I would suggest, simply not there.

How then is the Harvard legal process school an ancestor of the proposal here presented? Its open recognition that courts not only make law but that they also do and should update statutes, broke down simplistic views of automatic, hard and fast barriers between written law and judicial roles. At the same time, its equally fervent pleas for honest recognition of what judicial roles in fact *are* made untenable the patchwork of solutions and fictions by which courts and commentators have adapted to the statutorification of American law. The very honesty Hart and Sacks called for demands an open examination of a doctrine that their perceptive and subtle analysis of judicial and legislative functions clearly foresaw could not, *ipso facto,* be beyond the pale.

Let me step back a moment and say that I am not as clear in my own mind that the kind of honesty, the kind of destruction of subterfuges they seemed to call for, is always desirable. In particular, I am far from agreeing with Justice Frankfurter that Justice Black's "lack of candor" was appropriately described in that way or was undesirable even if so describable.[32] I will not reach the same conclusion about the subterfuges, fictions if one wishes, which permit courts to update laws while denying that they do so. Those are subterfuges I can do without, but my own views on candor will be outlined later.[33] For it is Hart's and Sacks's abhorrence of dishonesties, combined with their perception of what courts really do in interpreting statutes, that make them ancestors of the proposal here presented.

The dilemma they left us is well represented in a fine old case, *Sorrells v. United States.*[34] The case involved entrapment, but a form of entrapment that, however noxious, was not considered unconstitutional. Speaking for the majority, Chief Justice Charles Evans Hughes interpreted the law to avoid an "absurd or glaringly unjust result," even though it was pretty clear that the Congress that passed the law had intended that harsh result and had used words appropriate to it.[35] Justices Roberts, Brandeis, and Stone rejected Hughes's interpretation as dishonest, but concurred in the result and said that the Court should simply refuse "to lend the aid of the court's own processes to the consummation of a wrong."[36] In effect, they would have nullified the law as completely as if they had held it unconstitutional. Hughes's retort, still in his majority opinion, is enlightening: "Judicial nullification of statutes, admittedly valid and applicable, has, happily, no place in our system."[37] To interpret the statute rigidly and then to refuse to enforce it is equivalent to a finding of constitutional invalidity when we are unwilling to use the Constitution. In contrast, if we interpret the law to bar the harsh result, Congress by legislation can always alter our interpretation. Hughes preferred a dishonest interpretation that Congress could reject; the concurrers preferred an undue assertion of judicial power.

What was missing was an honest and open judicial decision that nonetheless permitted a legislative reconsideration, not because the words or the intent of the statute were uncertain, nor because the Constitution forbade the law, but because the statute was out of line with dominant principles, with the fabric of the whole statutory and common law. If that conflict was so patent in 1932, in so traditional a statutory area as criminal law, we would be blind indeed to deny its existence today.

Pomeroy, the restaters, Landis, and Henry Hart, then, are the ancestors; and the followers of Hart, in courts and colleges, have made inevitable the consideration of a doctrine permitting judicial common law review of statutes, whether they like it or not. The current proponents, nevertheless, are different. I mention two because they have independently focused on the problem and suggested solutions very close to my own. The first is Grant Gilmore, whose powerful writings have both defined the problem and, in their skepticism of final solutions to any legal problem, demanded an approach that furthers continuous change.[38] The second is a legislator and also a law professor. For some years now, Senator Jack Davies, chairman of the judiciary committee of the Minnesota senate, has proposed a law empowering the Minnesota courts to review and revise private law statutes more than twenty years old. I shall later consider whether a strict time rule is the best one. But in his clear perception of the problem and his down-to-earth legislator's response to it, Senator Davies must rank with Grant Gilmore as one of those closest to the birth.[39]

The Doctrine:
A Question of Legitimacy

The existence of identifiable ancestors does not guarantee legitimacy; that is always a separate question. It must be asked in several different ways, and quite apart from the need for such a doctrine or from its feasibility in relation to different types of statutes. Ancestors and proponents were mentioned to suggest its need; feasibility, limits, and techniques designed to make it workable with respect to different types of statutes will be discussed in later chapters. Legitimacy is our immediate concern.

I should like to raise that issue by discussing several related questions. The first is: What is the basis of a court's power to make or evolve law in a democracy? The second is: Can this basis justify the occasional use of judicial powers to allocate the burden of inertia, to define starting points for legislative action, in statutory areas as well as in those parts of the law to which legislatures have not spoken? The third is: Even assuming that judicial power can be justified in statutory areas, is the burden of inertia best assigned in our democracy by decisions of old or passing legislative majorities, by courts, by other institutions, or by a mixture of all these? The fourth is: Do our constitutions permit the allocation of the burden of inertia by courts, even if that should be desirable? And the last is: Can the power to revise statutes be properly asserted by courts on their own or must it be given to them by legislatures?

The Legitimacy of Court-Made Law

What, if anything, entitles judges to make law in a democracy? That they do is by now an accepted fact,[1] but on what basis? The answer to this question has long been a source of concern among legal scholars and judges; I cannot do it justice in a few paragraphs. Yet without some discussion of the issue, it will be impossible to see whether the same basis applies where judges act in statutory areas as at common law.

There are several different grounds for the judicial power to make or evolve law. The first is that this power has been implicitly delegated to courts by majoritarian bodies.[2] In purely formal terms such a justification suffices — a democracy can surely at times choose to act through agents.[3] But this justification is neither very helpful nor very interesting. It immediately pushes us back one step to other questions. Has there in fact been any delegation — implicit or explicit — and if so, what is its scope? And, most important, why would the legislatures or the people in a democracy wish to make such a delegation of authority to courts?

Since I am talking about judicial power to make or evolve ordinary laws — and not about the judicial power of constitutional nullification or review — these questions become almost identical to the original question I asked. If it makes sense in a democracy to give courts the power to evolve or to make the common law, then that very fact will go a long way toward legitimating the power, given the long history of legislative acquiescence in judicial making of the common law and the fact that any exercise of the power is subject to legislative revision.[4] The trouble is, of course, that none of this tells us anything about why, whether, and when it makes sense to give such power to courts, and therefore can be of no use in analyzing the problems with which this book is concerned: Can or should this power extend to statutory areas?[5]

The second ground is only slightly more interesting. It would justify judicial power to make law because such judge-made rules are all in a sense conditional, that is, they are subject to legislative or popular revision and hence are acceptable in a democracy.[6] The trouble with this argument is that, taken literally, it can justify any law, however instituted or arrived at, so long as a legislature or other majoritarian body can reject it. It says lawmaking by any body, of any sort, is consistent with democratic theory if the people can have the last word.

There is of course something to this. Indeed, if there were no inertia and if it made no difference to anyone what the conditional or temporary rule was, because such a rule could immediately and at no cost to anyone be revised according to the popular will, the argument would be valid as well as tautological.[7] Since there is inertia and since even conditional rules have enormous effect, the argument fails by itself. Despite inertia, however, the argument is not meaningless or foolish, for the amount of inertia does set a boundary on the "undemocratic" effect of allowing a nonmajoritarian body to make conditional rules.[8] It allows us to restate the question of judicial power to make ordinary laws: What justifies court power to make temporary rules and thereby to assign the burden of overcoming inertia and of getting those rules revised?[9] Or to put the issue in a slightly different way: What justifies courts in making law within the boundaries set by legislative inertia?

The answers to these questions necessarily depend on the way in which courts are constituted and the way in which they exercise the powers they have. As a result we are thrown back, as we were by the "implicit delegation" rationale, to the question of why one would in a democracy give courts the power to make conditional rules and to assign the burden of overcoming the inertial force that such rules have.

The third justification of judicial lawmaking power emphasizes the notion that courts do look at the election returns. Judges are, after all, either elected or appointed and ratified by elected officials. Their manner of selection suggests that they can both discern and respond to the popular will. The fact that their response is neither direct nor governed by immediate popular will is of little consequence in any democracy that rejects direct majoritarianism. The degree of independence accorded to judges—like the manner of their selection—leads them to follow longer-run majoritarian sentiments than, say, congressmen. But in the end, in a system in which senators have six-year terms, presidents four, congressmen two, and committee chairman indefinite ones,[10] what is so disastrous or peculiar about having elected or appointed judges—with long or life terms—also shape our law, at least at the level of making conditional rules that can be revised by legislatures?[11]

There is, again, something to this justification, but again not enough. Insofar as it says that judges are not immune from majoritarian pressures, it is surely correct. And insofar as it says that—apart from any judicial subservience to principles[12]—the judiciary as a whole, *because* of the way it is chosen, tends to respond to a delayed majoritarianism, it is not only correct but significant. A democratic polity might well wish its conditional rules to reflect such delayed majoritarian trends. The argument is made more significant by the fact that judicial lawmaking takes place in case-by-case situations and therefore is of necessity accretional, incremental, and the product of many judges. Thus delayed majoritarianism is served even by judges who seek to respond to their own view of the immediate popular will because no one of them can make the common law and all of them together do represent (in a literal sense) our evolving majorities.

Why, though, do we want delayed majoritarian wishes to be the source of conditional rules? Conversely, if capacity to discern majoritarian wishes—current or delayed—is what we want, do we really believe that courts are suited for that task? Their capacity to figure out what current majorities wish is surely limited, and their memory of what was wanted when they were appointed or elected is bound to fade. Their terms are too long, their staffs are too limited, and their manner of selection too bizarre to give much support to the notion that judges work well as makers of the common law because they seek to follow the wishes of the majority; and end up doing so with a bias toward those majorities that dominated at the time they were selected.

If, in other words, we wanted the burden of inertia to be assigned primarily on the basis of a delayed majoritarianism, it seems unlikely that we would assign the job to judges. Other institutions, such as independent administrative agencies, less hampered by principles, with more limited terms, and supported by a staff that can be used to discern trends in popular desires, would seem more suitable.[13] Still, the fact that courts are not divorced from political pressures, especially long-term ones, does form an outward boundary. Like the fact that the common law can be reversed by legislatures, it tends to limit the allegedly undemocratic effect of judicial lawmaking. For me, the limit is not sufficient.

The fourth justification of lawmaking by judges looks to their alleged capacity to "do what [is] right for the country."[14] Under such a theory judges would be justified in following their own values in evolving the common law since it is their educated and disinterested sense of what is right that we are seeking. At first blush, this justification is distinctly antidemocratic; it seems to put lawmaking power in the hands of "wise people" because they are wise, and not because they represent current, delayed, or long-term majoritarian wishes. This first impression is rather too strong. We are not, after all, talking about final rules. We are talking about rules that are subject to legislative revisions and about allocating the burden of inertia. There is nothing in itself deeply inconsistent with democracy in the delegation to a group of wise people of the job of setting the starting points, so long as the polity can reject the decisions of its guardians which it dislikes.[15] Such a "realistic" (and, without much refinement, false) view of judicial power may not be appropriate. But it cannot be dismissed out of hand. It is no more inconsistent with ultimate popular rule than is the appointment by an individual of an expert to make those preliminary decisions that the expert thinks best, subject to review by the individual.

Are judges, however, expert enough in what is right for society to justify even such temporary authority? That I trust my doctor or butcher to make preliminary suggestions on my behalf, which I sometimes do not have time to review adequately, does not mean that I would be wise to trust my doctor to make preliminary suggestions about a cut of beef or my butcher to prescribe a headache remedy. It is the qualifications of judges to decide society's wishes — even temporarily — that one properly questions.

Again, we should not exaggerate. There are many people less suited than judges to make decisions as to conditional rules based on their own values. The manner in which they are slected, their relative freedom from political pressures, the fact that they are required to be personally disinterested in the result, and most of all the fact that it takes so many of them to act effectively in shaping law, all combine to make them more suitable as temporary guardians than one might think. For me there is enough to be said for judges' disinterested values as a guide to policy that I am not shocked to read that one of France's leading scholars instructed judges to follow their own sense of right whenever the written law gave no directions.[16] It is hard for me to believe, however, that judges' capacity to discern what is best for the country can justify more than this kind of very limited allocation of power. Like their responsiveness to a delayed popular will and the fact that they can be overruled by majoritarian bodies, their disinterested and occasionally wise sense of right and wrong does not justify the enormous power that judges came to exercise at common law.

Most classic justifications of judicial common law power do not, in fact, look to the previous rationales. Instead they emphasize the subservience of courts to principles, to rational decision making, and to the whole fabric of the law, as explaining and justifying judicial lawmaking power.[17] As Chief Judge Charles Breitel put it: "The judicial process is based on reasoning and presupposes — all antirationalists to the contrary notwithstanding — that its determinations are justfied only when explained or explainable in reason. No poll, no majority vote of the affected, no rule of expediency, and certainly no confessedly subjective or idiosyncratic view justifies a judicial determination. Emphatically, no claim of might, physical or political, justifies a judicial determination."[18]

All this is well and good, but it leaves unanswered the crucial issue: what there is about principles of law, about the legal fabric, and about rational decision making which suggests that a body, selected for its capacity to discern these principles and to act rationally on them, should make the conditional rules for society and, at common law at least, set the starting points for legislative reaction. I will readily agree that courts are better than other institutions at discerning principles of law and at working out the demands of the ever changing legal topography.[19] I will concede that the way judges are trained and selected, their relative independence, the limitations imposed on their staff,[20] the fact that they make law incrementally in response to specific situations, and the requirement that they explain the grounds of their decisions,[21] all seem designed to lead them to perform this job and not others. In other words, principled decision making within a legal landscape is the primary judicial task. But unless legal principles and the legal topography are sensible starting points for legislative reaction, reliance on judges to make the common law because of their skill at discerning the landscape is still misplaced.

Why does a democracy care about the rational application of legal principles? The answer must lie in the belief that the legal fabric, and the principles that form it, are good approximations of one aspect of the popular will, of what a majority in some sense desires. It cannot be an exact fit, but it must reflect enough of what is wanted so that it is a good starting point for lawmaking. Then it follows that those who by training and selection are relatively good at exploring and mapping the legal landscape can appropriately be given the task of evolving the law, and inevitably of allocating the burden of overcoming the inertia of that law.

It is, I think, this belief that characterizes most justifications of judicial common law power.[22] Each judicial decision, at its best, is meant to represent a reasoned attempt to adapt a past set of decisions to a current problem. It tries to treat like cases alike when what is "alike" changes constantly because of ideological, technological, or even constitutional or statutory change. Common law rules become dominant slowly over time in response to many separate decisions in real cases by many disparate judges as to what has changed in the underlying framework.[23] In seeking to apply that framework to new circumstances, each judge inevitably brings to the task some sense of the majority that selected him or her and some sense of what is right for the country, and this, together with the fact that what a "like" case is depends on the level of generality at which one asks the question, helps the fabric to change. But the judge does not directly seek to apply his or her sense of the popular will or of right and wrong except as it seems to fit in the fabric. As a result, the judge's lack of skill at guessing the popular will or the court's possibly bizarre sense of values becomes relatively unimportant. At any moment consistency with the fabric can be taken to be a reasonably accurate account of what has evolved from past popular desires, and the judge's task is to do what is needed to accommodate that account to present needs.

It is, of course, impossible to prove that the legal fabric does, at any given moment, reflect the underlying desires of a society as these have evolved.[24] But the notion is not implausible, and it is not therefore outlandish to suppose that consistency with the legal fabric is an appropriate starting point for lawmaking. Insofar as groups or individuals are to be treated differently, because current majorities wish to favor or disfavor them, that can be done.[25] The ease with which it will be done, the burden of inertia to be overcome, depends on the number and size of obstacles that the particular legal system puts on majoritarian overruling of the fabric. But the idea that this slowly

woven fabric can represent a starting point from which more immediate majoritarian preferences must move is certainly understandable in a democracy that values continuity as well as change.

The moment one accepts the legal fabric as an acceptable starting
point, because it reflects underlying values of a people, it becomes
easy to understand why a legal system might give the power to make
conditional or temporary rules to people who by training, selection,
and relative independence are reasonably adept at discerning that
framework and its changes. The eighteenth- and nineteenth-century
view of the legal fabric seemed to be that *only* judges could discern it
and that changes in it could happen only through accretion of judicial reactions to changed conditions. This aspect of the common law
and of the evolution of the legal fabric has come under successful attack in this century.[26] It is one thing to say that judges are best suited
to map the legal landscape and to adapt new cases to it; it is quite
another thing to limit that mapping to a topography of judicial decisions.

If the object is to treat like cases alike, to adapt to changed technologies and ideologies, and to reflect the evolving values of a people, why should the input be only that of previous common law
cases? Statutes, no less than the common law decisions, reflect
changes in underlying popular attitudes.[27] The gravitational force of
such statutes should surely affect courts seeking to keep their map
current.[28] Nor should the input be limited to statutes. Scholarly
criticisms (both in law and derived from such related fields as philosophy, economics, and political science), jury actions that nullify or
mitigate past rules, even administrative determinations, all can be
appropriate reports of changes in the landscape in response to
changed beliefs or conditions.[29] Allowing courts to take such reports
into account does not change the judicial task—the role of courts
continues to be the accurate placing of new situations and cases in
the map—but the map can change more rapidly and can be a more
accurate reflection of popular desires because it considers more
manifestations of those desires. If the balance in our legal system is
thereby tilted slightly more toward change, so much the better; the
process still gives a starting point—subject to direct popular revision—which reflects both continuity and change.

I do not mean to suggest that the picture is this simple. One can
believe that a legal topography made up purely of common law deci-

sions vaguely reflects a mapping of societal desires or values. One can agree that, if that topography includes statutes, scholarly criticisms, and jury actions, it is more accurate and in some sense more responsive to popular wishes. But one can also question whether, once the landscape is enlarged in this way, judges are indeed limited or able enough in their mapping to be trusted. Treating like cases alike and having to explain one's results "in reason" may limit courts when the landmarks are relatively few, when the analogies are limited. Yet what restraints are there once a judge can be guided not only by precedents, and by the gravitational pull of deep constitutional principles,[30] but also by statutes, scholarship, and what have you?

As the "sources of law" expand, so, it would seem, does judicial power. Chief Justice Roger Traynor noted that only some statutes should exert a gravitational force—but which ones?[31] Should the court follow a series of new statutes in neighboring jurisdictions, or should it stay with its own state's precedents? Should the court follow the trends or vectors of change, the "emergent" over the "recessive,"[32] the predominant rules in recent statutes and judicial decisions, or should preponderant but increasingly dubious decisions be followed? When we combine all these different sources of law with the fact that the nation has fifty-one jurisdictions, and with the fact that there is a pull on ordinary lawmaking exerted by constitutions as well, we may well ask: What kind of confused landscape, what kind of a ragged map, have we got? Is it realistic to assume that courts are limited at all? Can they instead—under the guise of seeking to map the landscape or to weave the fabric of the law—do precisely what they wish, responding primarily to their own values or to the majorities that selected them?[33]

The criticism is well taken, though I think it goes too far. It is not realistic to believe that courts are free and unguided by principles because there are too many guidelines. One need not agree with Ronald Dworkin that there is always one right answer dictated by the legal landscape, which a court if it were able and dedicated enough could find,[34] to accept the notion that many answers are excluded by the obligation to follow legal principles.[35] The task is made harder perhaps, the temptations to follow one's own desires is greater, the areas in which those desires may appropriately be followed is larger,[36] because the guidelines are now so numerous; but limits as a practical matter remain.[37] And courts still are about as well suited as any institutions we might devise for mapping out this extraordinarily complex landscape.

Does this fact suffice to justify judicial power to make and evolve the common law? By itself it might not but, together with the other, inadequate justifications and limits already discussed,[38] it has. Let us assume that conformity with a complex legal landscape continues to be viewed as a good starting point for rules because that muddled map reflects society's changing and conflicting wishes. That is the traditional common law premise. Should we then be concerned by the fact that those most suited to make and follow the map are apt to be misled or liberated by the existence of too many conflicting signs and go off in their own direction? So long as we can expect them to try to follow and update the map in a changing landscape, and can criticize them for failing to do so, we should not be too worried.

We are, after all, still talking about conditional rules and burdens of inertia, to be overcome by legislative bodies with whatever ease we wish to establish. We are, moreover, when we assume that judges may have too much discretion because the map is so complex, still talking about incremental lawmaking arising out of case-by-case adjudication. Each judge can go only so far. If a judge cannot find guiding principles or willfully ignores them, it is not the end of the world. On what basis would such a judge decide the case? If he or she responded to a delayed majoritarianism or to a guess about to-day's popular desires, we might say that other institutions would have guessed better, but we would not for all that have an absurd starting point. If, instead, judges sought to do what they thought was right for society, we might be concerned with their capacity to make that judgment, but again there would be limits to our concern. One judge's views would win out only if enough other judges either found that they conformed to the legal landscape or, finding no adequate guidelines in the landscape, still shared the judge's guess of what the majority wanted or of what was right for the country.[39]

Thus, if the object were to pick experts on what is right for the country, or to pick a body that could discern the current majority's wishes, and make these our conditional rules, we almost surely would not pick judges for the task.[40] But if the object instead is to make such rules accord to a legal landscape, in the knowledge that the multiplicity of sources and the confusion of the map make that task extraordinarily hard, then using judges, courts, and the common law remains a good start.[41] Courts *are* best suited to discern and apply the principles. At times the topography will be too unclear to guide them; at other times they will choose to ignore it. They will fail and follow the election returns or their own values, but these values, and their guesses on majority wishes, are not all that bad. So long as courts act cumulatively, and so long as most of them seek to do what they are good at and follow the legal landscape, a system that gives them this power to evolve the common law — subject to legislative revisions — may still be a sensible one.[42]

We have, in any event, allowed such an approach to determine the making of the common law. The question we must now ask is ought the same approach to apply in areas where legislatures have acted, or should it be limited, as it traditionally was said to have been, to those parts of the law that the legislatures had left untouched.[43]

Can Common Law Power Apply to Statutes?

Should an old legislative decision determine the starting point, the allocation of the burden of inertia, or should that be decided on the basis of conformity to the legal landscape? I don't think one can give an all-or-nothing answer to the question. Too much depends on the type of statute, the type of majority and legislature that enacted it, and the statute's relation to fundamental or constitutional principles, not to mention the obvious question of how old the statute is.[44] All these factors will be important in any attempt to develop limits appropriate to the kind of doctrine we are now analyzing.[45] For now, however, I am more concerned with the question of whether there does exist a significant category of cases in which the burden of inertia is, in a democratic society, better assigned by courts acting in a principled, common law fashion than by leaving the burden where a long past legislative majority placed it.

If one accepts the authority of courts to make the common law, the answer to this question must be that a significant category of cases does exist. (And, by implication, the existence of the category explains the courts' use of subterfuges to deal with it.)[46] On what does the majoritarian legitimacy of an old statute rest? No more and no less than on two facts: in a system of checks and balances it has gone unrepealed; and it once commanded a majoritarian basis. The first is of no consequence, for the same argument applies to any rule that does no more than allocate the burden of legislative inertia. So long as the legislature can alter judge-made law, a judge-made law immediately commands the identical majoritarian basis as an old statute, if the statute's claim of legitimacy is grounded on no more than the negative fact of nonrepeal. It would follow that judge-made common law rules should also be outside the scope of judicial revision. And that has never been our law.[47]

I do not mean to suggest that nonrepeal is irrelevant. Deriving a current legislative intent from inaction is, as Hart and Sacks have taught us, dangerous.[48] But it is not without different shades of validity in different situations. In fact, one of the functions of the doctrine under discussion is precisely to strengthen the legitimacy of a statute from this "negative" point of view. A court could, by threatening to revise an old statute, force the legislative agenda. It could make legislative reconsideration, in the light of current majoritarian requirements, more likely than usually occurs when an old statute is simply on the books. Indeed, some of the most dramatic (and most doctrinally doubtful) cases of nonconstitutional judicial intervention I have cited had precisely that intent and effect.[49] The result would be that nonrepeal could be taken as a sign that the statute is still wanted by the legislature. As a general basis for legitimacy, however, the fact of nonrepeal is not sufficient and does not distinguish statutes from common law rules.

The second argument is more important. Is there, in a democracy, a special significance that ought to attach to a law because it was once passed by a majoritarian body? If enough time or other circumstances have intervened, undercutting a presumption that the same majority persists, I do not understand why any great significance should attach to a majoritarian origin. This, however, is quite different from saying that courts are suited to determine that the majoritarian basis has faded.

There is, and always has been, in our legal system a significant conservative or retentionist bias. Other things being equal, old statutes remain in force; and other things being equal, old common law rules remain in force. Without more, neither have any greater basis for their validity than the negative fact of nonrepeal. And, without more, that is quite sufficient. One could design a system that abolished this conservative bias and required all rules (common law and statutory) to be "currently majoritarian." In a way, that is precisely what the radical sunsetters, like Jefferson, seek.[50] Still, theirs is not our system, and it never has been.

So the issue is not whether there ought to be a conservative bias in our system, or whether the past ought to carry a presumption of validity that the present must overcome. It is, rather, the far narrower question of whether old statutes ought to be entitled to a greater presumption of validity than old common law rules. There is also the subsidiary issue of whether in considering the validity of specific old rules (whether statutory or common law) courts, legislatures, or other institutions are best suited to call into doubt the continued appropriateness of the particular conservative bias and bring about a reconsideration. My own conclusion is that there is nothing in democratic or majoritarian theory which supports the notion that old statutes, as a group, are more entitled to a conservative bias than old common law rules, or that courts are less suited than legislatures (at least checked and balanced ones) to question the appropriateness of that bias in a particular rule or statute.

Let us consider each of these points separately. The principal advantage a statute has (from a democratic point of view) is that it once commanded majoritarian support.[51] Over time, or over changed circumstances, the likelihood that such support persists inevitably becomes slim. Why then a special bias in its favor? In contrast, an old common law rule is almost inevitably the result of a slow accretion of Burkean social attitudes or of societal morality.[52] Again time and circumstances may change these.[53] But speaking realistically, which is more apt to retain the support that caused it to become a rule of law in the first place: rules that have grown to be dominant slowly over varied times and circumstances, or laws enacted by a specific legislature at a particular moment? It seems to be inevitable that as a general matter, the likelihood of change in support, and hence in majoritarian basis, is greater in such time-dependent legislative acts than in common law rules.[54]

There are of course court decisions that represent *ad hoc* responses to particular societal demands. And these, even if correct when made, ought not to benefit from any presumption of long-run validity.[55] Conversely, as Landis demonstrated, there are collections of statutes passed over time and over differing legislatures which are as

Burkean in their foundations as the most deeply seeded common law rules. Such statutes and the "equity" (to use the old, old term) that surrounds them are certainly entitled to the highest presumption of validity against temporary changes in conditions.[56]   But all this merely reinforces my point. It is the artesian source of the rule that entitles it to a long-run conservative bias in a democratic polity, rather than the immediate ground or institution from which it springs. Direct majoritarianism would give support for no such retentionist biases. The Burkean majoritarianism that is ours would distinguish among rules, but cannot on the ground that one was statutory and the other common law. If it were forced to make that simplistic distinction, it might even be inclined to give greater presumption to the common law rules and less to the statutory.

This does not necessarily mean, however, that a change in either type of rule should be judicial rather than legislative. Nor does it necessarily mean that the best determiner of the burden of inertia is judicial rather than legislative. It does imply that the current set of *nominal* doctrines — that courts can change time-honored common law rules but cannot touch statutes — is very peculiar indeed. Unless we are prepared to let only legislatures update the common law as well as statutes, we are driven to letting courts force the updating of both statutes and the common law. And that is just what, by indirection, is occurring. (Perhaps this is why Chief Justice Hallows in the Wisconsin case I have so often mentioned justified his position with the words "otherwise the death of the common law is near at hand").[57]

The consequences of permitting only legislative changes in both old common law and statutes are worth noting. They would imply one of two things: an extraordinary conservatism if our current checks and balances were retained, for then both common law rules and the cornucopia of modern statutes would go into the legislative deep freeze; or an extraordinary shift toward full majoritarianism, if the checks and balances that create that freeze were abolished. Neither is by itself inconsistent with a democracy of sorts: but neither is required by democratic theory and, more in point, both would represent great changes from the traditional form our democracy has taken.

Still, we are talking about legitimacy and so must go beyond listing the consequences of a move to a system in which all old laws (common and statutory) are subject only to legislative revision. We must consider whether judicial revision of statutes is itself consistent with democratic theory. The point here comes back to the nature of judicial lawmaking generally. If judicial lawmaking, of the sort envisioned at common law, is consistent with democratic theory because it is constrained by legal principles, is there anything that would make judicial allocation of the burden of inertia less consistent with democratic theory when statutes are involved?

Before examining the question, I should note that the reason I have put the issue this way is that the case for expansion of the judicial power to permit statutory updating is easier if one believes that the role of courts in common law making is legitimated by *any* of the other justifications listed earlier, easier than if one accepts the view that the common law power derives from the courts' capacity to map the legal landscape guided by principles of law. If the reason for courts' common law power is delegation by legislative bodies, then judicial power over statutes can be made legitimate simply by obtaining such delegation.[58] Similarly, if judicially made common law rules are legitimate because they are only conditional and can readily be repealed by legislatures whenever a judicial judgment about current support is incorrect, the same justification holds as to old statutes.[59] Finally, if we are willing to find that judicial common lawmaking is legitimate because courts can discern directly the will of the majority (current or delayed) or because their disinterested sense of what is right for the country is an expert judgment worthy of at least conditional respect, then judicial power to induce legislatures to reconsider statutes is no less appropriate.[60]

I have therefore chosen the hardest case by which to test the legitimacy of the doctrine. To the extent one believes that the above justifications have merit, the case for judicial power to sunset some statutes either follows *a fortiori* from the arguments I will make or can be made to follow by an appropriate delegation of authority from a legislature. The object of such judicial intervention would still be to make the starting point, from which legislatures are called to respond, as consistent as possible with the general fabric of common and statutory law. The technique and extent of such intervention remain to be discussed. But apart from such issues of limits, why should not this kind of starting point be generally appropriate to the updating of statutes?

Traditionally, of course, it has not been thought of as appropriate. And there are some good — though in the end not sufficient — reasons for the traditional point of view. These paradoxically lie in the very factors that tend to make statutes *more* time-bound than common law rules, and hence more likely to become obsolete. A statute when passed frequently represents a majoritarian decision to favor a particular group, or to compromise among groups despite any inconsistency of treatment this may create with the legal topography. Such a decision, as I have said, tends to lose its majoritarian basis over time and to become an illegitimate, even if constitutional, discrimination. But how are courts to tell that this majoritarian basis has faded?

If the law, when enacted, was inconsistent with the legal topography, does it tell the courts anything that twenty years later it is still inconsistent with that topography? Unless it does, courts will not be especially suited to decide that a reconsideration of the statute is warranted, since the basis for judicial power rests, by hypothesis, primarily on their particular skill at discerning the topography and not on their capacity to determine whether a current majority supports a given rule. If this were all, we would be forced to conclude that, while statutes date faster than common law rules and the problem of obsolescence is a real one, courts are not able to determine that statutes have dated and so cannot help us. We would then have to establish a body whose skill lay in deciding when statutes had become obsolete and leave to the courts their traditional role of updating only the common law.[61]

This conclusion, however, implies a much too simplistic view of what statutes are meant to do, of how they age and become obsolete, and even of how common law rules are made. In the first place, many statutes are meant to be elaborations of the legal topography. They may have been passed to create certainty or uniformity, or to pay out funds, but their bases remain consistent with our whole legal framework.[62] If time and circumstances make these statutes inconsistent, courts are capable of discerning that fact and are justified in calling for their reconsideration.

The same is true of those statutes that once favored a particular group, if the reason for their aging is that the whole legal landscape (common law and statutory) has caught up and surpassed them. Many of the examples of judicial activism or frustration cited earlier—workmen's compensation, the FELA cases, the Wisconsin comparative negligence rule—are of this sort.[63] As with another group of statutes, those whose whole impact is altered by changes in the rest of the legal or technological landscape,[64] courts do not need to guess at current majoritarian desires to decide that these statutes should be revised. Their skills at discerning the topography are precisely those needed to suggest that the basis of these laws has become doubtful.

I could list other types of statutes and circumstances in which the kinds of changes that would make updating appropriate are best discerned by common law courts. But to do so would be to get ahead of myself and to start the process of defining limits and guidelines for the doctrine under analysis. I would rather return to the hardest case, to the statute that was meant to derogate from the common law in order to favor a particular group, and to ask whether or not there is a role for courts in determining whether time has undercut the legitimacy of the statutorily ordained discrimination.

Let me start by looking at how courts have dealt with analogous judicial decisions. If we are realistic, we must admit that common law rules are not always simply an evolution of a legal topography. Like statutes they at times have been *ad hoc* responses to political pressures to favor certain groups.[65] How could common law courts tell that such judicial responses should be revised? One could call it easy. Such common law decisions were of dubious legitimacy because they did not fit the landscape. If over time the topography came to look like them, either through statutory or common law changes, courts would leave them alone.[66] If, instead, they remain anachronisms, courts are justified in saying that they were unprincipled and in overruling them.[67]

The last step is not so easy when we are dealing with a statute, because unprincipled preferences established by constitutional statutes are legitimate when made.[68] But some steps rather like the common law step remain available and appropriate. In the first place, many anachronistic statutes do come to fit in the landscape. Their gravitational pull, together with that of other statutes, changes the common law. These changes combine with further developments in the ideological or technological climate and in legal scholarship to make into a solid part of that fabric the very laws that at one time did not fit.[69] This is precisely what was meant by Landis and others when they asserted that some statutes become as much a part of "the law" as common law rules.[70] But if, still later, one such statute comes not to fit, or to fit awkwardly, courts are able to say so and are as justified in inducing a reconsideration of the statute as they are in reworking the common law. Just as the majoritarian basis of the preferential statute presumably was a factor leading to the change in the whole legal fabric, so does the subsequent lack of fit suggest the passing of that majoritarian basis.

Of course, the court may be "wrong." The legal framework and deep majoritarian desires are not by any means identical. Courts following the framework have been wrong at common law — and legislatures have had to overcome inertia and reverse them.[71] It may be that this danger should affect the techniques the court should use to induce a reconsideration.[72] But the skills the court would be called on to use in this situation remain judicial skills, and hence the legitimacy of their exercise remains the same as at common law. The power is legitimate because it results from the use of special judicial skills — analysis of the legal topography — and because employment of those skills tends, albeit indirectly and imprecisely, to adjust the law to deep majoritarian wishes.

The same statute that created a preference may, moreover, become obsolete in a second way that justifies court action. Instead of other statutes, doctrine, and common law moving to fit the statute, all these may move in the opposite direction. At first, courts — unless they are willing to guess at what current majorities want or to follow their own values — would not be able to make much of such a move. After all, the legislature intended the anachronism. It intended to derogate from the legal landscape and the "modern" common law. Still as more statutes, inconsistent with the first one, are enacted, as other jurisdictions repeal or reject analogous statutes — perhaps ones they had passed at the same time and in response to similar events — as scholarly criticism mounts and as juries or prosecutors use their power to ignore the law, the time approaches when a case can be made for sunset.

Again, the case is not made because the court can guess at what current majorities desire. Rather, the case is made because the lack of fit that the original legislature was willing to countenance has become magnified. The court still performs its principal task of looking for consistencies and analogies, the task for which it is trained. And, as with common lawmaking, the assumption that the result reflects an underlying majoritarianism and hence is legitimate in a democracy seems a sensible one, especially since the analogies have been broadened to include statutes as sources of law.[73]

Can we now go further and find a legitimate basis for judicial sunsetting with respect to statutes that have not become more inconsistent with the legal landscape since their enactment? Can we question statutes whose principal flaw is that they have not, over time, exerted a gravitational pull on other statutes or on the common law, and so have remained the anachronisms they were when passed? I am thinking still of a law designed to prefer a particular group but whose lack of fit remains, as it were, constant.

One may doubt that such a case exists. Most laws create their own landscape or become increasingly out of place. If, however, a law does neither, it is then that the difference between a court's power over a common law rule and a court's power over a statute seems most in point. An *ad hoc* common law rule that has, in time, failed to become principled is ripe for overruling. Yet only if one is prepared to say that courts are good at gauging current majoritarian feelings, or ought to follow their own values, can one feel easily comfortable with a judicially induced sunset of such a *statute*. The traditional basis of judicial common law power does not exist.

It does not, however, follow that such a statute should remain in force. After all the statute has, by hypothesis, found no new support in other statutes or in common law. It is, in a real sense, out of phase. Its basis, its legitimacy, depends simply on the fact that an old majority enacted it. Is this sufficient and, if so, for how long? Or is it better to allow courts after a time to force a reconsideration of such a law based on their direct judgment as to the existence of current majoritarian support for the law? Alternatively, would it be better to establish yet another judgmental body to decide when such a law was ripe for review?

An Old Majority, a Judicial Judgment, or Another Guardian?

Such a law poses starkly the problem of obsolescence, of allocating the burden of overcoming legislative inertia. To let the statute stand is frequently to perpetuate the will of a majority that no longer exists. To allow a court to force a reconsideration of the law is to ask the court to guess directly at current majoritarian feeling or to allow it to be guided by its own sense of the rightness of the statute. To cre ate another, more representative body whose job it is to decide either that the statute lacks a current majoritarian base or that it is no longer right invites that body to force reconsideration of other laws, which do fit the legal topography quite well and which the legislature does not wish to repeal.[74]

We are bound in the end to choose whether updating by an institution that has a fairly good sense of current majoritarian feelings, but is not bound by principles in its decision making, is preferable to updating by courts, which are good at discerning changes in the legal landscapes but which, we are still assuming,[75] have no great capacity for evaluating current popular desires. Alternatively we may choose to continue living with rules that have no more to be said for them than that they once commanded a legislative majority for the preferences they give. I have said enough to indicate why I believe the problem of legal obsolescence is a serious one, why simply living with anachronistic statutes is not really an option.[76] Not so readily resolved is the question of whether skill at discerning current popular support, capacity to analyze and follow the legal topography, or endowment with a trustworthy sense of values is most important in the updating of timeworn laws.

The decision must depend, in part, on how common are the situations that are well handled by each approach. It must also depend on how poorly each approach would deal with those situations it is not best suited to handle. How frequently, in other words, do statutes that do not fit the legal landscape lose popular support and hence their only basis for legitimacy? How often can the issue of whether a statute should be reconsidered by a legislature be decided by examining the legal landscape and its underlying principles, and how often instead must it depend on direct judgments as to the current majoritarian support or as to the rightness of the law? At times each skill is likely to be most relevant in our complex legal system. Ideally, the task of deciding when the burden of inertia should be shifted would be placed on a body that has all three qualities.

Such a body is not available. The very things that make administrative agencies reasonably adept at sensing current popular will — such as the existence of staff and therefore of budgetary dependence on elected officials — also make them ill suited to the task of discerning principles and call into question the disinterestedness of their judgments on the rightness of a statute. That is why giving power to update to them entails the danger that some statutes that still fit the legal landscape will be made subject to sunset prematurely and improperly, as a result of a temporary shift in the political climate.[77] Courts are trained to look to legal principles and hence are less likely to induce reconsideration of such statutes. They are, moreover, relatively disinterested even when influenced by their own values. But the representativeness of those values is certainly open to question, and their capacity to gauge what the current majority wishes is limited at best.

Courts do, however, have an advantage over alternative institutions. They are not clearly unsuited to the tasks at which they are not particularly good. Indeed, at times their power to make common law has been justified on the basis of their responsiveness to a delayed majoritarianism or on their capacity to be disinterested in applying their own values. More important, since these justifications have not traditionally been accepted, if they do follow their own sense of right and wrong or their judgments as to current majoritarian feelings, they immediately become subject to criticism. And this, combined with the accretional nature of their decisions, increases the chances that wrong guesses on their part will be corrected by other courts or by legislatures, even in a system with substantial inertia.[78] The fact that the court has decided a case in an unprincipled way becomes, by itself, a weapon for those who would overcome the inertia the decision created.

It may be well to reemphasize here that the accretional nature of judicial lawmaking remains a safeguard when courts are dealing with statutes. If a court modifies or begins to update a statutory rule, without thereby replacing it with a full-blown substitute, its misjudgments can readily be rejected or limited by later courts as they work out the new rule. These courts may do this on their own because they disagree with the earlier court, or in response to rejection of their view in other states, or in reaction to legislative or popular outcry. But, in all of these cases, the situation is no different from the usual one in common lawmaking. If instead the court seeks to induce legislative reconsideration by threatening to revise the statute unless the legislature does, the ensuing colloquy with the legislature gives much the same safeguards. The court and its successors can always back down, or start the process of revision more cautiously, if legislative lack of revision suggests danger. Again the process is the same as if an ancient common law rule were involved.[79] The issue is one of using techniques appropriate to obtaining the greatest advantages of colloquy and accretional lawmaking.[80]

All this leads me to think that giving courts the power to induce reconsideration of anachronistic statutes remains the best we can do, unless we are willing to accept some of the structural reforms discussed in Chapter VII and abolish those very checks and balances that have characterized our legal system. It remains the best we can do even though it inevitably entails the danger that courts will go beyond those situations in which their power is legitimated by analogy to the judicial power to evolve the common law, and will induce reconsideration of statutes whose lack of fit was legislatively intended and has simply persisted. Because it is impossible to draw neat lines and to employ other bodies that can update only in these cases, and because we are unwilling to live with such ill-fitting laws when their popular support has faded, courts will tend to sunset these laws as soon as they become convinced that popular support for them no longer exists.[81]

If one defines legitimacy in purely functional terms, as I suspect Hart and Sacks would do, then the fact that courts do the job better than others would be enough despite such dangers.[82] It is only if one grounds legitimacy of court power over statutes in analogies to the judicial power over the common law — and legitimates that power entirely in terms of subservience to principle — that the problem persists. Even then the problem can be solved if techniques and guidelines can be developed that would control the dangers of judicial sunsetting of those statutes whose lack of fit has remained constant. That will be one object of the next two chapters.

Let us take the hardest case, however. Can an argument be made for court power if it requires courts to decide whether what does not fit the legal fabric is no longer desired by a current majority? Did courts in evolving the common law have to make analogous judgments?

In part, of course, they always did,[83] though perhaps not so often as they would have to in supervising the sunsetting of statutes. One may go further and suggest that as the sources of law to which common law courts can look have expanded, and as more and more statutes have been passed, the number of times when it has become appropriate for common law courts to look to current majoritarian desires directly has also expanded. When statutes were few, and courts ignored them in defining the legal landscape, courts did not need to worry much about what a majority might wish and could simply fit each case in the evolving framework. Increasingly, however, it seems that courts are relying on their sense of what the majority wants to define the outward boundaries of their lawmaking. Why strike down a common law rule that seems not to fit if the legislature is sure to reenact it? Why develop a common law rule, to fill out the fabric, if it will immediately be abrogated by the people's representatives?

The fundamental job remains to find and follow the dictates of legal principles—because these reflect a deeper popular will. That is still the primary basis for judicial lawmaking authority. Unprincipled decisions, *ad hoc* rules that do not fit, remain in a sense outside the pale and subject to criticism. But with the increase in statutes such principled grounds for common lawmaking have tended to remain dominant only within the perceived boundaries of legislative inertia. The very fact that legislatures do act, more than they once did, makes courts at common law more hesitant to take actions that would only have the effect of inducing a legislature to reverse the court. Inevitably, it makes courts more sensitive than they once were to the demands of current majorities and to the outward limits these set on their own capacity to evolve the common law.[84]

The analogue to the situation of the statute which does not fit, which has not become anachronistic over time, and which may or may not be still wanted by a legislative majority is close. (Indeed, as at common law, even an old statute that has only recently become ill-fitting may be left alone if the court guesses that it is desired by the current majority.) The first task of courts in all instances remains to look to the landscape, to legal principles. If the statute can be said to fit, that settles the issue. If it does not, the guess, increasingly made at common law, as to majoritarian wishes will inevitably be made.

It is no answer to say that the reluctance of courts to abandon an old common law rule that does not fit (when they believe it to be supported by a current legislature) entails restraint by courts, whereas the judicially induced sunset of a statute that never fit (when a court believes it to lack legislative support) implies judicial activism. For though the first is conservative and the second revisionist in tendency, the issue of legitimacy is the same in both. The common law rule, since it doesn't fit and since it wasn't enacted by a majority, is illegitimate and should be struck down (unless the courts are correct in their direct guess about current legislative support). The statutory rule, whose lack of fit has remained constant since enactment, is legitimate and should remain in force (again unless the courts are correct in their guess about current legislative support). The judicial decision may lead to a conservative or revisionist result, but its propriety in both cases depends on a direct guess as to majoritarian wishes, and not on what traditionally legitimated judicial decisions — the desire to fill out the legal framework. One may argue that this fact undermines the legitimacy of judicial power over common law and gives even less support to the power over statutes. Unless, however, one is prepared to force courts to waste legislative time, and to invite legislative reversal when they believe such reversal to be nearly certain, or unless one is prepared to abandon court power to evolve the common law, one must come to accept this pragmatic boundary on the court's subservience to the legal fabric.[85]

There remain two issues of legitimacy to be discussed before we turn to the practical questions the doctrine requires us to face, whether the judicial power I have described is constitutional in our system (even if it is a legitimately democratic one); and whether the power must be delegated to the courts (through legislation like that proposed by Senator Davies)[86] or whether courts can assert its existence in a common law fashion, so to speak. The reason for the brevity of my treatment of these issues is simply that I do not think the first one raises serious issues, and the second one, though surely serious, seems not to be "ripe."

Is It Constitutional?

I cannot take a constitutional objection very seriously. Let us for the moment assume an explicit delegation by legislatures to courts of the authority I have described. Would that be invalid?

Legislatures have been permitted to delegate all kinds of authority to all sorts of institutions. In the end the major limits the Constitution has imposed on that delegation have been those deemed necessary to keep legislatures from ducking the responsibility of answering to the people, if, through delegation, rules that skirted close to the constitutional line were enacted. What legislatures may not do, in other words, is to delegate in ways that diminish their ultimate responsibility to the people for the enactment of constitutionally dubious laws.[87] But the kind of judicial power here described has as its primary function the forcing of legislatures to face up to their majoritarian responsibilities. As such it is not subject to a generic constitutional infirmity on delegation-of-power grounds.

It might, of course, be the case that an occasional exercise of the power might allow legislatures to avoid deciding a question that only a representative body ought to decide. But such an exercise would either be incorrect, in terms of the doctrine, or the result of sloppy techniques on the part of the court applying the doctrine. In any event, though such a case could be described as entailing an unconstitutional delegation, that description would add little to the fact that a higher court should strike down the particular exercise of the power.[88] Such possible abuses of the doctrine would be wrong and unfortunate, of course, but they would do nothing to undermine the constitutionality of the doctrine generally.[89]

The other major constitutional infirmity that might be charged to the doctrine is that it violates some general, structural notions of separation of powers. Other bodies could be delegees of this authority but not courts, precisely because they are courts and so must leave statutes alone.[90] It is hard to know quite what to do with that kind of statement. One can answer that courts were given power of this sort in many states by the very first codes that enacted the English common law.[91] And judges have always exercised power over statutes through subterfuges; to deny them the authority to do it openly would mean that the Constitution requires the use of fictions. One can also ask how courts can be empowered to make law, in the absence of a statute, and yet be precluded from continuing to make law by the existence of a statute when that statute expressly reserves that power to them. Finally, one can go deeper and question which of the aims and functions of separation of powers would be impeded by delegation of authority to the courts.

Is there anything that courts must do that they would do less well if they were given this authority?[92] It is hard for me to see what that would be — especially since the current use of fictions to achieve some results analogous to those here described itself seems more dangerous to traditional court roles than would the open exercise of this authority. Moreover, what courts would do in exercising this authority entails the same kind of examination of distinctions and analogies which has been the judicial task at common law. Is there anything, then, that legislatures must do that delegation of this authority to courts would impede? I think not, once one accepts the notion that the power must be used to induce rather than impede open legislative facing of semiconstitutional issues.[93]

Separation of powers is a serious structural doctrine in our constitutions. It demands great respect even though its imperatives are not expressed in detailed prescriptions.[94] But the respect it demands is substantive and not formal.[95] It asks us to consider the roles our institutions must play if we are to maintain that balance established by our governmental system. Judicial power to force legislative reconsideration of statutes serves precisely to maintain the balance between the traditional court role of keeping the fabric of the law consistent and up to date and the legislative role of reversing judicial misperceptions of majoritarian demands, while responding quickly to the constitutionally valid needs of special groups. As such it is, in a fundamental sense, fully consistent with the traditional balance of power imposed by our constitutions.

This does not, of course, mean that we will wish to give up the myth of a more formal, less functional separation of powers. We may have good reasons to want to preserve the fictions that myth entails.[96] Should we choose to give them up, however, our constitutions will not stand in the way.

Legitimacy Without Explicit Delegation

The question of whether the authority to allocate the burden of inertia must be expressly granted by the legislatures to the courts or can be arrived at by courts in a common law way is much more serious. But to treat it adequately one would have to spend more time than I wish to devote to it, and even then any conclusion would be premature.

First, one would have to develop a far more complete theory of when common lawmaking is appropriate than I can hope to do in this book. One would then have to analyze whether the indirect behavior (the subterfuges by courts and hints by legislatures) which had occurred to date would justify the courts in proclaiming as a doctrine what they could demonstrate had already occurred through the accretion of decisions and statutes. One would have to see, in other words, whether the gravitational field, which a theory of common lawmaking required, had become strong enough to permit this doctrine to be announced as an independent rule, which could in turn start exercising its own gravitational force; or if, instead, the field exerted a force sufficient to permit courts to act over statutes, but only if they continued to do so by indirection and subterfuge.

I prefer to get on with the task of beginning a consideration of the limits and techniques appropriate to the judicial role I have been describing. That courts, in a common law way, have come to the point of exercising the authority here described through fictions, subterfuges, and indirection is, I think, manifest. Whether that way of dealing with the authority is more desirable than an open acknowledgment of the power will be discussed in the last part of the book.[97] Whether it is then permissible for courts to make that declaration themselves or necessary to wait for a legislative sanction seems to me not ripe for discussion.

It would obviously be infinitely preferable to have a legislative sanction for the power. And under some justifications of judicial lawmaking it would be essential. (The straight-delegation theory is but the most obvious example.) And it is not clear that legislatures, if presented with the doctrine as a form of limited sunsetting, would necessarily freeze it. Senator Davies, for example, is optimistic about the enactment of his broad bill.[98] This by itself would argue for waiting and seeing before urging any judicial declaration of the rule—even if one were to conclude that such a "common law" declaration could be appropriately made. To reach such a dubiously second-best conclusion before it is clearly needed would seem hasty.

Perhaps, in other words, the very suggestion that a problem currently exists will suffice to force the agenda in some legislatures. If enough legislatures act, that fact might itself strengthen the argument for common law adoption of the doctrine elsewhere. In the circumstances, a premature analysis of whether the courts could, in the absence of legislative action, declare the power themselves seems wasteful and even misguided.[99]

Legitimacy — Conclusion

In the end the question of legitimacy, like all legal questions, is a profoundly practical one. We cannot avoid a decision on who should bear the burden of inertia in lawmaking, but we can choose among several possible approaches. The first would let the burden automatically fall on those who would change the will of a past majority or majoritarian body. This is the system that makes old rules untouchable (except by legislatures). The second would, just as automatically, put the burden of inertia on those who would keep in force any law that was enacted more than a fixed number of years before. This is the radical sunsetter's approach.[100] If the first position presumes a *continuation of majoritarian support in all cases,* until proven otherwise by an overcoming of inertia, the second approach presumes *the absence of such support after a set period,* unless proven otherwise. The third approach would let a semirepresentative body decide where the burden would lie. It would allow an administrative agency or a legislative or executive committee to decide which laws must be reconsidered and tested for current support in the legislature.[101] Such an approach is the hardest to justify in majoritarian terms, for it relies on the essentially unfettered desires of members of an only partly majoritarian body to determine the burden of inertia. The last approach would make the allocation of the burden a judicial function. It would ask courts to look at statutes, as they did common law rules, and decide which are ripe for reconsideration.

The first two approaches would both be clearly democratic if our system were a fairly direct majoritarian one. With checks and balances, they are majoritarian only by chance, for the first presumes (even where it is unrealistic) the continuation of support for an old law, and marshalls inertia and checks and balances behind that presumption, while the second presumes the exact opposite. The third approach is not mechanical. It permits a judgment on which old laws are entitled to a presumption of validity and which are not. But it allows this judgment to be made through the unfettered discretion of only partly majoritarian institutions and therefore gives little democratic control over the placement of the burden of inertia. Only the last permits judgment as to where the burden should lie and also hems in the exercise of that judgment in ways that have traditionally been viewed as democratic. The hemming in is, of course, achieved through the requirement that courts should not follow their own predilections in allocating the burden, but should look to which allocation creates a starting point that is most consistent with the whole fabric of the law, judge-made and statutory.

We can be skeptical about the courts' capacity to do this; but we must at the same time admit that this is precisely what the courts were said to be doing at common law and what, according to the jurists and scholars, explained and justified that kind of judicial lawmaking in a democracy. A judicial power to allocate the burden of inertia on the basis of how a timeworn statute fits the legal fabric involves courts in a task much like the one they have been trained to perform and gives them an authority that functionally is like the authority they had at common law. It asks them to do no more than what we have always expected them to do. It is, then, a legitimate allocation of power.

X

The Doctrine:
Limits and Guidelines

We are dealing with the slow adaptation of our whole legal-political system to a major change: the preponderance of statutory law. The current trend is to try to fit this fundamental change into a traditional legal-political mold and to reject both those reactions that would move our system away from one of checks and balances and those that would simply allow us to remain dominated by out-of-date legislation. The integration of a major change into an existing legal-political system is, however, an immensely complicated phenomenon. It has involved shifts in the formal relationships between courts and legislatures. The coming into being (whether openly or not) of the doctrine I have described is an important part of those shifts. The precise form and limits of that doctrine can only be determined over time and by many people. This is especially true because the limits and techniques appropriate to the judicial power to force legislative agendas will vary widely with the type of rule involved and hence with the field of law. And no one writer can adequately suggest what is appropriate in every field of law. I can only hope, then, that this and the next chapter will represent a start in the development of an appropriate doctrine.[1]

The Relevance of Legislative Inertia

Some general considerations are in order. The first is that the courts in exercising the power to induce the updating of statutes should

THE DOCTRINE: LIMITS [121

only deal in areas of legislative inertia. That is, if exercise of the power does more than take the form of a threat to reconsider an old rule judicially (of "blackmailing" so that the legislature is led to take a new look at an old statute), and entails instead a nullification or a modification of an existing rule, then that judicial action must generally be deemed to have been wrong if the legislature responds by reenacting the old rule. In that case the court was, by definition, going beyond a shifting of the burden of inertia. It misread the majoritarian support for the old rule, whether or not it was correct in its judgment that the rule was out of phase and did not fit the legal fabric. (There is one notable exception to this notion; that is the case in which the judicial object is not to question the present validity of the old law, but to force a current legislature to take responsibility for that law. I will discuss later this variant of the semiconstitutional ground for exercise of judicial authority.)

Does this mean that the courts should never modify or nullify a rule and then be reversed by a legislature? Not at all. To require correct employment of the doctrine in all cases would be to guarantee that it would fail to be used in some appropriate situations. It is like a player doubling at bridge or a bank deciding when to issue a loan. Every time a player doubles and the contract is made, we can say he was wrong to double, even though on the cards the double was warranted and even though a player who never doubles a good contract surely doubles too rarely. Similarly, all loans that go bad are criticizable and are wrong, even if they were within good banking practice when made. Yet a bank that has no bad debts is too conservative, is not doing its business correctly, and is clearly failing to make some loans that should be made.

The court's judgment must be based primarily on whether the statute fits the legal landscape, because that is what a court is good at discerning and because "fit" is correlated with majoritarian support. The two are far from the same, however, for legislatures can properly want a rule that is out of phase with the topography. The court must therefore do the best it can to avoid following the requirements of the legal landscape when that would conflict with powerful legislative desires. It dares not stray too far from subservience to the landscape, though, because it is unsure of its capacity to gauge majoritarian support.[2] Accordingly it is bound to make some decisions based on the fit of the statute which the legislature will want reversed. The same tension existed at common law. Application of the common law power to statutes, like the greater willingness of legislatures to act in traditionally common law areas, merely means more frequent possibilities of legislative reversals of court judgments. It calls for greater awareness on the part of courts of majoritarian wishes; it does not reduce the responsibility of courts to put subservience to the legal framework first.[3]

When a court nullifies a statute or modifies it, and then is reversed by a legislature, the court has misjudged — it has made a bad debt; it has doubled a good contract. At best it has followed what it thought was the legal landscape further than it should have, and that itself is a justifiable ground for criticism. But, unless it does this too frequently, it cannot be charged with abuse of power any more than the bank can be charged with reckless lending when it follows the rules and makes a bad debt. Still the fact that an easily identifiable misjudgment has occurred, and the fact that the misjudgment is by itself ground for criticizing the courts, can serve as significant restraints on the courts' tendencies to abuse the doctrine.[4] At the very least it will push the courts toward use of those techniques (often the appropriate ones for other technical reasons) which induce the legislature to reenact or revise the old law before an actual modification or nullification takes place.[5]

Does this mean that any judicial action within the area of legislative inertia is, in retrospect, correct? Can we accept the converse of the proposition discussed in the last paragraphs; that judicial behavior which modifies or nullifies a law and is left undisturbed by the legislature is, by that very fact, justified? I think not. Such a result implies only that there were no majoritarian pressures sufficient to overturn the judicial decision. It does not support in any positive sense the judicial reallocation of the burden of inertia. It is no answer to repeat my earlier statement that no special majoritarian significance should be attached to the fact that the old law had remained in force and unrepealed. There is just as little majoritarian significance to the fact that the absence of that law is also left undisturbed. Neither inertial result tells us much about what situation is currently preferable.

Does the fact that the court chose one of them (in this case, modification or nullification) help us to prefer that result? Unless the court's conclusion can be justified, on grounds other than on its own predilections, the choice simply indicates that one or two nonmajoritarian bodies (courts) preferred one solution to another. Unless the court has principled grounds for its choice, there is no special reason for giving any more weight to the preferences of judges than to that of any other expert.[6]

Retentionist and Revisionist Biases

Where modification or nullification cannot be justified in the same terms that traditionally supported the modification of common law rules, we are left with several options. We can—as a general concept—prefer our traditional conservative bias and leave the old law undisturbed, not because it has a majoritarian basis but because our bias is to retain in effect what is already in effect. Or we can have the opposite, radical bias and require that, unless retention of a rule finds positive support in the whole fabric of law, the rule must be abolished (subject always to legislative reenactment).

We must not be confused by the terms "conservative" and "radical," however. They represent basic notions about change and not current political predilections with respect to particular types of laws. For example, the radical bias would sunset all dated regulatory laws, however pleasing to the current political left. And the conservative bias would keep in effect many laws to which the political right might strongly object. For these reasons I prefer the terms "retentionist" and "revisionist" to the more traditional "conservative" and "radical," though I shall in fact use both. Under either approach, the court's own bias with respect to the particular law would be largely irrelevant.

Between opting either for undisturbed retention or for nullification, in those cases where the legal topography requires neither and where legislative inertia will leave either result in place, lie those approaches that allow court actions to force legislative reconsideration and require that these be tried before modification or nullification can take place. Such actions are clearly justified when the court believes, but is not sufficiently certain, that an existing law is out of step. They are also often justified when the court is sure that a law is out of phase but does not know or cannot (for technical reasons or limits in its competence) determine the appropriate substitute rule. But even these actions do not avoid the basic problem of choosing between a retentionist or a revisionist bias when the court simply has no basis for preferring the existing law or its absence. For in such cases, to force a legislative reconsideration is to choose the radical bias, while to fail to force a reconsideration is to choose the retentionist approach.

My own preference is for the conservative bias, which is also the one traditionally dominant in our legal-political system. It restrained common law courts from overturning common law precedents they disliked, even when these precedents were no longer mandated by the legal topography, unless the precedents *clashed* with that topography. It did this regardless of whether the precedents were rightist or leftist. And, I would think, it should do the same with respect to statutes, not because that is required by majoritarian theories but because most of us prefer stability and reject change that is made only for its own sake or that has no greater basis than the personal predilections of nonelected officials. By analogy, then, this conservative bias would permit a statute, which when passed was clearly meant to clash with the legal topography, to remain in force and unreviewed, unless the court found that no retenionist bias was warranted.[7]

What are the reasons that would justify courts in nullifying, modifying, or forcing reconsiderations of dated statutes? Some are general; others specific to specific types of statutes or rules. To state them is, in effect, to begin to delimit the doctrine. In general, though, the reasons are much like those that justified courts in abandoning dated common law rules. The fact that the court is dealing with statutes may alter somewhat the application of the reasons. It may emphasize those techniques that facilitate a legislative-judicial colloquy, but it does not change the basic notion that the court's job is to evaluate how the rule fits in the legal landscape.

Asymmetries in Inertia

Since the courts are seeking to create a dialogue with legislatures in order to bring about the updating of those laws that do not fit *and* whose lack of fit is not currently wanted by the legislature, courts must be concerned with the possible existence of an asymmetry in the effect of a retentionist or revisionist bias. Specifically they must examine how the nature of either the statute under consideration or the legislature involved may create the asymmetry.

The force of inertia is frequently not symmetrical in lawmaking and revision. At times reconsideration by a majoritarian or representative body, and hence possible reenactment, can easily be achieved without having to overcome major obstacles if a statute is nullified or cast into doubt. But legislative review of the same statute may require the bypassing of severe, nonmajoritarian obstructions if the statute is left undisturbed or unquestioned by the courts. Conversely, there may be statutes that once nullified can only with great difficulty be reconsidered in a majoritarian way; the same laws, if left in effect, are subject to almost constant review by a representative body. Obviously, a lack of symmetry of this sort, since it alters the practical effect of the court's decision should affect whether a retentionist or revisionist bias should be applied, and hence whether use of the doctrine is appropriate.

This factor is reminiscent of one that I and others have suggested should influence courts in deciding appropriate allocation of costs.[8] Can polluters, if charged with the cost of pollution, readily initiate negotiations with the neighboring householders; or can the latter without difficulty combine to deal with the polluting factories? Much that has been written about asymmetry in transaction costs as a ground for allocating substantive cost burdens can be applied here. For what we are dealing with is also the allocation of a substantive burden (the burden of an unfavorable law) to a particular group and the existence of asymmetrical transaction costs. Other things being equal, the burden is less onerous and the chance of a permanent bad result less great, if the initial allocation of costs places the burden on the party who has ready access to a free-market renegotiation. Similarly, the chance of a permanent bad result is less great if those on whom the court puts the burden of overcoming the effects of its decision have ready access to legislative reconsideration.

This, however, assumes that a single legislative reconsideration is the desideratum, just as transaction-cost literature assumes that free-market negotiation is the goal. If one doubts that the market negotiation is fair or efficient,[9] one is apt to place the initial burden so as to make that market renegotiation unlikely. Similarly, if a court believes that a one-shot legislative review of a rule is unlikely to cope adequately with an area, whereas accretional, common law development is more appropriate to the issues involved, it is likely to issue a rule that impedes immediate legislative review.

Obviously, a decision that makes legislative reconsideration less likely must be an unusual one. It must be based either on a clear notion that the decision accords with the legislative will or on clear indicia, based on principles, that the area is more suitable for accretional lawmaking than legislative review. Such situations are certainly possible and go a long way toward explaining a recent important federal court decision on the applicability of the Administrative Procedure Act to prisons.[10] Most of the time, however, courts will be well advised to err in the direction that makes legislative correction easy.

Asymmetry in the capacity to obtain majoritarian consideration does not generally justify court action or inaction that violates the other guidelines I will outline. If one knows that the polluters can avoid the cost of pollution more cheaply than the neighboring homeowners, it makes no sense to allocate the pollution cost to the homeowners simply because they could, by negotiation, easily overcome any error in the original allocation. Why, when the opposite allocation is clearly right, should any negotiation or transaction costs be countenanced? Similarly, why should a review be forced if the courts are sufficiently sure that the old law still fits, or that review would merely lead to cheap (but still unnecessary) reenactment? Only in the limiting case in which burdening one party leads to no transaction costs whatever or no obstacles involved in reenactment of a nullified law, could asymmetry be the sole factor in the judicial allocation of burdens.

Yet the existence of asymmetries remains important. Often there is doubt as to what cost allocation leads to optimal cost reductions, and equally often there is doubt as to whether an old law fits and even if it doesn't fit whether it is still supported in a majoritarian way. In the presence of such doubts, the judicial role must be to make easier the achievement of the appropriate (but unknown) substantive result. In cost allocations, this means charging the party who has easier access to free-market renegotiations; in the issues with which we have been concerned, it means putting the burden of inertia on the side that can more easily obtain majoritarian reconsideration of the allocation.

Asymmetries in majoritarian review may be due either to the nature of the law involved or to the nature of the legislature empowered to reconsider the law. As an example of the first, let us assume that some laws require funding by the full legislature every year in order to remain effective. These laws could rather easily be made subject to legislative review even in the absence of court-induced reconsideration. But the same laws, if nullified by courts, might only get reconsidered at the pleasure of a legislative committee. (I don't mean to suggest that under current procedures "funding" in fact encourages such substantive reconsideration — but the example still suggests how the nature of the law itself can render reconsideration asymmetrical.) Conversely, the threat to nullify a law that is manifestly needed, but some parts of which are anachronistic, is bound to create a full legislative reconsideration of the law. Leaving the same law undisturbed may, instead, mean that the dubious parts of the statute will only be reviewed if a strong inertial burden is overcome. (Again, to give a rather wild example, if a court believes that some parts of a murder statute no longer fit, a threat of nullification over the whole statute will almost certainly bring about a legislative review; but leaving the statute untouched may make it unlikely that the legislature will ever reconsider the specific parts the court believes to be out of phase.)[11]

Examples of asymmetries because of the nature of the legislature are also easy to find. Treaties may be abrogated by an executive act but may only be modified or reenacted with the consent of two thirds of the Senate.[12] This very fact, together with the complex process of international revisions that treaties entail, could suggest grounds for some particular court roles or restraints in treaty interpretations which would be inappropriate in other areas. Indeed, the New York Court of Appeals not long ago suggested just that kind of justification for employing an extraordinarily strained interpretation of the Warsaw Pact dealing with injuries in international flights.[13]

Closer to home, the behavior that was appropriate for the D.C. Court of Appeals in its one-time role as Supreme Court of the District of Columbia, had little to do with what would have made sense for the Supreme Court of Massachusetts in considering statutes of that commonwealth.[14] The District of Columbia then had no representative legislature. Its laws were made by Congress. As a practical matter, Congress did not get to review D.C. laws unless the House District of Columbia Committee let it do so. That committee in turn was disproportionately made up of southern congressmen who were about as far from representative of the population of the District as one could imagine.[15]

In such a context, reconsideration of D.C. laws by a body that was representative of the majority of the district was virtually impossible. And this in itself would have justified judicial lawmaking that did not fit into the Hart-Sacks legal process mold.[16] But beyond this, an asymmetry existed that could support a revisionist bias. If a D.C. law were struck down (or threatened with nullification), that law could be reconsidered by the whole Congress. (As a practical matter, the House District of Columbia Committee would relatively quickly push for a reenactment — and the whole Congress would get to vote on the issue.) If, instead, a D.C. law were left unquestioned, the whole Congress could not in practice decide if changes were warranted, unless the House committee also believed that changes were needed.

Is it any wonder that a court could believe that, among unrepresentative bodies, the Congress was more representative of District opinion than the House committee? And is it surprising that such a court might react with a high degree of "judicial activism"? The effect of this activism by the D.C. Court of Appeals, operating through the full arsenal of judicial tricks, was to assure that the whole Congress would review some old D.C. laws.[17] To that extent, the court was simply reacting to a situation of asymmetry and facilitating review of its actions (and of old statutes and rules) by the most nearly representative body available.

In fact, of course, the D.C. Court of Appeals went further and often sought by constitutional adjudication or other techniques to substitute its own judicial judgment for that of Congress.[18] I cannot say whether it did that because the doctrine we have been discussing was not available, and hence the court was at times driven *faute de mieux* to the Constitution, or whether it acted because it believed that even Congress was not an appropriate legislature for the District, or whether, instead, it believed that the issues involved were essentially judicial and nonmajoritarian. It is, in any event, to the side of our current discussion. What is interesting is the fact that, with all the extraordinarily able law clerks Judge David Bazelon has had, none has examined that court's role, and his own preeminent position in it, on the basis of the unique "legal process" context in which he worked.[19] All of us, I fear, remained too wedded to a model for Massachusetts even where the premises of that model made no sense, to see what influence the absence of those premises might play.

Be that as it may, the role of the Court of Appeals for the D.C.

Circuit has changed, as has, to some extent, the governance of the District and even perhaps the composition of the House District of Columbia Committee.[20] All that, then, is not really crucial. What is crucial, is that asymmetries in legislative capacity to deal with old laws that are questioned or nullified by courts, as against those that are left undisturbed, do affect the propriety of judicial use of the doctrine we are considering. And since it does, courts faced with asymmetries, by hook or by crook, by fiction and by subterfuge, have acted in ways that reflect the asymmetrical effect of their decisions.

The Legal Topography: Post-Enactment Changes

Asymmetries come into play only when the court has reason to believe that a statutory or common law rule needs reconsideration. Awareness of them certainly facilitates the legislative-judicial dialogue that seeks to make modern lawmaking as responsive to the need for continuity and change as common law adjudication was said to have been in another age.[21] But such awareness does not tell us when the dialogue is needed. It does not by itself justify courts to induce the review of a dated statute. That justification must still derive from how the statute fits in the current legal fabric and, in the first instance, on what has happened to that fabric since the statute was passed.

The questions courts should ask themselves in deciding whether to overcome the retentionist bias and force reconsideration of an old rule are therefore ones we have all heard before, for they are strikingly similar to those which at common law determined when old precedents should be discarded.

Has the common law surrounding the statute so altered that the old rule no longer fits in its current form? This, the traditional common law question, would have been highly relevant in the FELA-Jones Act cases, the California guest-statute situation, and the cases involving the comparative negligence laws of both California and Wisconsin.[22]

Have other statutes been passed which indicate the same type of change in the legal landscape and which, therefore, support a revisionist rather than retentionist bias? In this sense a single statute may not have much gravitational force, but, as Landis notes, a collection of statutes in one's own and other jurisdictions surely must create a strong revisionist pressure. "The task of distinguishing between the deliberate and the *ad hoc* pronouncements of a legislature is not too difficult," he said. "A course of legislation dealing continuously with a series of instances can be made to unfold a principle of action as easily [as a long series of common law judgments]."[23] This type of change justified Justice Harlan in *Moragne v. States Marine Lines*[24] in doing for marine wrongful death something like what Chief Justice Hallows did for comparative negligence in Wisconsin.[25] It would also have justified the negation of a retentionist bias with respect to Connecticut's absolute prohibition of birth control devices, a prohibition that applied even when contraception was needed to save a woman's life. For surely the passage of statutes permitting abortion in such life-and-death cases in all jurisdictions including Connecticut had to undermine any retentionist bias.[26]

Has the constitutional law surrounding the statute so changed that it no longer fits as written? This is different from the question of whether the old statute or rule is now of doubtful constitutional validity. The law may clearly be valid and yet make little sense in the new context. Indeed, this question is more like the issue of whether the technological world has changed sufficiently around the statute so as to make any bias in favor of its retention less desirable than a bias for reconsideration.

Examples of all these types of changes that overcome our retentionist bias are easy to come by. In Connecticut statutes were passed making it very hard for townships to leave regional school districts once they had joined them.[27] These statutes were, and probably still are, clearly valid. Subsequently the Supreme Court ruled that one-man-one-vote was required for elections to regional school boards.[28] The continued appropriateness of the statutes governing the withdrawal of townships from regions (now that the consequences of membership were completely different) became, to say the least, doubtful. Similarly, if the status of women in our society has sufficiently altered, because of social changes as well as constitutional holdings, so that the kind of absolute presumption of dependency made by the social security laws seems unwarranted, why should not the statutory validity of such a presumption be questioned, *quite apart from whether the presumption is constitutional?*[29] And if a technological change, such as the development of photocopying machines, has made copyright laws anachronistic, why should a retentionist bias hold rather than one that allows courts to force a legislative reconsideration of old copyright statutes?[30]

Finally, has there been a sufficient accretion of scholarly criticism of the bases of the old rule? In a sense this is analogous to the last set of questions, for the legal landscape can change as much because of intellectual revolutions as because of technological or social revolutions. An old rule or statute may not fit because the intellectual premises on which it was based are no longer considered valid. If that is the case, yet another argument exists for abandoning the retentionist bias and permitting courts to force legislative reconsideration.

In all these cases it is unlikely that a single change suffices to undercut the old statute. It usually takes a series of constitutional decisions, ideological changes, technological innovations, or intellectual revolutions to make an old rule anachronistic. Yet sometimes an event is sufficiently dramatic that it, by itself, makes old rules doubtful and overcomes the retentionist bias. Again as Landis said about statutes, in practice it is not too hard to see if changes have been *ad hoc* or if instead they have changed the whole legal topography.[31] Like changes in morality,[32] it is rare that any one factor will alter the legal landscape; it is rarer still that any one decision or theory will do it. A combination of events, decisions, and theories, however, changes the topography all the time, and usually in easily recognized ways.

The Landscape of Enactment

Still at the general level is another set of factors that can justify a court to force reconsideration of an old statute. In the last section I discussed the effect that changes around the statute can have. Here I am concerned with the nature of the statute under consideration — the time and circumstances in which it was enacted and what these have to say about obsolescence.

Most obviously, courts should be concerned with how old the statute is. I am not talking here about whether in order to limit the danger of judicial abuses a minimum age should be required — as in Senator Davies' bill[33] — before courts can decide whether to force reconsideration of statutes. I am talking about the relevance of the age of the statute apart from the danger of abuse.

The point here goes beyond the mere issue of conservative versus radical bias.[34] A recent statute deserves a presumption of majoritarian support, even if it is "different" and out of phase with the rest of the law. One should normally assume that the coalition behind it still obtains and, unless the preferences it created skate close to the constitutional line, that the discriminations it made were intended by that majority. An old statute, without more, remains valid primarily because of our retentionist bias and not because of any great sense that a presumption of majoritarian grounding is sound.

Yet one should not, perhaps, make too much of the mere chronological age of a statute. There are statutes that age early, because of intrinsic characteristics, and others that do not age at all. That is what makes general sunsetting a rather pointless approach and a judgmental control over the burden of inertia desirable. Indeed, the old common law doctrine of strict interpretation of statutes in derogation of the common law dealt primarily with new statutes. And Wellington's modern version of that approach based on a statutory-common law landscape seems likewise to center on the recent legislative aberration as appropriate for court review.[35] Similarly, Levi's theory of interpretation gives far greater scope to courts in dealing with new statutes than with old ones.[36] New statutes, moreover, are often the ones which, for semiconstitutional grounds, require a second legislative look.[37]

All of these traditional sources of judicial power over statutes focus on the fact that a newborn statute may be the result of inadvertence, overreaction to a particular set of events, or a legislative response to a temporary majority at war with more persistent societal views. The existence of such traditional views suggests that, as with people, the life expectancy of a statute, and of a judicial decision too,[38] is relatively low right after birth, becomes very high after the rule has survived a few years, and then diminishes as it ages. As a result I would not be inclined to limit the doctrine *absolutely* to statutes of a certain age unless that is necessary to prevent abuse.

Still, it should be emphasized that *true* interpretation (without any new doctrine) does permit a fair degree of judicial control over new aberrant statutes (as do *true* vagueness and delegation theories). At the same time, the likelihood that a new statute is based on distinctions that are not currently valid is much less than if the statute were

old. So, without exaggerating the significance of age, the date of enactment must remain a major factor influencing the propriety of
shifting away from a retentionist bias.

More interesting is the question of whether or not the statute was
made for an emergency, crisis, or specific problem. One reason for
the shift to statutes, as I noted, was the legislature's capacity to deal
quickly with crises—real or imagined—engendered by rapidly
changing technologies and ideologies.[39] It should be obvious that
such statutes are likely to age more quickly than other, more organic
laws. Such crisis laws are the product of quick changes, and other
quick changes can render them anachronistic. Such laws deserve little conservative bias, once the event, the crisis, the technological
change, is overcome. They are in fact the very statutes that most
justify the use of the doctrine here described.

Examples again are easy: fair trade laws passed during an economic crisis against a background of antitrust laws;[40] emergency
rent controls in the context of a still predominanty "free price" society;[41] emergency malpractice laws that place restrictions on recoveries alien to the rest of tort law and that could become dated as a result of relatively minor reorganizations in the medical profession or
in the insurance industry.[42] These laws when enacted were all at war
with the then prevailing legal fabric. They were justified because
majoritarian bodies are there precisely to make new and even *ad hoc*
distinctions that do not fit the legal landscape. They may become the
source of further common law and statutory change, and serve as
landmarks in a whole new topography. Or they may not. Emergency
rent control may or may not be the precursor of a regulated price
system. Restrictions on malpractice recoveries may or may not represent the beginning of a whole new way of trying to balance safety,
accidents, and compensation. Fair trade laws may or may not signal
a general move toward protection of competitors.[43]

Even if the principles these laws reflect do not come to prevail generally, there may remain instances in which bodies that are at least
majoritarian by representation choose to perpetuate distinctions in
favor of special groups. And then it is irrelevant that these distinctions originated in a particular time-limited set of circumstances.
But reenactment or reconsideration is required once those time-limited circumstances are past. And courts can justifiably force legisla-

tures in such situations to show whether or not they mean to keep in force the distinction which does not fit the law at large and is no longer supported by the circumstances that engendered it.

One should distinguish this kind of time-bound preference from those statutory discriminations that remain supported by the general circumstances existing at the time of enactment. These laws whose lack of fit has stayed constant present the most difficult case for the doctrine. Their justification rests directly in the persistence of the coalition that enacted them, and this becomes increasingly doubtful over time. Yet to determine that the support for these laws has faded, the courts have to make more direct guesses as to legislative support than was traditionally countenanced.[44]

When such laws seem to represent an attempt of a transient majority to write its views in stone, or when they seem to be the last gasp of a dying majority that seeks by legislation to foreclose the future,[45] such statutes create enormous temptations for judicial intervention. Most of the time, if the majority was transient or dying, that intervention will be justified by other visible changes in the landscape. If no such clear changes exist, traditionalists will prefer to stay with a retentionist bias; those who are more comfortable than I with justifications of judicial power based on court capacity to reflect current majorities or disinterested values will permit courts to induce legislatures to reconsider the preferences.

At the other end of the scale from all these ill-fitting laws are those statutes that instead work a reorganization of a whole area of law. Let us for the moment leave aside the issue of whether they do so statutorily because they involve government fundraising and spending, or because they constitute an all-encompassing compromise between major societal interests, or because they represent a kind of restatement of what were essentially common law solutions but which, in order to assure uniformity among jurisdictions, are enacted into a broad, uniform law.[46] These questions are important in deciding whether the doctrine should apply to parts of these codes and when judicial common law development is appropriate. (This is the kind of behavior in which European judges have always engaged in dealing with their broad codes; they can teach us a great deal, both good and bad.[47]) Since, however, such overarching laws themselves create the legal framework, courts should be reluctant to abandon the retentionist bias and to nullify such acts.

Reluctance does not mean abstention. Time and circumstances change even for broad codes. And it is possible that a code can become so out of phase with everything else in the law that a forced legislative reconsideration becomes appropriate. Yet one must assume a really extraordinary set of legal, technological, ideological, and intellectual changes around a code that clearly was the last gasp of a dying majority to make this seem plausible.[48] (Again, I am not talking about interstitial development within such broad laws, however detailed the language of the code. That, as I have suggested, may be demanded by technological or other changes and be highly appropriate.)

More plausible is a situation in which paraconstitutional doubts make even a broad code a correct subject for legislative reconsideration. For now it is enough to point out that even this basis, when applied to a broad code, is likely to be highly controversial and dangerous for the courts. And this remains true even if the courts are justified by the subsequent failure of legislative reenactment. An example of judicial nullification of a broad code on semiconstitutional grounds was the Supreme Court's invalidation of the National Recovery Act. That decision, though it did not lead to reenactment, certainly engendered controversy and hurt the Court, despite the fact that, since it was partly based on delegation of powers, it did not preclude a legislative second look.[49]

Constitutional Infirmities

The last general factor affecting the propriety of using the doctrine is the one that has had the most complete treatment in the literature. It is the existence of constitutional, paraconstitutional, or deep structural doubts about the statute or rule under consideration. The point is quite a simple one. When a law comes close to violating a constitutional imperative or threatens some organic or structural principle of our system, the appropriate bias is, almost by hypothesis, revisionist. This does not mean that such a law is unconstitutional or should be nullified so long as it fits the current legal fabric or is clearly supported by a representative body. It means that without evidence of such support, a court may well be justified in "sending that law back" even if there is no evidence of the absence of such support. It is enough that such a law is out of phase, or nearly so, with that longer-standing (and perhaps antimajoritarian) legal landscape that is sometimes called the penumbra of the constitution. To be valid, such a law must have more to support it than a simple retentionist bias.

Once the issue is put in this way it becomes quite easy to see the place of passive virtues (both true and fictitious), classic theories of strict interpretation of constitutionally doubtful laws, Wellingtonian notions of second look, and cases like *Sorrells v. United States*.[50] Even a recent law of dubious constitutional or organic validity benefits from the majoritarian support necessary to overcome the appropriate revisionist or nullificatory bias only if it is clearly, openly, and responsibly enacted by a legislature. Hence delegation, vagueness, and even strict interpretation in their true sense are appropriate doctrines. Sometimes, however, a clearly written law that was passed by a clearly representative body may have been enacted hastily and without the full consideration that would suggest more than temporary majoritarian support. Judicial intervention in such a situation is more dangerous, because the courts may too readily impute hastiness or thoughtlessness where they do not exist, but it still may give rise to appropriate judicial demand for a legislative second look. In such a case, interpretation, vagueness, and delegation are manifestly inappropriate doctrines to use. The true justification for imposing a second look would be the judicial authority to assure itself that, to the extent that the law clashes with the legal topography in a fundamental way, the clash is the result of the genuine and *considered* wishes of majoritarian bodies.

As such a statute becomes older (if time has not mitigated the constitutional doubts), the courts ought to feel freer to ask for reconsiderations than they would for statutes that do not clash with underlying principles. Again, no ground for a retentionist bias exists precisely because of the statute's clash with the legal environment. Now time may well show such a statute or rule to have been the precursor of change in our basic structure. And a statute that was of doubtful constitutionality when passed may subsequently fit as well as any law in the organic structure. That is surely what happened to those New Deal laws that were at the borders of the commerce power but that presaged a fundamental constitutional shift and now seem to fit the constitutional landscape very comfortably.[51]

When, however, no such constitutional or structural change occurs to make the statute fit, forced reconsideration is frequently appropriate even years after the statute has been passed and interpreted. Only as a result of majoritarian or legislative reconsideration can the polity be assured that such a law, which deserves no retentionist bias, is nevertheless to be retained because it has current majoritarian support. It is rare, I think, in such cases that doctrines like interpretation, vagueness, and delegation are likely to be appropriate. A more direct and open recognition of what is involved is called for. The Smith Act can serve as an example of a law that was clearly on the fringes of validity, did not become any more suited to the constitutional landscape with the passage of time, and therefore would have justified judicial action designed to induce a legislative reconsideration.[52]

The same is also true when constitutional or structural changes have made an old statute, which once fit the constitutional landscape, infirm in this deeper or structural sense. In such cases techniques like interpretation, vagueness, and delegation seem singularly inappropriate. The law was, in all probability, interpreted and upheld earlier when it presented no constitutional problems. To say that now it has become vague seems transparently false. It is much better to recognize the situation for what it is and note that, since no retentionist bias is warranted because the law is now constitutionally doubtful, it can only be upheld if it reflects a current, open, and clear majoritarian sentiment. Both the Connecticut birth control law and the Social Security Act's sex distinctions could have been examples of precisely such an infirming of a law as a result of postenactment constitutional changes.[53]

None of this should be taken to suggest that clearly unconstitutional laws should only be sent back for legislative reconsideration rather than be invalidated on constitutional grounds. That some judges, reluctant to use the ultimate constitutional power even when it is appropriate, may rely on the doctrine discussed (just as now they rely on the passive virtues) is undoubtedly the case. Whether or not they are acting improperly depends on one's view of when use of the ultimate constitutional power is appropriate in our system; and views on this differ widely.[54] My point is only that open affirmation of the doctrine under discussion is in no way inconsistent with use of the full constitutional power. It may lead some judges to shy away from what they see as an abuse of constitutional power (to which they had been driven by absence of an acceptable alternative). But, like the passive virtues properly understood, it represents no theoretical undercutting of traditional judicial review.

What the doctrine does permit is a more self-conscious consideration of what techniques will lead to an intelligent and considered review of the constitutionally doubtful statute by the legislature. Open recognition of the doctrine allows courts to shape the judicial-legislative dialogue so as to obtain information from the representative bodies which can help to shape ultimate constitutional decisions. More important, it can lead the legislative reconsideration to take place within guidelines that distinguish between what, if doubtul in a deep sense, would nonetheless be admissible if the majority truly wants it and what is invalid regardless of majoritarian demands.[55]

In the end, constitutional or structural infirmity becomes just one more factor that determines the appropriateness of the doctrine under consideration. Like asymmetry and nonconstitutional changes that serve to deprive a rule of the benefit of a retentionist bias, constitutional infirmity is not an all-or-nothing matter. The degree of dubiety of a statute varies and must in many cases be weighed against other factors. There are also instances where this factor is so dominant that by itself it warrants judicial nullification or forced reconsideration. But more often it will be one of many indications that together make clear that a law ought not remain on the books simply because it is there.

Specific Factors

In addition to the general factors that suggest when use of judicial power is appropriate, there are a host of specific factors. These have to do, for example, with how a specific rule or subrule fits within the particular framework of a field of law. They are closely related to the nature of the rule involved, the field of law in which it fits, and the reason why the rule or the field has become statutorified. They are different from the question of techniques and judicial competence. But like these they require a degree of specificity for full analysis which is not appropriate to this book. I will therefore simply mention a few, more as examples of possibly relevant factors than as true definers of the doctrine. Most of them, as I said, stem from the reason why statutorification occurred in the particular area.

If the reason for statutorification was, say, that government moneys were involved, then direct attention should focus on the rigidity of the figures used. Does the context suggest a relational or growing statute (like the workmen's compensation laws), which would warrant court efforts to force legislatures to bring the fixed money figures into line after a severe inflation? Or was the statute "intended" (as shown either by its context or by the later common law and statutory developments in the area) to represent a one-time and diminishing payoff to a powerful interest group or to a group that needed transitional aid?[56] If the latter, judicial intervention and forced reconsideration would only reopen an issue that ought to be left closed. (All this is apart from how easy or hard it is for courts to deal with specific figures, which I leave to the next chapter.)

If, instead, the statute was passed to achieve a generalized compromise between major interest groups, the courts might properly consider the following question: Have changes occurred that render some part of the compromise out of phase? Legislative reconsideration of that part may be inappropriate because it would reopen the whole compromise (something that may not be desirable from a general point of view or even from the standpoint of the parties themselves). Yet it may nonetheless be the case that a court could work interstitially within the general compromise and, taking changes into account, bring the anachronistic part up to date without causing the whole compromise to fall.

Still more obviously, if a statute was enacted to achieve uniformity, any event that affected the bite of the statute only in some jurisdictions might, all else being equal, justify a judicial reworking to restore the lost uniformity. And this, again, would be independent of what techniques would be most appropriate to the task at hand.[57] Yet here too the courts must beware the possibility that the break in uniformity might be a reversion to a more general point of view in the jurisdiction, and that it was the uniform statute that represented a temporary aberration. The whole context, the whole landscape, is crucial, even when one speaks of specific statutes and factors.

The same point can be made with respect to another factor. In many cases it is appropriate for courts to consider whether the statute when passed represented an expansion of a preexisting right or a restriction of an earlier common law or statutory right. Was it, like the Wisconsin comparative negligence statute of the 1930s, the

FELA law, and the workmen's compensation laws, an attempt to enhance plaintiff's chances to recover, or was it like the guest statutes
an attempt to cut down on what had come to be viewed as incorrect
jury verdicts?[58] If an expansionist statute is followed by a further expansion in the common law and in other statutes around it, then
court use of the doctrine is particularly appropriate. The courts
should be somewhat more cautious in their use of a general pro-
plaintiff (say) common law and statutory development as a ground
for overturning or questioning a statute that did represent a legislative attempt to limit an earlier form of that same type of common law
development.

Context, however, is once more all-important. What is an expansionary, as opposed to a limiting, statute or rule is only a matter of
point of view. A guest statute that restricts certain plaintiffs' rights
expands certain defendants' protections. If that statute is followed by
a common law or statutory development that further limits plaintiffs'
rights in analogous fields, it must be viewed as a statute whose pro-
defendant tendencies are appropriately subject to judicial expansion, and whose limits on its pro-defendant tendencies ought readily
to be subjected to forced legislative review.

Conversely, even statutes that represented a legislative move
against an otherwise dominant common law or statutory trend should
not be deemed immune from judicial reworking, or forced legislative
reconsideration, if that trend develops further. Consider, for example,
a case in which an expansionary law (like the Wisconsin comparative
negligence statute[59]) has been called into question because its limits
seem no longer to fit the general common law and statutory
movements in the jurisdiction and in other states. Suppose further
that the court misjudged the mood in the jurisdiction and that the
same statute is reenacted, *now* as a legislative affirmance of a desire to
run against the general trend. Suppose finally that more years pass,
and the same general trend becomes ever more dominant in both the
specific jurisdiction and at large. Should the existence of the once majoritarian restriction be left unquestioned? To do so would lead to the
odd result of making the slightly premature judicial intervention a
source of permanent preclusion of judicial action. (After all, if the
court had let the original expansionary statute alone, it would be easy
for a later court, given the continuing trend, to judge the old law out
of date and hence appropriate for reconsideration.)[60]

Perhaps a premature judicial action should serve as a warning to later courts to be more careful in seeing whether the statute is really out of date, despite the growing context. But that is achieved by the notion that expansionary statutes are more appropriate for further expansion than restrictive statutes. To add stronger limits than that is likely unduly to restrain courts when they review expansionary statutes (for fear of bringing forth "untouchable" restrictive statutes). It is also likely to cause legislative jockeying with language, in order to control the future precisely in ways that the future does not readily permit.

Three Cautionary Notes

All these specific examples are really part of the more general question of when, in the particular case, the legal context has changed sufficiently to warrant a shift in the burden of inertia, a dropping of the retentionist bias. We have now seen many factors that call into question the appropriateness of such a bias. It may therefore be well to end this chapter with some cautions.

The first situation I have in mind is one in which a whole new code or general statutory arrangement is enacted. Despite its attempt to be all-encompassing it leaves a few old statutes or old common law rules which used to fit well in the earlier legal landscape. How quickly should courts move to adjust these to the new dispensation? To move too fast causes us to lose a chance to experiment with the old. It causes us to jump to what, because it is all-encompassing, seems to be the legal landscape and yet may represent only a transitory approach. Again we must remember that the gravitational force of statutes, though clearly a significant and appropriate basis for the use of the doctrine, depended, even for Landis, on whether they were one-shot statutes or represented a course of development over time.[61] The breadth of a code may suggest the culmination of a series of developments, but it need not. Some other more organic evidence may be appropriate before the courts take the new statutory scheme as adequate grounds for dismantling what remained (in a backwater, so to speak) of the old approach.

This caution, significantly, applies regardless of whether the remnants of the old were statutes or common law rules. The doctrine would therefore induce change with the same caution that was sensible in evolving the common law, for in both some retentionist bias may be warranted as many different courts consider, by adjudicating real cases, whether the new code is a new legal fabric or is itself a short-lived manifestation of a passing majority.[62]

The second cautionary note goes to the question of which courts should be given the power to modify or force the reconsideration of anachronistic statutes. Those who wanted restatements to be enacted into law suggested that they have the same authority as a well-reasoned decision of the highest court of the jurisdiction.[63] Presumably, this would have limited most subsequent evolutions of the restatements to those sanctioned by the highest court of that jurisdiction. It seems likely that most states would similarly want to limit updating power to the highest court of the state, in much the same way they generally reserve to the state supreme court the power to reverse its own outdated precedents. Some states might, nevertheless, give greater scope to their lower courts.

As interesting an intellectual matter as this may be, I will not pursue it here. For, at bottom, it does not seem that the task of the lower court with respect to the modification of statutes is much different from the traditional task of lower courts of deciding when an old higher-court decision is so obviously dead that even the lower court can bury it. Common law courts have long been conscious of their limited role in avoiding old authority of higher courts. I can see little intrinsic reason why the problem of the obsolescence of a statute should be more intractable. Caution is warranted lest any judge in any court believe that he or she has the power to set the legislative agenda. But again it is the same caution that properly characterized the process by which common law rules were discarded.

The third cautionary note is perhaps the most important. Unless the doctrine is applied with restraint, there is a danger that it may result in overburdening both courts and legislatures. There are, however, some factors to suggest that an appropriate use of the doctrine may have the opposite effect.

Though it is certainly true that open recognition of the doctrine entails the danger that lawyers will seek to invoke it in many situations where it is not apt,[64] and hence overburden the courts, correct use of the doctrine may do away with out-of-date statutes that are themselves a major cause of court congestion. One of the leading sources of court congestion today is personal injury litigation. No small part of this stems from the inability of our legal system to keep up to date those more efficient statutory ways of dealing with such injuries, such as workmen's compensation, that we have on the books. To get around outworn compensation laws, injured employees have, with a high degree of success, brought suits against "third parties" based on product liability and other theories. The typical example is the employee's product liability suit against the third-party manufacturer of the machine that injured the employee in the course of employment. In many such cases, the losing defendant can in practice pass the cost of the verdict back to the employer, who could not have been sued except under a workmen's compensation law. The net result is that the same party pays who would have paid through an updated workmen's compensation law; but the payment is swollen by the higher cost of the product liability suit, and the courts are overwhelmed by the number of such suits and the time they take. Since, however, courts have not been able to make recoveries under workmen's compensation laws reflect the pro-plaintiff changes in the general law of torts, the expensive and court-burdening end run represented by product liability suits has been inevitable. The courts have not been able to adapt such injury cases to the changing topography by inducing reform of workmen's compensation, and they have been driven — in their desire to treat like injuries alike — to other solutions that are both expensive and time-consuming.[65]

One does not, moreover, need to look only at recent developments. Justice Frankfurter's objections to the FELA suits reflected precisely the same problem. Because the Supreme Court was not free to impose or induce a modern system of recovery in that area, he argued, it was misled into abusing *certiorari* jurisdiction, thereby overcrowding the docket and diminishing the time that could be spent on cases involving important issues of principle.[66]

Frankfurter may or may not have been correct in that particular set of cases, but the point is a valid one nonetheless. Laws that do not fit lead to litigation, as lawyers and litigants seek desperately and imaginatively to get around the anachronistic results the timeworn laws seem to impose. Courts trying to treat such litigants in ways that fit the legal fabric tend to encourage just such litigation. A direct attack on the dated statutes would take more time in the beginning but would, soon enough, deprive second-best litigation of much of its appeal and hence help to clear the dockets.

An analogous factor may reduce the tendency of the doctrine to overburden legislatures. To the extent courts seek to get around dated laws by second-best solutions, they often create crises, which then lead to the introduction of special-interest statutes designed to lessen the effect of the admittedly inadequate judicial solution. Such statutes typically do not resolve the underlying problem, since they focus on the immediate judicial solution rather than the anachronistic statutes that gave rise to it. (Those who push for such statutes are generally adversely affected by the judicial solution, but are not concerned with what led to it.) Thus they take up a great deal of legislative time without really solving the basic problem. As *they* become increasingly dated, one can predict that the process will repeat itself, and still more legislative time will be used up. Again, the host of statutes recently introduced to cope with the product liability crises, itself derived in part from inadequate judicial attempts to get around the dating of earlier statutes, can serve as an example.[67]

As we might expect, a similar effect is also created when courts attempt to get around dated statutes by holding them unconstitutional.[68] To the extent that some part of the dated statute represents a still dominant position in the legislature, the holding of unconstitutionality makes the legislative job of reestablishing that policy more difficult and time-consuming than would have been the case if the court, acting under the doctrine, had merely induced a second look. Legislative struggles with problems of school financing are examples of this last situation.[69] It has been extraordinarily difficult for legislatures to find school financing formulas that meet court-imposed constitutional requirements and yet conform to the political majoritarian demands of the particular state. If the nullification of the traditional form of school financing was meant to impose constitutional strictures, then the difficulties were inevitable and, in a sense, warranted. If, instead, the courts were seeking primarily to force legislatures to take another look at a system of financing of schools that had become discriminatory, then the fact that they were driven to use the constitutional weapon resulted in an unnecessary waste of legislative time.

The point is again a simple one. Subterfuges, because they are not fashioned to cope with a problem, are apt to lead legisltures no less than courts to wasteful ways of dealing with the problem. The existence of timeworn laws has led to a myriad of subterfuges and, therefore, to unnecessarily complicated legislative-judicial dialogues.[70] Open recognition of the doctrine may expand the number of instances in which the court engages in a dialogue with the legislature and induces legislative action; and this will tend to crowd legislatures. But it will also make that dialogue easier and less time-consuming than it is now.

The cautionary note still stands, however. If the doctrine is to be applied, the courts must, in deciding when and how to use it, be jealous of their own time and that of the legislatures. They must use it first and foremost in situations in which the statutes to be updated are themselves a source of legislative and judicial congestion. And they must employ those techniques that not only help to clear the ways but do not impose unnecessary constraints or time-consuming obstacles on the courts or on legislatures.

Judgment is once again called for. But as with the other cautionary notes it is a judgment akin to what courts have always had to exercise in the prudent evolution of the common law. For the abandonment of an old common law rule presented analogous dangers of overburdening and — if done right — analogous opportunities to reduce congestion.

XI

The Doctrine:
Techniques and Feasibility

Courts are not suited to do many things because they do not have the data necessary to know what should be done; because action in some areas requires detailed regulatory language; because not all the issues a legislative reconsideration would reveal to be at stake can be made apparent in an adversary setting; because judicial action in some areas has to be retroactive and hence may defeat justified expectations or fail to give needed warnings; or because judicial intervention fosters legislative abrogation of responsibility. A chapter on the feasibility of having courts use a power like that described in the last chapters must acknowledge these facts. It does not, however, have to reach any conclusions on what kinds of jobs courts can and cannot do. For in the end, the problems that would beset courts in trying to allocate the burden of inertia and in trying to keep written laws up to date are not different in kind from the problems they face, and have long faced, in trying to do the same job with respect to common law rules.

One may or may not agree with Abraham Chayes and Robert Keeton in their approval of increased judicial action within the present legal framework through use of new types of opinions and decrees.[1] The more one does agree with them, the more one can ask courts to be aggressive in carrying out the task of keeping the law consistent with a changing world and a changing legal topography. The less one agrees with them, the less one will be able to rely on courts as opposed to legislatures and agencies to keep our law current. For example, if courts cannot overrule prospectively, they will find updating very difficult in all situations — whether statutory or common law — in which legitimate expectations created by the old rule are involved. So the need to keep law current helps explain why courts have been asserting, and commentators have been urging, new modes of deciding which enhance judicial capacity to act prospectively and hence aggressively. But my own view on this crucial issue is somewhat beside the point of this book. For the judicial power to set the burden of inertia for statutes, and to decide whether a retentionist or revisionist bias should apply to an old law, requires in itself almost nothing in the way of judicial judgment that is not traditional to adjudication, and little in the way of judicial behavior that is not already needed if courts are to exercise the same power effectively over common law rules.

Courts must ask themselves first whether they are capable of deciding whether the currently operative rule or law should be revised or reconsidered; that is, whether there is something that keeps them from being able to decide in favor of a retentionist or revisionist bias. This was the question analyzed in the last two chapters. Only when they have decided that they are suited to allocate the burden of inertia (and that the burden should favor revision, for otherwise no action is needed) does the issue of techniques arise. How can a court best bring about a sensible reconsideration of the rule before it? This will depend on the degree to which any of the various technical limitations that adhere to all judicial lawmaking apply in the given instance. But it will also depend on the degree of assurance the court can have on the merits of the particular issue it faces. The techniques a court will appropriately use to update a statute or a common law rule, in other words, depend as much on whether the court is capable of defining the rule that does fit the legal landscape (instead of only being able to say that the existing one does not) as it does on whether the court is technically competent to bring forth the new rule.

As a practical matter, the courts can do any of several things when they have decided that an old rule is out of phase. They can strike down the existing rule and substitute a new one. They can strike down the rule and declare a new rule not of their own making to be applicable. They can, in other words, attach themselves to an existing statute whose gravitational pull formed part of the field which caused the court to conclude that the old law was out of phase in the first place. And they can do the same with respect to an existing set of administrative regulations which, they conclude, fit better than the statute or regulations they have found to be out of phase. They can strike down the existing rule and begin a process of developing a new rule (allowing later courts, agencies, or legislatures to flesh it out). They can revise part of the old rule and leave the rest in a state of uncertainty — to be reaffirmed or revised, either legislatively or judicially, in the future. Finally, they can strike down a rule and leave no rule in effect.

They can, moreover, do most of these things with an amazing degree of difference in the retroactivity or prospectivity of application of the change.[2] Perhaps most important, they can *do* none of these things, but *threaten* to do any or all of them, if a legislature or administrative agency does not act quickly. They can shape that legislative or administrative action by announcing, or by failing to announce, what they will do in the absence of such action. (An announcement creates a new inertia and therefore suggests rather more judicial assurance on what the well-fitting rule would look like than does a failure to announce, which leaves all interested groups uncertain and hence tends to force compromises.)[3] Finally, a court can do all these things with or without constitutional rhetoric, as it deems appropriate, to influence legislative or administrative response.

When are these techniques most appropriate? I can give only some examples of when courts have in fact used these different techniques in coping with outdated rules and statutes. And these will, I hope, serve both to suggest the factors that different courts with different views of appropriate judicial behavior consider to be relevant to the choice of techniques and to show that, once the decision to update a statute was made, the existence of a statutory rather than common law context made little difference in choice of technique.[4]

In general, the choice of judicial techniques used has depended on the interplay of five factors: (1) The degree to which the old rule — whether statutory or common law — could be deemed so out of phase that any reliance on it was misguided. (2) The difficulties inherent in the judicial writing of a new rule. (3) The degree of discomfiture that would be caused by a temporary absence of a rule or of a complete rule (in cases in which the alternative of a slowly developing rule might be available). (4) The degree of certainty the court could derive from the legal topography as to what would be the appropriate new rule to replace the outdated one, and hence of the desirability of establishing a single-shot judicial solution, as against either opening an explicit colloquy with the legislature or beginning a process of accretional lawmaking through adjudication. (5) The court's own view of its appropriate role, of the source of its authority.

The Interplay — Examples

My first set of examples involves, once again, comparative and contributory negligence. The first thing to note is that the decision on whether old pro-defendant rules in these areas should be left undisturbed or whether reconsideration should either be forced or new rules decreed — the issue we were concerned with in the last chapter — seems to have had very little to do with whether an old statutory or an old common law rule was involved. In Illinois, for instance, where the old rule was clearly common law, the court, after asking for briefs on the issue of revision, decided to leave the rule alone because it had stood too long to be changed by a court.[5] (Since the Illinois court has been willing to overturn other longstanding common law rules, one can only conclude that the problem was not so much the age of the common law rule as residual doubts about whether the rule was out of phase, or a reluctance to act in view of the technical problems that revision entailed.)[6]

By way of contrast, both the California and the Wisconsin supreme courts, even though faced with a statute, had no problem in deciding that a retentionist bias was not warranted in the same general area.[7] The techniques these two courts used were different and, interestingly, were mirrored by two other courts — the supreme courts of Hawaii and Florida. Hawaii dealt with its common law rule in much the same way in which Wisconsin dealt with its statute;[8] Florida chose techniques to alter its common law rule much like those employed by the California court to amend its code.[9]

Both the Hawaii and the Wisconsin courts decided that the combination of the five factors facing them made it more appropriate to induce a legislative reconsideration than to strike down the old rule and begin developing a new one. In both states, the court refused to act, but suggested that it might act unless the legislature reconsidered the old rule within a set time. Wisconsin, as we saw, forced this reconsideration without clearly saying what it would do in the absence of legislative action. The Hawaii court created a new, revisionist inertia by indicating, in dicta, what steps it might take toward a new rule if the legislature failed to act.[10] That difference is more than one of detail, of course, and reflects a different degree of judicial self-assurance as to what the legal topography was. But for our immediate purposes it is not too important. What matters more is that both approaches achieved their aim of getting the legislatures to write a new statute and to do it quickly. In this respect both techniques suggested a high degree of awareness of the difficulties inherent in a judicial promulgation of a new rule, a belief that a slow development of a new rule would not be desirable, some doubts as to precisely what the new rule should be, a desire to enter into a dialogue with the legislature, and considerable certainty that a retentionist bias was not warranted.

The California and Florida supreme courts viewed the matter differently. Again, one court could be said to have been dealing with a common law rule, the other with a statute.[11] And again this fact made no difference. Both courts agreed that a retentionist bias was unwarranted, that they knew — in general terms — what kind of new rule would fit the topography; that some legitimate expectations attached to the old rule; and that a fully developed and detailed new rule could not yet appropriately be issued by a court. They did not, however, believe that the field required a fully developed rule. For that reason they found it unnecessary to abstain and threaten to act only if the legislature remained somnolent, or to adopt a completed rule from elsewhere. Accordingly they did not need to use the Wisconsin-Hawaii technique or the one used by Justice Harlan in the Moragne case.[12] They preferred to opt for incremental adjudication over either form of dialogue with the legislature.

On the other hand, their recognition of a reasonable if diffuse reliance interest caused them to start developing a new rule for the most part prospectively.[13] In a sense a shift to comparative negligence from contributory negligence was ideally suited to the partial retroactivity doctrines employed. Those who had a right to rely on the old rules were primarily insurance companies who, allegedly, based their premiums on a "contributory negligence" actuarial experience. Awarding comparative negligence damages in one case —

that which brought about the prospective change — would only minimally affect insurers whose rates depended on a great mass of cases. Only a wholesale retroactive application of comparative negligence would have had any significant effect on those who properly relied on the old rule. Thus, even the quite sloppy treatment given to the issue of prospective versus retroactive application by both the California and Florida courts was probably adequate in the particular area they faced.[14]

With these cases one can usefully compare the techniques employed by the Supreme Court in the Moragne case and in the FELA-Jones Act cases, and by the New York Court of Appeals in the Eck case.[15] In *Moragne* the Supreme Court of the United States was faced with the fact that the many wrongful death statutes passed by Congress and by the states had failed to provide any relief for those killed in certain maritime accidents. One could have viewed the exception of these accidents from wrongful death laws as intended by legislatures,[16] or one could have viewed the mass of laws (as Hallows read the 1930s Wisconsin comparative negligence law)[17] as extending a recovery to some decedents but not barring those who were not covered. The Supreme Court, in a brilliant opinion by Justice Harlan, chose to view the situation in the latter way and, therefore, to derive a judicial power to act even in a predominantly statutory field. What barred recovery, Harlan said, was the ancient outdated common law and not the equally outdated statutes. He then had no trouble in declaring that the common law rule that failed to permit wrongful death damages was out of phase with the modern legal topography and could not stand.

It was, he judged, so far out of step that no expectation or reliance interest in the old rule was justified. Not for him, then, any problems of prospective or partially prospective overruling. Indeed, it was objectionable to continue to apply the old rule for any time, since to do so would treat *this* set of victims unlike similar victims.[18] As a result judicial abstention, coupled with a threat to act if Congress did not fill the gap, was not the appropriate technique. The technical difficulty was that no common law wrongful death recovery existed. All such recoveries were governed by statutes that had, like most statutes, a myriad of detailed limits and provisions. These provisions, moreover, differed from one wrongful death statute to another. Harlan could say that there was such unanimity in allowing recovery for wrongful death that a right to recovery existed and that it should not be delayed until Congress acted, but he had no equivalent assurance on the limits of the right and he was, given the specificity of these limits in analogous contexts, reluctant to let the limits be developed over time. He was, in addition, reluctant to have the Court try to write a detailed statute on its own.

His solution was to pick one statute as "probably" the most appropriate and declare it to be applicable. He then, in effect, asked the legislature to alter his choice if they preferred another statute.[19] In this way, he avoided the difficulties of judicial law writing and of slow common law rule development, while at the same time avoiding any delay in the application of the rule to a situation in which reliance on the old rule was unwarranted. Since recovery by the decedent, rather than reliance on the old rule, clearly fit the topography better, it should be granted immediately. But the nature of wrongful death statutes indicated that a relatively clear rule was preferable to common law incremental adjudication, and that was what Harlan established. More than any other case, perhaps because the opinion is so hard-headed, perhaps because it is written by so traditional a judge as Harlan, *Moragne* stands as a monument to what courts, aware of the fullness of techniques available to them, can do to update laws.

The Eck case (involving jurisdictional rules for bringing suits for damages in international flights under the Warsaw treaty) and the FELA-Jones Act cases (involving injuries to railroad and maritime employees), both of which I have already discussed,[20] show a different mixture of the same factors listed earlier.[21] In both of these sets of cases dramatic changes external to the written rules had made those rules outdated. The widespread pro-plaintiff developments, in tort law generally, had made the original FELA and Jones Act obsolete; the total change in airline ticketing practices, since the Warsaw treaty, had made the jurisdictional rules of that treaty nearly absurd (to the New York Court of Appeals). In both these situations the old rule was sufficiently out of phase so that reliance on it was not justified. Accordingly, no problem of retroactivity needed to be faced, even though the old rule certainly seemed "clear."

Retroactivity was less of a problem for another reason as well. The rules involved in these cases fit in the category of many pro-defendant rules, which even if not out of phase do not warrant reliance by wrongdoers (though they may by their insurers). Contributory negligence, many exclusionary rules of evidence, and the roadblock in the way to recovery discussed in the Eck case are not intended to affect the conduct of potential defendants, but only to affect the standard of care of others — plaintiffs in the case of contributory negligence, policemen in exclusionary rule cases. Defendants are not meant to rely on plaintiff contributory negligence or police misconduct to excuse their own substandard behavior. For this reason, the courts did not need to give much weight to claims of reliance made by such defendants and could change the rules with greater freedom — worrying perhaps about insurers but not about the individual "wrongdoer."[22] (Once again, rules of this sort that engender only very limited reliance can with equal likelihood be of statutory or common law origin.)

The courts moreover, in both the Eck and the FELA-Jones Act cases, were quite sure of what new rule would fit snugly in the current legal topography. In the FELA-Jones Act situation, a rule of jury supremacy seemed to the majority to suit the changes that had occurred in tort law, and to retain for injured seamen and railroad employees their preferred position.[23] In the Eck case a simple allowance of jurisdiction to hear damage suits (which would have been banned by the treaty language) would adequately respond to the technological changes in the airline industry. Both responses were, technically, well within the traditional capacities of the courts. Hence the courts opted for an aggressive technique (on its face simply traditional interpretation) that modified the old rule and, at the same time, promulgated a new one without explicitly inviting a legislative response.

The dissenters in the FELA-Jones Act cases agreed that the old rule was out of phase. Their disagreement, if I can be a bit cavalier about it, was primarily with what the new rule ought to be. They were far from clear that an advantageous position in the "new" tort law as determined, case by case, by juries represented a treatment of rail and sea employees like that afforded others similarly situated. Their plausible viewpoint, as expressed by Justice Frankfurter, was that workmen's compensation was the correct model.[24] But they either were not sufficiently sure of this fact or, more likely, had doubts about the Court's power to impose the result, and so did not urge judicial adoption of their preferred solution. Instead of doing what Harlan did in the Moragne case, they sought to force legislative action, but did so in a way quite different from and more dangerous than that employed by the Hawaii and Wisconsin courts in the comparative negligence cases.

The dissenters said that the FELA and Jones Act statutes allowed recoveries but only if negligence (tightly defined) existed. Without such clear negligence, the cases should have been withheld from the jury. Had they wished, they could then have adopted, as a common law matter, a "nearby" workmen's compensation law and awarded limited no-fault damages in those cases in which insufficient evidence of negligence existed to go to a jury. Like Harlan, they would have altered the no-recovery common law (here in the absence of negligence, in *Moragne* in the presence of death) by attaching themselves to an appropriate statute that would have defined and limited the recoveries to be awarded. Like Harlan, too, they could have implicitly invited a legislative reaction.

As I said, however, they either were not so sure of the topography or they doubted their institutional authority to adopt a nearby statute, and so they proposed to issue results sufficiently harsh and antimajoritarian, coupled with a plea to Congress, in order to break the legislative inertia.[25] Passing the matter of the "fairness" of such an approach to the injured workers whose rights would have been unnecessarily narrowed in the interim, the dissenters' aim was simply to force the legislature to act when the exact form of the appropriate new rule was both uncertain and too difficult for the court to establish on its own. The technique was the extraordinarily dangerous but not unusual one of moving the law *away* from the legal topography, of creating an even greater misfit, so as to make legislative reaction almost inevitable.

This technique is surely almost always wrong. It can take the form — as the dissenters in the FELA cases suggested — of going back to a strict interpretation or rule that the court believes to be so far out of phase as to be intolerable, or it can take the form of striking down a statute — because part of it is anachronistic — in the belief that total absence of the statute will be so out of line that the legislature will be forced to reconsider the issue immediately.[26] Because, in the first instance, it makes the law less consistent and moves away from the dictates of the legal fabric, it is only appropriate in situations in which the losers (pending the legislative reaction) are not unduly harmed by a failure to obtain relief for a time. It seeks to force rather than request a legislative response and to hold the temporary losers hostage until such a response is obtained, thereby making them lobbyists, as it were, for legislative action.

For this reason it is singularly dangerous — whether it takes the seemingly traditional, Frankfurterian, abstentionist form of a return to "the letter of the law" or the activist form of leaving an area that needs a rule without any rule. A court can never in fact be sure that the legislature will respond, and if it does not the hostages remain in captivity to a rule that is clearly out of line.[27] It is, moreover, totally inappropriate in cases in which the loser suffers severe harm from even a temporary loss. This is not just because that loser is being treated in a way inconsistent with the legal fabric, and hence *prima facie* unfairly, but because such one-shot losers are no longer hostages and have little incentive to lobby for change in the rule.[28] Senator Davies astutely notes that one major reason for legislative failure to update laws is that if the updating is, like most legislation, prospective only, those who have already lost have little reason to urge legislators to update.[29] Only if there exist powerful people who know ahead of time that they will lose from the out-of-phase result can this technique bring about the legislative reaction it seeks.[30]

A milder version of both forms of this technique exists. This version entails a judicial threat to return to a strict interpretation or to strike down a statute or rule. Here too the object is to get the legislature to cure a rule that the court is sure is somewhat out of phase but which the court does not feel it is able to replace, perhaps because the legal landscape does not give it sufficient guidance. But rather than moving directly to a position that is still more out of phase, the court "stays" its action and continues to apply the mildly — if clearly — outworn rule while the legislature has time to act. This more restrained approach, which was used in *American Bankers Ass'n v. Connell,* an important set of banking cases,[31] treats the parties before the court more fairly, that is, more in accordance with the legal landscape. It also has the advantage of allowing the court to back down — or try the opposite tack of making incremental improvements — if the legislature refuses the invitation to reconsider the law.[32] And this lessens the danger that the court, in order to cure an anachronism, will end up creating a greater one. But it still is likely to work only if there exists a group of future losers who are self-conscious enough to know that they will suffer if the court is allowed to carry out its threat. And since the court only threatens to impose an out-of-phase result and then stays its hand, it may lessen the pressure on the legislature to act. The threat to blackmail may not be as effective as actual blackmail.

A court, which cannot define or feels it cannot evolve a new rule to fit the landscape, may on occasion be justified in threatening to move to a rule—or to a nonrule—that it can impose, even though such a rule or nonrule does not fit the landscape, in order to force the legislative hand. But it seems very unlikely that the actual imposition of a self-consciously outworn rule or nonrule without a prior threat will ever be justified simply because it puts more heat on the legislators. The fact that so restrained a justice as Frankfurter suggested the move in the FELA cases must, therefore, be attributed to the fact that no doctrine was available to permit him simply to threaten and to stay a return to the admittedly ill-fitting strict interpretation.

One should contrast this inappropriate judicial move, with another—seemingly similar—move. This arises in cases like Eck or Moragne in which the court imposes a new rule it is quite certain fits the landscape better than the existing rule. But it also arises in the reverse situation, in which the court believes that the absence of a rule or law fits the landscape better than the existing law. In such cases the court will simply nullify the old law.

Most often this technique has been employed in criminal cases or against laws impinging on the penumbra of fundamental rights of speech, religion, free press, travel, and so on. The old rule is either out of date or for other paraconstitutional reasons deserves no retentionist bias, in whole or in part. Continuation of the law, with a threat to act if the legislature does not, is not appropriate because few justifiably rely on the old law and, perhaps, because some are unjustifiably harmed by its continued, unaltered application. Judicial modification of the law, or promulgation of a new one by Harlan-like adoption, is not appropriate because the court is unsure of what the new rule should look like or cannot write a sufficiently detailed law and has no adequate adoptable models near by. Slow common law development of a new rule won't work because foreknowledge and forewarning (especially if the context is of criminality) are necessary. Absence of any law, for a time, fits the topography best and is not, in any event, catastrophic. The court appropriately nullifies the old rule and, under the doctrine proposed in this book, invites the legislature to write a new one, if it cares to.

This technique can be said to have been the one the Supreme Court was looking for in the Sorrells case, but could not find in the absence of the doctrine I have been discussing.[33] It is the one Bickel recommended in the Connecticut birth control situation and in *Lincoln Mills*.[34] It was, finally, the approach taken by Judge Newman in the Connecticut abortion case, especially when he failed to stay his decree.[35] It is, as I said, in a sense the same approach taken in *Eck, Moragne,* and by the majority of the Court in the FELA cases,[36] for it too imposes a result the court believes to be more in keeping with the landscape — all at once — and invites legislative action to alter or further define the result. Unlike these cases, however, the change it imposes is the absence of a rule rather than a judicially promulgated rule.

Such a technique is more often justified than a return to an admittedly ill-fitting strict interpretation of an old rule, or a move to an equally ill-fitting absence of a rule in order to force legislative action, since the result in the first instance is to make the law conform more — rather than less — closely to the legal landscape. Like the inappropriate, blackmail technique, however, it has a milder form that may be preferable unless the court is quite certain that the absence of any rule or the new rule it imposed fits the topography. This milder version again takes the form of threatening to move to the new better-fitting rule unless the legislature acts. Alternatively, it strikes down the old rule in the belief that absence of any rule gives the best fit, but it stays its holding to give the legislature a chance to disagree.

This would have been the effect of Newman's decision in the Connecticut abortion case, had he been willing to stay his decree. [37] It was, in fact, what the Hawaii court did in its comparative-contributory negligence case.[38] It bespeaks less certainty than a direct move to a new rule or to the absence of any rule. And it takes a different view of the importance of the reliance interests based on the old rule. On both counts it is more conservative and less self-assured than the Eck, Moragne, or FELA cases. But it still goes beyond what the Wisconsin court did in its comparative negligence case,[39] because it tells the legislature what the court will do if the legislature fails to act. For this reason it is most appropriate when the court is sure the old rule does not fit; believes it knows what would fit better but is either not that confident of this or of its capacity to do a good job technically of creating a new rule; is concerned with reliance on the old rule; and does not believe that case-by-case evolution of a new rule is desirable.[40]

It is the last that distinguishes this approach from that employed by California and Florida in their moves away from contributory negligence.[41] Because it presupposes that a slow evolution of a rule is not suitable, this approach rejects traditional common law adjudication (even as modified by California and Florida to protect reliance interests in the old rule). But because it wishes a substitute for the legitimacy given by common law incrementalism, given that the landscape is not obvious, it seeks that substitute by delaying its action and explicitly inviting a colloquy with the legislature.[42] In its own way, it is as sophisticated and appropriate on many sets of facts as was Harlan's approach in *Moragne* on the facts before him.[43]

Detailed Statutes, Precise Numbers

Rules involving government payouts and receipts of moneys present particular technical problems for courts in carrying out updating functions, as do rules involving precise figures. Once again, however, the problems are technical ones, which guide the form of the appropriate judicial intervention, rather than any particular difficulties that attach to having courts determine whether such rules are out of date and should be deprived of a retentionist bias. Moreover, as we have seen, the technical problems that do exist are really independent of whether the rule to be questioned is common law or statutory. (It is as manifestly difficult for a common law court to cope with a needed change in a common law rule that uses figures, like the rule against perpetuities, as it is for such a court to cope with inflation-gutted statutory figures.)[44] One should acknowledge, however, that as a practical matter these problems arise most often in statutory contexts.[45]

In these situations reliance interests, difficulties in judicial promulgation of new detailed rules, and uncertainty as to what precisely the new rule should be combine with the manifest need for a complete new rule before the old one is abandoned, to pose the least attractive situation for judicial intervention. For here the gap between the court's ability to say that no retentionist bias is warranted and its capacity to update the law by itself is at its greatest. It is here that prospective modifications and limited retroactivity have had the most play. The case involving the prospective reversal of the use of descendants of Queen Victoria as acceptable "lives in being" for the rule against perpetuities is an early common law example of these techniques.[46] It is in this type of case that the inventiveness shown by Harlan in *Moragne* is most needed.[47] But even that does not suffice. New techniques would need to be developed — such as prospective decrees accompanied by a mandate to an administrative agency to carry out the detailed law-writing tasks the court is not suited to perform — if full use were to be made of the judicial capacity to determine that a rule is out of date.

Nevertheless, one should not despair of filling the gap. The context is somewhat different (because it was not age that made the statutory language inappropriate), but the celebrated income tax case, *Helvering v. Clifford*, is nonetheless instructive of what could be done.[48] In that case the Court needed detailed rulings in order to carry out what it believed to be the appropriate thrust of a statute. It did what it could on its own, and then in effect left it for the appropriate agency (the Treasury) to complete the job.[49] Is it too far-fetched to assume that courts, when faced with laws that are out of date in their technical details, could likewise start the process of updating and request — or even require — the appropriate agency to carry out the matter?[50]

A more recent example of court and agency cooperation in rehabilitating an obsolete statutory scheme is *American Bankers Ass'n v. Connell*.[51] Congress' carefully considered statutory scheme of some years ago expressly carved out special roles for credit unions, savings and loan associations, and commercial banks.[52] These statutes prohibited banks from giving interest on checking accounts and prevented credit unions and savings institutions from issuing negotiable drafts (the functional equivalent of checks) against interest-bearing accounts.

New techniques of record keeping and fund transfer developed, and each type of financial institution sought successfully to attain an advantage over the others through administrative regulations authorizing what the statutory scheme prohibited. The court struck down these regulations and said that "[neither we nor the regulatory agencies are] empowered to rewrite the language of statutes which may be antiquated in dealing with the most recent technological advances, nor are we empowered to make a policy judgment as to whether the utilization of these new methods of fund transfer is in the overall public interest. Therefore, we have no option but to set aside the regulations."[53]

If this had been all the court had done, the cases would have been a traditional example of the judicial blackmail technique advocated by Frankfurter in the FELA cases.[54] But the court did more and issued an eight-month stay of its decision. It is this additional factor that makes *American Bankers* an example of the more inventive techniques a court can employ in implementation of the doctrine proposed here. The court stayed its decision, it said, to give Congress a chance to "declare its will upon these matters."[55] This willingness to delay enforcement was remarkable in view of the court's language emphasizing its, and the regulatory agencies', required subservience to the timeworn statutes. Presumably the Court believed special circumstances warranted the extraordinary stay, since the stay amounted to no more and no less than the kind of judicial power over statutes I have been discussing.

Under the doctrine I am proposing, a court would also need special reasons to refuse to enforce a statute's clear command, but when the reasons exist — when the landscape dictates it — such action would clearly be appropriate. In fact, the court in *American Bankers* acted no differently. I cannot say whether it did this because the financial community had relied on the regulations and had made huge investments in the new fund transfer methods, or because the court felt the regulations it struck down fit the modern landscape better than the original statutory scheme, or finally because the court believed it could discern that the then current Congress favored the new methods. That the court had gauged the landscape correctly, and by its decision helped Congress to enact legislation to conform to it, is indisputable.[56]

If the court had been operating under the doctrine, its decision striking down the regulations, but only in eight months, would still have been correct. The opinion would have read slightly differently, and more honestly. The language, denying that the courts and the agencies had the power to make such changes, without legislative action, would be replaced by language asserting the wisdom of abstaining *pending* legislative action. But the result would be the same. Conversely, if agencies had resisted the importunities of their client industries in the first instance (as they did not here), a court could in a proper case and upon a sufficient showing of the obsolescence of the statutory scheme have induced an agency review, or if more appropriate a legislative reconsideration of the problem, but openly and without falsely protesting its powerlessness before the offending statutes.

Again, whether the court decision is retroactive (as in *Clifford*), or prospective-permissive, to induce agency action, or finally prospective-restrictive, in order to force legislative reconsideration of past regulations that clash with statutory language (as in *American Bankers*) will depend on factors that may differ even in closely related laws. (The federal courts have expressly refused to make *Clifford*-like moves in the context of estate and gift taxes, for instance, probably because they have deemed reliance to be more crucial there.)[57] But that is somewhat beside the point. More significant is that the same techniques that can be used to ask legislatures to act — or face the consequences of judicial intervention — can be expanded and applied to administrative agencies as well.

In dealing with agencies no less than with legislatures, the court can change the law (leaving it to them to work out the details) or abstain, but threaten to act if no action is taken (thereby inducing the agencies to come up with detailed revisions). Either way the judiciary can seek to make legislatures and administrative agencies alike use the skills it lacks to achieve the goal of reconsideration of anachronistic rules. Of course, a very high degree of self-consciousness of the capacities of all the institutions involved would be needed to apply such techniques. But the result would be to take full advantage of the court's ability to gauge when rules are out of phase with the legal topography, without asking of them technical tasks they cannot perform.

There is, then, no apparent reason why we cannot take full advantage of the court's ability to gauge when rules are out of phase simply because there are technical tasks they cannot perform. The dialogue between courts and administrators, and courts and legislatures, which would be needed to deal with obsolete and technical statutory or common law rules, would seem peculiar for a while, but it would be far less radical structurally than many of the developments in "public law litigation" that have occurred recently with relatively little hue and cry.[58]

The Relevance and Irrelevance of Technique

We face a serious problem of legal obsolescence. We have institutions that are eminently suited, in a system of checks and balances, to determine what is and what is not obsolete, what needs and what does not need to be reconsidered by majoritarian and technically expert bodies. We have traditionally, though only nominally, failed to make use of this capacity when the old rule was statutory, though we often relied on it when the old rule was court-made. If we are willing to abandon that distinction, we can then focus on the important but separate problem of which institutions are, in our democracy, most suited to carry out the updating, and proceed to develop techniques that permit us to make the best use of the capacities of each. And these questions will not be very different whether the updating involves statutory or common law rules.

In the end what does matter is not the nature of the old rule, but rather which behavior on the part of courts in updating leads to legislative abrogation of responsibility and which leads to legislative taking of responsibility; which techniques foster judicial casualness in information seeking and writing of laws; which methods protect legitimate expectations; which devices deprive parties of important substantive rights during the updating; and which approaches lead to serious and sober legislative consideration of constitutional and deep structural issues. We will have to do much more than I can do here in developing appropriate judicial devices and techniques to accomplish intelligent updating. If we fail, we will have to accept timeworn rules or rely on approaches to updating that are either inadequate or inappropriate to our system. And we may fail. But if we do, it will be a general failure and will only in small part be due to the fact that updating sometimes involves statutes rather than common law rules.[59]

XII

The Role of the Courts in
an Age of Statutes

I am now in a position to describe the common law function, the role of courts, in this age of statutes. It is not a nostalgic restoration of courts as the primary makers of law, in our system. The reasons for statutorification are too profound to be reversed, for courts are not capable of writing speedily enough most of the rules that a modern society apparently needs. Nevertheless, there will remain situations in which courts can make law. Sometimes this will be in areas that have remained common law, and sometimes this will be in areas governed by statutes. That is not a significant distinction. It will occur in areas in which the new rule to be promulgated is clearly mandated by the legal landscape and in which a statement of the rule does not involve detailed language and technical data beyond a court's competence. It will also occur in areas in which, despite the usual demands of modern society for quick and certain rules, a slow judicial development of a new rule is still acceptable or even desirable. Yet, even if a fair number of such areas remain, it is unrealistic to expect that courts will be able to play the kind of lawmaking role they once played. For there will be too many situations in which, for example, the writing of a new law will simply be beyond the capacity of a court and in which, nonetheless, a new law must be promulgated all at once.

Also I do not believe that the new common law function can require courts to take on an aggressively antimajoritarian role as revisers or reviewers of legislative lawmaking. Legislatures may have become the primary sources of law, but this does not mean that courts can take on the one-time legislative function of revisers of ordinary law, and through frequent constitutional adjudication become the holders of the last word with respect to such law. That job must belong to a majoritarian body.

The true antimajoritarian role that our tradition of judicial review does assign to courts is too crucial and too chaste to permit its promiscuous application in circumstances that are trivial, as in guest statutes. Such use can only endanger (either by fostering easy constitutional amendments or out-and-out destruction of judicial review) the role courts must play as guardians of fundamental constitutional rights. Whatever common law role can remain for the courts in our age of statutes must, like the traditional common law role, leave to the legislatures the last say, unless constitutional guarantees are involved. It must, in other words, be separate from the ultimate power of constitutional adjudication.

What, then, is the common law function to be exercised by courts today? *It is no more and no less than the critical task of deciding when a retentionist or a revisionist bias is appropriately applied to an existing statutory or common law rule.* It is the judgmental function (which cannot successfully be accomplished by sunset laws or automatic updatings) of deciding when a rule has come to be sufficiently out of phase with the whole legal framework so that, whatever its age, it can only stand if a current majoritarian or representative body reaffirms it. It is to be the allocator of that burden of inertia which our system of separation of powers and checks and balances mandates. It is to assign the task of overcoming inertia to that interest, whose desires do not conform with the fabric of the law, and hence whose wishes can only be recognized if current and clear majoritarian support exists for them. It is this task (so like that exercised by courts in updating the common law) which desperately needs doing in a checked and balanced statutory world like ours, and it can be done by courts using traditional judicial methods and modes of reasoning.

The task can be accomplished by courts regardless of whether they are capable of carrying out the updating on their own by promulgating new rules or whether they must use techniques designed to influence the legislative and even the administrative agendas, and induce these bodies to act and to write new, or reaffirm old, rules. It can be achieved without in any way depriving popular or representative bodies of their last say, of their right to assert and impose new distinctions that do not fit the fabric of the law and that do not, merely on this account, violate constitutional guarantees. Indeed, it encourages the legislatures to act responsibly to affirm precisely such distinctions when, despite the fact that in the courts' judgments they do not fit in the legal landscape, the distinctions are nonetheless wanted. As a result, this judicial function—like its common law equivalent—can ask for consistency among what scholars call policies as well as among principles.[1] Or it can ask for firm, current majoritarian support for such "inconsistent" policies, rather than allowing them to remain in force simply on the basis of an inappropriate retentionist bias. It can do all this without confusing this job with that of constitutional adjudication which our system also assigns to the courts, and without ignoring the relevance that must be given to the fact that a rule—even if in the end it is constitutionally valid—is entitled to little or no retentionist bias when it comes close to violating constitutional guarantees.

In carrying out this task the courts would, as I have said, be doing little different from what they have traditionally done. Their main job would still be to give us continuity and change by applying the great vague principle of treating like cases alike.[2] They would exercise the same capacity to define what are "like" cases at different levels of generality, in terms of different sources of law (statutory, jurisprudential, case, scholarly comment) and in response to technological, societal, and even ideological changes. Some courts would presumably be aggressive and even willful in their use of such data; others would not. But that has always been the case with the common law function, and whether the aggressive or the passive mode is preferable is not really germane to this book. What is relevant is that in carrying out this task, passively or actively according to their own judicial philosophies, the courts would be establishing a modern version of the traditional American judicial-legislative balance.

To establish such a modern balance, two principal changes would be needed. First, the courts would not be bound to declare or promulgate the new in order to find that the old fails to fit. To some extent that has always been the case, for often an old rule was destroyed at common law while the new one was only hinted at by the courts. In a statutory world, that may occasionally be appropriate. Often, however, the appropriate technique will be to enter into a dialogue, to ask, cajole, or force another body (usually the legislature but sometimes the agencies) to define the new rule or reaffirm the old.[3] Second, and this is the change with which I have been most concerned, the judicial common law would attach to statutory rules that are out of phase just as much as to common law precedents or doctrines. This last may be less of an innovation than it seems, for courts through subterfuges, fictions, and willful use of inappropriate doctrines have already been anything but reluctant to deal with obsolete statutes.

The first change may, in fact, be more significant because it entails a separation of functions that were united in the old common law judicial roles. The role of maker of new law was intimately tied to the job of deciding when the old rule no longer deserved the benefit of a retentionist bias. To abandon the old the courts had to be willing at least to start making the new. The same reasons that have made our system statutory tend to make the lawmaking role much harder for courts to perform. This fact (rather than the existence of statutes as such) calls for new judicial techniques designed to bring forth legislative and administrative revisions in old rules, and would call for them whether the old rules are statutory or court-made.[4] It in no way diminishes the capacity of courts to tell when old rules are out of phase, however. And the same fact, since it has led to the existence of a multitude of statutes, makes the need to employ this judicial capacity all the greater if we are to preserve a system that can, at the same time, give us continuity and change.

If the courts and legislatures openly accept this common law function as appropriate to the age of statutes, they will be recognizing some significant changes in our legal-political system. But they will only be recognizing the changes, not making them. The statutorification and the concomitant tendency toward obsolescence of American law have already occurred. So have the judicial reactions to these changes. What remains to be done is only the taking of the last step, the seeing of the world as it is, and the giving of a name to what is already happening in indirect and often careless ways. But such a last step is by no means insignificant, and also by no means necessarily desirable. Candor gives benefits, but it surely entails risks. Are they justified?

XIII

The Dangers of the Doctrine

The reader may not yet be convinced that an open promulgation of the doctrine I have been analyzing is appropriate. Assume we agree on these points: (1) A judicial power to allocate the burden of inertia would be useful in our system and might even be essential. (2) In part because of this, courts are doing much of what I am proposing, but by indirection and through legal fictions and subterfuges. (3) What needs to be done can be achieved without pushing courts to do what is technically difficult for them to do. (4) The indirections that have been used are not especially helpful in limiting courts to what they can do well. (5) Explicit and limiting legislative authorization for such a doctrine could be made a prerequisite to its use. Still, what seems to be the most open and direct way of doing something in the law is not always the best way to do it. So we will have to consider whether open assertion of the judicial power entails such dangers that subterfuges and tricks are better ways of achieving the common law function than honest recognition of the doctrine.

The principal danger, other than the overburdening of courts and legislatures,[1] is that if the doctrine is there, it will be used even when we would not want it to be. In one of his last major works Alexander Bickel not only made a routine criticism of Justice Black's use of absolutes and concluded that they would not have restrained the Supreme Court from overreaching, but more important he also catalogued the failures of Justice Frankfurter's notions of restraint to control judicial self-aggrandizement.[2] The honest way, in Bickel's view, failed because no matter how much justices reiterated the need for limits, they always went beyond those limits when a particularly pressing case presented itself. That is, of course, the danger of any noncategorical language, however we try to hem it in with cautions; and it is an inevitable risk that would be entailed if we recognized a judicial power over statutes, however limited by doctrinal niceties.

Many less strictly "legal" examples than Bickel's can be given. How often have we all seen a committee, appointed to decide if a search should be undertaken to fill a job, immediately become the search committee for filling the job. The very fact that the possibility of a vacancy is admitted goes a long way toward creating the vacancy. And the very fact that a judicial power over statutes is recognized goes a long way toward justifying its exercise. This tendency is aggravated in an adversarial system. To admit a doctrine or a possibility is to encourage lawyers to argue for it. Lawyers will, if they are doing their job, frequently argue the possibility even where it ought not to apply. At best this becomes an expensive waste of time and energy. But it usually will be more than that. The very fact that the argument has been made can suggest to the press and to the people that the argument has won; this in turn causes it to win more often in the future. (We all have seen the simple transposition by which an outlandish tort case, with a request for huge damages, loses but gets reported ambiguously and then is taken by people at large—including future jurors—as a judgment upholding the outlandish result.) Nor need the harm stop there—the fact that a doctrine can be argued creates an aura of respectability that, at least in a tough case, puts pressure on a court to accept the argument.

There is little doubt that open admission of the doctrine would occasionally result in its use in situations where judicial review of statutes should not take place, and in others where it would not take place if courts were deprived of counsel's arguments in its favor and had to rely on their own imagination to find ways of achieving it. At law, to recognize a doctrine is to give it weight, to endow it with gravitational force, and to permit it to exert influence in parts of the landscape as yet unknown.

It is not a sufficient answer to say that the danger of overuse is small since such judicial abuse can (unlike judicial abuse of the power of constitutional adjudication) always be remedied by legislative action.[3] To the extent that the only practical alternative to recognition of the doctrine of common law supervision *is* a flight to the Constitution, then that answer is true enough. And, as we shall see, that will be a strong argument for recognition of the doctrine. But we must nonetheless recognize the fact that judicial abuse is not adequately compensated for simply because a legislature has the last word. Acceptance of such judicial abuse implies acceptance of the doubtful proposition that a past legislative starting point has no greater claim of legitimacy than the court's own willful preference.[4] Or it implies denying that legislative inertia is a major factor in our system, and hence denying that allocation of starting points has a crucial effect on results, on what the law will be.

There are, moreover, other reasons why the legislative ability to reverse "willful" judicial abuses of the doctrine cannot fully allay our fears. The first is that if legislatures get into the habit of reversing courts too easily, this will tend to hamper important judicial functions that depend on the finality of court judgments. One could conceive of the extreme situation in which legislatures have become so accustomed to reversing courts that litigants as a matter of course seek to have results in ordinary litigation reversed at the legislative level. Some of that does occur, inevitably and even appropriately; but certainly our system is not one of general appeals to a supreme *legislative* court from the rulings of the supreme judicial courts.

The second danger is that legislatures, in order to avoid the first risk, will be reluctant to reverse courts even when they disagree with the judicial decision, even when the court was incorrect in ruling that a statutory rule needed revision. The creation of such an aura around judicial common law decisions (analogous to that which exists around constitutional rulings[5] would increase the force of inertia, even beyond what it is today, and could make judicial common law rulings much more powerful than would be appropriate.

Finally, it is conceivable that courts themselves, aware of these two dangers, would become reluctant to use the doctrine even when its use would be appropriate. A kind of "save it for when it is really needed" philosophy might arise which could put us right back to where we started — choking on obsolete statutes.[6]

I am not saying that the equilibrium that would be reached at the end of such a process would be worse than what we are now moving toward. After all, judicial power over common law rules exists and its use entails many of the dangers I have catalogued. When this is combined with the judicial supervision of statutes which derives from interpretation, passive virtues, and direct constitutional adjudication, it is more than possible that we are already flirting with the tension between too much judicial determination of results and too ready legislative reversal of court decisions. My point is not to choose among possible second-bests. It is to recognize, emphatically, that to admit the existence of a doctrine like the one we have been considering is not a matter of indifference and cannot be rendered indifferent by the fact that the legislature does retain its ability to have the last say.

Still, in the end, we will have to engage in second-best analysis. We will need to consider whether the possible dangers from recognition of such a doctrine are matched by dangers that flow from its continued lack of recognition. And we will need to speculate about whether the dangers of recognition are more or less capable of correction, if they become severe, than would be those of nonrecognition. We have already examined the dangers of nonrecognition which adhere to each of the doctrines that are being used to give courts power over statutes. We have not, however, looked at the sum of these dangers—at the uses and abuses of subterfuges—and compared them to the sum of the dangers entailed by recognition of the doctrine.

Before we do that, however, we must ask ourselves whether taking all of the doctrines that have been used to achieve some judicial control over out-of-phase statutes, and applying each of them *only* when each would fit properly within its own doctrinal limits, would give us an adequate weapon to fight statutory obsolescence. We must, in other words, ask whether the job of allocating the burden of inertia can be achieved honestly, and without creating a new doctrine by applying all of the doctrines already available to courts.

The answer to this question is essentially an empirical one that can be found by looking at current judicial behavior. Consider whether courts exercise only within proper limits these powers: their traditional right to review common law rules; their authority to interpret statutes honestly, but in ambiguous cases also functionally; their power to send back for reconsideration vague or broadly delegative or inconsistent laws that infringe on the penumbra of the Constitution; and their duty to nullify statutes that violate the Constitution. The answer in each instance must be no. We have seen the race to use equal protection doctrines to strike down laws that are clearly constitutionally valid; the use of interpretations that would do honor even to the greatest of casuists; and the development of the passive virtues into devices for a "virulent variety of free-wheeling interventionism."[7] We have seen, in other words, that the tools at hand are nowhere near sufficient to the task courts feel pressed to do. Let us add: the persistence of laws that are obviously out of phase, which — were they common law rules — would be altered and would only very doubtfully be enacted by a current legislature; and the popularity of notions like that of sunset laws which are manifestly inadequate to the job of coping with legal obsolescence.[8] The conclusion must be that the problem we face is not being solved.

XIV

The Uses and Abuses of Subterfuge

We must, therefore, return to a second-best analysis and ask ourselves whether the dangers in further stretching other doctrines, in order to achieve a degree of success in overcoming timeworn laws and in allocating the burden of inertia, are greater or less than the admitted dangers of honest recognition of judicial power to decide in favor of the retentionist or revisionist bias. Such a discussion inevitably requires some preliminary consideration of the role of subterfuges and indirection in the law. This topic is vast. It is at the root of such diverse legal debates as that currently taking place on the uses and abuses of law and economics and cost-benefit analysis in law,[1] and those that are not long past on the desirability of utilitarian or balancing language as against the language of categoricals or absolutes in constitutional adjudication.[2] Just to mention these two is to suggest why a full treatment of the problem is beyond the scope of this book. Yet some general discussion is needed in order to make some judgments on whether, in dealing with the doctrine explored here, indirection or candor is better.

The first thing to note is that there are at least two types of subterfuges frequently used in law. The most important, and in a way more clearly dishonest, kind of subterfuge is that designed to hide a fundamental value conflict, recognition of which would be too destructive for the particular society to accept. Dishonesty, whether chosen or through a failure to look far enough into dark corners, is preferred because total candor is given less weight than the other values involved in the conflict, one of which would be undermined by honesty. This is the kind of subterfuge found in those situations Philip Bobbitt and I have called "tragic choices."[3] It is too damaging to admit that jails are so bad that some recidivist rapists are willing to be castrated to get out of jail; yet society is not willing to improve jails sufficiently to make castration a choice rapists would abjure. So we lie and say that those prisoners who opt for castration cannot be exercising a free choice, even though, if we but looked, we might see that the convict preferred castration to jail and would not subsequently regret his choice.[4]

The second argument for subterfuge or indirection is a generalization of the slippery-slope argument for absolute language. It is result-oriented and relies on the fact that sometimes use of indirection and of "technically incorrect" language can bring us closer to the desired result than would use of more precise language. If we admit that the state can regulate religion, we are psychologically, if not logically, more likely to allow such regulation than if we say that there can be no regulation of religion and then from time to time define behavior by some cults as not religious and hence subject to regulation. The refusal to permit polygamy among Mormons in the nineteenth century was certainly regulation of religion, but the denial that it was such regulation may have lessened the impact of the decision and led to less regulation of religion than would have followed from an "honest" admission that some religious beliefs *are* in practice subject to state prohibition.[5]

Many situations in which subterfuges are used rely on both justifications. The classic example of this is the one given by Charles Black in his masterful defense of absolutes in constitutional adjudication.[6] After posing a situation in which we would all doubt the applicability of a powerful societal absolute—that against torture—he dramatically suggests why we have chosen nonetheless to describe torture as absolutely forbidden in our system.

A judge is faced with the claim that a prisoner is being tortured. The police, remarkably, admit the fact but demonstrate beyond a doubt that the prisoner has hidden a hydrogen bomb, set to explode in an hour, in a major city and that the only thing the prisoner fears is hideous pain. The judge, Black indicates, may waffle, may adjourn court, may subsequently resign, but the one thing he or she is not apt to do is to enforce the supposed absolute against torture and let the city be destroyed. Are we then correct in characterizing our rule against torture as an absolute one? Yes, Black suggests, because the opposite rule — which would say we balance the need for torture against its harm — would be totally inaccurate. Whom would you trust more to decide both the case of the hydrogen bomb and torture cases generally, *as we want them decided,* he asks rhetorically: a judge who in hard and easy cases is always declaring that we must balance the costs and benefits of torture, or the judge who announces that our system has an absolute prohibition against torture? Which in practice, if not in definition, is using words more nearly correctly; which use of terms, in other words, leads us closer to the desired result?

In fact, Black's example does not depend solely on greater precision of result to justify its lesser linguistic precision. The choice between permitting torture and sacrificing many lives is precisely one of those tragic choices that frequently lead to subterfuges in order to allow society to hold to two conflicting ideals.[7] We do not wish even to admit our willingness to torture (quite apart from our fear that to admit it would lead to more torture than we would wish), but at the same time we are unwilling to let lives be lost. Because it relies on both grounds for absolute language, Black's example is a particularly strong one, though some may doubt whether even it justifies linguistic imprecision. In fact, neither ground can *always* justify a lack of candor, for lack of candor is in itself always harmful. At the same time, it is only honest to admit that frequently the presence of either ground, and more frequently the conjunction of both, does lead to the use or toleration of subterfuges.[8]

We should be careful not to overstate the case, however. Often different words are used simply to suggest that different sources or different justifications should be looked to in making decisions. Language that declares free speech, as worded in the Constitution, to be absolute, might be taken to suggest that interpretation of the charter's words is appropriate, that historical meaning is crucial, and that present benefits and risks of speech are only relevant if the historical meaning is unclear. As such it signals a particularly strong judicial role. A language of reasonableness, in deciding what restrictions on speech are appropriate, suggests instead that a current weighing of costs and benefits is in order and hence implies a greater legislative role. If both uses of language are so understood and if the

"absolutist" is, in fact, willing to abide by the honest if vague meaning of history and interpretation,[9] neither usage can be said to be a
subterfuge. The same is not the case if the absolutist then stretches
history and interpretation in order to achieve what may in fact be an
eminently sound result.[10] Speech, like torture, does have a meaning,
and it would not be forthright to say that Charles Black's absolutist
can get out of the dilemma, honestly, by interpreting the ex-
cruciating pain inflicted on the hypothetical prisoner as not being
torture.[11]

The justification, which might support fictions and tricks in order
to permit courts to allocate the burden of inertia, is not primarily the
first or ideal-preserving, conflict-denying, tragic-choice justification.[12] Nor can the fictions used by courts be argued away — as
in the last paragraph — by saying that what is going on is only interpretation, plus passive virtues, plus constitutional adjudication.
Courts and scholars have gone too far and asked for too much in the
way of judicial supervision of out-of-phase laws to permit this
wishing away of the problem of honesty. If the current approach,
which relies on indirection, is to be justified in these terms, it must
be on the second, result-oriented ground. It must depend on the fact
that to admit this judicial power would be inevitably to admit its
abuse; that we come closer to achieving the amount of judicial supervision we want by denying that it is permitted at all than we would
by acknowledging what is going on and trying to control it by doctrine and language; that, like the judge in the torture example, we
decide better, in practice, by denying that it ever takes place at all.

Again a caveat is useful. Is language that is descriptive of what
goes on more honest than language that, *because* it is *more* restrictive
than what goes on, approaches more closely the results we want?
Who is to say which would be more misleading, Justice Black's absolutes or Justice Frankfurter's balances, if the former better achieve
the societally desired results?[13] Both are actually misleading and inaccurate, though in very different ways. And who is to say that linguistic accuracy must hold sway over accuracy of result? Certainly
much of our ordinary speech is not premised on any such a simplistic
view of language and its literal accuracy.[14]

Still, linguistic inaccuracy has its costs. Too much of it destroys
the credibility of communications in general. And too much use of it
by courts destroys their credibility, especially since the major effec-

tive control on courts stems precisely from their duty to explain what they are doing.[15] We may therefore wish to save the linguistic inaccuracies that we allow courts to employ for those situations in which they are either essential to accuracy of result or in which they are indispensable for the preservation of ideals and the handling of fundamental conflicts in values.[16] We have already seen that this last justification does not apply very well to the use of indirections or tricks by courts in the updating of laws. We must now see whether indirections and subterfuges are needed to achieve accuracy of result to a degree sufficient to overcome the strong presumption in favor of openness and candor.

In fact, if open admission of the doctrine of judicial sunset tends to its abusive use, so failure to recognize it has led to abusive use of each of the alternate possibilities. If recognition of the doctrine would have lawyers arguing its applicability where it should not apply, so interpretations, passive virtues, and, most dramatically, constitutional invalidity are routinely argued where they should not stand a chance. If it is true that abuse of the doctrine might lead to either too many or too few legislative tendencies toward reversal of judicial decisions, so it is the case today that legislatures are faced with precisely the same problems, with the added factor that to reverse the court may in some instances call into question truly constitutional rulings, while in others it seems to require calling the courts liars.

In addition, the tendency for courts to use the Constitution to nullify trivial laws, which are simply out of phase, raises problems beyond those that would be created by an open recognition of the doctrine. For such decisions inevitably assert a form of judicial power that is hard to square with democratic primacy in most areas.[17] As such it creates a danger, both for true constitutional judicial review and for legislative supremacy in nonconstitutional areas, which has no analogue in an open recognition of common law power over statutes.

It may nevertheless be the case that such a danger is well borne. It is possible that the opportunity for abuse is too great with any doctrine that would ask courts to decide, as to statutes and as to common law rules, whether a retentionist or revisionist bias is appropriate. We cannot simply assume that the tendency for the alternate approaches to give false limits, and occasionally no limits, is more dangerous. We cannot even be sure that, if the doctrine were to be abused, we could control it by limiting it in mechanical ways (as Senator Davies would propose) to "private" laws more than, say, twenty years old.[18]

In the end, however, I believe that we need not resolve these uncertainties to reach a conclusion about the desirability of openly recognizing such a doctrine. We are not comparing a certain harm-benefit with an uncertain one. We do not know the ultimate dangers of the road — use of subterfuges and constitutional adjudication — we are currently taking, any more than we know the ultimate risks that would flow from recognition of the doctrine. Both may work, but each has its obvious pitfalls. How then can we choose? At least when we are uncertain about whether or not linguistic imprecision leads to greater precision of result, we must choose linguistic precision. The burden must be on those who would argue for indirection. The choice must be for candor.[19]

The Choice for Candor

To choose candor in situations of uncertainty is not, despite the surface appeal, inevitable. Ultimately it is justified by our need occasionally to be less than candid and hence by the great importance to be candid whenever we can. The pressure to use subterfuges, as I have said, can come from the desire to preserve great ideals or aspirations, such as the sanctity of life or the total integrity of human bodies. Or it can come from more prosaic grounds, say the need to use ambiguous language in order to achieve particular results.[1] But it can also come from a desire in situations of uncertainty to slow down change until we are sure we want it.

The use of absolute or categorical language, even when it is inaccurate and leads to inaccurate results, may have substantial merit for this last reason. To affirm the myth of an absolute separation of powers between courts and legislatures is to make use of this kind of delaying subterfuge. A language of rights, of justice, of absolute separation of powers, tends to put roadblocks in the way of too simple a balance, too quick and ahistorical an analysis. It is useful, for it keeps us from disregarding as "vague generalities" those real fears and dangers we do not understand.[2] It is the language of evolution or of revolution and is, understandably, abhorred by those who long for rational and radical reform. It does not lend itself to modeling or to careful rational planning, but responds in complex ways to diffuse pressures. It is, in fact, the language of the common law. And one could say that our courts are developing a judicial power over statutes today, slowly and in a common law fashion. They are not trying to model such power or to control it rigorously as they would were they to recognize such a doctrine openly. This fact might be good or bad depending on one's general bias toward evolutionary as against rationalist modes of thought.

We should not forget, however, that the language of categoricals, of subterfuges, is particularly prone to manipulation. It allows those who are in a position to employ the absolutes to mask what they are doing, to hide whose interests they are trading off. And too often such hiding becomes self-serving or exploitative. If a court denies that it is modifying or forcing review of a statute it deems out of phase, it is usually more able to serve its own ends than a court that must openly admit to what it is doing and justify its behavior rationally. The charge made by the followers of the legal-process tradition against Justice Black, that he could use his absolutes as he wished and that this was dangerous, has obvious merit.[3] The same charge, in miniature, can be leveled against judicial tricks that accomplish allocations of the burden of legislative inertia.[4]

Still, not all uses of categoricals or of aspirations are equally subject to manipulation and exploitation. Some are more dangerous than others, just as some are more useful than others. Even Bickel and Wellington, in their *Lincoln Mills* article, recognized this when they admitted the utility of legal fictions and then denied that these could be used except on a "few occasions" by the Supreme Court; courts may lie, they said, but the Court can't. (It is ironical but not very important that their solution in that article did nevertheless involve use of a jurisdictional gimmick, or trick, by the Supreme Court.[5])

My own instinct, if one is to make a general statement on when subterfuges are appropriate, is that they were wrong on both counts. The Supreme Court must occasionally lie; the courts by and large should not. We may need absolutes at the constitutional level for precisely the reasons Charles Black's essay indicates. They serve to preserve, nominally untouched and subject only to slow change, great aspirations, ideals in conflict; and they keep us from foolhardy action where wrong results really matter. When such fundamental issues are at stake, the danger of exploitation, of evolutionary bias, and even of manipulation may well be worth bearing. But the fact that we must occasionally lie at such a level makes it all the more imperative that we do not lie, that we be candid, at more prosaic levels.[6]

Without honesty and candor we cannot even know where we are. If we do not speak precisely and describe as openly as we can what we are trying to do in all those cases where basic conflicts are not at stake, then even the statement of ideals in categorical terms in those basic conflicts will sound hollow and false. We will have made the language of fiction and aspirations our common currency, and we will not be able to reserve it for those few situations where it, and it alone, can slow us down and help us preserve our conflicting ideals. For this "weak" reason then, I conclude that we should recognize openly that courts are exercising the power to allocate legislative inertia and to decide whether statutes deserve a retentionist or a revisionist bias. To deny what we are doing, to use tricks here, is to destroy by overuse a language that is easily cheapened, a language that should be reserved for the Court, in matters of high principle, and not the courts in low-level tasks.

In the end, however, my view on this is of little significance. For whether our legal system openly adopts the doctrine I have here described or continues to use devices and tricks to approach the same results is hardly up to me. As a scholar, it is my job to look in dark places and try to describe, as precisely as I can, what I see. Others, men and women of the world, have different roles. They will either consciously or unconsciously accept a language or a doctrine which tells us (too clearly to be accurate) just what we are doing, or reject it for one which idealistically, but misleadingly, tells us that we are not doing it.

Justice Hugo Black, on hearing of Charles Black's defense of absolutes, once said to me, "You realize, Guy, I cannot agree with that." I wondered at the time why he had chosen just those words, why he had not said, "Charles Black is *wrong,* there *are* absolutes." Many years later I read his son's book of reminiscences about the Judge. In one passage the younger Hugo, graduated from Yale Law School and waiting for his bar results, asks his father what is in essence the student's eternal question: "Hold on, Daddy, what *is* the right?" And his father, the great absolutist, speaking now as teacher and not as Judge, gives the ultimate balancing answer: "Son . . . doing right is whatever contributes the greatest good for the greatest number — that's all there is to it."[7] He could say that to his son when speaking as a father, as a scholar even,[8] and yet feel that for him as a judge to agree with Charles Black would be to admit the possibility of tradeoffs, to compromise the essential utility of absolutist language, and to alter the very balance that he had sought to preserve through his refusal to use balancing language.

In a way Charles Black and Justice Black were both right. Each was doing his job, playing his role. Should we, to return to relatively easy matters, develop and model a doctrine of judicial power to allocate the burden of legislative inertia? Or should we try to reach some or all of its results slowly, by indirection and subterfuge? That is not for me to say, though my own preference for openness should be clear. Should we as a society own up to the fact that we price lives whenever we set a compensation level for auto accidents or fail to require whatever device, at whatever cost, could make driving safer?[9] That again is not for me to say. It is for me and for all scholars to think about the tradeoffs involved in such decisions, to expose them, and even to argue the costs and benefits of using a language that hides them. We must *think*, lucidly and openly, about a doctrine of judicial power over statutes, about the common law function in the age of statutes. If we do our job well, society may answer, "You are wrong," but will mean what Justice Black said of Professor Black, "You realize *I* cannot agree with that."

Notes

I. Choking on Statutes

1. All agree that modern American law is dominated by statutes. See, e.g., Traynor, "Statutes Revolving in Common-Law Orbits," 17 *Cath. U. L. Rev.* 401, 401-402 (1968): "A judge's responsibility is the greater now that legislatures fabricate laws in such volume. The endless cases before him increasingly involve the meaning or applicability of a statute, or on occasion its constitutionality. Such statutes, reflecting their sponsors or draftsmen or author-legislators, are of infinite variety in purpose, range, and quality . . . [A statute] may cast a heavy shadow on the common law or a light one, or it may idly plane until some incident sends it careening into action. The hydra-headed problem is how to synchronize the unguided missiles launched by legislatures with a going system of common law." His statement and metaphor can be taken to define the issues with which this book deals. Traynor is not alone among great modern judges in focusing on this problem, see Chap. VIII, note 15. See also G. Gilmore, *The Ages of American Law* 95 (1977).

There is, however, room for debate on the extent of common law dominance in the early nineteenth century. Grant Gilmore gracefully expresses the traditional view of postrevolutionary American jurisprudence: "We did set out to create a rationally organized system of law. We did have to adjust that system — somehow — to the dizzying pace of social, economic and technological change. We did have to cope, in the real world, with the complicated problems that arose from the obscure metaphysical concept of an indissoluble union of indestructible states. The federal Congress did little; the state legislatures did less. The judges became our preferred problem-solvers." G. Gilmore, supra, at 35-36.

Two elements may be distinguished in this portrait of the nineteenth century: great activity by the courts and inactivity by legislatures. The first element is not open to serious question: judges, between the start of the nineteenth century and the Civil War, creatively manipulated and changed common law rules in reaction to changing circumstances to a degree that the subsequent period of formalism and judicial modesty has made us almost forget. See G. Gilmore, supra, at 35-36. L. Friedman, *A History of American Law* 17, 99-100 (1973); M. Horwitz, *The Transformation of American Law, 1780-1860* 1-4 (1977); W. Nelson, *The Americanization of the Common Law: The Impact of Legal Change on Massachusetts Society, 1760-1830* 171-172 (1975).

Recent scholarship, however, has questioned the idea that there was little statutory activity before the Civil War. The accounts of Horwitz and Friedman, for example, portray early legislatures as fairly active in generally promoting the same policies that the common law was serving: commercial convenience and economic development. See M. Horwitz, supra, at 1, 47-53; L. Friedman, supra, at 99-100. While these statutes occasionally did amend the common law, see W. Nelson, supra, at 91-92, most of them concerned matters generally considered inappropriate for common lawmaking, such as distributing land to private parties, see, e.g., Fletcher v. Peck, 10 U.S. (6 Cranch) 87 (1810); issuing special corporate charters, see L. Friedman, supra, at 166-167, and Liggett Co. v. Lee, 288 U.S. 517 (1933); granting licenses, franchises, and monopolies, see M. Horwitz, supra, at 122-139; and subsidizing particular transportation systems, see L. Friedman, supra, at 158, 159-161. Taxes and direct government expenditures were at extremely low levels, see id. at 163-164, so any statutory ventures would have to be either self-supporting or virtually costless. Consequently, effective enforcement of direct regulation was rare at the local level, even more so at the national. See id. at 163-166. Moreover, large areas of private law—tort, contract, commercial law, and insurance law—were almost immune from legislative interference. See id. at 232-238, 409-427, and M. Horwitz, supra, at 160-237.

For the purposes of this book, Gilmore's picture of the nineteenth century, as dominated by the common law to the near exclusion of statutes, need not be accurate. There is very little, if any, dispute that the common law played a much more significant role in the nineteenth century than it does in our own day. See Frankfurter, "Some Reflections on the Reading of Statutes," 47 *Colum. L. Rev.* 527, 527 (1947). But all that is essential to my argument is that in some areas of private law, the common law was openly and legitimately kept up to date by common law courts.

2. G. Gilmore, supra note 1, at 95.

3. See Chaps. IX, X, and XI.

4. Each of these proposals and their limitations will be discussed in Chaps. II-VII.

5. Similar proposals have been made by Senator Jack Davies of Minnesota and Grant Gilmore. The idea occurred to each of us more or less simultaneously and has been developed by each independently. See Davies, "A Response to Statutory Obsolescence: The Nonprimacy of Statutes Act," 4 *Vermont L. Rev.* 203 (1979); Gilmore, "Putting Senator Davies in

Context," 4 *Vermont L. Rev.* 233 (1979); Calabresi, "The Nonprimacy of Statutes Act: A Comment," 4 *Vermont L. Rev.* 247 (1979). See also G. Gilmore and C. Black, *The Law of Admiralty* §6-56, at 446-448 (2d ed. 1975); G. Gilmore, supra note 1, at 97, 143-144.

6. I will consider these and other techniques the courts might use, including methods for allocating the burden of legislative inertia to promote legislative reconsideration of a law, in Chap. XI.

7. See Chaps. X and XI.

8. See Chaps. X and XI for a discussion of the various techniques and limits appropriate to the doctrine.

9. See, e.g., R. Dahl, *Pluralist Democracy in the United States: Conflict and Consent* 370 (1967): "Given the existence of a two-party system, it follows that unless attitudes are highly polarized, each of the two parties can hope to win only by constructing an electoral coalition made up of people whose views coincide on some questions but diverge on others . . . " Dahl adds that "there is substantial reason for thinking that low polarization has been the usual condition" of politics in America, where "Large socio-economic groups have generally been heterogeneous in political attitudes." Id. See also D. Mayhew, *Party Loyalty Among Congressmen* 146-168 (1966), for an account of how the dynamics of coalition building — and not legislator preference — explains whether particular legislation will be passed. This process may actually be more theoretically desirable than one that would have on each issue a referendum of legislative, or even of popular, preferences, since the building of coalitions provides a means by which intensity of preference can be recognized.

10. See, e.g., G. Gilmore, supra note 1. I would hasten to add here that I am not really concerned with the historical accuracy of this tradition, of this "received wisdom." Indeed, parts of it have been criticized recently as simplistic. See note 1, supra. It remains, nonetheless, an adequate statement of American aspirations about how continuity and change should be balanced. See note 11, infra. For this reason, whether that system ever really existed in its simplistic form is not as important to me as the fact that it can appropriately be used as a benchmark from which to compare modern legal-political phenomena. Throughout this book, then, when I refer to the "common law system," the "nineteenth-century balance," or the "traditional paradigm," I mean to refer to this idealized legal-political system.

11. See, e.g., Lum v. Fullaway, 42 Hawaii 500, 502-503 (1958): "[T]he genius of the common law, upon which our jurisprudence is based, is its capacity for orderly growth . . . The vehicle by which such growth is accomplished is what may be described as judge-made law. This is evident in the utterances of [the] learned oracles of law." (Citations omitted.) "Perhaps, the recent trend is to rely more on legislatures, and less on courts, for the growth of law. Nevertheless, judicial lawmaking continues inexorably." Id. at 504. See also note 1, supra.

12. "The fact is that we have never known the strict doctrine [of *stare decisis*] in the United States. It was only reached in England in the nine-

teenth century. Our lax regard for precedent represents an older—which is not necessarily to say more regressive—doctrine." Wise, "The Doctrine of *Stare Decisis,"* 21 *Wayne L. Rev.* 1043, 1046-47 (1975).

While as late as the middle of the nineteenth century the force of *stare decisis* was uncertain, the House of Lords decided in 1898, London Tramways Co. v. London County Council, [1898] A.C. 375, that they could not alter precedents laid down by the House of Lords acting as the supreme court in previous cases, but that such precedents could only be altered by an Act of Parliament. To do otherwise would mean that the courts would usurp the legislative function. See also Beamish v. Beamish, 11 Eng. Rep. 735, 760-761 (1861).

In 1966, Lord Chancellor Gardiner announced in a "Practice Statement"—a kind of general memorandum from the court—that, while "Their Lordships regard the use of precedent as an indispensable foundation upon which to decide what is the law," they "nevertheless recognise that too rigid adherence to precedent may lead to injustice in a particular case and also unduly restrict the proper development of the law. They propose, therefore, to modify their present practice and, while treating former decisions of this House as normally binding, to depart from a previous decision when it appears right to do so." [1966] 1 *Weekly L. R.* 1234 (H.L.(E.)). For a brief account of this turnabout, see Leach, "Revisionism in the House of Lords: The Bastion of Rigid Stare Decisis Falls," 80 *Harv. L. Rev.* 797 (1967).

13. See Chap. IX. Here and later, "majoritarian" will be used in a rather special sense. I will assume that whatever a current representative legislature would decide on a question to which it gives its full consideration represents majoritarian preference regardless of how a majority of the public at large (however that is defined) would decide the same issue. This not very realistic assumption permeates most American political rhetoric, and there is little to be gained by questioning it in this book.

14. The federal Constitution, which was much imitated by the states, see L. Friedman, supra note 1, at 102, placed many roadblocks in the path of passage of statutes. See Chap. VII, note 8, and accompanying text. At least at the federal level, the committee system early provided an additional nonconstitutional barrier to easy passage of statutes. See H. Hart and A. Sacks, *The Legal Process: Basic Problems in the Making and Application of Law* 727-730 (MS 1958). See also Traynor, supra note 1, at 424-425.

15. In traditional common law thinking, legislatures were presumed to seek only particular results when passing statutes; they were thought to lack intent (or even competence) to make more fundamental changes in the common law. Thus each new statute underwent a process of interpretation by courts which often considerably narrowed the potential scope of the statute's impact. For a classic criticism of such judicial "jealousy" of the legislative branch, see Pound, "Common Law and Legislation," 21 *Harv. L. Rev.* 383 (1908). For a sympathetic view of the proper use of statutes as sources of law by common law courts, see Landis, "Statutes and the Sources

of Law," in *Harvard Legal Essays* 213 (1934), and Stone, "The Common Law in the United States," 50 *Harv. L. Rev.* 4 (1936), discussed in Chap. VIII. See also Traynor, supra note 1.

16. Marbury v. Madison, 5 U.S. (1 Cranch) 137 (1803), is the celebrated case in which the Supreme Court asserted the right to invalidate federal statutes found to violate the Constitution. The judicial power of constitutional review had occasionally been exercised by state courts in state cases before the Supreme Court's epochal decision. See Nelson, "Changing Conceptions of Judicial Review: The Evolution of Constitutional Theory in the States, 1790–1860," 120 *U. Pa. L. Rev.* 1166, 1167-74 (1972).

17. See, e.g., L. Friedman, supra note 1, at 107. Nelson, in his article on changing conceptions of judicial review, supra note 16, at 1181, counts over 150 cases of exercise by either federal or state courts of this ultimate power by 1860.

18. For a classic expression of this view, see Snowden v. Snowden, 1 Bland. 550 (Md. 1829) (on whether the longstanding practice of ignoring statutory requirements for the serving of process on an infant defendant constituted constructive overruling of the statute): "These precedents would seem to sanction the position, that a positive legislative enactment may be virtually repealed by a long, general, and uninterrupted course of practice. But they are precedents which I should feel a great repugnance to adopt and enlarge upon. I hold it to be my duty to treat the acts of my predecessors with respect; and to yield implicit obedience to my superiors; yet I cannot lose sight of the sphere assigned to the judiciary, and allow myself, by any suggestion arising from the case, or by following any lightly considered precedent, to overstep the limits constitutionally prescribed to the judicial department to which I belong. No judge or court, either of the first or last resort, can have any right to *legislate;* and there can be no difference between the power to declare an act of Assembly obsolete, and the power to enact a new law. The power to repeal and to enact are of the same nature. I shall therefore always consider an express provision of a constitutional act of Assembly as an authority superior to any usage or adjudged case whatever." Id. at 556.

19. As Grant Gilmore has stated, middle age is the most dangerous time in a statute's life, for then it still has relevance and bite in real situations but its thrust is no longer desired or desirable. "The most difficult period in the life of a statute — as in the life of a human being — is middle age. Admittedly the statute is no longer what it once was but there is life in the old dog yet. An occasional subsection still has its teeth and subparagraph (3) (b) may burn with a gem-like flame. We are now passing through our statutory middle age." G. Gilmore, supra note 1, at 96.

20. The reasons for the movement to statutes are discussed in Chap. VII.

21. "Unfortunately, with the New Deal, a style of drafting which aimed at unearthly and superhuman precision came into vogue, on the state as well as the federal level." G. Gilmore, supra note 1, at 96.

22. The "case law codes" proposed by the "American codifiers" active in the nineteenth century and into our own were, as Gilmore puts it, "not statutes at all. That is, they were not designed to provide rules for the decision." G. Gilmore, supra note 1, at 71. According to Gilmore, Llewellyn, the principal draftsman for the Uniform Commercial Code, envisioned the case law code as "a statute whose principal function would be to abrogate obsolete rules, thus leaving the courts free to improvise new rules to fit changing conditions and novel business practices. Llewellyn's code, as he conceived it, would have abolished the past without attempting to control the future." Id. at 85. For a discussion of the success of codification efforts in commercial law, see Gilmore, "On Statutory Obsolescence," 39 *U. Colo. L. Rev.* 461 (1967).

The original restatement movement wished to go beyond the vague language of codes and to attempt to provide solutions that would, if followed, give guidance in concrete cases. The American Law Institute thus served as history's mediator between the early codes and the modern wave of statutorification. Although the restatements were to be "made with the care and precision of a well-drawn statute," they were not to be enacted as statutory law. 1 *ALI Proceedings* 20-28 (1927). See H. Hart and A. Sacks, supra note 14, at 748-771; see also Chap. VIII.

23. G. Gilmore, supra note 1, at 95: "One of the facts of legislative life, at least in this country in this century, is that getting a statute enacted in the first place is much easier than getting the statute revised so that it will make sense in the light of changed conditions."

24. As we shall see, e.g., Chap. X, impossibility of reenactment is one but not the only test of the obsolescence of a statute (and is by itself certainly not a sufficient condition) for obsolescence.

25. Once again, I do not mean that this balance existed at such-and-such a time in the nineteenth century, but rather that it came to be the received wisdom that this was what the system had achieved at common law, how its functioning came to be perceived and understood.

26. See, e.g., Behrns v. Burke, 229 N.W.2d 86 (S.D. 1975), refusing to follow the dubious equal protection analysis of Brown v. Merlo, 8 Cal. 3d 855, 106 Cal. Rptr. 388, 506 P.2d 212 (1973), discussed in text at Chap. II, notes 15-18, and to invalidate the South Dakota guest statute. The Court made no secret of its disdain for the statute: "We are inclined to agree [with the Court in *Merlo*] that the guest statute is unreasonable . . . In fact, unreasonable may be too kind an expression." Yet its validity was upheld. See also Louisville and Nashville Ry. v. Atkins, 390 F. Supp. 576, 579 (M.D. Tenn. 1975), *aff'd mem.,* 423 U.S. 802 (1975) (rejecting the argument that changed profit circumstances made the high property tax rate on railroads unconstitutionally arbitrary, although other business rates were lower, with the traditional statement: "This evidence, however persuasive and appropriate it might be if presented to a legislative body, simply does not sustain the plaintiff's claim of invidious discrimination.").

27. See Chaps. II and IV. Since interpretation is defined convention-

ally as a search for original legislative intent, circumstances arising after a definitive interpretation of a statute has been made are frequently not accepted as arguments for changing the statute's construction, even where, as in Phillips Petroleum Co. v. Wisconsin, 347 U.S. 672 (1945) (forcing the Federal Power Commission to regulate the field price of natural gas), the result of the original interpretation proves to be a total disaster. Cf. E. Levi, *An Introduction to Legal Reasoning* 31-33 (1949), discussed at Chap. IV, note 29. Courts are thus left with this rather odd set of limits: if a problem arises for the first time, a result that seems wise to the court may frequently be attained through "functional" interpretation regardless of "original legislative intent," see Chap. IV, but if the problem has arisen before, the court is prevented from taking into account changes and reaching the result it deems best (unless the problems with the original construction should have been apparent at the time of the original ruling, in which case the original construction can be overruled as "erroneous"). Cf. Fugate v. Urban, 16 Ill. App. 3d 191, 305 N.E.2d 295 (1973) (following an earlier interpretation believed by the Court to be unwise), and Swendsen v. Brighton Building and Maintenance Co., 35 Ill. App. 3d 987, 343 N.E.2d 42 (1976) (overruling *Fugate* and refusing to follow the earlier interpretation).

28. Several commentators have recently taken up the theme of "judicial usurpation." See, e.g., R. Berger, *Government by Judiciary* (1977); but see Murphy, "Book Review, of Berger, Government by Judiciary," 87 *Yale L. J.* 1752, 1768-71 (1978); Alfange, "On Judicial Policymaking and Constitutional Change: Another Look at the 'Original Intent' Theory of Constitutional Interpretation," 5 *Hastings Const. L. Q.* 603 (1978). See also Deutsch, "Neutrality, Legitimacy and the Supreme Court: Some Intersections Between Law and Political Science," 20 *Stan. L. Rev.* 169 (1968). For a comparative perspective, see Dahrendorf, "A Confusion of Powers: Politics and the Rule of Law," 40 *Mod. L. Rev.* 1 (1977).

29. One judge, see text at Chap. IV, note 24, argued that "the death of the common law is at hand" if courts do not scrupulously avoid finding legislative preemption of common law activity, even where a fair reading of original legislative intent would indicate preemption.

30. R. Keeton, *Venturing To Do Justice* 82 (1969): "A court's refusal to acknowledge its inevitably creative role in statutory interpretation is unrealistic and crippling even in the disposition of a single case. From a long range point of view, such refusal freezes reform. When legislatures intrude into an area of private law, the court considers itself no longer free either to overrule or to innovate interstitially. In view of the ever increasing impact of inertia in legislatures, the effect in most cases is a deep freeze."

31. This book is a common law book in more than just its subject matter. The structure of the first twelve chapters follows that of a fairly typical common law opinion. First, the problem is identified; then past judicial solutions are surveyed. Once these are found to be unsatisfactory, the question becomes: Can the problem be left to other branches of the government without more? The conclusion that it cannot leads to a consideration of

whether a new judicial solution might be appropriate. The antecedents of that solution are then examined: Is the new approach consistent with precedent, indeed is it new at all, or has it already been commonly used without explicit recognition? In the common law, innovation must make its peace with history. Fuller elaboration of the rule follows, but, as in many common law decisions, no attempt is made to define its ultimate scope and limits or to resolve all the problems it entails. Finally the question is raised whether the courts ought to develop the new judicial solutions themselves or whether they ought to wait for a clearer delegation of the task from the legislatures.

The last three chapters of the book, by contrast, concern matters that do not normally surface in common law opinions: what are the costs and benefits of honest and self-conscious adoption of a new, possibly far-reaching doctrine, as against those of continuing to use unselfconscious and occasionally uncandid or dishonest alternatives? The dangers of the doctrine, even refined and limited, may make its open adoption undesirable, despite its apparent superiority over other approaches. This question will entail a brief discussion of the role of subterfuges in the law. The discussion, while incomplete, will suffice for me to conclude, tentatively, that this is an area where acting openly is the preferred approach.

II. The Flight to the Constitution and to Equal Protection Clauses

1. On reapportionment, see L. Tribe, *American Constitutional Law* 738-761 (1978).

2. Griswold v. Connecticut, 381 U.S. 479 (1965). The statute under attack, *Conn. Gen. Stat.* §53-32 (1960), read as follows: "Any person who uses any drug, medicinal article or instrument for the purpose of preventing conception shall be fined not less than fifty dollars or imprisoned not less than sixty days nor more than one year or be both fined and imprisoned." Section 53-32 had been the subject of litigation before in Poe v. Ullman, 367 U.S. 497 (1961). There the Court dismissed the case, refusing to consider plaintiffs' contention that the statute was unconstitutional, because the Court could find no "case or controversy" involved: "We were advised by counsel for [plaintiff-appellants] that contraceptives are commonly and notoriously sold in Connecticut drug stores. [Footnote omitted.] Yet no prosecutions are recorded . . . The undeviating policy of nullification by Connecticut of its anti-contraceptive laws throughout all the long years that they have been on the statute books bespeaks more than prosecutorial paralysis." 367 U.S. 497, 502 (Frankfurter, J.).

3. At the time of *Griswold,* Connecticut's abortion law allowed a woman to have an abortion if it was "necessary to preserve her life or that of her unborn child." *Conn. Gen. Stat. Ann.* §53-30. The anticontraceptive law forbade "absolutely" such devices, even in life-or-death situations. See, e.g., Buxton v. Ullman, 147 Conn. 48 (1959), *appeal dismissed sub nom.* Poe v. Ullman, 367 U.S. 497 (1961), and Tileston v. Ullman, 129 Conn. 84

(1942). Yet no one was prepared to argue that Connecticut viewed abortion as preferable to contraception. The "absolute" anticontraception law was clearly a vestige of views that were no longer dominant — that were indeed nearly nonexistent — in the state.

4. "In the course of its opinion the Court refers to no less than six Amendments to the Constitution: the First, the Third, the Fourth, the Fifth, the Ninth, and the Fourteenth. But the Court does not say which of these Amendments, if any, it thinks is infringed by this Connecticut law." 381 U.S. 479, 527-528 (Stewart, J., dissenting).

5. Justice Goldberg, concurring in *Griswold*, noted, "The State of Connecticut does have statutes, the constitutionality of which is beyond doubt, which prohibit adultery and fornication." 381 U.S. 479, 498. And Justice Harlan had noted earlier in Poe v. Ullman, "The right of privacy most manifestly is not an absolute. Thus, I would not suggest that adultery, homosexuality, fornication and incest are immune from criminal enquiry, however privately practiced." 367 U.S. 497, 552 (Harlan, J., dissenting).

While the Court in Eisenstadt v. Baird, 405 U.S. 438 (1972), extended the right protected in *Griswold* to unmarried couples, it held in Doe v. Commonwealth's Attorney, 425 U.S. 901 (1976) (mem.), that claims of privacy were no bar to statutes criminalizing private consensual homosexual behavior. The Court summarily affirmed a decision by a three-judge district court, 403 F. Supp. 1199 (E.D. Va. 1975), rejecting the arguments of District Judge Merhige, who in dissent found the privacy rationales in *Griswold* and *Eisenstadt* compelling. Id. at 1203-05.

6. Califano v. Goldfarb, 430 U.S. 199 (1977).

7. Id., 430 U.S. 199, 217 (Brennan, J.; joined by White, Marshall, and Powell, JJ.) (quoting Schlesinger v. Ballard, 419 U.S. 498, 508 (1975)). This plurality opinion held that the distinction between widows and widowers constituted "invidious discrimination against female wage earners affording them less protection for their surviving spouses than is provided to male employees." Id. at 202.

8. Justice Rehnquist (joined by Burger, C.J., Stewart and Blackmun, JJ.) found two rational grounds 'for the distinction: first, there were arguments of administrative convenience; second, there was an intent to confer a special benefit on widows, a motive approved in Kahn v. Shevin, 416 U.S. 351 (1974). Califano v. Goldfarb, 430 U.S. 199, 224-242 (1977).

9. Id. at 223 (Stevens, J., concurring).

10. Id. at 223 n.9: "Perhaps an actual, considered legislative choice would be sufficient to allow this statute to be upheld, but that is a question I would reserve until such a choice has been made."

11. "I consider it clear that Congress never focused its attention on the question whether to divide nondependent surviving spouses into two classes on the basis of sex. The history of the statute is entirely consistent with the view that Congress simply assumed that all widows should be regarded as 'dependents' in some general sense, even though they could not satisfy the statutory support test imposed on men." Id. at 222 (Stevens, J., concur-

ring). Recommendations to revise the statute and abolish the discrimination had previously been considered by Congress, see, e.g., *Hearings on Financing the Social Security System before the Subcommittee on Social Security of the House Committee on Ways and Means,* 94th Cong., 1st Sess. (1975), but had never been enacted.

12. The House bill to amend the Social Security Act following the Court's ruling in *Goldfarb* directed the Secretary of HEW to study the problem of gender-based discrimination and to report findings on the prospects of securing equal treatment to Congress within six months. The bill also provided for measures immediately designed to implement such equal treatment. See *H. Rep. No.* 95-702, Part 1, 95th Cong., 1st Sess., at 4, reprinted in [1977] *U.S. Code Cong. & Ad. News* 4155, 4161. The Senate rejected the measures designed immediately to eliminate discrimination, but agreed to the six-month study by HEW. *H. Conf. Rep. No.* 95-837, 95th Cong., 1st Sess., at 73, reprinted in [1977] *U.S. Code Cong. & Ad. News* 4155, 4319. The amended bill was enacted as the Social Security Amendments of 1977, Pub. L. No. 95-216, 91 Stat. 1509.

13. Nor is this use of constitutional adjudication as a means of updating the law limited to the United States. The West German constitutional court in 1975 faced almost the identical issue involved in Califano v. Goldfarb, 430 U.S. 199 (1977). The German social security law gave widows an automatic pension, but required proof of dependency before widowed husbands could receive them. This law had been upheld against constitutional challenge in 1963. Since then, the same widespread entrance of women into the job market observed in the United States had occurred in Germany so that, the court noted, "it is no longer assumed that the woman must be primarily a housewife." The court held that the statute was still constitutional, but stated that "grounds for constitutional complaint would exist in the future if the legislature failed to work intensively toward a solution more reasonably in accord with actual conditions, a solution which would eliminate those effects of the current statute which are tending toward unconstitutionality. The current situation thus sets forth a constitutional mandate for the legislature, namely, to fashion a new regulation of this area which will bar any conflict with [the constitutional clause relevant to legislative discrimination on sex]. Given the difficulty of this assignment, wide-ranging and time-consuming preparations will be necessary. This Court, however, starts with the principle that the new regulation must be put into effect by the end of the second following legislative session." Judgment of Mar. 12, 1975, Bundesverfassungsgericht, W. Ger. [1975] BVerfGE 39,169 (195).

This approach takes the "actual purposes" equal protection analysis Justice Stevens employed in *Goldfarb* one step further. Not only does it declare that a law can become unconstitutional when the original justification for it is eroded by time (at least if no new, equally forceful one replaces it), the approach also authorizes courts to tell the legislature that, while as of the time of decision the law is valid since its justification retains some rational basis, it is moving "toward unconstitutionality." This kind of declaration that a law will soon be unconstitutional seems not to be an uncommon technique in the West German constitutional court. See, e.g., Judgment of Mar. 14, 1972, Bundesverfassungsgericht, W. Ger. [1972] BVerfGE 33,1 (13) (prisoners' rights); Judgment of May 10, 1972, Bundesverfassungsgericht, W. Ger. [1972] BVerfGE 33,171 (189f.) (regulation of physician's fees); Judgment of Apr. 3, 1974, Bundesverfassungsgericht, W. Ger. [1974] BVerfGE 37,104 (118) (admissions to state medical school); Judgment of Feb. 8, 1977, Bundesverfassungsgericht, W. Ger. [1977] BVerfGE 43,291 (321) (admissions to state university). I am indebted to Angelo Winkler of the European University Institute for pointing out these cases to me, and to Steven Heimann, Yale Law School, for providing the translation I am here quoting.

14. Rowland v. Christian, 69 Cal. 2d 108, 70 Cal. Rptr. 97, 443 P.2d 561 (1968).

15. Brown v. Merlo, 8 Cal. 3d 855, 506 P.2d 212 (1973).

16. The law at stake in *Merlo* allowed automobile guests to recover from owners only when drunken driving or willful misconduct was involved. *Cal. Veh. Code* §17158 (West). The court examined two rationales upon which the distinction might rest: protection of hospitality and prevention of collusive lawsuits. Neither was found to be sufficiently furthered by the statute to permit the prohibition of recovery for negligence. A second portion of the statute prohibited recovery from a driver by an owner/passenger; it was this portion of the statute that the court refused to consider. Brown v. Merlo, 8 Cal. 3d 855, 862 n.3 (1973). Following the decision, the legislature repassed that portion of the statute that was not expressly declared unconstitutional by the court, thus continuing to prohibit recovery by an owner/passenger from a guest driver. 1973 *Cal. Stats.*, c.803, p. 1426, §4.

17. In Schwalbe v. Jones, 120 Cal. Rptr. 585, 534 P.2d 73 (1975) [hereinafter cited as *Schwalbe I*], the California Supreme Court in an opinion by Justice Tobriner held that the remaining bar to recovery by an owner/passenger was unconstitutional as well. On rehearing, however, Schwalbe v. Jones, 16 Cal. 3d 514, 128 Cal. Rptr. 321, 546 P.2d 1033 (1976) [hereinafter cited as *Schwalbe II*], Justice Sullivan, writing for the Court, adopted the view expressed by the minority in *Schwalbe I,* finding the distinction between owner/passenger and nonowner passenger constitutional. Finally, in Cooper v. Bray, 21 Cal. 3d 841, 148 Cal. Rptr. 148, 582 P.2d 604 (1978), the Court, once again in an opinion by Justice Tobriner, returned to the holding in *Schwalbe I* and declared the denial of recovery to an owner/passenger unconstitutional. It held that the legislature had added the owner/passenger clause to *Cal. Veh. Code* §17158 in 1961 to treat an owner/passenger and other social guests equally, that the holding in *Brown v. Merlo* had eliminated that rationale for the statute, and that since there was no independent rationale for denial of recovery of an owner/passenger, the remaining clause of §17158 fell to equal protection objections.

18. Note, "The Supreme Court of California, 1975-1976" 65 *Cal. L. Rev.* 257, 501 (1977).

19. The fact that the legislation "upheld" the court by failing to reenact the statute may be taken to suggest that the court correctly judged the "will of the people," but it is by no means conclusive. See Chap. X.

20. Stewart, J. (joined by Black, J.), dissenting in Griswold v. Connecticut (the Connecticut birth control case): "I think this is an uncommonly silly law." 381 U.S. 479, 527 (1965).

21. See text at notes 6-12, supra.

22. For example, in the 1979 Holmes Lectures, Charles Black persuasively suggests that the protections against discrimination provided to blacks and other racial minorities by the Equal Protection Clause have been significantly weakened by the distortion of equal protection doctrine engendered by recent uses of that doctrine to accomplish other tasks. C. Black, *Decision According to Law* (1981).

23. One of the objections raised to a constitutional amendment to overturn *Roe v. Wade* is that the amendment procedure should be used only *in extremis*. Supporters of the amendment agree that it is indeed a serious step to alter the Constitution, but argue that it is just such conflicts for which the amendment process was designed. See, e.g., Bernardin, N.Y. Times, Feb. 26, 1977, at 19, col.3. See also A. Bickel, *Politics and the Warren Court* 155 (1965): "the practice of hastening or confirming [by constitutional amendment] the demise of unwanted judicial doctrines would lead to a pestilence of amendment that would destroy the value of our Constitution as a symbol and as a cohesive force in society."

24. Thus Congress recommended and the states ratified the Twenty-Sixth Amendment, which states, "The right of citizens of the United States, who are eighteen years of age or older, to vote shall not be denied or abridged by the United States or by any State on account of age," shortly after the Supreme Court in Oregon v. Mitchell, 400 U.S. 112 (1970), had held unconstitutional an amendment to the Voting Rights Act compelling states to extend the vote in state elections to eighteen-year-olds. Cf. A. Bickel, *The Least Dangerous Branch: The Supreme Court at the Bar of Politics* 244, 254-272 (1962).

25. See, e.g., Gunther, "Foreword: In Search of Evolving Doctrine on a Changing Court: A Model for a Newer Equal Protection," 86 *Harv. L. Rev.* 1, 8-12 (1972). See also G. Gunther, *Constitutional Law: Cases and Materials* 674 (10th ed. 1980): "[Equal protection] has come a long way from being the 'last resort of constitutional arguments'; instead, it is a prolific source of modern constitutional litigation." For an example of judicial recognition of the recent activity in the equal protection field, see Brown v. Merlo, 8 Cal. 3d 855, 106 Cal. Rptr. 388, 506 P.2d 212 (1973). See also C. Black, supra note 22. Cf. Perry, "Modern Equal Protection: A Conceptualization and Appraisal," 79 *Colum. L. Rev.* 1023 (1979). See also Harris, Equal Protection Nullification in Washington State: A Case Study (unpublished paper on file in Yale Law School Library) (detailing the increased use

of equal protection clauses to strike down out-of-phase statutes in Washington state).

26. Cf. Chap. IX. See also Raz, "Professor Dworkin's Theory of Rights," 26 *Pol. Stud.* 123, 135 (1978) (attacking the soundness of the principle of treating like cases alike).

27. See Chap. IX.

28. Such an equal protection analysis, aimed at removal of statutes felt to be out of date, may come to be used increasingly against economic regulation, especially regulation that was the product of now unpopular philosophies, such as fair trade laws. Substantive due process is another way of reaching the same result: if there is no rational basis to support a classification for equal protection purposes, it is not more difficult to say that there is no basis for allowing invasion of the harmed individual's liberty or property. See Defiance Milk Products Co. v. Du Mond, 309 N.Y. 537, 132 N.E.2d 829 (1956), which invalidated on substantive due process grounds a New York law preventing evaporated skimmed milk from being sold at retail. A somewhat similar statute had been upheld by the Supreme Court in Carolene Products Co. v. United States, 323 U.S. 18 (1944), on the ground that consumers were sometimes confused between two types of milk products. The dissent in *Defiance Milk* applied traditional deferential standards and would have allowed the law: "At the time this restriction was enacted in 1922 there was proof before the Legislature of deception or confusion [between skimmed and whole evaporated milk]." 309 N.Y. at 550, 132 N.E.2d at 836. The majority decided, however, that "it is incredible that *as of this date* shoppers do not know what is meant by 'condensed skimmed milk.' " 309 N.Y. at 542-543, 132 N.E.2d at 831. It seems clear that the New York Court of Appeals was much less assiduous than usual in searching for a sustaining rational basis for the law because of its longevity and apparent obsoleteness.

29. See note 22, supra, and accompanying text.

30. See, e.g., Pound, "Common Law and Legislation," 21 *Harv. L. Rev.* 383 (1908).

III. The Passive Virtues

1. See A. Bickel, *The Least Dangerous Branch: The Supreme Court at the Bar of Politics* 111-198 (1962). See also Bickel and Wellington, "Legislative Purpose and the Judicial Process: The Lincoln Mills Case," 71 *Harv. L. Rev.* 1 (1957); Bickel, "The Supreme Court, 1960 Term—Foreword: The Passive Virtues," 75 *Harv. L. Rev.* 40 (1961); Wellington and Albert, "Statutory Interpretation and the Political Process: A Comment on *Sinclair v. Atkinson*," 72 *Yale L. J.* 1547 (1963); Wellington, "Common Law Rules and Constitutional Double Standards: Some Notes on Adjudication," 83 *Yale L. J.* 221 (1973).

2. See, e.g., Kent v. Dulles, 357 U.S. 116 (1958); Barenblatt v. United States, 360 U.S. 109, 134 (1959) (Black, J., dissenting); and

Greene v. McElroy, 360 U.S. 474 (1959).

3. Perhaps the most notorious example of openly subconstitutional constitutional law is provided by the Supreme Court's recent exclusionary rule jurisprudence. In United States v. Calandra, 414 U.S. 338 (1974), the Court described its rule preventing states from using illegally obtained evidence as a mere "judicially created remedy designed to safeguard Fourth Amendment rights generally through its deterrent effect, rather than a personal constitutional right of the party aggrieved." Id. at 348. The clear implication is that the rule, while consitutional, is subject to revision by any legislature that would design its own remedy. See Monaghan, "The Supreme Court, 1974 Term—Foreword: Constitutional Common Law," 89 *Harv. L. Rev.* 1 (1975) (attempting to provide a general rationale for open and explicit constitutional second-look doctrines), and Schrock and Welsh, "Reconsidering the Constitutional Common Law," 91 *Harv. L. Rev.* 1117 (1978) (attempting to refute the Monaghan rationale).

Vagueness has remained an attractive means for courts to invalidate laws without stating final limits on a legislature's constitutional power. See, e.g., Colautti v. Franklin, 439 U.S. 379 (1979), striking down a Pennsylvania statute, with criminal sanctions, that imposed a duty on doctors performing an abortion to determine whether the fetus was viable and, if it was, to exercise care to abort the fetus alive and further preserve its life and health. The Court held the concept of viability to be unconstitutionally vague, although as Justice White pointed out in his dissent, id. at 401-403, the term and the given application of it were almost certainly derived from the Court's earlier decision in Roe v. Wade, 410 U.S. 113 (1973).

A possible reemergence of the recently rarely invoked concept of undue delegation may be presaged by Industrial Union Department, AFL-CIO v. American Petroleum Institute, 448 U.S. 607, 100 S.Ct. 2844 (1980), discussed in Chap. V, note 37. A plurality of four justices invalidated a strict OSHA standard limiting occupational exposure to benzene because OSHA had not found a significant risk of harm from present levels of benzene. The OSHA Act, giving the agency power to formulate regulations for worker health standards, was interpreted to require a threshold finding that present standards were unsafe before the exercise of regulatory power. Four members of the Court purported to adopt the interpretation to avoid a constitutionally dubious construction, for otherwise "the statute would make such a 'sweeping delegation of legislative power' that it might be unconstitutional under the Court's reasoning in *A.L.A. Schechter Poultry Corp.* v. *United States*, 295 U.S. 495." Id. at 646. Justice Rehnquist, in an opinion concurring in the result, would not have reached the construction of the statute, but would have simply invalidated the relevant provision of OSHA as unconstitutional under the *Schechter* doctrine. Id. at 671 (Rehnquist, J., concurring). The four dissenters were quite sure that the majority was willfully misinterpreting the statute. On delegation, see Chap. IX, text at notes 87-89.

4. See note 13, infra, and accompanying text.

5. See, e.g., A. Bickel, supra note 1, at 29-33, 129-133.

6. See, e.g., Bickel and Wellington, supra note 1.

7. A. Bickel, supra note 1, at 143-156, argues that the concept of desuetude was implicit in Frankfurter's opinion in Poe v. Ullman, 367 U.S. 497 (1961). In *Poe* the Supreme Court dismissed appeals from the dismissal of complaints seeking declaratory judgments that the Connecticut birth control statute violated the Fourteenth Amendment. On Bickel's view: "The prevailing opinion by Mr. Justice Frankfurter in *Poe v. Ullman* did not in so many words hold that the Connecticut anti-birth-control statute had been nullified by desuetude in its application to the use of contraceptives by a doctor's prescription. But it did rest on this flat statement: 'The undeviating policy of nullification by Connecticut of its anti-contraceptive laws throughout all the long years that they have been on the statute books bespeaks more than prosecutorial paralysis.' And the opinion declined on this ground to reach what would otherwise be a ripe, justiciable issue. There might have been nothing amiss in language a shade more explicit. But the guarded expression is characteristic of our law in the initial stages of a doctrinal development. The consequence of the opinion, nevertheless, must be that a prosecution of persons situated as are Dr. Buxton and his patients would fail on the grounds of desuetude." Bickel, id. at 154 (citing opinion of Frankfurter, J., 367 U.S. at 502). See also District of Columbia v. John R. Thompson Co., 203 F.2d 579 (D.C. Cir. 1953), *reversed and remanded,* 346 U.S. 100 (1953). In the D.C. Circuit opinion, one of the issues dividing Judge Prettyman, concurring, and Judge Fahy, in dissent, was whether the Reconstruction antidiscrimination ordinances at issue in that case had become invalidated by desuetude.

8. Section 2 of the Canadian Bill of Rights, 8-9 Eliz. II, c.44 §§1-3, as amended by 19-20 Elizabeth II c. 38 s. 29 (1971), R.S.C. Appendix III, at 457 (1970), states that "Every law of Canada shall, unless it is expressly declared by an Act of Parliament that it shall operate notwithstanding the Canadian Bill of Rights, be so construed as not to abrogate, abridge or infringe, or to authorize the abrogation, abridgement or infringement of any of the rights or freedoms herein recognized and declared." The Minister of Justice of Canada is charged with the examination of every proposed bill or regulation to ascertain if it is inconsistent with the "purposes and provisions" of the Bill of Rights. Cf. Chap. IV, note 30 (discussing principles of "clear statement" in interpretation of statutes).

9. See Bickel and Wellington, supra note 1.

10. See, e.g., the effect that Justice Frankfurter expected from a denial of *certiorari* in FELA cases, Chap. IV, note 14. The dangers of using this particular technique to induce legislative reconsideration are discussed in Chap. XI.

11. See, e.g., Wellington and Albert, supra note 1, at 1555.

12. See Bickel and Wellington, supra note 1. See Chap. VI for a discussion of the sunset movement.

13. Gunther, "The Subtle Vices of the 'Passive Virtues' — A Comment

on Principle and Expediency in Judicial Review," 64 *Colum. L. Rev.* 1 (1964).

14. See Chap. IV for a discussion of interpretation.

15. Gunther, supra note 13, at 21 and 25.

16. See Chap. IV, note 35, discussing an attempt to find a constitutional infirmity in a workmen's compensation law which limited recovery to $35 per week and which took the place of all torts remedies against the employer. See also Chap. VI, notes 23–24. In fact, while inflation dated many fixed schedule workmen's compensation laws, some of these laws would have become out of phase even without inflation. As a country becomes wealthier it tends to give a higher monetary value to safety (risk avoidance), just as it does to the environment. Quite apart from inflation, then, as the country's wealth increased, employee recoveries that were fixed by statute tended to become increasingly out of line with recoveries at common law for analogous injuries. Indexing (see Chap. VI), though it might deal with the problem of inflation, could only with great difficulty deal with this more complex aging of a statute.

It is not surprising that some courts, faced with much lower recoveries for workers under compensation laws than they regularly see at common law for the same injuries, have been sympathetic to doctrines that create, in effect, an end run around the workmen's compensation statutes. The development of product liability for machine tool manufacturers is but one example of this kind of judicial reaction to dated laws. Unfortunately, like much judicial updating by indirection, this development is substantially inferior to what would be achieved if workers' compensation laws were updated directly. For product liability substitutes a very expensive, time-consuming, and uncertainty-creating remedy for one which, were its recovery schedules not out of line, would compensate far more speedily and cheaply. See Chap. V, note 28. See Calabresi, "Product Liability: Curse or Bulwark of Free Enterprise?," 27 *Cleveland State L. Rev.* 313 (1978).

17. See Wellington, supra note 1, at 221–229; R. Dworkin, *Taking Rights Seriously* 82–86 (1977). When equal protection doctrines are used to invalidate an out-of-date statute, it may be unclear whether the statute's invalidity comes from its use of an unconstitutional distinction among persons or, instead, from its being obsolete. The constitutional challenges to school financing through property taxes are examples of just this ambiguity. See, e.g., San Antonio Independent School District v. Rodriguez, 411 U.S. 1 (1973). Where schools are financed through property taxes , the legislature is allowing distinctions in per-pupil expenditures to take place between towns on the basis of wealth. Wealth distinctions between towns and hence in per-pupil expenditures may not have been large when the system of school financing was initially adopted. They may have become large only through changes in towns' wealth over time. See id. at 7–8, and Robinson v. Cahill, 62 N.J. 473, 303 A.2d 273, 287, *cert. denied sub nom.* Dickey v. Robinson, 414 U.S. 976 (1973). Yet the now significantly unequal, in some sense unintended, system of school financing may still remain in force

because of legislative inertia.

In such a case, if the court believes that wealth distinctions may be constitutionally permissible, but only if they are clearly supported by a current majority, or only if they are not too extreme, the appropriate judicial tactic might be to force a legislative reconsideration of the issue. The object would be to put the burden of overcoming inertia on those who want town wealth differences to affect per-pupil expenditures. If, however, the only way a court can do this is by using equal protection, the result is not simply to mandate legislative reconsideration with the burden on those favoring inequality. It frequently is not even to order such a reconsideration constrained by a constitutional requirement that inequality be contained within relatively small bounds. Using equal protection too readily implies that *no* inequality, except truly minimal ones, can be tolerated. Such an implication may make any legislatively acceptable system of school financing very difficult to come by. This may be fine if the court really intends a "constitutional" prohibition on any but minimal differences. It clearly is not desirable if, as I hypothesized, the court instead only intends to force a legislative reconsideration.

The danger in a use of equal protection doctrine in a case where the court means mainly to force a legislative reconsideration is not limited to the fact that the reconsideration most acceptable to the legislature may seem constitutionally suspect and hence be inhibited or blocked. For the very use of the doctrine in such a case inevitably suggests that similar distinctions are constitutionally suspect in other areas. Thus wealth distinctions outside of education come to seem constitutionally doubtful. See Michelman, "The Supreme Court and Litigation Access Fees: The Right to Protect One's Rights, Part II," 1974 *Duke U. L. Rev.* 527, esp. 563-567 (1974). Again, this is fine if the court intends to cast doubt on such distinctions in general. It is exceedingly undesirable if the only aim is to make sure that major distinctions based on wealth are supported by current majorities and not merely by inertia.

18. That a statute is out of phase neither entails nor requires that the statute be old, in terms of the number of years since its enactment. Rather, a statute is out of phase when it no longer fits in with the legal landscape, and it can become out of phase upon the advent of social, technological , or political changes. See Chaps. I and X.

19. See, e.g., Wellington, supra note 1, at 285-287 (approving the invalidation of anti-birth-control statutes that offended "conventional moral standards") and Newman, J., concurring in Abele v. Markle, 342 F. Supp. 800, 805 (D. Conn. 1972) (invalidating the Connecticut abortion statute because "the only interests which the 1860 legislature was seeking to advance are not today sufficient to justify invasion of the plaintiff's constitutionally protected rights").

20. See note 7, supra.

21. See Bickel and Wellington, supra note 1.

22. See Abele v. Markle, 342 F. Supp. 800, 805.

23. Roe v. Wade, 410 U.S. 113, 93 S.Ct. 705 (1973). See, e.g., G. Gunther, *Constitutional Law: Cases and Materials* 609-610 (10th ed. 1980) (discussion of post-*Roe* congressional activity), and 33 *Cong. Quar. Weekly Report* 917-922 (May 3, 1975) (debates on proposed constitutional amendments and statutes). See also note 46, infra.

24. See Chaps. X and XI for a further discussion of how colloquy can be fostered.

25. It should be made clear that I am taking no position here on the constitutional propriety *vel non* of the abortion decision. My point is only that, whatever one's view on the merits of the antiabortion laws, another type of judicial response might have led to a *current* reconsideration of the issue, with less anguish and division. See Chaps. XI and XII.

26. See Chaps. X and XI for a discussion of occasions when nullification may be appropriate and when, instead, legislative reconsideration seems preferable. See also Chap. XI on the judicial techniques most suited to achieve each of these.

27. See Chap. VI for a discussion of sunsetting. See also note 18, supra.

28. See supra note 1: Wellington; Bickel and Wellington; Wellington and Albert.

29. See Landis, "Statutes and Sources of the Law," *Harv. Legal Essays* 213 (1934), and text at Chap. VIII, notes 15-20. But cf. R. Dworkin, supra note 17, at 105-123, discussed in Chap. IX, note 18.

30. See Pound, "Common Law and Legislation," 21 *Harv. L. Rev.* 383 (1908), for a classic criticism of such judicial abuse.

31. Cf. Wellington, supra note 1, at 277-295 (defending substantive due process in the economic realm and applying conventional morality as a test of constitutional validity), and Bickel and Wellington, supra note 1, at 39 (limiting the second-look argument advanced in the article).

32. See G. Gilmore, *The Ages of American Law* 96 (1977): "[T]he more tightly a statute was drafted originally, the more difficult it becomes to adjust the statute to changing conditions without legislative revision. Unfortunately, with the New Deal, a style of drafting which aimed at an unearthly and superhuman precision came into vogue, on the state as well as the federal level." (Footnote omitted.)

33. To be sure, a legislature's clear statement limits the use of gimmicks. For example, the use of interpretation would be curtailed in the face of a clear statement by the legislature, since to get around the clear statement by means of interpretation would involve the destruction of language. And courts are well aware of the importance to judicial independence of being limited by language or, at the very least, of acting as if language imposes limits on their power. Cf. H. Hart and A. Sacks, *The Legal Process: Basic Problems in the Making and Application of Law* 1412-13 (MS 1958). But a requirement of a clear statement by the legislature does little to help us identify anachronistic statutes, and may stand in the way of an attempt to update an avowedly anachronistic one.

34. But cf. E. Levi, *An Introduction to Legal Reasoning* 6-7, 29-33 (1949),

discussed in Chap. IV, note 29.

35. Bickel and Wellington, supra note 1, at 34.

36. Furman v. Georgia, 408 U.S. 238 (1972).

37. Bickel and Wellington, supra note 1, at 34.

38. In his opinion in Gregg v. Georgia, 428 U.S. 153, 179 (1976), Justice Stewart noted: "Four years ago, the petitioners in *Furman* and its companion cases predicated their argument primarily upon the asserted proposition that standards of decency had evolved to the point where capital punishment no longer could be tolerated . . . The petitioners in the capital cases before the Court today renew the 'standards of decency' argument, but developments during the four years since *Furman* have undercut substantially the assumptions upon which their argument rested." Stewart then went on to speak of the legislative response to *Furman* as the "most marked indication of society's endorsement of the death penalty for murder." In his earlier concurring opinion in *Furman*, 408 U.S. 238, 306 (1972), Justice Stewart, while claiming it was not the sole basis of his decision, did note that the death sentences at issue in that case were clearly both "cruel" and "unusual, in the sense that the penalty of death is infrequently imposed for murder, and that its imposition for rape is extraordinarily rare." Id. at 309.

39. See note 38, supra.

40. *Conn. Gen. Stat.* §§53a-46a (West 1980 Supp.); 1973, P.A. 73-137 §4. See Fellows, *Connecticut Legislature Votes Death Penalty for Six Crimes,* N.Y. Times, Apr. 20, 1973, at 1, col. 7 (describing the circumstances of the Connecticut vote).

41. The *Furman* decision was perceived by many to mean that no capital punishment statute, except those applying to such specialized circumstances as the military in wartime, would be constitutionally acceptable. See Note, "Furman v. Georgia: Will the Death of Capital Punishment Mean a New Life for Bail?," 2 *Hofstra L. Rev.* 432, 432-433 (1974): "*Furman v. Georgia* has effectively abolished capital punishment in the United States for the time being." See also Note, "Is the Death Penalty Dead?," 26 *Baylor L. Rev.* 114, 122 (1974): "Is the death penalty dead in Texas? It seems difficult to reach any other conclusion."

42. See Abele v. Markle, 342 F. Supp. 800 (D. Conn. 1972), esp. concurrence of Newman, J., id. at 805.

43. But how are federal courts to respond to obsolete state legislation without a constitutional predicate? To participate in a colloquy with a state legislature, the federal courts must at least be able to assert jurisdiction. And it is highly doubtful that jurisdiction could generally obtain to nullify or force the reconsideration of a *state* statute, without a constitutional predicate. (Michael Perry of the Ohio State University Law School posed this very useful question to me.)

At least two responses may be available to circumvent such a jurisdictional block to federal updating of state laws. First, the block would be circumvented if, as Charles Black has suggested to me, there may occasionally be a constitutional right to have laws updated even if there is no constitutional right to define what the updated law will say. In that case, federal courts could assert jurisdiction to nullify or to force the reconsideration of an outdated, and hence constitutionally unacceptable, state law. This intriguing notion requires more space for development than can be provided here. See Chap. IX, note 99.

A second, perhaps less ambitious judicial option would take advantage of the ways in which state and federal laws often influence one another. While the federal judiciary might not be in a position to force the reconsideration of state laws directly, the federal courts can influence state legislatures by acting with respect to related federal legislation. Just as the enactment of new federal legislation in the area of, say, automobile safety or medical insurance may motivate state legislatures to reexamine state statutes dealing with those matters, so might federal judicial updating affect state lawmaking. Thus the federal judiciary's updating of a federal safety or health care statute could also produce a pressure on the state legislature to reconsider state enactments. Similarly, it might lead state courts to induce such legislative reconsideration. By exercising its jurisdiction over federal statutes, the federal judiciary might, then, by a kind of ripple effect, affect state laws as well.

44. To reemphasize, I am making no judgment on the correctness of the Supreme Court's ultimate views concerning abortion legislation. The issue, rather, is what they might have done, and what we might have been spared, if there had been available another approach to the problem of an obsolete statute.

45. The attacks have been legion. On the scholarly side, see, e.g., Ely, "The Wages of Crying Wolf: A Comment on *Roe v. Wade*," 82 *Yale L. J.* 920 (1973). The *Roe* decision has also triggered a continuing popular outcry, annual demonstrations against the decision on its various anniversaries, see, e.g., DeWitt, *Abortion Foes March in Capitol on Anniversary of Legalization*, N.Y. Times, Jan. 23, 1979, at C10, col. 1, and calls for legislative and majoritarian responses, most particularly calls for a constitutional amendment, see, e.g., Destro, "Abortion and the Constitution: The Need for a Life-Protective Amendment," 63 *Calif. L. Rev.* 1250 (1975). Rubin, "The Abortion Cases: A Study in Law and Social Change," 5 *N.C. Central L. J.* 215 (1974), canvasses the immediate legislative responses to the *Roe* decision, both proposed constitutional amendments and state statutory changes. See also note 23, supra.

46. It is, however, just possible that a politically viable compromise might have emerged even if none seems plausible now. Once a question has polarized into an issue of my fundamental value against yours, it is hard to back down from the confrontation. But if the question has not yet become polarized, inconsistent views can sometimes coexist. For example, states once allowed abortions in order to save lives, even though that was a compromise of sorts among views. What this shows is not that compromising on deeply held values is the right thing to do. I'm not saying that here. Rather, it suggests that sometimes an accommodation among the sets of

values can be reached if the issue is not polarized, if a confrontation of competing sets of values is avoided.

The lack of an appropriate doctrine precluded the courts from initiating what could have come to be a nonpolarizing response to the question. Framed in terms of the Constitution, the issue had to be addressed at the level of fundamental rights, and it had to be addressed for everyone. So the courts were precluded from involving the legislatures and the populace in a search for an accommodation that might have avoided a direct confrontation of deeply held values. And they were also precluded from allowing different jurisdictions to reach their own individual accommodations within some broad constitutional guidelines. Examining these alternatives, the Court might well still have come out as it did and found all of them unacceptable on a fundamental, constitutional level. Or it may be that even if the Court found some mixed solutions acceptable, the same confrontation of values would have occurred. But surely making available the possibility of considering other ways of resolving the issue would not have been wrong. Even that was precluded for the lack of a doctrine.

IV. Interpretation

1. H. Hart and A. Sacks, *The Legal Process: Basic Problems in the Making and Application of Law* (MS 1958). Hart and Sacks define the task of interpretation as deciding "what meaning ought to be given" to the directions of a statute in the respects relevant to a given case. Interpretation should not be ascertainment of the "intention of the legislature with respect to the matter at issue," id. at 1410, for in many cases there was no such intention. (It is this fact that the fiction of legislative "total prescription" hides, they assert.) Nor is interpretation wise which literally applies statutory language to fringe cases, Hart and Sacks say, since in passing a bill the legislative majority, like the draftsman, fix their minds only "on the propriety of the *general policy* expressed in the bill, as tested by a few representative *examples* of application and non-application." Id. at 1153 (emphasis in original). The interpreting court's primary goal in statutory construction, Hart and Sacks argue, is to "attribute" a statutory purpose to the original legislature. In doing this a court must make use of legislative history and reflect on the problems that led to the bill's passage, in this way trying "to put itself in imagination in the position of the legislature which enacted the measure." Id. at 1414. The court should "[r]espect the legislature as the chief policy-determining agency of the society," id. at 1410, and apply the legislative purpose thus attributed to the fact situation before the court.

There are, however, constraints on the application of the attributed purpose. Hart and Sacks would not apply the attributed purpose if its expression "would violate any established policy of clear statement," see note 30, infra, nor if purposive construction would give the statute's words "a meaning they will not bear." Id. at 1200. Thus, within a framework which describes interpretation as application of *original* legislative purpose,

Hart and Sacks nevertheless intend interpretation to be used for other functions: the preservation of language and the promotion of consistency between the statute to be construed and the legal landscape.

Hart and Sacks say the latter function (with which we are principally concerned in this book) should dictate the court's result when a court cannot locate any purpose relevant to the matter at hand, and there is no earlier respectable interpretation available. "The court's last resort, when doubt about the immediate purpose of a statute remains, is to resort to an appropriate presumption drawn from some general policy of the law. This is likely to be its only resort when the question concerns more nearly ultimate policy, or the mode of fitting the statute into the general fabric of the law." Id. at 1416.

2. R. Keeton, *Venturing To Do Justice* 78-97 (1969). "I do not understand Hart and Sacks to imply that the purpose to be attributed to the statute need be one that was or even could have been consciously formulated at the time the statute was enacted." Id. at 82. Although Keeton eclectically agrees that "if the statute contains evidence that a legislature has considered a question and prescribed an answer to it, the court must respect and apply that answer," he also takes as given that legislatures leave courts a large area in which to "resolve the problem at hand in a way that in the court's view produces the best total set of rules," id. at 94. Keeton is thus more aggressive than Hart and Sacks in delineating a "responsible" and "creative" role for courts in statutory interpretation. Keeton would also be somewhat more ready than Hart and Sacks to overrule prior interpretations of a statute, perhaps when such interpretations are "unwise" as well as "unfaithful to the legislative mandate." Cf. H. Hart and A. Sacks, supra note 1, at 1416, and R. Keeton, supra, at 79-80. See also Wellington, "Common Law Rules and Constitutional Double Standards: Some Notes on Adjudication," 83 *Yale L. J.* 221, 262-265 (1973).

3. See, e.g., H. Hart and A. Sacks, supra note 1, at 1156, and R. Keeton, supra note 2, at 81.

4. One reason Keeton advises creative or activist interpretation is that otherwise, "In view of the ever increasing impact of inertia in legislatures, the effect [of a court's refusal to acknowledge its creative role in statutory interpretation] in most cases is a deep freeze." R. Keeton, supra note 2, at 82.

5. Two cases in the 1958 Supreme Court term first brought the problem to my mind: Baker v. Texas Pac. Ry. Co., 359 U.S. 227 (1959), and Dick v. New York Life Insurance Co., 359 U.S. 437 (1959). On the gestation of the ideas, see Calabresi, "The Nonprimacy of Statutes Act: A Comment," 4 *Vermont L. Rev.* 247, 248-250 (1979). See also the interesting parallel development of Senator Davies' proposal, in Davies, "A Response to Statutory Obsolescence: The Nonprimacy of Statutes Act," 4 *Vermont L. Rev.* 203 (1979).

6. G. Gilmore, *The Ages of American Law* 97, 143 n.58 (1977).

7. Neither state regulatory laws nor other state laws, including work-

men's compensation laws, could be extended to railroad employees because any such extension of state statutes or common law was viewed as a restriction upon interstate commerce. Thus, in Baltimore & O. R.R. v. Baugh, 149 U.S. 368 (1893), the decision of the United States Circuit Court for the Southern District of Ohio was reversed. The Circuit Court had awarded recovery to an employee of the railroad who was injured by the negligent act of an engineer in a suit against the railroad applying Ohio common law. The Supreme Court held that the question was not one of local law but of general (i.e., federal) law, since the railroads were instruments of interstate commerce. "Commerce between the States is a matter of national regulation, and to establish it as such was one of the principal causes which led to the adoption of our Constitution. To-day, the volume of interstate commerce far exceeds the anticipation of those who framed this Constitution, and the main channels through which this interstate commerce passes are the railroads of the country . . . The lines of this [railroad] extend into half a dozen or more States, and its trains are largely employed in interstate commerce. As it passes from State to State, must the rights, obligations and duties subsisting between it and its employés change at every state line? . . . The question is not local but general." Id. at 378-379. See also Mississippi R.R. Comm. v. Illinois Cent. R.R., 203 U.S. 335 (1906), and Atlantic Coast Line v. Wharton, 207 U.S. 328 (1907), striking down state statutes requiring trains to stop at certain places as repugnant to the Commerce Clause.

Early federal attempts to fill the gap in the workmen's compensation protection failed. The Employers Liability Act of 1906, 34 Stat. 232, was held unconstitutional in The Employers Liability Cases, 207 U.S. 463 (1908). The 1906 Act imposed liability upon the railroads to employees who suffered damages resulting from the negligence of any of the railroads' employees, agents, or officers or from any defect or insufficiency of equipment, but did not limit this liability to damages suffered while participating in interstate commerce. The Supreme Court held that although Congress could regulate employer-employee relations under the commerce power, they could only do so "to the extent that regulations adopted by Congress on that subject are solely confined to interstate commerce." Id. at 495. The narrowness of the perceived commerce power of the federal government was in stark contrast to the breadth of the limitations in dealing with commerce imposed upon states by the earlier court decisions. That the Supreme Court's view of the commerce power was a determinedly narrow one was underscored by its decision in Adair v. United States, 208 U.S. 161 (1909). That case, decided in the same term as The Employers Liability Cases, invalidated a federal statute forbidding interstate railroads from discharging employees for participating in union activities on the grounds that this activity was beyond the commerce power. "What possible legal or logical connection," the Court asked, "is there between an employee's membership in a labor organization and the carrying on of interstate commerce?" Id. at 178.

It was in the context of these decisions that Congress considered FELA, and there was considerable doubt in Congress as to whether any broadly drafted workmen's compensation statute for railroad or maritime employees would be constitutional. In the Senate debate on FELA, one participant noted, "I doubt whether we are at liberty to say every time a man goes into the employ of a common carrier that we insure him against accident"; he was only silenced upon the assurance that FELA did no such thing. 42 *Cong. Rec.* 4533 (1908) (comments of Sen. Teller). Oddly enough, then the FELA, which was drafted to fit within what was perceived to be a narrow Court conception of the commerce power, was broadly construed and upheld in that broad form. The Act was comprehensive and exclusive, preempting all state workmen's compensation acts applying to interstate railroads. New York Central R.R. Co. v. Winfield, 244 U.S. 147 (1917).

The course of the Court's decisions in the maritime sphere followed a similar pattern. In 1917, the Supreme Court reversed a New York court decision applying the nonfault-based New York workmen's compensation laws to an action arising out of the death of a stevedore. Southern Pacific Co. v. Jensen, 244 U.S. 205 (1917). The Court reasoned that the Constitution and Judiciary Act of 1789 created exclusive federal authority over all admiralty and maritime cases, "saving to suitors, in all cases, the right of a common law remedy, where the common law is competent to give it." Section 9, Judiciary Act of 1789, 1 Stat. 76, 77. Although this "savings clause" meant that some parts of the maritime law might be changed by state legislation, liability for injuries to employees was not such a part. Here, too, the interest in uniformity of laws was paramount and any attempt to impose non-fault liability was seen as a restriction on interstate commerce. Id. at 216-217. Congress responded by expanding the savings clause to include not only the right of a common law remedy, but also "the rights and remedies under the workmen's compensation law of any State." Act of Oct. 6, 1917, c. 97, 40 Stat. 395. The Supreme Court, in Knickerbocker Ice Co. v. Stewart, 253 U.S. 149 (1920), refused to apply the New York workmen's compensation laws to a suit arising out of the death of a bargeman. The Court noted that the purpose of the framers of the Constitution in committing the control of admiralty to the federal government was to promote uniform laws, and held that the 1917 amendment, delegating the power to legislate in the maritime sphere to the states, promoted inconsistent laws and was hence beyond the power of Congress. "To say that because Congress could have enacted a compensation act applicable to maritime injuries, it could authorize the states to do as they might desire, is false reasoning." Id. at 164.

8. The Federal Employers Liability Act of 1908, 35 Stat. 65 (1908), *now codified at* 45 U.S.C. §§51-59 (1976) (FELA), provided a federal cause of action for harm to employees in the scope of their employment due "in whole or in part" to the negligence of officers, agents, or employees of railroads engaged in interstate commerce. The "fellow servant" rule of the common law was abrogated, and contributory negligence was replaced by com-

parative negligence. The defense of assumption of risk was taken away from railroads by subsequent amendment of FELA. 53 Stat. 1404 (1939). The Jones Act, 38 Stat. 1164 (1915), *now codified at* 46 U.S.C. §688 (1976), incorporated the FELA standard of liability by reference; it created a cause of action for negligence in favor of a seaman injured or killed "in the course of his employment."

Early decisions of the Supreme Court interpreting FELA found that the intent of Congress had been to apply common law standards of negligence to FELA cases. The common law placed a rather demanding burden of proof on plaintiff both as to negligence and proximate cause. See, e.g., Bailey v. Central Vermont Ry., 319 U.S. 350, 352 (1943) (FELA liability "rules have been largely fashioned from the common law . . . except as Congress has written into the Act different standards"), and Pennsylvania R.R. Co. v. Chamberlain, 288 U.S. 333, 339 (1943) (under common law standards plaintiff did not present a jury question on negligence "where proven facts give equal support to each of two inconsistent inferences; in which event, neither of them being established, judgment, as a matter of law, must go against the party upon whom rests the necessity of sustaining one of these inferences as against the other, before he is entitled to recover"). See also New York Central R.R. Co. v. Ambrose, 280 U.S. 486, 489-490 (1930): "[The plaintiff], upon whom lay the burden, completely failed to prove that the accident was proximately due to the negligence of the company. It follows that the verdict rests only upon speculation and conjecture and cannot be allowed to stand . . . The utmost that can be said is, that the accident may have resulted from any one of several causes, for some of which the company was responsible, and for some of which it was not. This is not enough." (Citations omitted.)

9. Broad change in the common law, in response to changing views of justice and optimal risk distribution, was not a novelty in the law of torts or the common law generally. The nineteenth century had seen a dramatic change from the earlier dominance of the no-fault tort of trespass to liability based almost exclusively on fault, so much so that in the celebrated case of Ives v. South Buffalo R. Co., 201 N.Y. 271, 94 N.E. 431 (1911), an early workmen's compensation law was held unconstitutional as violating an employer's fundamental right to be free from liability without fault. See 2 F. Harper and F. James, *The Law of Torts* §§12.1-12.2 (1956).

10. Starting in the period of 1943-1948 and continuing throughout the 1950s, the Supreme Court began remodeling the law of negligence under FELA to lighten plaintiffs' burden under the Act. In case after case directed verdicts for railroads were reversed. Of twenty FELA *certiorari* petitions granted between 1943 and 1948, nineteen were granted at the instance of employees, and in sixteen of those nineteen, the lower court was reversed for setting aside a jury verdict for an employee or taking the case from the jury. See Wilkerson v. McCarthy, 336 U.S. 53, 70 (1949) (Douglas, J., concurring). See also Alderman, "What the New Supreme Court Has Done to the Old Law of Negligence," 18 *Law & Cont. Prob.* 110 (1953); Note,

"Supreme Court Certiorari Policy in Cases Arising Under the FELA," 69 *Harv. L. Rev.* 1441 (1956).

For many years the Court remained unwilling to state explicitly that it was changing the standard of FELA liability. It still purported to be applying well-settled common law principles in a case-by-case review of sufficiency of the evidence. Invariably, earlier and wholly inconsistent (often unanimous) Supreme Court decisions were ignored. Thus Lavender v. Kurn, 327 U.S. 645, 653 (1946), and Ellis v. Union Pacific Ry., 329 U.S. 649 (1947), seemed to overrule Pennsylvania R.R. Co. v. Chamberlain, 288 U.S. 333 (1943), *sub silentio*, in holding it was no objection to a verdict that it involved speculation. "The choice of conflicting versions of the way that the accident happened . . . the inferences to be drawn from uncontroverted as well as controverted facts are for the jury." Tennant v. Peoria & P. Union Ry. Co., 321 U.S. 29 (1944), openly authorized speculation as to proximate cause without mention of New York Central R.R. Co. v. Ambrose, 280 U.S. 486 (1930), and similar cases. See discussion, note 8, supra.

Doubts as to whether the Supreme Court had been candid in its treatment of the FELA cases surfaced in Wilkerson v. McCarthy, 336 U.S. 53 (1949). Justice Douglas, in a concurring opinion, stated that the early rash of FELA cases, overturning jury verdicts rendered in favor of employees, were the result of judicial hostility to the change in the common law negligence standard for liability, and that continued Court stewardship of these cases was a fitting attempt to correct its earlier action. Id. at 68-69. Not until eight years later, however, was a majority of the Court willing to admit that "special features of [the FELA] statutory negligence action" made it "significantly different from the ordinary common law negligence action." Rogers v. Missouri P. Ry. Co., 352 U.S. 500, 510 (1957). In *Wilkerson*, Justice Black (for the majority) still purported to be applying well-known law from the general jurisprudence of negligence. In his dissent in *Wilkerson*, Justice Jackson sardonically observed, "If in this class of cases, which forms a growing proportion of its total, this Court is really applying accepted principles of an old body of liability law in which lower courts are generally experienced, I do not see why they are so baffled and confused at what goes on here. On the other hand, if this Court considers a reform of this law appropriate *and within the judicial power to promulgate*, I do not see why it should constantly deny that it is doing just that" (emphasis added). 336 U.S. at 76.

11. Since the Supreme court was not forthright in explaining the changes it was making in FELA liability, many lower courts continued to apply well-settled principles of negligence law and to hand down directed verdicts, albeit with a substantial risk of case-by-case reversal. Two typical cases in which the lower court majority did not even mention the by now well-developed line of Supreme Court cases were Cahill v. New York, N.H. & H. R.R. Co., 224 F.2d 637 (2d Cir. 1955), *rev'd per curiam*, 350 U.S. 898 (1955), and Anderson v. Atchison, T. & S.F. Ry. Co., 31 Cal. 2d

117, 187 P.2d 729 (1947), *rev'd per curiam*, 333 U.S. 821 (1948).

12. At the time of the Supreme Court's FELA decisions, while the common law of negligence was much more liberal toward recovery by plaintiffs than it had been in 1908, the common law still granted directed verdicts more frequently than the Supreme Court majority in FELA cases. Whether the present common law of negligence is as hostile to such verdicts for defendants as the "reinterpreted" FELA standard is not clear. Cf. Conda v. Plain, 222 So. 2d 417 (Fla. 1969) (jury entitled to consider all possible inferences arising from the evidence), and Ashe v. Acme Builders, 267 N.C. 384, 148 S.E. 2d 244 (1966) (holding that the sufficiency of the evidence to support a material issue is a matter of law).

13. Some courts were quick to see that the Supreme Court would not tolerate directed verdicts against plaintiffs in FELA actions. Griswold v. Gardner, 155 F.2d 333, 333-334 (7th Cir. 1946), noted as early as 1946, "Any detailed review of the evidence . . . for the purpose of determining the propriety of the trial court's refusal to direct a verdict would be an idle and useless ceremony in light of the recent decisions of the Supreme Court. This is so regardless of what we might think of the sufficiency of the evidence in this respect. The fact is, so we think, that the Supreme Court has in effect converted this negligence statute into a compensation law." See also Atlantic Coast Line R.R. Co. v. Floyd, 227 F.2d 820, 822 (4th Cir. 1955) ("The Supreme Court has made crystal clear its manifest unwillingness to sanction the taking of cases under the FELA away from the jury by directed verdicts in favor of defendant railroads"). After the *Rogers* decision, see discussion at note 10, supra, for lower appellate courts to tolerate directed verdicts for railroad defendants or to reverse jury verdicts for plaintiffs would have amounted almost to open rebellion. The Supreme Court's need to oversee FELA jurisprudence on a case-by-case basis thus lessened, although occasional FELA sufficiency cases were still taken in the 1960s. See, e.g., Ferguson v. St. Louis-San Francisco Ry. Co., 307 S.W. 2d 385, *rev'd per curiam*, 356 U.S. 41 (1958), Moore v. Terminal R. R. Ass'n, 312 S.W. 2d 769, *rev'd per curiam*, 358 U.S. 31 (1958), and Gallick v. Baltimore & O. R. Co., 327 U.S. 108 (1963).

14. Justice Frankfurter believed that " 'the remedy for an obsolete and uncivilized system of compensation for loss of life or limb of crews on ships and trains is not intermittent disregard of the considerations which led Congress to entrust this Court with the discretion of certiorari jurisdiction. The remedy is an adequate and effective system of workmen's compensation,' adequate in amount and especially prompt in administration . . . The persistence of [the] archaic and cruel system . . . is attributable to many factors. Inertia of course . . . [But] one cannot acquit the encouragement given by this Court for seeking success in the lottery of obtaining heavy verdicts of contributing to the continuance of this system of compensation whose essential injustice can hardly be alleviated by the occasional 'correction' in this Court of ill-success." Ferguson v. Moore-McCormack Lines, 352 U.S. 521, 538-40 (1957) (dissenting opinion).

As the above quotation indicates, Frankfurter believed that the majority's decision to review determinations of fact in so many FELA and Jones Act cases was an abuse of the Court's discretionary power of granting *certiorari*. See, e.g., Dick v. New York Life Ins. Co., 359 U.S. 437, 458-61 (Frankfurter, J., dissenting). Frankfurter's objection, even if plausible when the Court claimed that it did no more than review questions of sufficiency of the evidence on the facts of particular cases, lost much of its force after *Rogers*. See note 10 supra. For in that case, the Court announced that it was protecting the rule of law embodied in the FELA from systematic erosion by lower courts. Even after *Rogers*, it remained possible to argue about whether the Court was using its resources wisely in accepting so many FELA cases; but after *Rogers* the practice was certainly consistent with the Court's rule of practice that it will only take cases in its *certiorari* jurisdiction if a rule of law, rather than the mere correctness of a decision upon particular facts, is at issue in a given case. In light of this, the most plausible explanation for Frankfurter's continued behavior in FELA cases was his perception that a workmen's compensation system to deal with injuries to railroad employees fit better in the legal fabric than did a "liberalized" FELA.

15. See Chap. XI.

16. The statute, former *Wis. Stat. Ann.* §895.045 (West), passed in 1931, provided that "Contributory negligence shall not bar recovery in an action by any person or his legal representative to recover damages for negligence resulting in death or in injury to person or property, if such negligence was not as great as the negligence of the person against whom recovery is sought, but any damages allowed shall be diminished in the proportion to the amount of negligence attributable to the person recovering."

17. F. Harper and F. James, supra note 9, at §22.1.

18. In 1970, when the Wisconsin Supreme Court reevaluated the state's comparative negligence statute, twelve states had some form of comparative negligence. Five states had just passed statutes of the sort in 1969 and 1970, and the Wisconsin court seemed to feel the gravitational force of the recent trend. By 1980, thirty-three jurisdictions had become subject to comparative negligence; eight employed the "pure" sort. See W. Schwartz, *Comparative Negligence* §§1.1-1.7 at 1-30 (1974), §§1.1-1.5 at 1-6 (1978 Supp.). See also Placek v. City of Sterling Heights, 405 Mich. 638, 653n.5, 275 N.W.2d 511, 515 n.5 (1979).

19. Pure comparative negligence was adopted judicially in Florida, California, Alaska, and Michigan. See Hoffman v. Jones, 280 So.2d 431 (Fla. 1973); Li v. Yellow Cab Co., 13 Cal. 3d 804, 119 Cal. Rptr. 858, 523 P.2d 1226 (1975); Kaatz v. State, 540 P.2d 1037 (Alaska 1975); Placek v. City of Sterling Heights, 405 Mich. 638, 275 N.W.2d 511 (1979). Courts had earlier modified the contributory negligence rules in Georgia and Tennessee. See Smith v. American Oil Co., 77 Ga. App. 243, 495 S.E.2d 90 (1948) (holding that the plaintiff cannot recover if the negligence of the plaintiff was greater than or equal to that of the defendant); and Bejach v.

Colby, 141 Tenn. 686, 214 S.W. 869 (1919) (holding that contributory negligence leading directly to the injury will bar an action, but remote contributory negligence only serves to mitigate damages). See Annot., 78 A.L.R. 3d 339 (1977). See also discussion of judicial adoption of comparative negligence in Chap. XI.

20. Vincent v. Pabst Brewing Co., 47 Wis. 2d 120, 177 N.W.2d 513 (1970). Three of the four opinions, see note 21, infra, rehearsed the standard arguments in favor of pure comparative negligence, although the author of one of the three opinions insisted that the change, however desirable, was for the legislature to make. Chief Justice Hallows was most vocal in his insistence that Wisconsin's limited comparative negligence statute was "not now in accord with modern concepts of social justice." 47 Wis. 2d at 135, 177 N.W.2d at 520.

21. Justice Hanley, joined by two other justices, was unsure as to whether pure comparative negligence was preferable to the modified comparative negligence embodied in the statute, but indicated that it was in any event inappropriate for the court to overturn a statute. He went on to note that the legislature then in session was considering a pure comparative negligence bill. Chief Justice Hallows, at the other extreme, was quite certain that changing to pure comparative negligence was both desirable and within the court's power and that the change should be made without regard to legislative activity on the subject. Justices Wilkie and Beilfuss agreed with Hallows on the merits of pure comparative negligence and that a change was within the court's authority, but preferred to wait until the legislature had a full chance to address the issue of pure comparative negligence. Justice Heffernan concurred in the result, refraining from altering the rule "in view of the legislature's present study of comparative negligence problems." 47 Wis. 2d at 131, 177 N.W.2d at 517. In his view adoption of pure comparative negligence was in the court's power, but, unlike the other three justices holding the majority view that the court could change the law, he expressed no opinion as to whether he would favor such change. Thus the legislature could predict that, if it did not act to change the law, the court would—but it was uncertain as to what rule the court would adopt. Neither Heffernan nor the other justices who refused to decide the case in view of legislative activity on the subject mentioned that a comparative negligence bill had in fact been introduced, to no avail, in both houses in the prior legislative session. (1969 Senate & Assembly Journal Index.) It seems apparent that it was the court's action in *Vincent* that induced a decisive legislative reconsideration in the 1971 session. See note 22, infra.

22. "After the mandate of *Vincent* . . . the legislature enacted ch. 47 of the Laws of 1971, published on June 22, 1971. That statutory modification struck from the statute the words 'as great as' and substituted therefor the words 'greater than.' Under this statutory modification, plaintiffs found 50 percent negligent will be able to recover 50 percent of their damages from a defendant who is found to be equally at fault. The point at which a plaintiff is barred from recovering has been raised by one percentile point." Lupie v.

Hartzheim, 54 Wis.2d 415, 417, 195 N.W.2d 461, 462 (1972).

23. Chief Justice Hallows quoted Frankfurter's witticism: "Wisdom too often never comes, and so one ought not to reject it merely because it comes late." 47 Wis.2d at 141, 177 N.W.2d at 523. The cite of Frankfurter by Hallows is ironic in a second sense as well. In the FELA cases, as we saw, note 14, supra, Frankfurter argued for a narrow interpretation so that Congress would be induced to enact workmen's compensation. Hallows agreed with Frankfurter's view of legislative dynamics, but was much less convinced of the merits of nonfault liability. Hallows's stated reason for advocating comparative negligence was his "fear . . . that if the doctrine of pure comparative negligence is not adopted, the whole fault system in torts will be repudiated and a no-fault system akin to workmen's compensation adopted." 47 Wis.2d at 138, 177 N.W.2d at 521.

24. The full passage reads: "The history of this statute is clear that it was a reaction against the doctrine of contributory negligence but there is nothing in its history or in its language which evinces any intent to preempt this field of common law to the exclusion of this court . . . The doctrine of pre-emption applied to common-law areas should rest only on affirmative action; otherwise, the death of the common law is near at hand." Vincent v. Pabst Brewing Co., 47 Wis.2d 120, 140-141, 177 N.W.2d 513, 522-523 (1970). By this hyperbolic language Hallows meant that the mere fact that the legislature recognizes a common law distinction as incidental to legislation need not be taken as legislative preemption of further common law development. In this case, however, his analysis of the intention of the original legislature is, to say the least, debatable. See note 27, infra.

25. It is significant that even after the legislature had rejected pure comparative negligence, Chief Justice Hallows continued to urge the court to alter the statute. See his lone dissents in Lupie v. Hartzheim, 54 Wis.2d 415, 418, 195 N.W.2d 461, 462 (1972), and Gross v. Denow, 61 Wis.2d 40, 53-60, 212 N.W.2d 210-13 (1973). His staunch support of pure comparative negligence leads one to believe that when deciding *Vincent*, had he been unable to claim that the legislative intent to preempt was not explicit, he would have been willing to listen to constitutional arguments. A decision overturning the statute on those grounds would have been an act of "virulent interventionism", but because of the availability of interpretation techniques and a call for legislative reconsideration, the Wisconsin court did not face this question.

26. Moragne v. States Marine Lines, 398 U.S. 375 (1970), discussed in Note, "The Legitimacy of Civil Law Reasoning in the Common Law: Justice Harlan's Contribution," 82 *Yale L. J.* 258 (1972). See also discussion of *Moragne,* Chap. XI, text at notes 15-19.

27. The legislative draftsman, in an article written after the 1931 statute was passed, gave no hint that the legislature had left any room for court action on the rule of comparative negligence itself. "Under Chapter 242, inquiry must be made to ascertain who is most negligent in order to fix liability on him." Padway, "Comparative Negligence," 16 *Marquette L. Rev.* 3, 7 (1931).

28. There are two reasons why one might be concerned with the words of a statute in interpretation. One might believe that legislative language is an indication of legislative intent. See note 30, infra. Aside from this, one may not wish to allow courts to flout the social conventions of language, which is after all an artifact of all of society, not just of the judiciary or the law. If it is impossible to control the judiciary with language, then passage of statutes is a waste of time — as is the promulgation of common law rules. See H. Hart and A. Sacks, supra note 1, at 1218-26. Thus, although Wellington admits that sometimes a court should ignore a discernible legislative intent — where the statute is close to a constitutional line, would subvert a common law principle, or delegates to the courts a role for which they are unsuited — he believes that, nevertheless, courts should do nothing "incompatible with a decent respect for the English language. The result must be containable in the words of a statute." Bickel and Wellington, "Legislative Purpose and the Judicial Process: The Lincoln Mills Case," 71 *Harv. L. Rev.* 1, 30 (1957). See also Wellington and Albert, "Statutory Interpretation and the Political Process: A Comment on Sinclair v. Atkinson," 72 *Yale L. J.* 1547, 1559-66 (1963); Wellington, supra note 2, at 262-264. Wellington's concern for preserving the social conventions of language does not go so far as to endorse literalism; there is no indication that he would feel compelled to follow a literal reading where purposive interpretation indicates a different construction. See note 30, infra. If this is true then, despite his protestations, the words of a statute are important to Wellington also because they suggest something about legislative intent.

29. A distinction is frequently drawn between statutory and constitutional interpretation. Justice Roberts stated the classical view of flexibility of constitutional construction: "though the words . . . have remained essentially what they were in 1787, the high bench itself has come to recognize that the proper interpretation of that instrument does change to meet the new demands imposed by changed external conditions. The Constitution must be capable of adaptation to needs that were wholly unforeseen by the Founding Fathers; else, it is less a document intended to endure through the ages than a government's suicide pact." B. Schwartz, *The Reins of Power* 156-157 (1965). Yet few if any argue consistently that "changes in external conditions" are sufficient reason to overrule prior statutory interpretations. The contrary, orthodox view is given by E. Levi, *An Introduction to Legal Reasoning* 32 (1949): "Once a decisive interpretation of legislative intent has been made, and in that sense a direction has been fixed within the gap of ambiguity, the court should take that direction as given." This is said to be true, *a fortiori*, when the legislature spoke clearly on a particular issue in the first instance.

What is the the source of the difference between constitutional and statutory construction? The obvious answer is that statutes are much easier to amend than the Constitution, which we want to maintain as a stable document for the protection of some of the rights on which it does speak clearly. Equally important, however, is subject matter: the Constitution concerns basic issues and is written at a fairly high level of generality.

There is no compelling reason why organic statutes (such as the Judiciary Act, Title 28, U.S.C.) or broad codes cannot be interpreted much like a Constitution. And indeed they have been. As we have seen, however, clearly worded statutes, loaded with obstacles for those judges who would make their interpretations evolve with the times, have replaced the common law and even broad codes over much of their original territory. Since the legislature does not, and probably cannot, amend the great variety of statutes it has created when the forces that brought them about change, the need arises for some new manner of keeping statutes, as well as constitutions and codes, up to date.

30. There is no consensus on what courts should be doing when they interpret statutes. For the purpose of this book, it does not matter which of various theories of interpretation is accepted; some alternative mechanism to update statutes would still be desirable.

The broad proposition that courts in interpreting statutes seek the "original legislative intent" finds support in countless cases. If this view of interpretation is accepted, it follows that statutory obsolescence cannot be dealt with by honest interpretation. For honest interpretation would require that the court apply the law as envisioned by a legislative body that met in the past.

The framework of original legislative intent permits widely different degrees of freedom in interpretation. Some courts apply a "plain-meaning test" and only look for legislative purpose if statutory words are not clear on their face. Other courts search for the original congressional purpose. A third group of courts adhere to the "last-resort" approach.

The plain-meaning test, which argues that an unambiguous statute leaves no room for interpretation, is still popular, despite much justified criticism. See H. Hart and A. Sacks, supra note 1, at 1144-1200. A notorious example of the application of this test is Caminetti v. United States, 242 U.S. 470, 489-90 (1917), which interpreted the Mann or White Slave Traffic Act (banning the taking of women across state lines for immoral purposes) as applying to the taking of a "concubine and mistress" to a neighboring state: "it has been so often affirmed as to become a recognized rule, when words are free from doubt they must be taken as the final expression of legislative intent."

This literalist approach has been disapproved by the Supreme Court and replaced with the second approach mentioned above, which seeks to discern and apply the original legislative purpose. See, e.g., Train v. Colorado Public Interest Research Group, 426 U.S. 1, 10 (1976): "When aid to construction of the meaning of words, as used in the statute, is available, there certainly can be no 'rule of law' which forbids its use, however clear the words may appear on 'superficial examination.' " In Boys Market, Inc. v. Retail Clerks Local 770, 398 U.S. 235 (1970) (creating an exception in the absolute language of §64 of the Norris-La Guardia Act barring certain types of antistrike injunctions), this approach was used to apply the "core purpose" of a statute to new facts even though the statute, read literally, forbade such application.

This by no means new approach, see text at notes 2 and 3 supra, will give acceptable results when a still-valid legislative purpose confronts new fact situations. It is of no help, when changes in the legal fabric render even the legislative policy-determination outdated.

The third approach, the 'last resort' of H. Hart and A. Sacks, supra note 1, is taken up by R. Keeton, supra note 2, and Wellington, supra note 2, at 262-265. This approach would have the courts take responsibility for creating the best rule of law in a situation in which a statute is said to govern. The court should use common law policies, augmented by statutory ones, to make the "best" law. All concede that exercise of this power is only legitimate when original legislative intent is not clear. Even under this view, therefore, it is still extraordinarily difficult to use inter-pretation to modernize statutes whose application to a given situation is un-questioned, whether because of precise language or legislative history, or because intent was made explicit, or, finally, because there has been a definitive prior interpretation.

I am much more sanguine than some — e.g., Wellington, supra note 2, that such meaningful original intent can often be found if one honestly sear-ches for it. But it is far from clear that a court will be anxious to seek for an "original governing legislative will" if finding it only serves to prevent the court from imposing the rule it considers most consistent with current conditions. See, e.g., Eck v. United Arab Airlines, 15 N.Y.2d 53, 203 N.E. 2d 640 (1964). The Warsaw Convention barred plaintiffs from suit against a foreign airline except where the airline "has a place of business *through which the contract has been made"* (emphasis added), but the New York Court of Appeals in effect excised the italicized words from the treaty. It seems obvious that one of the purposes of the parties to the Convention was to limit the places at which an air carrier could be sued. This intent was ig-nored in the court's analysis. Whatever the merits of the *Eck* decision — the rule rejected by *Eck* may well have been an appropriate subject of judicial sunsetting, see Chap. X — it should serve to remind us that by misidentify-ing purpose or by making a purpose inquiry at a sufficiently high level of generality ("The Convention was intended to promote air traffic"), a court can obtain almost any result it wishes. Such a view may lead to some results closer to those that would flow from adoption of the doctrine I shall discuss than would occur if the court sought to find "legislative intent."

Legislative intent is not the sine qua non of interpretation in all cases. It is accepted that the legislature may not approach constitutional invalidity without being explicit; it is not enough, as in Kent v. Dulles, 357 U.S. 116 (1958), that a constitutionally dubious result was most likely intended. See A. Bickel, *The Least Dangerous Branch: The Supreme Court at the Bar of Politics* (1962), and Chap. III, text at notes 6-8. That "statutes in derogation of the common law are to be strictly construed," and that "statutory repeal by implication is disfavored," are other examples of court imposed "clear state-ment" requirements. See also Wellington, supra note 2. While application of all these various clear statement principles is normally coupled with a dubious bow to legislative intent (e.g., the legislature must be deemed to intend to avoid constitutionally doubtful statutes), it is obvious that in many cases they supersede the most likely but not explicitly stated legislative intent. See H. Hart and A. Sacks, supra note 1, at 1412-13. Such clear-statement principles, in short, are a form of functional interpretation designed to maximize the consistency of a given statute with the constitutional, statutory, and common law landscape. But even if such a clear-statement principle came to be freely employed outside its most frequent area of application, the constitutional sphere, the principle would still apply comfortably only to statutes that are *at the time of their passage* inconsistent with some part of the legal landscape. As a result it would fail to keep up to date many statutes whose incongruity developed only over time, unless one invented a fictional legislative intent that statutes be always kept current. See also note 39, infra.

31. Gunther, "The Subtle Vices of the 'Passive Virtues' — A Comment on Principle and Expediency in Judicial Review," 64 *Colum. L. Rev.* 1 (1964). While not all statutes are constitutionally doubtful, all of them need interpretation, so that a court willing to interpret creatively enough could make the "virulent variety of free-wheeling interventionism" of constitutionally active courts seem timid by comparison. Id. at 25.

32. For example, New York does not permit the recovery of damages for pain and suffering, loss of society, and grief of relatives in its wrongful-death action. *New York Est. Powers & Trusts Law* §§5-4.1 to 5-4.5 (1967). On the general problem of wrongful death and survival statutes, see W. Prosser, *The Law of Torts* §§126-127 (1971), and S. Speiser, *Recovery for Wrongful Death* 103-116, 407-55 (2d ed. 1975).

33. See S. Speiser, supra note 32, at 689-695, §§7:1-7:4.

34. Some states maintain limits on wrongful death recovery for special circumstances. Colorado, Kansas, Maine, and Wisconsin, for example, limit nonpecuniary damages recoverable by relatives. See *Colo. Rev. Stat.* §13-21-203 (1973), *Kan. Stat. Ann.* §60-1903 (1976), *Me. Rev. Stat. Ann.* tit. 18A, §2-804 (1980 Supp.), and *Wis. Stat. Ann.* §895.04 (West 1979 Supp.). Most other states allow the jury full leeway in awarding damages for each category of damages recoverable, subject of course to general rules of *additur* and *remittitur.*

35. For example, in 1968 I received a letter from Haywood Burns of the NAACP Legal Defense Fund, asking for advice on the constitutionality of the Louisiana Workmen's Compensation Law. Since the nonfault compensation remedy was exclusive, injured workers like Burns's client were barred from instituting tort actions; yet the workmen's compensation benefits were limited to a maximum of $35 a week. As he put it, "this arrangement has the effect of statutorily impoverishing large numbers of injured employees." In the FELA cases, discussed in notes 5-14, supra, Justice Frankfurter was quite sure that workmen's compensation statutes should

replace the "archaic and cruel" FELA negligence action remedy. In theory he may well have been right, but plaintiffs like Burns's client have discovered that a rapidly aging statute can become older and much more stingy than the "archaic" common law. See also Chap. III, note 16.

36. See, e.g., W. Prosser, supra note 32, §74, at 488-491.

37. Even apart from explicit statutory language, however, courts frequently are reluctant to update death statutes. See, e.g., Justus v. Atchison, 19 Cal. 3d 564, 139 Cal. Rptr. 97, 565 P.2d 122 (1977), in which the California Supreme Court denied recovery for the wrongful death of a stillborn child. The court found that the action for wrongful death was a creature of statute and that interpretation of the statute must rely on the original legislative intent rather than on the "evolving common law." Following this rule the court held that a fetus was not a person within the meaning of the wrongful death statute. It did this notwithstanding the contrary weight of recent authority and the fact that its own holding, in Keeler v. Superior Court, 2 Cal. 3d 619, 87 Cal. Rptr. 481, 470 P.2d 617 (1970), that the intentional killing of a viable fetus was not homicide, had been speedily reversed by the state legislature. 1970 *Cal. Stats.*, ch. 1311, §1, p. 2440, amending *Cal. Penal Code* §187.

38. See the California cases declaring guest acts unconstitutional, Chap. II, notes 15-18.

39. Courts sometimes do act (though rarely talk) as if the scope of interpretation were limitless. But cf. People v. Daniels, 71 Cal.2d 1119, 80 Cal. Rptr. 897, 459 P.2d 225 (1969) (overruling earlier court interpretations of the California kidnaping statute: "It continues to be our duty to decide each case that comes before us; in so doing, we must apply every statute in the case according to our best understanding of the legislative intent; and in the absence of further guidance by the Legislature, we should not hesitate to reconsider our prior construction of that intent whenever such a course is dictated by the teachings of time and experience." 71 Cal.2d at 1128, 80 Cal. Rptr. at 902, 459 P.2d at 230. If this position were held consistently, so that changes in the legal landscape were taken as arguments for reinterpreting statutes, whatever their history or language, courts would approach the doctrine I describe in this book. But then limits on the practice of interpretation, analogous to those I will discuss in Chaps. X and XI, would become imperative. At present, when courts claim that interpretation is no more than an analysis of language or a backward-looking search for legislative intent, it is unlikely that such essential limits will be developed. And, since no appropriate guidelines are developed and used as a standard for decision, some "willful" courts may reinterpret a statute to suit themselves, although the original intent is both discernible and valid and the old law still fits the legal landscape. Other "rigid" courts may refuse to update a statute that is hopelessly out of phase with prevailing conditions, when that updating cannot honestly be done through interpretation.

40. See Gunther, supra note 31, at 6-10.

V. The New Deal Response: Administrative Agencies

1. See, e.g., Stern, "The Commerce Clause and the National Economy, 1933–46," 59 *Harv. L. Rev.* 645 (1946) (reviewing legislative activity in response to the depression); Schlesinger, "Sources of the New Deal," in *Paths of American Thought* 372-391 (A. Schlesinger, Jr., and M. White, eds. 1963) (describing Roosevelt's program as a pragmatic middle course between the adherents of the ideological left and right); and J. Landis, *The Administrative Process* 30 (1938) (describing the New Deal's distrust of the ability of the judicial process to make necessary adjustments in the development of law).

2. This faith was encapsulated in President Roosevelt's second inaugural address: "The essential democracy of our Nation and the safety of our people depend not upon the absence of power but upon lodging it with those whom the people can change or continue at stated intervals through an honest and free system of elections." Quoted in Holt, "The New Deal and the American Anti-Statist Tradition," in *The New Deal* 27, 43 (J. Braeman, ed. 1975). Further accounts of the New Deal's characteristic faith in a simple majoritarianism are found in Holt, supra, at 43-46, and in Hubert Humphrey's c.1939 master's thesis, published as H. Humphrey, *The Political Philosophy of the New Deal* (1970), esp. at 45-52.

3. The work of Herman Finer provides an example of this hope. In 1932, before the New Deal but after the onset of the Depression, Finer argued the desirability of the European cabinet system of government over the American system of separation of powers; see 1 H. Finer, *The Theory and Practice of Modern Government* 153-180 (1932). He also criticized the rigors of the American constitutional amendment process, id. at 196-200. In a 1946 update of his earlier work, Finer argued again that the presidency suffers from a "permanent weakness" — the separation of powers. See H. Finer, *The Future of Government* 126-127 (1946).

4. See Landis, "Statutes and the Sources of Law," *Harvard Legal Essays* 213 (1934), and especially his analysis of the effect that nineteenth-century bastardy laws had on the interpretation of wills and on the appropriate construction of wrongful-death statutes, discussed in Chap. VIII, note 17. See also Stone, "The Common Law in the United States," 50 *Harv. L. Rev.* 4 (1936).

5. See J. Landis, supra note 1. See also Friendly, "A Look at the Federal Administrative Agencies," 60 *Colum. L. Rev.* 429 (1960), and H. Friendly, *The Federal Administrative Agencies: The Need for Better Definition of Standards* (1962), which sketch the development of certain of the independent agencies — ICC, NLRB, FTC, CAB. Perhaps the dominant explanation for the growth of agencies is the perception that they were needed to respond to the economic catastrophe of the times. See, e.g., Stern, supra note 1. Agencies were thought to have greater institutional capacity than legislatures to examine technical, specialized problems and to frame an appropriate response. See, e.g., Jaffe, "An Essay on Delegation of Power, Part I,"

47 *Colum. L. Rev.* 359, 361-363 (1947). In addition, Congress then and since has been described as simply unable to handle the full load of its legislative responsibilities without help. See, e.g., H. Friendly, supra at 167; see also Jaffe, "Administrative Process Re-examined: The Benjamin Report," 56 *Harv. L. Rev.* 705, 725 (1943) (Congress has "other fish to fry"). These theories, and indeed the bulk of my discussion, apply to both dependent and independent agencies (those agencies over whose members the President has no formal power, see K. Davis, *Administrative Law: Cases — Text — Problems,* 12-18 (6th ed. 1977)). However, it is worth noting that part of the justification given for the independence of some agencies is the desire to have agency commissioners be less subject to political influence, because in some of their functions they were to behave like judges. See id. at 13.

6. See Friendly, supra note 5, at 431, and Final Report of the Attorney General's Committee on Administrative Procedure, S. Doc. No. 3, 77th Cong., 1st Sess., 20 (1941) ("Taken together, the various Federal administrative agencies have the responsibility for making good to the people of the country a major part of the gains of a hundred and fifty years of democratic government"), and sources cited supra note 2. See also President's Committee on Administrative Management, *Administrative Management in the United States* 36 (1937): the administrative agencies "constitute a headless 'fourth branch' of the Government, a haphazard deposit of irresponsible agencies and uncoordinated powers. They do violence to the basic theory of the American Constitution that there should be three major branches of the Government and only three."

7. See, e.g., Stewart, "The Reformation of American Administrative Law," 88 *Harv. L. Rev.* 1667, 1671-88 (1975); Freedman, "Crisis and Legitimacy in the Administrative Process," 27 *Stan. L. Rev.* 1041, 1041-64 (1975). On the difficulties of deriving a determinate "legislative intent," see Chap. IV.

8. The paradigmatic New Deal statute delegated to the agency the power to act "in the public interest" as new problems arose. See, e.g., Communications Act of 1934, ch. 652, title III, §307, 48 Stat. 1083, codified at 47 U.S.C. 307(a) (1976) ("public convenience, interest or necessity" standard for licensing radio stations). A more recent example is found in the Occupational Safety and Health Act of 1970, Pub. L. 91-956, §6, 84 Stat. 1593, codified at 29 U.S.C. § 655b (1976) (provision for modifying safety standards as a result of, inter alia, new "research, demonstrations and experiments" so as to "serve the objectives of this chapter").

Even when the statutes do not seem to delegate such a flexible power, courts have allowed agencies a fairly broad "discretion" to implement statutory terms flexibly when circumstances are viewed by the agency as changing. The National Labor Relations Act section codified at 29 U.S.C. §152(3) (1976), for example, which defines "employee" for the purposes of the Act, contains no mandate to the agency to reinterpret in line with changing conditions. Yet the Supreme Court in National Labor Relations Board v. Hearst Publications, 322 U.S. 111 (1944), held that the Wagner

Act definition of employee was not a question of "statutory interpretation for the courts to resolve" but one of "specific application of a broad statutory term" for the agency. By this means, the Court noted, the intent of Congress could be effected in new situations. The refusal to speak of statutory interpretation allowed agencies flexibility to keep statutory mandates up to date. See also Packard Motor Co. v. National Labor Relations Board, 330 U.S. 485 (1947), esp. at 491-492 (novel application of "employee" to foremen accepted by Court); National Labor Relations Board v. Bell Aerospace Co., 416 U.S. 267 (1974) (clear intent of Congress and settled administrative construction prevented agency from making a particular expansion of "employee").

The agencies' responsibility to adapt to changing circumstances explains other legal doctrines, such as the reluctance of agencies to apply rules of *stare decisis*. There can be no quarrel with the Interstate Commerce Commission's early statement that it does not have "the same reason for applying the maxim *stare decisis* which exists in courts of law." Board of R.R. Comm'rs v. Atchison, T. & S.F. Ry., 8 I.C.C. 304, 308 (1899). For example, the ICC would surely be justified in taking a different view today as to the degree to which a reduction in rail competition should preclude approval of a merger from the view it would have taken when railways had a near monopoly. But cf. American Glue Co. v. Boston & M. R.R., 191 I.C.C. 37, 39 (1932).

9. See, e.g., the FCC's regulation in the mid-1960s of community antenna television (CATV) systems. A challenge to the FCC's power to enact these regulations under the Communications Act of 1934, 48 Stat. 1064, 47 U.S.C. §151, was upheld by the Ninth Circuit in Southwestern Cable Co. v. United States, 378 F.2d 118 (9th Cir. 1967), but a unanimous Supreme Court reversed, 392 U.S. 157 (1968). While conceding that "certainly Congress could not in 1934 have foreseen the development of community antenna television systems," the Court held that Congress in passing the act had recognized "the rapidly fluctuating factors characteristic of the evolution of broadcasting" and "the corresponding requirement that the administrative process possess sufficient flexibility to adjust itself to these factors." Id., 392 U.S. at 172-173. H. Friendly, supra note 5, cites two more examples: the Federal Reserve Board's regulation of margin requirements, authorized by 15 U.S.C. §78g, and the SEC's laying down rules to govern short sales, authorized by 15 U.S.C. 78j. "Here it is plain — that the legislature did not 'bring to a close the making of the law,' and that the agency is doing the kind of thing the legislature might well have done on its own account were it not for the need of frequent and rapid change. In such cases the very lack of any effective action by the legislature usually compels the agency rather speedily to frame rules and regulations which supply the needed definition . . . In such instances the regulators have stated in fairly definite terms what the regulated may do and what they may not; if the regulated do not like the prescription, they may endeavor to have it changed either by the agency or, failing that, by the Congress; meanwhile they

know where they stand and that they all stand alike." Id. at 7 (citations omitted) (citing Justice Jackson's dissent in FTC v. Ruberoid Co., 343 U.S. 470, 486 (1952)).

10. See text at notes 44-45, infra, and at Chap. XI, notes 44-58.

11. See, e.g., Cutler and Johnson, "Regulation and the Political Process," 84 *Yale L. J.* 1395, 1408 n.43 (1975) (citing Justice Black's suggestion that every statute creating a new agency should limit the life of the agency to fourteen years); id. at 1414-17 (outlining their own recommendation of greater presidential intervention in the regulatory process); T. Lowi, *The End of Liberalism* 309 (1969) (proposing a Tenure of Statutes Act requiring agencies to be renewed every five to ten years). For a more complete discussion of sunsetting, see Chap. VI.

12. Cf. note 36, infra.

13. Cf. H. Friendly, supra note 5, and Gardner, "The Administrative Process," excerpted in W. Gellhorn and C. Byse, *Administrative Law: Cases and Comments* 24, 28 (6th ed. 1974) (agency most interested in bringing to life its own program). See also text at notes 32-43, infra.

14. See Chap. IX.

15. Cf. R. Dworkin, *Taking Rights Seriously* (1977); Wellington, "Common Law Rules and Constitutional Double Standards: Some Notes on Adjudication," 83 *Yale L. J.* 221 (1973).

16. See, e.g., R. Nader, *Unsafe at Any Speed* 232-294 (1965), and T. Lowi, supra note 11. Even such a stout defender of agencies as James M. Landis noted, as early as 1938: "The pressing problem today . . . is to get the administrative to assume the responsibilities that it properly should assume . . . The assumption of responsibility by an agency is always a gamble that may well make more enemies than friends. The easiest course is frequently that of inaction." J. Landis, supra note 1, at 75. Cf. H. Friendly, supra note 5, at viii: "the basic deficiency, which underlies and accounts for the most serious troubles of the agencies, is the failure to 'make law' within the broad confines of the agencies' charters." For another criticism, see Hector's letter to President Eisenhower, announcing his resignation from the CAB, published in Hector, "Problems of the CAB and the Independent Regulatory Commissions," 69 *Yale L. J.* 931 (1960): "The CAB is a creature imprisoned by its own structure and procedures. It is unable to form clear policy. It is unable to make sound and comprehensive plans. It is unable to administer its affairs with vigor and dispatch." Id. at 931.

17. For an example of aggressive agency action see note 36, infra, and Chap. XI, notes 51-56. See also note 30, infra. For a recent and on the whole favorable chronicle of agency action see R. Kagan, *Regulatory Justice: Implementing a Wage-Price Freeze* (1978).

18. See, e.g., American Automobile Parts & Accessories Association v. Boyd, 407 F.2d 330 (D.C.Cir. 1968). Plaintiffs were independent parts manufacturers of, among other things, automobile head restraints. They sought to invalidate (on grounds of irregularities in violation of the Administrative Procedure Act) the Federal Highway Administrator's regulation

requiring factory installation of head restraints. As the Court noted, 407 F.2d at 332, the real issue was the plaintiff's competitive position once the regulation was official. If head restraints were factory-installed, the automobile purchaser would buy the head restraint from the automobile manufacturer at the time of the car purchase, and not from the independent manufacturers. The Administrator, seeking to ensure that every automobile was equipped with an adequate restraint system, mandated factory-installed restraints rather than plaintiff's proposed alternative of equipment standards for the head restraints. That the Administrator's solution might adversely affect the competitive structure of the industry seemed of little interest to him, since, one assumes, the statute was concerned with safety and not competition. The Court found no violation of the Administrative Procedure Act, however, and so it rejected the plaintiffs' case without reaching what it had described as the real issue.

19. See, e.g., Peltzman, "The Benefits and Costs of New Drug Regulation," in *Regulating New Drugs* (R. Landau, ed. 1973). Peltzman describes the 1962 amendments to the Food, Drug and Cosmetic Act as resulting, at least in part, from the impact on the public consciousness of the thalidomide drug episode of 1961–62. Even though the tragedies resulting from the use of thalidomide were largely confined to Western Europe, reports of the episode aroused concern that testing of new drugs was insufficiently regulated. In his article, Peltzman tries to calculate the overall costs and benefits of the 1962 amendments to the consumer and concludes that the pre-amendment arrangements were better, largely because of the loss of innovation in drugs as a result of the amendments. He continues: "If, as now seems likely, there will be no substantial reduction of the formal restraints embodied in the Amendments, one must be pessimistic that any substantial reduction in the costs they have generated will be accomplished by purely administrative changes. The FDA is, after all, confronted by the same political forces that militate in favor of legislative inertia. Moreover, the FDA can expect little of the reward for extremely successful innovations, but substantial cost for wrongly certifying an unsafe or ineffective drug." Id. at 208.

There are at least two distinct factors that could conspire to make agencies avoid taking risks. The first centers on the greater risk involved in acting than in failing to act. Harm resulting from action is more readily attributed to the bureaucrat than harm from inaction. Cf. Calabresi, "The Problem of Malpractice: Trying to Round Out the Circle," 27 *U. Toronto L. J.* 131, 136 (1977): "In almost every instance, for every treatment which, if it goes wrong as sometimes it will, gives rise to a compensable loss, there exists a substitute treatment or non-treatment whose harm in practice would not be recognized as a compensable loss. This problem in the decision-makers is compounded by the fact that the victim is equally 'biased' in what he or she can recognize as a cost which can give rise to compensation. In other words, almost inevitably, the fault-malpractice system penalizes some medical maloccurrences and some avoidance costs while systematically failing to penalize the medical maloccurrence and avoidance costs of substitute approaches." The second centers on the tendency for the agency to retain past approaches as a source of power, regardless of their present desirability. See A. Downs, *Inside Bureaucracy* 96-101 (1967), describing the bureaucrat he labels the "Conserver": one who rises to the top of the hierarchy by eliminating as few as possible past programs of that bureaucracy, thereby maintaining or possibly expanding the bureaucracy's sphere of influence.

20. See, e.g., Peltzman, supra note 19; A. Downs, supra note 19; J. Landis, supra note 16.

21. See, e.g., M. Bernstein, *Regulating Business by Independent Commission* 183-187 (1955).

22. This is obviously apparent in the cases of those agencies designed to, or which had come to, protect the regulated industries. See, e.g., Jaffe, "The Effective Limits of the Administrative Process: A Reevaluation," 67 *Harv. L. Rev.* 1105 (1954) (discussing the CAB and ICC). It is also true of other agencies that exist mainly to burden the regulated industries for the benefit of conflicting interests, such as consumers. The stability the agency bestows may well be deemed worth the cost by all but the marginal firms. See, e.g., Freedman, "Crisis and Legitimacy in the Administrative Process," 27 *Stan. L. Rev.* 1041, 1069-72 (1975) (discussing the SEC).

23. Cf. H. Friendly, supra note 5, at viii (administrators need to recognize legislators whose "bark is worse than their bite"), and Senator Dirksen's forthright statement of his practice of calling agencies. 105 *Cong. Rec.* 14057-59 (1959). See also J. Landis, supra note 1, at 60-61. In commenting on the response to their task by agencies that are more subject to political influences, Judge Friendly suggests that agencies are most likely to resolve problems in a piecemeal fashion, through *ad hoc* responses to particular pressures rather than by reference to the legal topography. Friendly's solution is for the legislature to provide "general legislative standards" to direct the agencies in their lawmaking. Id. at 22-23. See also Friendly, "A Look," supra note 5, at 437-439, 444-446. But see note 35, infra (questioning Friendly's solution). Occasionally, of course, well-placed legislators can induce an agency to make a change that they could not get through the legislature. The problem in such a case is not one of obsolescence but one of the legitimacy of the change. Cf. text at notes 28, 29, infra.

24. Cf. note 18, supra.

25. J. Schumpeter, *Capitalism, Socialism and Democracy* 99 (2nd ed. 1946): "pure cases of long run monopoly must be of the rarest occurrence."

26. Cf. M. Bernstein, supra note 21, at 74-102 (on the life cycle of an agency), esp. at 95: "The period of old age is unlikely to terminate until some scandal or emergency calls attention dramatically to the failure of regulation and the need to redefine regulatory objectives and public policies. In this fashion, the historical pattern of regulation might come full circle, although no important regulatory function of a commission has actually been eliminated." For another version of the life cycle of a regulatory agency see A. Downs, supra note 19, at 5-23.

27. See, e.g., R. Dworkin, supra note 15, and Wellington, supra note 15. See also Chap. IX.

28. See Chap. IX. We respect the courts' actions in part because courts share some, though only some, of the attributes of juries which have caused us to give juries wide powers. See text at notes 41-42, infra. The most important of these shared attributes is the incremental nature of court and jury decisions. One court's decision might be skewed with respect to the law or the legal topography, but that court's decision is not even the last judicial word on the subject. Other courts will render decisions with respect to similar cases in the same area of law, and those courts may distinguish or even ignore the one problematic result. Or other courts might well follow the first court's impetus, in which case the first decision will have triggered a slow reevaluation of that area of the law. The point is that developments in the landscape come about bit by bit, as a result of the actions of many courts, after a process of integration of that initial change. Juries are even more *ad hoc* or case-by-case; they are also in a deep sense majoritarian in their incremental lawmaking. See note 42, infra. In place of this last attribute, courts should substitute the promotion of consistency in the legal landscape. See note 27, supra.

29. I use these terms interchangeably.

30. These capacities — expertise, relative insulation from politics but responsiveness to broad policy guidance from the legislature — lead two observers to recommend the New Deal agency, with a specific form of statutory mandate, as one solution to the problem of making government activism work in general and, no doubt, with regard to updating in particular as well. Ackerman and Hassler, "Beyond the New Deal: Coal and the Clean Air Act," 89 *Yale L.J.* 1466, esp. 1471-79, 1566-71 (1980). This study of the Clean Air Act experience leads the authors to conclude that future policymakers would do well to consider legislation that would force agencies to define appropriate objectives and take steps to implement them, by a certain deadline. Cf. Chap. XI, text at notes 48-58, infra.

31. In this sense, at least, an agency's responsiveness to political influence may well be useful. Where a contrary course is not indicated by bureaucratic self-interest, an agency may respond flexibly in a manner that reflects current and rapidly shifting majoritarian sentiments. Even Kenneth Davis, perhaps the foremost advocate of limiting and structuring administrative discretion, argues that some such discretion is crucial to the adequate functioning of the administrative-legislative task. He has gone further: "When major policy under a statute containing no meaningful guides on the question is worked out through cooperation between a legislative committee and an agency, the governmental machinery may be operating as it should. Even when lobbyists are influencing the committeemen to oppose the agency's effort to protect the public interest as the agency sees it, the system may be sound; to condemn responsiveness of administrative policies to the strongest pressures would in some circumstances mean condemning the heart of democratic government." K. Davis, *Discretionary*

Justice: A Preliminary Inquiry 148 (1969). This accountability holds for independent agencies and, of course, even more for dependent agencies. Whether close accountability makes the agencies sensitive to changes in external social conditions, or, instead, only responsive to special interests that are politically well placed vis-à-vis that agency, depends on the nature of the accountability and on the nature of those who have the political influence. See note 23, supra, and note 35, infra.

32. For two examples where an agency failed to seek a broad consistency in the legal topography, see NLRB v. Virginia Electric & Power Co., 314 U.S. 469 (1941), and Textile Workers Union of America v. Darlington Manufacturing Co., 380 U.S. 263 (1965). In each case the Supreme Court remanded orders of the NLRB for further fact finding because the Court was concerned that the Board's finding of an unfair labor practice might inhibit certain important rights of the employer. In *Virginia Electric,* the Court was concerned that the Board not interfere with the employer's free speech rights; in *Darlington,* that the Board not interfere with the employer's right to close its business. I am not here concerned with whether the Court's view of those rights was correct. What is of interest to me is that the Supreme Court's decision was made with reference to a broader legal topography than that represented by the National Labor Relations Act.

More recently the Supreme Court has struggled, in interpreting congressional intent and specific language in the Occupational Safety and Health Act of 1970, 29 U.S.C. §651 et seq., with the question of whether safety standards under that law should reflect primarily the goal of the statute to protect workers at any cost, as the agency ruled, or those balances between the benefits and costs of safety which are said to prevail in our legal system at large. See Industrial Union Department, AFL-CIO v. American Petroleum Institute, 448 U.S. 607, 100 S.Ct. 2844 (1980). Once again I am less concerned with the correctness of either the agency's or the Court's viewpoint than with the different focus of attention of the two.

33. This is, at the least, one apparent explanation of the Federal Trade Commission's recent struggle to control advertising aimed at children. Congress' resulting attempt to "clip its wings" certainly shows that the FTC's goal was not fidelity to the congressional will. See *Senate Panel Backs Curbs on F.T.C.,* N.Y. Times, Nov. 21, 1979, at 5, col. 4; *House Votes, 321 to 63, to Allow Congress to Veto F.T.C. Rulings,* N.Y. Times, Nov. 28, 1979 at 1, col. 1. See also J. Landis, supra note 1, at 75: "One of the ablest administrators that it was my good fortune to know, I believe, never read, at least more than casually, the statutes that he translated into reality. He assumed that they gave him power to deal with the broad problems of an industry and, upon that understanding, he sought his own solutions."

34. See text at notes 41-43, infra (comparing our willingness to grant broad powers to juries).

35. See note 23, supra. It is true that H. Friendly, *The Federal Administrative Agencies,* supra note 5, argues that better definition of standards would diminish political pressures on administrators. Judge Friendly complains

that agencies fail "to develop standards sufficiently definite to permit decisions to be fairly predictable and the reasons for them to be understood."
Id. at 5-6. It may well be that this failure is unfair to those whose lives or
properties are regulated by agencies. But it would be wrong to believe that
what would correct the failures would also suffice to make agencies good
updaters of outworn laws. It is plausible that the most important focus of
political influence on agencies is covertly exercised with respect to what is
unseen about agency behavior, and indeed what is *not* done by an agency,
where standards are hard to formulate. See K. Davis, supra note 31, at
3-26. Finally, sometimes it would be impossible for Congress to frame standards that would at the same time provide guidance to agencies and approach sensible substantive results. See Ackerman and Hassler, supra note
30.

36. One recent dramatic example of this kind of agency action was examined by the D.C. Circuit Court of Appeals in American Bankers Ass'n
v. Connell, (1978-1979 Transfer Binder), *Fed. Banking L. Rep.* (CCH)
Para. 97,785 (D.C. Cir. Apr. 20, 1979), *disposition noted,* 595 F.2d 887.
(Copy on file at Yale Law School Library). At issue were three different sets
of regulations, promulgated by three different regulatory bodies, that con-
verged in allowing the same piece of updating: the development of Automatic Fund Transfer systems for banks, credit unions, and savings institutions. Notwithstanding the convergence, and the apparent societal need for
the regulations, the Circuit Court played its own hand in the game of
legislative reconsideration. After suggesting that the law, unaltered by the
regulations, was likely to be out of date, the court nevertheless set aside all
three sets of regulations as having no legislative basis. The court discoursed
on the importance of legislative supremacy and lectured the agencies on the
undesirability of substituting their judgments for that of the legislature. It
then, rather startlingly, stayed its own order for eight months: "We do so
with the firm expectation that the Congress will speedily review the overall
situation and make such policy judgment as in its wisdom it deems necessary by authorizing in whole or in part the methods of fund transfer
involved in this case, or any other methods it sees fit to legitimize, or conversely, by declining to alter the language of existing statutes, thus sustaining the meaning and policy expressed in those statutes as now construed by
this court." Id., opinion at 3. The net effect of announcing that in eight
months the court would return to what was generally accepted to be an out-
rageously outdated starting point was to force Congress to reconsider the issue without permitting the agencies to shape or delay that congressional review by imposing what, to them, seemed a desirable updated set of rules.
See Chap. XI, notes 51-56, and accompanying text.

37. See note 32, supra.

38. Cf. R. Dworkin, supra note 15, at 71-80, 90-100, and Wellington,
supra note 15, at 230-254.

39. See Chap. IX.

40. See Chap. VII.

41. One can raise some questions when a new law skates close to the line of constitutional invalidity, represents the last gasp of a dying majority or the attempt of a temporary coalition or majority to give permanence to its policies, or perhaps is the modern equivalent of a statute in derogation of well-established common law principles. See Chaps. III and IX. All in all, however, such instances do not detract fundamentally from the notion expressed in the text. Cf. Davies, "A Response to Statutory Obsolescence: The Nonprimacy of Statutes Act," 4 *Vermont L. Rev.* 203 (1979) (act applying only to statutes that are twenty years old).

42. Cf. G. Calabresi and P. Bobbitt, *Tragic Choices* 57-59, ch. 3, nn. 30-31 (1978) and Calabresi, "*Bakke* as Pseudo Tragedy," 28 *Cath. U. L. Rev.* 427, 429-432 (1979).

43. This is of course the aim of the extraordinarily interesting proposal made by Cutler and Johnson, supra note 11, at 1414-17. Cutler and Johnson would give the President power to intervene in the regulatory process, subject to the veto of either house of Congress. The single-house veto is designed to place some checks on the Executive, but the thrust of the suggestion is clearly to allow the updating of rules, in the regulatory area, on the basis of the President's view of current majoritarian needs. But such updating, which would surely give us change, might violate the traditional American desire for continuity and for strictly limited power, even in majoritarian bodies. It would do so to a greater extent if the President were permitted to issue a detailed new set of regulations to which the legislature had to react — a "decree law" subject to a one-house veto. It would do so considerably less if the President were limited to forcing a legislative reconsideration of the offending regulation. Cf. Chap. XI. We might not always be comfortable with the assumption that the President speaks as one with the current majority. Similar doubts may be responsible for Cutler's recent move toward advocating a parliamentary system. See Chap. VII, note 2, and Chap. IX, note 74. Even apart from the issue of presidential power, one would have to ask whether the Cutler-Johnson approach, if extended beyond the regulatory area, would solve the problem of legal obsolescence. This in turn depends on whether legal obsolescence demonstrates itself primarily in statutes that a busy executive decides are no longer majoritarian, or also in laws whose lack of popular base is demonstrated by the fact that they no longer fit in the legal fabric. See Chap. IX; also Chap. VI, text at notes 11-20.

44. See notes 8, 9, and 30, supra. Given a statutory mandate and a subject matter that allow the agency "clarity of definition in the statement of . . . most basic policies," one could expect an agency to keep its statute up to date in terms of its basic policies. See Freedman, supra note 22, at 169-172 (attributing SEC success to manageable mandate and resulting "steadiness of vision").

45. See Chap. XI, text at notes 35-58.

VI. Legislative Responses

1. See, e.g., Price-Anderson Act, Pub. L. 85-256, 71 Stat. 576 (1975), codified at 42 U.S.C. §2210 (1976), which by its terms would have expired in ten years were it not reenacted. In fact, it has twice been reenacted for additional ten-year periods. See Duke Power Co. v. Carolina Environment Study Group, 438 U.S. 59, 64-67 (1978).

2. 5 *The Writings of Thomas Jefferson* 121 (Paul Ford ed. 1895): "no society can make a perpetual constitution, or even a perpetual law. The earth belongs always to the living generation. They may manage it then, and what proceeds from it, as they please, during their usufruct. They are masters too of their own persons, and consequently may govern them as they please. But persons and property make the sum of the objects of government. The constitution and the laws of their predecessors extinguished them in their natural course, with those whose will gave them being. This could preserve that being till it ceased to be itself, and no longer. Every constitution, then, and every law, naturally expires at the end of 19 years. If it be enforced longer, it is an act of force and not of right."

3. See Chap. X for a discussion of the bases of our retentionist bias.

4. "According to Washington folklore, Justice Black suggested that every statute creating a new agency should limit its life to 14 years." Cutler and Johnson, "Regulation and the Political Process," 84 *Yale L. J.* 1395, 1408 n.43 (1975). Justice Black said as much to me in personal conversation and, indeed, in his view statutory obsolescence was not limited solely to statutes setting up regulatory agencies. The proposed but rejected sunset law of 1977, S. 2, would have subjected virtually all federal programs to sunset and would have codified such a notion of universal statutory obsolescence. See *The Sunset Act of 1977: Hearings before the Subcommittee on Intergovernmental Relations of the Senate Committee on Governmental Affairs,* 95th Cong., 1st Sess. (1977). S. 2 was criticized on just this ground in Note, "Zero-Base Sunset Review," 14 *Harv. J. Legislation* 505, 535-537 (1977).

5. T. Lowi, *The End of Liberalism* 309 (1969) (proposing a "tenure of statutes act"). Justice Douglas, when chairman of the Securities and Exchange Commission, suggested to President Roosevelt that every agency should be abolished within ten years of creation. Adams, "Sunset: A Proposal for Accountable Government," 28 *Admin. L. Rev.* 511, 520 (1976). Douglas thus explained the reasons for cutting short agency life: "The greatest creative work of a federal agency must be done in the first decade of its existence if it is to be done at all. After that, it is likely to become a prisoner of its own bureaucracy." W. O. Douglas, *Go East, Young Man* 297 (1974). In Colorado the Sunset Law applies only to thirty-nine boards, divisions, and commissions, not to the general body of laws. 1976 *Colo. Sess. Laws,* ch. 115, §1(2)-(4). This narrowed focus was also found in the proposed but rejected Texas Constitution of 1975, which sought to limit all statutory state agencies to a ten-year life span unless renewed by law. Of the ten states that have enacted sunset laws, six are primarily concerned

with regulatory agencies. "Zero-Base Sunset Review," supra note 4. The *Harvard Journal of Legislation*'s model sunset act is such a limited act, Note, "A Model Federal Sunset Act," 14 *Harv. J. Legislation* 542 (1977), and Common Cause, a major supporter of sunsetting, would favor a sunset act limited to regulatory programs, see Adams, supra.

6. See "A Model Federal Sunset Act," supra note 5, at 542.

7. S. 2, 95th Cong., 1st Sess. (1977), provided for review every five years, with agencies in related fields coming up for review simultaneously. It was passed by the Senate Oct. 11, 1978, and referred to the House Committee on Government Operations and Committee on Rules, where it died at the close of the Congress. A similar bill, H.R. 2, 96th Cong., 1st Sess. (1979), has been proposed, which as of this writing has not yet gone into committee. The Colorado sunset bill, discussed in note 5, supra, reviews all affected agencies over a six-year period.

8. Many "potential" majorities are quiescent in the face of organized minority opposition, but can galvanize themselves to pass legislation when a crisis, scandal, or catastrophe occurs.

The muckrakers of the early 1900s were experts at using scandal to rouse action, appealing not directly to the social needs but to mass sentiments of responsibility, indignation, and guilt. See R. Hofstadter, *The Age of Reform* 203-204 (1955). Through his well-published exposes of corruption in various American cities, Lincoln Steffens roused a popular movement against political corruption. See L. Steffens, *The Shame of the Cities* (1904). Recently, Ralph Nader has demonstrated the use of scandal and catastrophe to arouse support for automobile safety regulation. Catastrophe was supplied in the form of the Corvair: by October 1965 over one hundred suits alleging instability in the Corvair had been filed, and it was partly by capitalizing on these suits that Nader was able to arouse national interest in regulation of automobiles. See R. Nader, *Unsafe at Any Speed: The Designed-In Defects of the American Automobile* 9 (1965); Nader and Page, "Automobile Design and the Judicial Process," 55 *Cal. L. Rev.* 645 (1967). Nader may also have been aided in his crusade to raise popular attention by the clamor that arose when he claimed to have been spied upon and otherwise harassed by one automaker. See *Critic of Auto Industry's Safety Standard Says He Was Trailed and Harassed; Charges Called Absurd,* N.Y. Times, Mar. 6, 1966, at 94, col. 1. This charge culminated in a leading invasion of privacy case, Nader v. General Motors Corporation, 25 N.Y.2d 560, 255 N.E.2d 765, 307 N.Y.S.2d 647 (1970).

A further area in which catastrophe has been particularly effective in rousing dormant potential majorities is that of air pollution. Although pollution had long been a problem in many major cities, no federal action was taken until the 1948 smog that settled on Donora (a small town in the Steel Valley upriver from Pittsburgh), killing twenty and leaving over 6000 sick. Only then did the U.S. Public Health Service begin an extensive study of the effects of pollution. J. Krier and E. Ursin, *Pollution and Policy* 102-104 (1977). Other examples of catastrophe-reactive legislation are abundant.

Flood control programs have, for the most part, only arisen after a disastrous flood and not as the result of coordinated planning. H. C. Hart, "Crisis, Community and Consent in Water Politics," 22 *L. & Contemp. Prob.* 510 (1957). Recently the crash of a DC-10 plane sparked extensive Federal Aviation Administration studies on plane and flight safety, and a near catastrophe at the Three Mile Island nuclear plant led to studies of what safety regulations should exist in that industry. Krier and Ursin list four reason why crises are the impetus for legislation: (1) they overcome governmental inertia and uncertainty by making the expense of inaction suddenly appear too high; (2) they provoke citizen demands for action; (3) the press emphasizes crises, intensifying the first two effects; and (4) crusaders with a longstanding commitment, such as Upton Sinclair, Rachel Carson, and Ralph Nader, are able to capitalize on these crises. See J. Krier and E. Ursin, supra at 263-277. Krier and Ursin go on to note: "the roles of crisis can be expected to weaken with time. For example, if episodes increase the costs of doing nothing and thus encourage doing something because citizens suddenly find the problem intolerable and fear it will persist, experience might reveal that the conditions are in fact tolerable and do not persist — precisely because they are episodic. Similarly, if episodes become familiar (but not too familiar, not persistent), citizens may undergo a sort of acclimatization, such that the episodes are no longer crises but rather events not out of the ordinary at all." Id. at 272-273. A crisis-born law that still fits the fabric of the law and enjoys majority support but is in this post-crisis stage may, nevertheless, not survive sunset. Although the popular majority may favor the reform, it may no longer have the initiative to repass it.

9. The traditional rule for the interpretation of legislative intent in re-enactment or amendment is that reenactment of a law as part of a body of laws, and amendment of a law, with a typical boiler-plate clause reenacting the law as a whole, imply approval. This rule has been criticized as unrealistic and cumbersome, since in effect it tells the legislature that it cannot exercise the power to amend except at the risk of committing itself on all questions under the broad statute being amended. See, e.g., H. Hart and A. Sacks, *The Legal Process: Basic Problems in the Making and Application of Law* 1401-05 (MS 1958). The presumption that a legislature in amending a statute means to endorse what it does not change is in some ways akin to the presumption that the legislature in enacting a statute originally meant to speak on all aspects of the problem. In short, the legislature is treated as if it had all-inclusive vision, when, inevitably, its vision and attention are only partial.

For judicial recognition of the limited value of legislative reenactment as a means to determine legislative intent see, e.g., Girouard v. United States, 328 U.S. 61 (1946). In that case the Court had to construe the effect of an oath required under the Naturalization Act of 1906. Since its original enactment, the Court had thrice interpreted the Act to say that an alien who refuses to bear arms will not be admitted to citizenship. Subsequent efforts to amend the law died in committee, and in 1940 the oath was reenacted in its preexisting form as a part of the Nationality Act. The Court refused to accept the argument that Congress, in reenacting the law as written, had accepted the Court's interpretation of it: "It is at best treacherous to find in congressional silence alone the adoption of a controlling rule of law. We do not think under the circumstances of this legislative history that we can properly place on the shoulder of Congress the burden of the Court's own error. The history of the 1940 Act is at most equivocal. It contains no affirmative recognition of the rule of the [previous three] cases. The silence of Congress and its inaction are as consistent with a desire to leave the problem fluid as they are with an adoption by silence of the rule of those cases." 328 U.S. at 69-70.

Justice Black makes an analogous point in his dissent in Barenblatt v. United States, 360 U.S. 109, 134 (1959) (Black, J., dissenting). In that case the Court sustained the conviction of a teaching fellow who refused to answer questions put to him by the House Committee on Un-American Activities. The Court reasoned that Barenblatt knew with sufficient certainty at the time of his interrogation that there was so compelling a need for his replies that infringement of his rights of association was justified. Black argued that the need for the investigation was by no means clear, "since Congress expressed it neither when it enacted Rule XI [establishing the Committee] nor when it acquiesced in the Committee's assertions of power." 360 U.S. at 139. See also discussion of Price-Anderson Act, note 24, infra.

10. For example, the *New York Times* reported that as a result of Colorado's sunset law, $212,000 was spent to review thirteen agencies. Of the thirteen, three were eliminated, saving the taxpayers a grand total of $6,810. See *With New Law, Colorado Spends $212,000 to Abolish 3 Agencies*, N.Y. Times, Apr. 23, 1978, at 46, col. 3. A more optimistic but still guarded report notes that the sunset laws did encourage agencies to make a thorough house cleaning before their review and that some of the reviewed agencies were retained only after substantial changes. "Zero-Base Sunset Review," supra note 4, at 513-514.

11. See Cutler and Johnson, supra note 4, discussed at Chap. V, note 43.

12. See Chap. V, note 43, and accompanying text for an analogous criticism of the Cutler-Johnson proposal and especially of the delegation of such power to dependent administrative agencies.

13. The idea of a commission that would exercise this kind of function was suggested to me by a letter of Professor Clifford S. Fishman of the Catholic University of America (Nov. 15, 1978) (on file in Yale University Law Library). See also Chap. IX, note 83.

14. For a discussion of the relationship between the judicial task of determining whether a law fits the legal landscape and the political task of ascertaining whether a law has majoritatian support, see Chaps. IX-XII. In fact, of course, the two tasks can never be completely separated, but which

one predominates will determine whether courtlike bodies or semirepresentative officials will take on the job of deciding what laws should be subject to sunset and where the burden of legislative inertia should lie.

15. This is indeed the solution Judge Friendly has proposed to the problem of statutory obsolescence and imperfection. "The same reasons for a permanent establishment devoted to critical study that have recently been emphasized as to the administrative agencies demand the creation of a group whose prime business it is to see that federal statutory law becomes what it ought to be." Friendly, "The Gap in Lawmaking—Judges Who Can't and Legislators Who Won't," 63 *Colum. L. Rev.* 787 (1963), at 803 (footnote omitted).

16. See Cardozo, "A Ministry of Justice," 35 *Harv. L. Rev.* 113 (1921). The New York Law Review Commission was established in 1934.

17. See H. Hart and A. Sacks, supra note 9, at 809-817; Sutton, "The English Law Reform Commission: A New Philosophy of Law Reform," 20 *Vanderbilt L. Rev.* 1009 (1967); MacDonald, "The New York Law Revision Commission," 28 *Modern L. Rev.* 1 (1956).

18. Cf. Chap. VII, for a discussion of the difficulties courts face in fashioning detailed laws as one reason for the proliferation of statutes.

19. See Chap. II, text at notes 2-5.

20. See Chap. V, text at note 43, and Chap. IX.

21. On this point, see Chap. IX, text at notes 2, 29, 30, and 43. See also Davies, "A Response to Statutory Obsolescence: The Nonprimacy of Statutes Act," 4 *Vermont L. Rev.* 203 (1979).

22. A common example in the past of statutes whose intended benefits were wiped out by inflation is workmen's compensation laws. The Pennsylvania workmen's compensation statute, what is now 77 *Pa. Cons. Stat. Ann.* §511 (Purdon 1980 Supp.), for instance, clung to fixed maximum awards until 1972. Although these maxima had been occasionally revised, at the time maximum weekly compensation was only $60 for a totally disabled worker. 1968 Pa. Laws 6 §1. It is not unlikely that the recent rapid development of product liability for manufacturers of machine tools represents an attempt by courts to get around outdated workmen's compensation laws. See Chap. III, note 16.

Usury laws also tend to rely on standard numbers. In Pennsylvania, for example, generally no interest greater than 6 percent can be charged for loans of less than $50,000. 41 *Pa. Cons. Stat. Ann.* §201 (Purdon 1980 Supp.). Two figures in this law will go out of date: the $50,000 limit is ever representing a smaller real sum of money, and the 6 percent interest rate becomes increasingly unrealistic. The decrease in the limit of the principal helps to mitigate the effects of the falling return on the money, but does not fully offset that decline. Hence Pennsylvania borrowers may be protected against high rates of interest, but they face a restricted money market. Understandably, lenders and borrowers try to get around this limitation, and courts sometimes help them. In one case, a Pennsylvania court upheld a private loan contract which provided that the principal be indexed as not being in contravention of the Pennsylvania usury statute. Olwine v. Torrens, 344 A.2d 665 (Pa. Super. 1975). But see Aztec Properties v. Union Planters Nat'l Bank of Memphis, 530 S.W.2d 756 (Tenn. 1975) (faced with the same problem under a restrictive Tennessee usury statute, the Tennessee Supreme Court refused to permit private indexing of the principal). The problem is discussed more fully in "Indexing the Principal: The Usury Laws Hang Tough," 37 *U. Pitt. L. Rev.* 755 (1976).

In other cases, although inflation may not harm the intended beneficiaries of the original law, it may have disproportionate and unintended adverse effects on other parties. Thus federal liability limitations for nuclear incidents, set at $560 million in 1957 so as to encourage the nuclear industry, may be an unrealistic and detrimentally low estimate of potential damages today. (In fact the statute, 42 U.S.C. §2210(e) (1976), was—unsuccessfully—attacked under the Fifth Amendment on precisely that ground, in Duke Power Co. v. Carolina Environmental Study Group, 438 U.S. 59 (1978).) Contribution limits set in the Federal Election Campaign Act of 1971 limit the maximum real value of contributions ever more strictly as years pass. The goal of the limitations was to discourage corruption; inflation increasingly adds the effect of forcing candidates to rely on an increasingly broader and shallower base of financial support. 2 U.S.C. §441a(a) (1)-(3) (1976).

23. Today many state workmen's compensation laws are indexed to the average weekly wages within the state. See, e.g., 77 *Pa. Cons. Stat. Ann.* §511 (Purdon 1980 Supp.); *W. Va. Ann. Code* § 23-4A-1 (Michie 1980 Supp.). Indexing of tort awards generally is an approach used in many foreign countries. Fleming, "The Impact of Inflation on Tort Compensation," 26 *Am. J. Comp. L.* 51 (1978); Hellner, "Indexing of Tort Awards in Sweden," 26 *Am. J. Comp. L.* 71 (1978). But on whether this solves the problem, see Chap. III, note 16.

Statutory rates of interest may also be indexed. Although the general ceiling rate of interest in Pennsylvania is 6 percent, residential mortgage rates are governed by a separate rule that ties the maximum rate to the Monthly Index of Long Term United States Government Bond Yields. 41 *Pa. Cons. Stat. Ann.* §301(b) (Purdon 1980 Supp.).

24. For an instance of this more technical type of delegated indexing see the Fair Labor Standards Act, codified at 29 U.S.C. §204(d)(1) (1976). The Secretary of Labor is to calculate annually a fair minimum wage and overtime coverage policy, taking into account changes in the cost of living, productivity, the level of wages in manufacturing, the ability of employers to absorb wage increases, and such other factors as he deems pertinent and recommend the resulting figure to Congress. On the state level, a common example of this technical delegated indexing is found in public utility laws. Thus in Pennsylvania, the legislature has delegated to the Public Utilities Commission the power to determine what fair rates are, using the costs of production as an index to guide them. 66 *Pa. Cons. Stat. Ann.* §1309 (Purdon 1980 Supp.).

25. The Internal Revenue Code is full of such "ambiguous uses of figures." Small businesses are permitted to take a deduction of 20 percent of the value of the tangible personal property used in the business up to a maximum of $10,000. I.R.C. §179. Individuals are entitled to deduct half of their payments for medical insurance up to a maximum of $150. I.R.C. §213. One suspects that these figures were meant to be real, or should have been so intended, since the need to encourage small businesses and self-protection by buying health insurance remains constant (or even increases) as the dollar depreciates. But one cannot be sure, for health insurance is itself often described as a cause of rising health costs.

One code provision that one must assume was clearly meant to stay constant with reality is the interest due on the late payment of tax. Until 1975, the interest charged on late taxes was 6 percent. Inflation surpassed this figure, and the tax code in effect gave a subsidy to those who paid their taxes late. To remedy this situation, Congress altered the law. I.R.C. §6601(a). The interest rate to be charged on late payments is to be determined yearly by the Secretary of the Treasury, who should round the adjusted prime rate charged by banks to the nearest full percent. I.R.C. § 6621(b).

Other deductions may well have been intended as temporary measures. Thus I.R.C. §182 permits farmers to deduct their expenses for clearing land not in excess of $5,000. Given that the overproduction of foodstuffs is a persistent market problem and that the need to clear more farmland is dubious, it may be that Congress intended that the value of this deduction should wane once the political support of the beneficiaries of the deduction was no longer necessary.

Other laws are even more confusing in their intent. For instance, I.R.C. §218(b)(1) limits the deduction for contributions to candidates for public office to $100. This seems to be in accord with the fixed limitation on the size of contributions found in the Federal Election Campaign Act, 2 U.S.C. §441a(a)(1)-(3) (1976), but not in line with the indexing of the spending limit, 2 U.S.C. §441a(c)(1). Whether the fixed limits in these laws, touching a subject so dear to the heart and consciousness of every legislator, will be periodically revised is also an unanswerable question.

The same uncertainty of purpose can be found in the Price-Anderson Act, 42 U.S.C. §2210(e) (1976). It is clear that $560 million in current dollars is not equal to that amount in 1957 dollars, that the nuclear reactors of today are much larger and more likely to cause widespread harm should an accident occur than those of 1957, and that we now have a much clearer idea of the extent of possible damage should that accident occur. Yet the retention of a $560 million liability limitation does not clearly define whether Congress believes that this limit is still sufficient, or whether the legislature believes that an ever growing subsidy (afforded by an ever declining *real* maximum liability limit) is needed or wanted to encourage the development of the nuclear industry. It seems that Congress has simply not faced this question, although the bill has been reenacted twice with only minor changes. Rather it appears that, having once settled on an arbitrary figure for a liability limitation, Congress is loathe to find another, necessarily arbitrary, figure as a replacement. Hence, although the statute is subject to its own sunset provision and is specific in its terms, it has not been given effective legislative reconsideration.

26. But see Matthews v. Allen, 360 S.W.2d 135 (Ky. 1962), in which the Kentucky Supreme Court interpreted a state constitutional limit of $8,400 on judicial salaries to mean $8,400 in real terms and hence to permit periodic increases in salaries according to inflation. A dissenter protested that the "majority opinion on this point does all but eradicate the ink with which Section 246 of the Kentucky Constitution is written." 360 S.W.2d at 139 (Bird, J., concurring).

27. See Chap. IV.

VII. Structural Responses

1. G. Gilmore, *The Ages of American Law* 40 (1977): "No golden age endures forever." This approach would have our judiciary behave as Gilmore says it did in the early nineteenth century, before Langdellian formalism temporarily destroyed judicial creativity. "Pure Mansfieldianism flourished: not only were his cases regularly cited but his lighthearted disregard for precedent, his joyous acceptance of the idea that judges are supposed to make law—the more the better—became a notable feature of our early jurisprudence." Id. at 24. Some have questioned whether this view is based on accurate history. On the problem of whether such a golden age of government by the judiciary existed at all, see Chap. I, note 1.

2. See, e.g., Geyelin, *Parliamentary Government Makes More Sense,* L.A. Times, July 14, 1980, part II, at 5, col. 3 (describing with approval the position he attributes to Lloyd Cutler). Cutler's own position is set out in a speech entitled "To Form a Government" (1980) (on file in Yale Law School Library) and is, characteristically, highly sophisticated. Cutler begins by criticizing the stalemate that so often arises when a President without outstanding leadership abilities faces a Congress whose members have their own individual goals. To the extent that the President cannot carry Congress with him, the programs the people elected when they voted for the President are not adopted, and there is no government, in the parliamentary sense, formed behind the leader. Thus there is an inherent cost in separation of powers. According to Cutler, the costs of separation have escalated in the past few decades as the need to react to domestic and international events with comprehensive plans has increased and as both the unifying effects of party loyalty and the seniority system in Congress have weakened. To correct this growing problem, Cutler advocates importing elements of the parliamentary system into our system in order to create greater government responsiveness to the desires of the public on particular issues. Proposals that he mentions would involve amending the Constitution (1) to require congressmen to be elected on the same nonseparable

ticket as are the President and Vice-President, (2) to require the President to select half of his Cabinet from congressmen of his party, or (3) most interestingly, to allow the President and/or Congress to call for a new national election in the event of a serious policy stalemate. See also H. Finer, *The Theory and Practice of Modern Government* 540-541 (rev. ed. 1949); Mazer, *Toward a United States Parliament?*, N.Y. Times, July 6, 1980, at 16, col. 5 (letter to the editor); and notes 3, 7, 8, infra.

3. A recent renaissance of this viewpoint can be found in the popular discussion on the merits of direct democracy spawned by California's Proposition 13. See, e.g., Segal, "You Can Fight City Hall: Take the Initiative," 133 *Read. Dig.* 106 (Oct. 1978). As distinguished a political theorist as Robert Dahl notes that a number of other countries allow more direct democracy than the United States and yet have comparable levels of "political liberty." He recommends that "political scientists need to begin a serious and systematic reexamination of the constitutional system, much beyond anything done up to now." Dahl, "On Removing Certain Impediments to Democracy in the United States," 92 *Pol. Sci. Q.* 1, 17 (1977). Our "elaborate systems of checks and balances, separation of powers, constitutional federalism, and other institutional arrangements," says Dahl, are "both adverse to the majority principle and in that sense to democracy, and yet arbitrary and unfair in the protection they give to rights." Id. at 5. See also proposals discussed in note 7, infra.

4. See, e.g., G. Gilmore, supra note 1, at 24, 96. Nostalgia for the past glory of the common law may have been one influence behind the original restatement movement, which at first resolutely refused to deal in statutory reform. Addressing the American Law Institute, parent of the Restatements, Justice Frankfurter praised it for its exclusive concentration on the common law, embarrassingly enough, after the ALI had already abandoned this exclusive common law orientation by work on a uniform commercial code. See G. Gilmore, *The Death of Contract* 132 n.162 (1974).

5. An interesting example of mournful resignation at the coming of the Age of Statutes comes from England. Lord Devlin, in *Samples of Lawmaking* 6 (1962), states that "the work done by the judges of England is not now as glorious as it once was," although "at its best, the common law is, I think, better than any statute could be." Id. at 117. His nostalgia does not become a call to action; in that book he seemed prepared to let judicial lawmaking drift into obsolescence.

6. Except, of course, for those arising out of true constitutional adjudication.

7. See, e.g., C. Black, "National Lawmaking by Initiative? Let's Think Twice," 8 *Human Rights* 28, 30-31 (Fall 1979), which argues that an initiative system would make impossible the kind of deliberation and compromise building that we expect and ideally obtain from our present method of enacting statutes. The public would be forced to make a "take it or leave it" decision on a law previously formulated and not subject to change in the course of public discussion. This would mean the losers

would lose totally rather than getting the quarter-loaf that a legislative compromise might yield them. Cf. note 34, infra. The result would be a polarization of society. Black also suggests that referenda would give inordinate importance to media budgets in the passage of legislation. Id. at 49.

Many observers have also noted that unpopular minorities are likely to be victimized by the polarization that may come with either a referendum or an initiative. See, e.g., Bell, "The Referendum: Democracy's Barrier to Racial Equality," 54 *Wash. L. Rev.* 1 (1978). Cf. Hunter v. Erickson, 393 U.S. 385, 390-391 (1969) (striking down a charter provision subjecting fair housing ordinances to a referendum before they would take effect) with James v. Valtierra, 402 U.S. 137, 141-143 (1971) (upholding a state constitutional provision requiring that a low-rent housing project be approved by a majority of qualified electors), and Eastlake v. Forest City Enterprises, 426 U.S. 668, 675 (1976), (upholding a city charter provision subjecting changes in zoning to a popular referendum), on the question of whether a referendum scheme limited to certain types of state legislation works a violation of the Fourteenth Amendment.

8. Advocates of change often have mourned the fact that reform can be stopped by a presidential veto, by vote of either house of Congress, or by a majority — or perhaps even an influential minority — of a congressional committee or subcommittee. See H. Hart and A. Sacks, *The Legal Process: Basic Problems in the Making and Application of Law* 726-735 (MS 1958) (on committees and bicameralism); and Dahl, supra note 3, at 17 (mentioning the veto and the bicameral Congress as two potential casualties of the constitutional reexamination he recommends). Lloyd Cutler has recently advocated careful consideration of changes in our constitutional structure which would lower, through any one of various plans, the current high likelihood of stalemate between the executive and the legislative branches. Cutler, supra note 2. Woodrow Wilson's *Congressional Government: A Study in American Politics* (1885) was an earlier scholarly critique of the American system which seemed to lean toward recommending the adoption of a parliamentary system. No doubt because of its lack of constitutional basis, the antimajoritarian effects of the committee system in the post-World War II years have received the most notoriety. Some have argued that events in the 1960s have left any given committee much less able to frustrate the will of the majority of the legislature than before. See Sundquist, *Politics and Policy* 506-537 (1968), as an example of an advocate of reform who draws this optimistic conclusion. Nonideological, undisciplined, centrist political parties have also been accused of defusing expression of the public will. "Toward a More Responsible Two-Party System: A Report of the Committee on Political Parties, American Political Science Association," 44 *Am. Pol. Sci. Rev.* Supp. No. 3, Part 2 (1950), argued for responsive political parties with coherent ideological programs so that voters would be presented with a significant choice. This report has apparently been the whipping boy of almost all subsequent writers in the field. See, e.g.,

Kirkpatrick, "Toward A More Responsible Two-Party System: Political Science, Policy Science, or Pseudo-Science?" 65 *Am. Pol. Sci. Rev.* 965 (1971), and works cited therein at 968 n.5.

As originally enacted, the constitutional system seemed much more concerned with representation of geographical entities than people. This, of course, has changed radically. Direct election of senators came with the Seventeenth Amendment. The Supreme Court's reapportionment decisions instituted a "one man, one vote" rule for representation in state legislatures. And, at least every four years, a movement arises to replace the electoral college system with the direct election of presidents. See, e.g., 123 *Cong. Rec.* S19297 (daily ed. Dec. 6, 1977) (article by Rep. Morgan on the constitutional amendment proposal then before Congress). But federalism and geographical representation have proven more durable than many have expected. For example, the expansion of federal power throughout the twentieth century and frequent imposition of federally set standards upon the states made it seem to many as if "the only aspect of state government that is beyond the reach of Washington is the very existence of the states with their present boundaries." M. Reagan, *The New Federalism* (1972). Those like Reagan who saw the national response to social and economic problems in the 1960s as both effective and progressive praised the development. But their burial of "constitutional," as opposed to functional, federalism now seems premature. See, e.g., Usery v. National League of Cities, 426 U.S. 833 (1976) (striking down amendments to the Fair Labor Standards Act extending that Act to cover employees of States and their political subdivisions as violative of the right of the states to function in a federal system). That decision set no clear limits on the scope of "integral [state] government functions" with which Washington cannot interfere.

Perhaps the most dramatic advocacy of direct democracy that recent years have seen is the constitutional amendment proposed by Senators Abourzek and Hatfield calling for a national initiative on any potential subject of federal legislation (other than declaring war) upon the petition of a number of citizens equal to 3 percent of the number of votes cast in the preceding presidential election. A majority of the people would then be able to enact laws directly, bypassing the whole existing legislative system. S. J. Res. 67, 95th Cong., 1st Sess. (1977), discussed in Bell, supra note 7, at 2; and C. Black, supra note 7.

9. See, e.g., Traynor, "Statutes Revolving in Common-Law Orbits," 17 *Cath. U. L. Rev.* 401, 424-425 (1968): "For all the vaunted responsiveness of legislatures to the will of the people, it is no secret that legislative committees, particularly those dominated by the elder statesmen of a seniority system, tend to dilute the reliability of statutes as expression of public policy." Cf. Sundquist, supra note 8, at 471-481. In the summer of 1978, for example, the federal no-fault auto insurance bill, which had already passed the Senate, was voted down in the House Committee on Interstate and Foreign Commerce. Whether it would have passed the whole House is hard to say, but given the action in committee we will never know. Its considerable ad-

vantages are discussed in *S. Rep. No.* 382, 93d Cong., 1st Sess. (1973). See also *Standards for No-Fault Motor Vehicle Accidents Benefits Act, Hearings Before the Senate Committee on Commerce, Science and Transportation on S.1381,* 95th Cong., 1st Sess. (1977).

10. An example may be the fate of the constitutional convention bill twice passed by the Senate and reported to the House Judiciary Committee, never to be heard from again. 117 *Cong. Rec.* 37141 (1971) (S.215, 92d Cong., 1st Sess.) (1971); 119 *Cong. Rec.* 23138 (1973) (S.1272, 93d Cong., 1st Sess. (1973)). Because the bill purported only to express the duty of future congresses to follow Article V's directions in calling a constitutional convention when two thirds of the states called for it, it might have been difficult for the full House to have voted it down. House members may well have preferred that the bill be bottled up in committee in order to avoid encouraging those who sought such a convention, with all its dangers and unknowns. On the dangers of S.215, the earlier constitutional convention bill, see C. Black, "Amending the Constitution: A Letter to a Congressman," 82 *Yale L. J.* 189 (1972).

11. See Chap. IX; cf. Cutler and Johnson, "Regulation and the Political Process," 84 *Yale L. J.* 1395 (1975).

12. See Chap. IX, for a discussion of the alleged majoritarian bases of judicial lawmaking.

13. On legislatures as predominantly reactive, revising bodies, see Davies, "A Response to Statutory Obsolescence: The Nonprimacy of Statutes Act," 4 *Vermont L. Rev.* 203 (1979).

14. See David, "The Civil Code in France Today," 34 *Louisiana L. Rev.* 907, 907-908 (1974), and Merryman, "The Italian Style, II: Law," 18 *Stan. L. Rev.* 396, 407 (1966).

15. On ways in which courts can work with legislatures and administrative agencies to bring about revision of such highly technical laws, see Chap. XI.

16. Expenses of all levels of government on public health, public assistance, workmen's compensation, and old age and retirement benefits were only 2.4 percent of GNP in 1890; in 1970 the figure was 15.3 percent. See Department of Commerce Bureau of the Census, *Historical Statistics of the United States* 340 (1975).

17. In torts this happy degree of uniformity in the common law was shattered by the coming of differing state no-fault automobile liability statutes. "The result is a checkerboard of rules of liability and insurance, with no national uniformity." *No-Fault Insurance: Hearings before the Senate Judiciary Committee on S.354,* 93d Cong., 2d Sess. 758 (1974) (testimony of E. Griswold). The resurrection of the earlier situation of national uniformity was cited by Dean Griswold as one of the bill's main benefits. Id. at 725-726, 757-760.

18. Two areas that created special problems of conflict of law in the torts field, before nonfault, see note 17 supra, were wrongful death statutes, see Chap. IV, note 33, and guest statutes, see Chap. II, note 15. As some

states began to repeal their guest statutes or raise the level of recovery under the wrongful death statute, courts became increasingly loathe to apply the limited laws of another jurisdiction. They were required to apply these limited laws under the traditional conflicts rule, that the law of the place of the tort should govern. Courts began to devise new conflicts rules in an attempt to avoid the traditional rule and apply their own law, with the consequence that these tort cases were left in hopeless confusion. Cf. e.g., Miller v. Miller, 22 N.Y.2d 12, 237 N.E.2d 877, 290 N.Y.S.2d 734 (1968) (refusing to apply Maine's limit to an accident involving New York residents in Maine, using an "interests" analysis), and McDaniel v. Petroleum Helicopters, 455 F.2d 137 (5th Cir. 1972) (giving effect, under Louisiana conflict-of-law rules, to the $110 limit of the Colombian wrongful-death statute using the traditional rule). Equally vexed was the problem of whether a state that had no guest statute should give effect to one of a sister state in any of various fact situations. Compare, e.g., Clark v. Clark, 107 N.H. 351, 222 A.2d 205 (1966) (refusing to apply the Vermont guest statute to an accident between New Hampshire residents in Vermont, using an "interests" analysis), and Cipolla v. Shaposka, 439 Pa. 563, 267 A.2d 854 (1970) (giving effect to the Delaware guest statute in a suit by a Pennsylvania resident against a Delaware resident arising out of a Delaware accident, applying an "interests" analysis).

19. One original aim of the American Law Institute's restatement movement was "to promote the uniformity of law among the several states," thereby serving to reduce both uncertainty and complexity, the "two chief defects" of the law. 1 *ALI Proceedings* 2, 6 (1923). As time went on, the ALI decided that its uniformity aim would be better served by advocacy of *binding* rules of law, i.e., statutes, and the uniform laws movement, which has now spawned more than ninety model statutes, was born. See *Uniform Laws Annotated* (West & 1979 Supp.).

20. "The few people—including myself—who have ever spent much time studying the judicial product of the period have been appalled by what they found." G. Gilmore, supra note 1, at 60. See also id. at 36–39, 60–67, and M. Horwitz, *The Transformation of American Law, 1780–1860* 253–266 (1977). Horwitz, in contrast to Gilmore, argues that a flexible, policy-oriented conception of law "was no longer needed once the major beneficiaries of that transformation had obtained the bulk of their objectives. Indeed, once successful, those groups could only benefit if both the recent origins and the foundations in policy and group self-interest of all newly established legal doctrines could be disguised." Id. at 254. One of the early responses to the persistence of this sluggishness of the common law was Roscoe Pound's plea that statutes be given full effect even if (and even because) they did change the common law. See Pound, "Common Law and Legislation," 21 *Harv. L. Rev.* 383 (1908). See also Landis, "Statutes and the Sources of Law," *Harvard Legal Essays* 213 (1934); and Stone, "The Common Law in the United States," 50 *Harv. L. Rev.* 4 (1936). Cf. Cardozo, "A Ministry of Justice," 35 *Harv. L. Rev.* 112 (1921).

21. See, e.g., G. Gilmore, supra note 1, at 91-98, and R. Keeton, *Venturing To Do Justice* 10 (1969).

22. Compare text at Chap. V, note 36, for an analogous criticism of too complete lawmaking by administrative agencies. See also Chap. IX, note 73, and Chap X, notes 3-5, on incremental lawmaking and statutes.

23. See Chap. IX for a critical discussion of justifications of judicial power based on court capacity to discern the will of the majority or to determine what rule is most desirable.

24. Cf. Chaps. XI and XII, discussing how courts can operate in colloquy with legislatures to solve this dilemma.

25. It is in recognition of this that legislatures are often spoken of as bodies that preeminently make law in crises. See e.g., G. Gilmore, supra note 1, at 95-96. One commentator has suggested that such "timely responsive" legislation is virtually the only sort legislatures should enact. See Morse, "Theories of Legislation," 14 *DePaul L. Rev.* 51 (1964). See also Chap. VI, note 8, on how legislation is often spawned by crises.

26. One congressional response was the Consumer Credit Protection Act, Pub. L. 90-321, 82 Stat. 146 (1968), codified at 15 U.S.C. §§1601-1681 (1976).

27. The Consumer Product Safety Act, Pub. L. 92-573, 86 Stat. 1207 (1972), codified at 15 U.S.C. §§2051-2081 (1976), preempts the field of minimum safety standards for certain consumer appliances; 15 U.S.C. §2075, leaves no room for inconsistent state regulation, except insofar as a state would demand stricter safety standards.

28. Analogous technological changes have made longstanding statutes outdated. Occasionally the crisis becomes severe enough so that the old law is reworked. Thus development of photocopying machines in the 1950s led in time to the Copyright Act of 1976, Pub. L. 94-553, 90 Stat. 2541 (1976), codified at Title 17 of U.S.C., which attempted to create a balance between an author's interest in protecting his intellectual property and the public's potential benefit from the new technology. The statute, which makes photocopying a problem of "fair use," leaves considerable room for further judicial development despite some relevant legislative history. See *Nimmer on Copyright* §13.05(e) at 13-73-13-75 (1980). See also Chap. X, note 30.

29. In reaction to the widespread perception that judicial change had created great uncertainty in the law of medical malpractice liability, resulting in exorbitant insurance premiums, many states passed laws in the 1970s: requiring that patient grievances be submitted for arbitration before a review board on which doctors could be represented before a tort action could be filed; guaranteeing that insurance would be available; establishing special short statutes of limitation, or dollar limits on recovery (applicable only to malpractice claims); and changing the substantive law to make recovery more difficult. See Comment, "Recent Medical Malpractice Legislation—A First Checkup," 50 *Tulane L. Rev.* 655 (1976), and statutes collected therein at 661 n.37. See also note 31, infra.

30. Gilmore states that the UCC's final acceptance is the result of

efforts of such a declining majority: "The Code, which in the 1940s had seemed much too 'liberal' to its conservative critics, had by the 1960s become an almost nostalgic throwback to an earlier period. The final irony in the Code project was that its eventual 'success' (that is, its enactment) can well be taken as an attempt by the most conservative elements in the bar to turn the clock back." G. Gilmore, supra note 1, at 86. More recent examples of attempts to limit uncertainty created by common law techniques are medical malpractice acts, discussed at note 29, supra, and note 31, infra, and recent attempts to codify the law of products liability, discussed at note 31, infra.

31. There was much reason for a disinterested observer to applaud the modest liberalization of malpractice law in the 1960s. See, e.g., Brune v. Belinkoff, 354 Mass. 102, 235 N.E.2d 793 (1968) (holding general medical practitioners to the standard of care expected of the average qualified practitioner, rather than allowing doctors to plead as a defense that they are no more incompetent than others in their locality), and Clark v. Gibbons, 66 Cal. 2d 399, 426 P.2d 525, 58 Cal. Rptr. 125 (1967) (allowing a jury to infer negligent harm from evidence that a given procedure is normally safe in combination with evidence that the physician committed "specific acts of negligence of a type which could have caused the occurrence complained of"). 66 Cal. 3d 413, 426 P.2d 534, 58 Cal. Rptr. 134. Nevertheless, the uncertainty that followed this liberalization did create a crisis in insurance premiums and availability. Cf. Calabresi, "The Problem of Malpractice: Trying To Round Out the Circle," 27 *U. Toronto L. J.* 131, 135-136 (1977). See also *American Enterprise Institute: The Economics of Medical Malpractice* (Rottenberg ed. 1978). As a result, medical and insurance groups were in many cases able to obtain a majority in the legislature long enough to codify their will. Some of the resulting statutes went beyond the need to cure uncertainty. If these are not repealed and become increasingly inconsistent with the legal landscape, it is easy to predict that courts in future years will deal with them by using constitutional adjudication, distorted interpretation, or other disingenuous methods. Indeed, in some instances they already have. See, e.g., Wright v. Central Du Page Hospital Ass'n, 63 Ill.2d 313, 347 N.E.2d 736 (1976); Arneson v. Olson, 270 N.W.2d 125 (N.D. 1978); and Note, "California's Medical Injury Compensation Reform Act: An Equal Protection Challenge," 52 *So. Cal. L. Rev.* 829 (1979). Product liability law has in recent years made great strides in generosity toward plaintiffs, often on the basis of liability without fault. This development is generally consistent with the aims of tort law; normally those held liable are both better able than the victims to reduce the occurrence of accidents and to spread over a broad spectrum of society the inevitable residual costs. See McKean, "Product Liability: Trends and Implications," 38 *U. Chi. L. Rev.* 3 (1970), and Calabresi and Bass, "Right Approach, Wrong Implications," 38 *U. Chi. L. Rev.* 74 (1970). In this move, there doubtless have been cases in which plaintiffs were allowed to recover from defendants who in fact had little opportunity for avoiding the harm in question. More important, the

manner in which product liability has come about has created enormous uncertainty costs. Nevertheless, the current rush toward statutorification has often seemed an attempt to freeze the law at a level that victims, as a group, cannot find tolerable. See Twerski, "Rebuilding the Citadel: The Legislative Assault on the Common Law," 15 *Trial* 55 (1979); *Draft Uniform Product Liability Law,* 44 Fed. Reg. 2996 (1979); and Symposium, "Product Liability Law: The Need for Statutory Reform," 56 *N.C. L. Rev.* 623 (1978). The net result of this move to codify product liability law may be yet more statutes, providing for *governmental* compensation schemes, coupled inevitably with governmental regulations of safety. See Calabresi, "Product Liability: Curse or Bulwark of Free Enterprise?" 27 *Cleve. St. L. Rev.* 313 (1978). Born as they are in the exigencies of a perceived crisis, these statutes if passed may be the start of a new and dominant (for me, undesirable) trend characterized by very low liability in tort conjoined with greater governmental compensation and regulation. If they do not signal a new trend, they are likely to become anachronistic and soon pose the kind of problems for courts which this book discusses.

32. Cf. Moragne v. States Marine Lines, 398 U.S. 375 (1970), discussed in Chap. XI, notes 15, 19.

33. For example, an *ad hoc* congressional panel on limitation of product liability concluded: "a product that might be immunized in some way by a statute in Ohio might still be subject to liability claims in all of the other states, thus negating any significant effect the state law might have on insurance rates. Consequently, we feel that any rapid, meaningful changes in product liability law must either come from the federal government or else be in the form of a readily-adopted uniform code. The dictates of time seem to point towards the federal approach." 123 *Cong. Rec.* H3897 (daily ed. May 2, 1977).

34. Thus it is argued that interest-group pluralism works because the participation of interest groups in the legislative compromise process helps to ensure their acceptance of the final result. See, e.g., D. Truman, *The Governmental Process* (1951). On this theory, the result of judicial decisions would not be accepted as readily by affected groups, particularly if they were not represented in the litigation that decided the issue, whereas they would have been able to participate in legislative hearings on the subject. See note 37, infra, and Chap. IX on the question of the appropriate role of courts and legislatures on political questions of choice among competing groups. To the extent that a situation of the sort described by Truman exists, if judicial action is needed courts would be well advised to use those techniques that force the legislative agenda and induce legislatures to resolve the problems, rather than those requiring a direct judicial resolution. See Chap. XI.

35. See note 37 infra, on the conflict between farmers and ranchers in the Great Plains.

36. See, e.g., the 1827-28 New York statutes revising property law. One of the changes made conveyance of land possible without the pre-

viously obligatory transfer of a piece of soil from the land. See L. Friedman, *A History of American Law* 207-211 (1973). Legislatures in some states also responded to prairie pressures for open range, see note 37, infra, and passed fencing-out statutes, declaring that farmers and other landowners could only recover for damage caused by rampaging cattle if they had erected a lawful fence, of material and dimensions calculated to prevent the entrance of cattle. See, e.g., statute discussed in Adams Brothers v. Clark, 189 Ky. 279, 224 S.W. 1046 (1920) (noting what constitutes a lawful fence to exclude trespassing cattle).

37. One example of the common law coping with a dramatic, political interest-group conflict is given in W. Webb, *The Great Plains* (1931). As the westward movement of settlers in the nineteenth century carried them into the Great Plains, the conflicting interest of farmers and ranchers came to a head over the problem of fencing. The common law of England, adopted by the more heavily populated and wooded seaboard American states, was that the owner of animals was liable for any damage they caused on another's land. In the West common law courts often held it was more appropriate that farmers bear this cost or avoid it by fencing out the cattle of the ranchers, which was not feasible until the invention of barbed wire. See, e.g., Delaney v. Erickson, 10 Neb. 492, 6 N.W. 600 (1880) (holding that "the principle of the common law of England . . . is not 'applicable' to the uncultivated, uninclosed wild prairie lands of this state"). When population increased and if the legislature did not act, some common law courts became willing to reimpose the older common law rule. See, e.g., Adams Brothers v. Clark, 189 Ky. 279, 224 S.W. 1046 (1920) (announcing that the time had come for enforcing the traditional rule in a case concerning trespassing chickens).

Whether or not courts should attempt to resolve such conflicts is, of course, a debatable question. Thus Wellington states that a policy of subsidy for an infant industry is not sufficiently "neutral" for the common law to adopt. Wellington, "Common Law Rules and Constitutional Double Standards: Some Notes on Adjudication," 83 *Yale L. J.* 221, 226 (1973). But the decisions of the Massachusetts Supreme Court, led by Chief Justice Lemuel Shaw, have been described as providing just such a subsidy for railroads. This was the apparent reason for and the effect of decisions modifying the notion of eminent domain so that, contrary to the earlier common law concerning common carriers, railroads could employ eminent domain and yet have exclusive use of their rails; similarly tort liability of railroads was limited through such inventions as the fellow-servant doctrine. See L. Levy, *The Law of the Commonwealth and Chief Justice Shaw*, 118-182 (1957). Cf. L. Friedman, supra note 36 at 157-61; and M. Horwitz, supra note 20, at 63-108. Apparently, as in the *Delaney* case, it was sufficiently clear to the court that the public interest was on the side of one interest group so that a political decision for that group seemed appropriate even for a common law court. Cf. Chap. IX.

38. This was realized as early as 1885 by Woodrow Wilson: "Legisla-

tion unquestionably generates legislation. Every statute may be said to have a long lineage of statutes behind it . . . Every statute in its turn has a numerous progeny . . . Once begin the dance of legislation, you must struggle through its mazes as best you can to its breathless end, — if any end there be." W. Wilson, supra note 8, at 297. Professor Wilson (as he then was) also quoted with apparent approval a contemporary who believed that "repeal was more blessed than enactment." Id.at 295.

39. Crimes were originally enforced without statutory sanction by the common law; the justification was that if an action was *malum in se* (wrong in itself), a wrongdoer needed no statutory warning that committing it might lead to criminal punishment. See W. LaFave and A. Scott, *Handbook of Criminal Law* §9, at 57-69 (1972). One could argue that the notice given by this notion of common law crime was preferable to what one can get from the current broadly drafted set of statutory crimes, which are made tolerable only by prudent exercise of unreviewable prosecutorial discretion. Cf. Fletcher, "The Metamorphosis of Larceny," 89 *Harv. L. Rev.* 469, 527-530 (1976). Even in America's early years, however, the idea of common law crime was attacked for leaving too much power in the hands of judges. See M. Horwitz, supra note 20, at 9-16. Thus the United States has never had a federal common law of crime. United States v. Hudson & Goodwin, 11 U.S. (7 Cranch) 32 (1812). Invocation by the states of the concept has been rare, and the current trend is definitely toward the total abolition of common law crimes. See W. LaFave and A. Scott, supra. Cf. Commonwealth v. Mochan, 117 Pa. Super. 454, 110 A.2d 788 (1955) (upholding common law crime against public morals). Criminal laws are, of course, only one example of those laws that have always tended to be statutory because foreknowledge and forewarning were deemed crucial.

40. G. Gilmore, supra note 1, at 95.

VIII. A New Approach: Antecedents and Roots

1. See Mark Twain, *The Adventures of Huckleberry Finn* 314-316 (Author's National Ed. 1976), in which Huck and Tom are trying to rescue Jim. While the "authorities" all require the use of case knives and a period of years for such an effort, the boys choose pickaxes and shovels instead for speed. Tom recommends, "We really dig right in, as quick as we can; and after that, we can *let on,* to ourselves, that we was at it thirty-seven years." This remark from Mark Twain's novel was pointed out to me by John Van Voorhis, then of the New York Court of Appeals, as a good description of what a court's role frequently must be.

2. Cf. Cutler and Johnson, "Regulation and the Political Process," 84 *Yale L. J.* 1395 (1975), and letter from Clifford Fishman (Nov. 15, 1978) (on file in Yale Law School Library), discussed in Chap. VI, note 13, and accompanying text, both suggesting other institutions to allocate the burden of legislative inertia. See also Chap. IX, note 83.

3. Senator Jack Davies of Minnesota has recently introduced a "Non-

primacy of Statutes Act" in the Minnesota legislature, which would give courts explicit authority to treat private law statutes more than twenty years old as common law. See Davies, "A Response to Statutory Obsolescence: The Nonprimacy of Statutes Act," 4 *Vermont L. Rev.* 203 (1979). Davies' conclusion that such a response is needed to cope with an age of increasing statutorification was arrived at independently of either my own or Grant Gilmore's conclusions. Davies was reacting to two different kinds of stimuli: his observations of the legislative process, made during his fifteen years' experience as a state legislator, and his reflections on such judicial activity as Justice Harlan's concurrence in Welsh v. United States, 398 U.S. 333, 344 (1970). I am somewhat skeptical of both Davies' twenty-year restriction and the statute's implication that use of full common law power over laws is frequently desirable or even feasible. I prefer to speak of "judicial allocation of burdens of inertia" and of "judicial sunsetting," and in many situations I would favor the use of techniques by courts to force the legislative hand rather than direct judicial amending of time-worn laws. See Chaps. X, XI, and XII. Nevertheless, the similarities between Davies' statute and my approach are striking and reassuring. See Calabresi, "The Nonprimacy of Statutes Act: A Comment," 4 *Vermont L. Rev.* 247 (1979).

4. Pomeroy, "The True Method of Interpreting the Civil Code," 4 *West Coast Rptr.* 109-110 (1884). Pomeroy's view was adopted by the California courts, but generally only implicitly. See Harrison, "The First Half-Century of the California Civil Code," 10 *Cal. L. Rev.* 185, 189-193 (1922). A much earlier analogous problem and solution can be found in the states that adopted the English common law by statute. See note 6, infra.

5. But cf., e.g., Nelson, "The Eighteenth-Century Background of John Marshall's Constitutional Jurisprudence," 76 *Mich. L. Rev.* 893 (1978) (implying that Marshall's view of the proper scope of judicial review included elements of a second-look doctrine).

6. There were, of course, earlier codes than the Field Code, arising from the desire to compile and adopt English common law as well as early colonial applications of that common law. At least on the civil side, these codes tried to suggest how English common law was to be incorporated into the developing American common law. See O'Connor, "Legal Reform in the Early Republic: The New Jersey Experience," 22 *Amer. J. Legal Hist.* 95 (1978). O'Connor chronicles the New Jersey codification experience from 1792-1800 and also cites accounts of the Virginia and New York revisions. Id. at 95, n.1. See W. Nelson, *The Americanization of the Common Law: The Impact of Legal Change on Massachusetts Society* (1977), and M. Horwitz, *The Transformation of American Law, 1780-1860* (1977).

7. See Chap. I, note 23.

8. See Chaps. IX and XI for a discussion of these technical problems and their effect on judicial lawmaking.

9. See Harrison, supra note 4 (discussing alternative approaches to code construction). See also H. Hart and A. Sacks, *The Legal Process: Basic*

Problems in the Making and Application of Law 780-787 (MS 1958), for a discussion of Pomeroy's enterprise and a general discussion of codification. For an alternative contemporaneous view of construction, see H. Black, *Handbook on the Construction and Interpretation of the Laws* 363-369 (1896) (giving maxims for code construction). The California Civil Code, §§3509-3548, sets out a variety of Maxims of Jurisprudence to aid in the "just application" of the other provisions of the Code. Among these are §3510, which prescribes, "When the reason of a rule ceases, so should the rule itself," and §3511, which states, "Where the reason is the same, the rule should be the same."

10. See *Report of the Committee on the Establishment of a Permanent Organization for the Improvement of the Law Proposing the Establishment of an American Law Institute,* in 1 *ALI Proceedings* 1-139 (1923) (hereinafter cited *Report*). The *Report* outlined the difficulties of American law and traced them to two chief defects: its uncertainty and its complexity. Id. at 1. A restatement of the law, it was urged, would not only serve to eradicate uncertainty and unnecessary complexity, but would also promote those "changes which will make the law better-adapted to the needs of life." Id. at 18.

11. Id. at 19-22.

12. The *Report* addressed this problem: "If the 'principles' in the restatement of the law were made with a view to their adoption by legislatures as a formal statutory codification of the law, one or other of these two distinctive features of the common law, its flexibility or its fullness of detail, would have to be sacrificed . . . *We fear that if the law stated in this detail were given the rigidity of a statute, injustice would result in many cases presenting unforeseen facts.*" Id. at 23-24 (emphasis added).

13. "If the principles of law set forth in the restatement are not to be adopted as a formal code it is nevertheless not impossible that they may be adopted by state legislatures with the proviso that they shall have the force of principles enunciated as the basis of the decisions of the highest court of the state, the courts having power to declare modifications and exceptions." Id. at 24.

14. Cf. note 12, supra.

15. Landis, "Statutes and the Sources of Law," in *Harvard Legal Essays* 213 (1934). See also Stone, "The Common Law in the United States," 50 *Harv. L. Rev.* 4 (1936), for a thoughtful contemporaneous discussion of the common law. While Chief Justice Stone cites Landis' work, it seems clear that he had arrived at many analogous conclusions independently. See note 17, infra. See also Traynor, "Statutes Revolving in Common Law Orbits," 17 *Cath. U. L. Rev.* 401 (1968). Cf. Cardozo, "A Ministry of Justice," 35 *Harv. L. Rev.* 113 (1921); Friendly, "The Gap in Law Making—Judges Who Can't and Legislators Who Won't," 63 *Colum. L. Rev.* 787 (1963). In a real sense all of these writers are precursors of the approach discussed in this book.

16. R. Dworkin, *Taking Rights Seriously* 111 (1977). Dworkin uses the term "gravitational force."

17. See Landis, supra note 15, at 224-225, where he discusses the effect of nineteenth-century bastardy laws on the interpretation of wills and on the construction of wrongful death statutes. The bastardy statutes generally did no more than permit an illegitimate child to take by intestacy from its mother. The equity or pull of these statutes led many courts, however, to read the word "child" in a will to include the illegitimate child, despite strong common law precedents to the contrary. In addition, such changes in the "principles of intestate distribution" had an important effect on who would be deemed next of kin for purposes of recovery under wrongful death statutes, which, although roughly contemporaneous with the bastardy laws, were not correlated with them. It did not matter to Landis whether the changes in the principles of intestacy and in the common law interpretations of wills preceded or followed the passage of wrongful death laws: "changes in the principles of intestate distribution, whether made prior or subsequent to the death statutes, should therefore carry through into the distribution of compensation effected by the death acts." Id. at 225. Changes in the legal landscape not only justified courts in giving an altered reading to a prior statute but had actually brought it about in this nineteenth-century instance.

Chief Justice Stone's focus is also on statutes as aids in updating the common law: "a statute is not an alien intruder in the house of the common law, but a guest to be welcomed and made at home there as a new and powerful aid in the accomplishment of its appointed task of accommodating the law to social needs." Stone, supra note 15, at 15. But, like Landis, he goes beyond this rejection of the principle of strict construction of statutes in derogation of the common law and argues that we should "treat a statute much more as we treat a judicial precedent, as both a declaration and a source of law, and as a premise for legal reasoning. We have done that with our ancient statutes . . . readily molding them to fit new conditions within their spirit, though not their letter." Id. at 13. He views this as part of the task of proper interpretation and regrets that "we cannot revise *ab initio* our philosophy of interpretation of statutes." He considers the "organization of judge-made and statute law into a coordinated system [as] one of the major problems of the common law in the United States." Id. at 15. The same theme reappears strongly in Traynor, supra note 15: "With perspective we see that for many centuries judges have been accommodating statutes to the common law openly or indirectly, expansively or warily," id. at 403; and "The hydraheaded problem is how to synchronize the unguided missiles launched by legislatures with a going system of common law." Id. at 402.

18. Cf. R. Dworkin, supra note 16, at 105-123, distinguishing the force exerted by an enacted statute from the gravitational force exerted by a common law precedent. The former force depends on the "canonical form of words" in the statute; that canonical form "sets limits to the political decisions that the statute may be taken to have made." Id. at 110. The gravitational force of common law precedent, however, may be explained by appeal to "the fairness of treating like cases alike"; this force, apparently as

distinguished from the force of a statute, "escapes the language of its opinion." Id. at 113. It is doubtful, however, that Dworkin is really saying that statutes have no gravitational effect at all. For he argues: "A precedent is the report of an earlier political decision; the very fact of that decision, as a piece of political history, provides some reason for deciding other cases in a similar way in the future." A statute, no less than a precedent, is the report of an earlier political decision and, as Landis has argued, the very fact of that decision should give some reason for treating later cases, even those not within the terms of the statute, in a similar way. See esp. Traynor, supra note 15.

19. It is important to remember that in Landis, Stone, and Traynor, supra note 15, no less than in Hart and Sacks, supra note 9, Dworkin, supra note 16, and Wellington, "Common Law Rules and Constitutional Double Standards: Some Notes on Adjudication," 83 *Yale L. J.* 221 (1973), the notion of a legal fabric that both justifies and limits judicial lawmaking is taken for granted. They may differ in the degree to which they believe that topography to determine the correct result in any given case, as against merely guiding courts or setting outside limits on appropriate judicial action, but they never doubt that it is there and that it properly exercises a powerful restraint on judicial behavior. And clearly the validity of arguments for, and against, a doctrine like the one we are considering, no less than of arguments for judicial power to develop the common law, depends on one's belief in the existence and force of such a legal fabric. See Chap. IX.

20. The approach of the legal process school finds its fullest description in the great unpublished work by Hart and Sacks, supra note 9. Bickel, Gunther, Wellington, indeed most current legal scholars, consciously or not, have followed its path.

21. See Hart and Sacks, supra note 9, at 1410-17 ("The Rudiments of Statutory Interpretation"). "The function of a court in interpreting a statute is to decide what meaning ought to be given to the directions of the statute in the respects relevant to the case before it. *Comment:* Before deciding that this statement is so nearly indeterminate as to be meaningless, notice what it does *not* say. It does not say that the court's function is to ascertain the intention of the legislature with respect to the matter in issue." Id. at 1410. See also Chap. IV.

22. Hart and Sacks, at 1225-26 ("Why should word meanings be respected at all"), and passim.

23. See, e.g., Hart and Sacks, supra note 9, at 1149-79 (discussing Whiteley v. Chappell, 4 Q.B. 147 (1868), London & India Docks Co. v. Thames Steam and Lighterage Co., House of Lords A.C. 15 (1909), Johnson v. Southern Pacific Co., 117 F. 462 (8th Cir. 1902), and Brown v. United States, 160 F.2d 310 (8th Cir. 1947), on the issue of the literal interpretation of statutory language.

24. See, e.g., Hart and Sacks, supra note 9, at 1203-17 ("New Applications of Old Enactments").

25. See A. Bickel, *The Least Dangerous Branch: The Supreme Court at the Bar of Politics* (1962), and Bickel and Wellington, "Legislative Purpose and Judicial Process: The Lincoln Mills Case," 71 *Harv. L. Rev.* 1 (1957).

26. See A. Bickel, *The Supreme Court and the Idea of Progress* 24-42 (1970), for a statement on Frankfurter's opposition to a literalist judicial posture: "He inveighed against the postulation of absolutes by anyone, most of all by judges." Id. at 31.

27. See, e.g., R. Keeton, *Venturing To Do Justice* (1969); Wellington and Albert, "Statutory Interpretation and the Political Process: A Comment on Sinclair v. Atkinson," 72 *Yale L. J.* 1547 (1963).

28. See Hart and Sacks, supra note 9, at 1411-17.

29. See A. Bickel, supra note 25. See Chap. III on the use of constitutional second-look techniques to update statutes.

30. See R. Keeton, supra note 27. See Chap. IV on the use of techniques of interpretation to update statutes.

31. See Wellington, supra note 19, at 262-264.

32. See Chaps. XIII, XIV, and XV. See also G. Calabresi and P. Bobbitt, *Tragic Choices* (1978).

33. See esp. Chap. XV.

34. Sorrells v. United States, 287 U.S. 435 (1932). See also Chap. XI, note 33.

35. Sorrells v. United States, at 448-451. The quotation is at 450.

36. Sorrells v. United States, at 453 (Robert, J., dissenting in part). The quotation is at 458.

37. Sorrells v. United States, at 450.

38. See G. Gilmore, *The Ages of American Law* 109-110 (1977): "The function of law, in a society like our own . . . is to provide a mechanism for the settlement of disputes in the light of broadly conceived principles on whose soundness, it must be assumed, there is a general consensus among us . . . so long as the consensus exists, the mechanism which the law provides is designed to insure that our institutions adjust to change, which is inevitable, in a continuing process which will be orderly, gradual, and, to the extent that such a thing is possible in human affairs, rational. The function of the lawyer is to preserve skeptical relativism in a society hell-bent for absolutes." See also Gilmore, "Putting Senator Davies in Context," 4 *Vermont L. Rev.* 233 (1979).

39. See note 3, supra, on Davies' approach and its origins.

IX. The Doctrine: A Question of Legitimacy

1. See, e.g., Traynor, "Statutes Revolving in Common Law Orbits," 17 *Cath. U. L. Rev.* 401 (1968): "Of course it was lawmaking to establish standards of reasonableness," id. at 404, and "judicial rules analogized from statutes are at one with other judicial lawmaking." Id. at 425. See also J. Ely, *Democracy and Distrust* 4 (1980): "Of course courts make law all the time."

2. See K. Davis, 1 *Administrative Law Treatise* §2.17 at 136-137 (2d ed. 1978), citing opinion of Marshall, C.J., in Osborn v. Bank of the United States, 22 U.S. (9 Wheat.) 738, 866 (1824): "Judicial power, as contradistinguished from the power of the laws, has no existence. Courts are the mere instruments of the law, and can will nothing. When they are said to exercise a discretion, it is a mere legal discretion, a discretion to be exercised in discerning the course prescribed by law; and, when that is discerned, it is the duty of the Court to follow it. Judicial power is never exercised for the purpose of giving effect to the will of the Judge; *always for the purpose of giving effect to the will of the Legislature; or, in other words, to the will of the law"* (emphasis added). Cf. J. Ely, supra note 1, at 67-68: "An appeal to consensus, or to consensus tempered by the judge's own values, may make some sense in a 'common law' context, where the court is . . . responding to a broad legislative delegation of decision-making authority."

3. The key words are "at times." Delegation may be improper if it allows legislatures to avoid facing issues that, under the Constitution, only majoritarian bodies can decide. And it may be improper if it requires institutions to perform functions that are inconsistent with their required constitutional roles.

4. See J. Ely, supra note 1, at 4-5, 67-69, distinguishing judicial common law power from that of constitutional adjudication.

5. Even if such power should extend to statutes, the desirability, and perhaps the necessity, of having any such delegation of authority made explicit by a legislature remains to be discussed.

6. See e.g., J. Ely, supra note 1, at 4: "in nonconstitutional contexts, the court's decisions are subject to overrule or alteration by ordinary statute. The court is standing in for the legislature, and if it has done so in a way the legislature does not approve, it can soon be corrected." See also id. at 67-69. Cf. discussion of Ely at note 60, infra.

7. Cf. Coase, "The Problem of Social Cost," 3 *J. L. & Econ.* 1 (1960); Calabresi, "Transaction Costs, Resource Allocation and Liability Rules—A Comment," 11 *J. L. & Econ.* 67 (1968), and Dahlman, "The Problem of Externality," 22 *J. L. & Econ.* 141 (1979) (analyzing an analogous tautology in the field of law and economics; for "popular will" substitute "efficiency," for "no inertia" read "no transaction costs," and the now classic Coase theorem applies directly).

8. Cf. Demsetz, "When Does the Rule of Liability Matter?" 1 *J. Legal Stud.* 223 (1972); and Calabresi, supra note 7, which make the analogous move in discussing the effect of transaction costs on Coase's theorem. See also Chap. X for a discussion of the relevance of asymmetries in inertia which relies on transaction costs theory.

9. One could put the question of judicial review under the Constitution in the same way. The crucial difference is, of course, that the burden of overcoming a holding of unconstitutionality is far greater than that required to reverse ordinary judicial lawmaking. See J. Ely, supra note 1, at 4-5, 67-69. Some perhaps could justify even the constitutional review

power in terms of its reversibility by majoritarian bodies. Cf. C. Black, *Decision According to Law* (1981) (defending congressional power to limit the appellate jurisdiction of the Supreme Court on the ground that the possibility of such action by Congress helps to justify judicial review in a democracy). See also Shapiro, "Judicial Modesty, Political Reality and Preferred Position," 47 *Cornell L. Q.* 175 (1961) at 192 (suggesting that constitutional adjudication may be no more final than ordinary judicial lawmaking), and A. Bickel, *The Least Dangerous Branch: The Supreme Court at the Bar of Politics* 244-272 (1962) (treating constitutional holdings as at the middle of the lawmaking process and not at the end).

10. Similarly in most state governments, and despite occasional recall statutes, extended terms of office diminish the immediacy of the response of popularly elected officials. Cf. Tyler, "Court Versus Legislature: The Sociopolitics of Malapportionment," 27 *Law & Contemp. Prob.* 390 (1962).

11. See Shapiro, supra note 9, at 185-194; cf. Tyler, supra note 10, at 404. J. Ely, supra note 1, at 67, admits that such undemocratic aspects of legislatures may be capable of blocking legislation, but he powerfully attacks the notion that this fact can justify judicial nullification of statutes at the *constitutional* level. His skepticism of judicial capacity to discern a kind of "filtered consensus" does not, however, cause him to reject ordinary lawmaking by courts but only the "transfer [of] analytical techniques [from common law fields] to the constitutional area without dropping a stitch." Id. at 68.

12. See text at notes 17-25, infra.

13. See Chap. V, for a discussion of the inevitable effect that the presence of staff has in making administrative agencies sensitive to political pressures.

14. The quotation is from Justice Hugo Black, who told one of his law clerks, now Professor Daniel Meador of the University of Virginia Law School, that if after trying as hard as he could to determine the intent of the Constitution or of a statute he could find no adequate guidance, he would then simply "do what was right for the country". Cf. Holmes's view that "Where there is doubt . . . even if it is disguised and unconscious, the judges are called on to exercise the sovereign prerogative of choice." O. Holmes, "Law in Science and Science in Law," in *Collected Legal Papers* 210, 239 (1921).

15. Thus J. Ely, supra note 1, at 67-68, while strongly critical of this approach as a basis of constitutional adjudication, admits its possible applicability as to common law, conditional, rules. Paul Freund, in passing, has suggested that even as to constitutional adjudication judicial power to review old laws to see if they conform to current values may be justified. See also Chap. X, note 34.

16. F. Gény, *Méthode d'interpretation* (1st ed. 1899). Gény, whose ideas concerning interpretation of the French Civil Code are summarized in J. Stone, *The Province and Function of Law* 149-160 (1946), argued in contrast to the then prevailing exegetical view that where (as often occurred) the legis-

lator's will could not be discerned concerning a particular problem of interpretation, the judge should resort to "free scientific research"—choosing a rule of law based on custom or his own standard of justice or utility. Such a method seems almost inevitable in view of Article 4 of the French Civil Code (Crabb. trans. 1977) which prohibits judges, on penalty of criminal conviction, from refusing to decide cases because of the insufficiency or ambiguity of the Code, and the insistence that earlier judicial decisions may not in theory serve as a source of law.

More frequently, the *ad hoc* response is defined in terms of a new principle that is not in fact applied in the particular case but ultimately becomes far more significant than the case that failed to apply it. In constitutional law, the Japanese internment cases of World War II are arguably of this sort. See, e.g., Korematsu v. United States, 323 U.S. 214 (1944). Decided while the war was still on, these cases were soon criticized as having been wrongly decided. See, e.g., Rostow, "The Japanese American Cases—A Disaster," 54 *Yale L. J.* 489 (1945). The ironic feature about *Korematsu* is that it was in this case that Justice Black first announced the doctrine that racial classifications are inherently suspect. 323 U.S. at 216. At the time, the doctrine was not much noticed. (For example, the Rostow article just cited has no discussion of the significance of the doctrine.) But *Korematsu* turned out to be one of the very few decisions in which the use of a suspect classification was upheld, and the doctrine came to be the basis for a plethora of equal protection cases striking down racial and other discriminations.

17. See, e.g., Landis, "Statutes and the Sources of Law," in *Harvard Legal Essays* 213 (1934); Stone, "The Common Law in the United States," 50 *Harv. L. Rev.* 4 (1936); H. Hart and A. Sacks, *The Legal Process: Basic Problems in the Making and Application of Law* (MS 1958); R. Dworkin, *Taking Rights Seriously* (1977); Wellington, "Common Law Rules and Constitutional Double Standards: Some Notes on Adjudication," 83 *Yale L. J.* 221 (1973); and Traynor, supra note 1.

18. Breitel, "The Lawmakers," 65 *Colum. L. Rev.* 749, 772 (1965), quoted with approval by Chief Justice Traynor, supra note 1, at 402.

19. See, e.g., Traynor, supra note 1, at 401: "A judge's . . . training for fitting pieces into a coherent whole makes him technologically indispensable in any age." See also R. Dworkin, supra note 17; Wellington, supra note 17, and H. Hart and A. Sacks, supra note 17.

20. Cf. Chap. V, text at notes 32, 33, suggesting that absence of staff paradoxically may help courts in this task.

21. See A. Bickel, *The Supreme Court and the Idea of Progress* 81-82 (1970); A. Bickel, supra note 9, at 69-70; Traynor, supra note 1, at 402.

22. See, e.g., authorities cited at notes 17 and 18, supra. It is skepticism on this point, I think, as well as doubt as to the existence of a legal fabric definite enough to control judges, that leads Ely to reject what he terms "the consensus approach" as a basis for judicial power to go beyond ordinary lawmaking and to create constitutional obstacles to legislation. J. Ely, supra note 1, at 67-69.

23. The fact that such rules arise out of "real" situations is, of course, linked to the incremental nature of judicial lawmaking. But it also provides a separate justification. Issues look different in real, individual cases than when they are posed at large or abstractly. We know that people vote differently on the same issue depending on how it is presented. It is not unreasonable to have among our lawmaking institutions one whose view of what is required is influenced predominantly by a presentation of the issues in individual contexts.

24. Edmund Burke distinguished between the momentary political expressions of the people and the more enduring attitudes and values of the people derived from the past. See, e.g., Burke, "Appeal from the New to the Old Whigs," 4 *Collected Works* 162-177 (1865-1867), and *Reflections on the Revolution in France* 95, 186-187 (Oxford 1907). In discussing Burke, Alexander Bickel described the function of these values: "The visions of good and evil, the denominations to be computed—these a society draws from its past and without them it dies." A. Bickel, *The Morality of Consent* 24 (1975). There is, of course, a long tradition of scholars of the common law who have pointed to these deeply rooted values as the source or the inspiration of common law rules. This tradition can be traced back at least as far as Blackstone's claim that the common law is the custom of the realm. See W. Blackstone, 1 *Commentaries,* Introduction, section 3 (Sharswood ed. 1868). See also Chief Justice Stone's comment: "We cannot examine critically the course of the common law in this country without acknowledging the varying, but at times far-reaching, effect upon it of a legal philosophy which looks to the past as the means, not only of securing a needful continuity of legal doctrine, but as affording the measure of experience which is to guide the development of the law." Stone, supra note 17, at 11.

25. I assume, of course, that the discrimination, the unequal treatment, stays within broad constitutional bounds. Cf. Chap. II.

26. See, e.g., Traynor, supra note 1, at 402-403: "we no longer can afford to have judges retreat into formulism . . . to shield wooden precedents from any radiations of forward-looking statutes while they ignored dry rot in the precedents themselves. There was a deep plunge into such formulism during the eighteenth century . . . under the spell of Blackstone's vision of the common law as a completed formal landscape graced with springs of wisdom that judges needed only to discover to refresh their minds for the instant case . . . The formulism of the eighteenth century, riding with the always strong force of inertia, continued to hold sway in the nineteenth century. Though it has long since been discredited by its cumulative inadequacies and distortions, it remains to haunt our own time." See also Pound, "Common Law and Legislation," 21 *Harv. L. Rev.* 383 (1908); Page, "Statutes as Common Law Principles," 1944 *Wisc. L. Rev.* 175; Stone, supra note 17; and esp. Landis, supra note 17. See also the discussion of Landis in Chap. VIII.

27. Landis, supra note 17.

28. Not all statutes are entitled to such gravitational pull. (The term

derives from Dworkin, who is more skeptical than most modern writers as to the role of statutes as sources of law. See Chap. VIII, note 18; and note 56, infra.) See Traynor, supra note 1, at 424-426, for a discussion of the problem of deciding which statutes are entitled to weight as sources of law. See also Landis, supra note 17, for an analogous discussion.

29. Cf. Wellington, supra note 17; R. Dworkin, supra note 17.

30. Common law rules and even statutes that conflict with our deep constitutional principles, even if they do not actually violate the Constitution, become suspect and vulnerable to change far sooner than rules that do not approach the penumbras of our fundamental charters. See Chaps. III and X.

31. See Traynor, supra note 1, at 425-426. He notes that in cases of common law decision making where a statute is arguably relevant, "The process of discriminating choice involves more than the usual deliberation characteristic of the judicial process. A judge may have to evaluate more than one policy and more than one model for a rule from whatever source, if they appear relevant, and in doing so he may decide to reject rather than accept one model or another." Characteristically Chief Justice Traynor is not troubled by this "freedom" since the choice to reject the model provided by a statute "signifies a considered judgment that it is not appropriate to govern the case, just as its acceptance would signify a considered judgment that it is." Id. at 425. In other words, judicial choice is necessary in any case.

32. Cf. Perry, "The Abortion Funding Cases: A Comment on the Supreme Court's Role in American Government," 66 *Geo. L. J.* 1191, 1234 (1978) (describing some recent controversial Supreme Court decisions as being in accord with dominant or emergent American values).

33. J. Ely, supra note 1, at 67, after listing some of the numerous sources of social values and techniques for identifying them, puts the point forcefully (if perhaps with some exaggeration, see note 37, infra): "it should by now be clear that . . . one can convince oneself that some invocable consensus supports almost any position a civilized person might want to see supported." His criticism, however, causes him to reject the social value or consensus approach only as a basis for *constitutional* adjudication, for "what courts may do properly in common law contexts [on the basis of the consensus approach], has nothing to do with the tasks they can legitimately set themselves in the area of constitutional adjudication." Id. at 69.

34. See, e.g., R. Dworkin, supra note 17, and Dworkin, *Book Review,* Times Literary Supplement (London), Dec. 5, 1975, at 1437 (reviewing R. Cover, *Justice Accused: Anti-Slavery and the Judicial Process* (1975)), discussed and criticized in Hart, "Law in the Perspective of Philosophy, 1776–1976," 51 *N.Y.U.L. Rev.* 538 (1976).

35. See Hart, supra note 34, and Wellington, supra note 17.

36. Cf. notes 14 and 16, supra. See also Hart, supra note 34.

37. See Chap. VIII, note 19. The very existence of limits which, not so long ago, were taken for granted is now frequently questioned. In more

than twenty years of teaching, I have seen a significant change in students' preconceptions on the matter. When I began to teach, many students came to law school assuming an almost mechanical judicial task that called for virtually no judgment, let alone discretion. Academic lawyers realistically emphasized all the room that the legal framework gives to judges. To make the point stronger, many stopped talking about frameworks or fabrics altogether, and the distinction between judgment in trying to map out the law and judicial authority to follow the judges' own values or their sense of popular wishes sometimes got lost in the shuffle. The object, after all, was to expose for the sham that it is any mechanical view of judicial lawmaking. We did our job all too well, and today many students assume that all limits are sham. It is only with some effort that one convinces them, by talking about specific judges in specific cases, that judges — for all the scope they have — do not decide cases as they would were they legislators or even disinterested guardians furthering their own view of right and wrong. The precise nature of the limits is a much more debatable question, of course. We do not need to agree with Dworkin's view that, while there is much need for judgment, there is no room for discretion. See note 34, supra. We can, for example, accept the notion of reasonably firm outward boundaries determined by principles, within which discretion — though not necessarily simply that of a legislator or a pursuer of personal values — can operate. Cf. note 35, supra.

All such approaches recognize that difficult judgments are called for and that there will be errors. But if there are errors, and, even if courts can exercise choice and act where the framework provides inadequate guides, the scope of such actions and errors is nonetheless limited by the existence of outside boundaries. As a result, the potential dangers of such actions and errors are also limited. There are advantages in giving authority to bodies whose exercise of power is constrained, even when those constraints do not always operate. From the standpoint of this book, however, all this is somewhat beside the point. If limits did not exist on judicial behavior, it might be hard to justify a system that gave courts conditional power to make *common law* rules. But once such power was taken for granted, it would be almost impossible to explain why it should not permit courts to force reconsideration of old statutes. See text at notes 58-60, infra.

38. See text at notes 2-17, supra.

39. Cf. Traynor, supra note 1, at 425. After discussing the freedom to make choices among models which at times characterizes judicial lawmaking in a world that includes statutory sources, see note 31, supra, Traynor states of a resulting rule that the continuing force of a choice made by analogy to a statutory rule, "like that of any other precedent, depends on its continuing fitness to survive as it ages. It may endure for generations or succumb to rapid obsolescence" (footnote omitted). Cf. text at notes 78-80, infra.

40. If our principal concern were current popular desires, we might, for example, choose an institution directly dependent on the executive, like

that suggested by Cutler and Johnson, "Regulation and the Political Process," 84 *Yale L. J.* 1395 (1975). But this fact ought to concern us no more than the fact that occasionally courts, in trying to discern the legal landscape, must act like economists or philosophers. I do not doubt that if the legal task were predominantly that of giving effect to economic principles, we would not assign it to judges selected and trained as ours are. (But cf., e.g., Landes and Posner, "The Independent Judiciary in an Interest-Group Perspective," 18 *J. L. & Econ.* 875 (1975), and Ehrlich and Posner, "An Economic Analysis of Legal Rulemaking," 3 *J. Legal Stud.* 257 (1974).) We might even choose economists! But given the many tasks we do assign our judges for which they are suited and trained (and which economists would mangle), the fact that judges must also take economics into account cannot be a major worry.

41. See Wellington, supra note 1. There are extraordinary situations where the map is necessarily contradictory. Philip Bobbitt and I examine some of these in our book, *Tragic Choices* (1978). The existence of such situations, however, renders all of our decision-making devices inadequate. As that book seeks to demonstrate, in such situations the open, majoritarian responsiveness that might ordinarily be viewed as the advantage of legislative decisions can become a reason for not having legislatures decide. At times in such situations we will use juries, at other times judges, and at still other times legislatures that mask their intentions. In any event, the absence of any consistency in a legal landscape to guide the making of choices does not exclude the occasional use of judges even in those cases. Id. at 39–40, 204 nn.13, 14.

42. See text at notes 10–16, supra, and at 78–80, infra.

43. See Traynor, supra note 1, at 425, emphasizing the duty of the judge to follow statutes where they govern. Cf. Landis, supra note 17, and Stone, supra note 17, suggesting some scope for judicial action even when legislatures have spoken. See Chap. VIII, note 17. The traditional view is, of course, contradicted by the many subterfuges courts have used to deal with statutes that do not "fit." See Chaps. II–IV. See also Pound, "Spurious Interpretation," 7 *Colum. L. Rev.* 379 (1907), and Pound, "Common Law and Legislation," 21 *Harv. L. Rev.* 383 (1908), for classic criticisms of such judicial behavior.

44. Cf. Davies, "A Response to Statutory Obsolescence: The Non-primacy of Statutes Act," 4 *Vermont L. Rev.* 203 (1979).

45. See Chap. X for a discussion of such limits.

46. See Chaps. II–IV for a description and criticism of such subterfuges.

47. At one time that was, nominally, the law in England. It is no longer the case even there. See Chap. I, note 7.

48. In the section of *The Legal Process,* supra note 17, entitled "Interpreting the Silences of the Legislature: Herein of the Use of Statutes by Analogy," at 1381–1401, Hart and Sacks raise the issue of the legitimacy of construing legislative silence as either a bar or as an invitation to overrul-

ing a judicial statement. In this section, like so many others of that work, Hart and Sacks offer very few answers, but they set the analytical stage by distinguishing three subsidiary questions: *"First.* In deciding whether to overrule the prior cases, what, if any, weight should be given to the fact that Congress had failed to override them by statute? . . . *Second.* In deciding whether to overrule the prior cases, what, if any, weight should be given to the fact that Congress had since reenacted the section interpreted, without saying whether or not it approved the interpretations? *Third.* In deciding whether to overrule the prior cases, what, if any, weight should be given to the fact that Congress had since enacted a special statute dealing with a related problem in a way which was inconsistent in principle with the earlier interpretations. Should the special statute be taken as marking the outer bounds of inconsistent action, and so as impliedly forbidding overruling? Or should the principle of it be taken as providing support for judicial correction of the inconsistent interpretation of the general statute?" Id. at 1381.

49. See the discussion of Vincent v. Pabst Brewing Co., Chap. IV, text and notes 16-25; and of American Bankers Association v. Connell, Chap. V, text and note 36. Cf. the discussion of Justice Frankfurter's dissenting opinion in Rogers v. Missouri Pacific R. Co., Chap. IV, text and note 14. See also Chap. XI.

50. See Chap. VI, notes 1-11, on Jefferson and the radical sunsetters. See also Chap. X on the bases for retentionist and revisionist biases.

51. Work in political science and political theory in the last twenty-five years has expanded the notion of what can be said to constitute majoritarian support. In his now classic treatment of democratic theory, Robert Dahl argued that the majority rarely rules on matters of specific policy; instead, the policies are selected by a process he termed "minorities rule." Thus majoritarianism (in what he described as a strict Madisonian sense) was not an adequate account of our governmental process, but majoritarianism was still an apt description in the sense that specific policies probably did accord with a consensus of values. See R. Dahl, *A Preface to Democratic Theory* (1956), esp. at 132-134. There is now a substantial literature that attempts to describe majoritarian processes along lines similar to Dahl's — for elections, see, e.g., D. Black, *The Theory of Committees and Elections* (1971), and J. Buchanan and G. Tullock, *The Calculus of Consent* (1974 ed.); for congressional actions, see, e.g., D. Mayhew, *Congress: The Electoral Connection* (1974).

52. See note 24, supra.

53. While time and circumstance may change these common law rules, their change is still accretional, just as their development was. Cf. H. L. A. Hart, "Changing Conceptions of Responsibility," in *Punishment and Responsibility: Essays in the Philosophy of Law* 186-209 (1968), where Hart chronicles the changes in the notion of responsibility for criminal acts. He describes how a rule of law can resist pressures for its change and then undergo a shift in response to cumulative pressures. No one challenge to the rule of law will force the change, but the weight of all the challenges may

bring about a new development. Hart has elsewhere sketched a conception of social morality in general that suggests that social morality, as well as individual moral rules, change accretionally. See H. L. A. Hart, *Law, Liberty and Morality*, 68-73 (1963); see also Hart, supra note 34.

54. Cf. R. Dworkin, supra note 17, at 90-100. Dworkin distinguishes principles from policies as he examines the nature of legislative, and of judicial, lawmaking. Policies, for him, express calculations of the best means of attaining some collective goal; principles, a content of a more deontological sort. Since calculations of utility will shift as underlying social facts change, it seems likely that policies will be extremely changeable when any society is in a time of flux. Principles, in contrast, should be more persistent, changing only in keeping with the sort of changes in the society that could be said to work a change in morality or social values. See note 53, supra. While it would not be accurate to equate the principle-policy distinction with the judicial-legislative difference, it nonetheless seems fair to conclude that for Dworkin principles play a significant role only with respect to the judicial task. Thus common law rules should be less time-dependent than legislative acts on Dworkin's view as well.

55. As a general proposition, we would of course expect that even a correct *ad hoc* judicial response would lapse into legal obscurity. We would expect that such cases would usually trigger no new developments in the law and would, instead, tend to wither away, choked by those legal developments that are more broadly based and more enduring. Not infrequently, however, a judicial decision that is *ad hoc* at the time it is made engenders a doctrine which, after a period of gestation, comes to term and to full judicial life. See, e.g., Scott v. Shepherd, 3 Wils. 403, 95 Eng. Rep. 1124 (Common Pleas 1773), and Rylands v. Fletcher (1868) L.R. 3 H.L. 330 (*affirming* (1866) L.R. Excheq. 265, *which reversed* 34 L.J. Rep. N.S. 177 (1865)), decisions that could be taken to be *ad hoc* responses to particular problems in torts law and that at other times and places became, instead, the bases for fundamental notions.

56. See Landis, supra note 17, discussed in Chap. VIII, text at notes 15-19 (statute's "equity" enables judges to slough off anachronisms in the legal structure). See also Traynor, supra note 1 (inappropriate statutes should be rejected as models for judge-made rules). Ronald Dworkin, supra note 17, suggests that statutes, unlike judicial decisions, do not have gravitational pull, a claim that, taken literally, seems doubtful. See note 28, supra, and Chap. VIII, note 18. It seems likely that what Dworkin had in mind were those statutory enactments that were merely *ad hoc* responses to specific developments in the society, or those that were inconsistent responses to particular societal demands. Such legislative enactments might properly have little or no gravitational pull.

57. See Vincent v. Pabst Brewing Co., 47 Wis. 2d 120, 131, 177 N.W.2d 513, 523 (1970) (separate opinion of Hallows, C.J.).

58. See Davies, supra note 44. See also text at notes 2-5, supra, and 87-99, infra.

59. See text at notes 7-9, supra. Cf. J. Ely, supra note 1, at 4, 67-68; Davies, supra note 44 (limiting the power to statutes twenty years old).

60. See text at notes 10-16, supra. It is these last justifications which, in the context of *constitutional* adjudication, John Ely derides as "the Führer principle." J. Ely, supra note 1, at 68. Ely seems less troubled by analogous justifications for common lawmaking and notes, perhaps too readily, that "appeals to this sort of filtered consensus may make sense." Id. at 67-68. It is not altogether clear, however, whether such judicial power may make sense at common law because "the legislature has [not] spoken," or because the court decision "can be undone" in ways easier than "by the cumbersome process of constitutional amendment." Id. at 68. Ely does not, of course, focus on problems of court power outside the constitutional context, and so one should not criticize the fact that he leaves his views on this point, expressed in passing, unresolved. Paul Freund seems much less troubled than Ely by these justifications, at least when applied to old laws. See Chap. X, note 34.

61. Cf. Cutler and Johnson, supra note 40, but see Freund's suggestion that courts may be such a body, Chap. X, note 34.

62. See Chap. VII on the many reasons for statutes.

63. See Chap. IV, notes 16-35 and accompanying text, for a discussion of these statutes.

64. An example of this might be a statute passed by a pro-rancher legislature which specified that liability for the trespass of cattle should exist, but only if the cattle broke through a fence. At the time such a statute was enacted, the absence of fencing materials meant that cattle could roam at will. Small gardens might be protected, but these posed no danger to a ranching industry based on freedom to pasture at large. The invention of barbed wire, which permitted the fencing in of enormous tracts of land at relatively little cost, converted such a statute into one that doomed the open range and favored those very farming interests who had lost in the legislature. See W. Webb, *The Great Plains* (1931), and Chap. VII, notes 35-37. For an example of legal change that alters the effect of a preexisting statute, see the discussion of the effect of one-man-one-vote rulings on Connecticut statutes dealing with withdrawals from multitown school regions, Chap. X, text at notes 12-13.

65. Rylands v. Fletcher, note 55, supra, has often been viewed as an *ad hoc* judicial decision imposing nonfault liability to favor traditional landowners over new industrialists who had won out in Parliament when the Corn Laws were repealed.

66. Thus Rylands v. Fletcher, note 55, supra, though perhaps *ad hoc* when decided, became one of the bases for a more general legal principle supporting nonfault liability for certain types of ultrahazardous activities.

67. Cf. Traynor, supra note 1, at 425.

68. One function of majoritarian bodies is precisely to make such *ad hoc* decisions as are wanted by a currently dominant majority or coalition of minorities and do not violate our basic charters. If such a preference, though valid, approaches constitutional invalidity, courts may be jusitfied

in requiring a legislative second look to reaffirm that the encroachment on the fringes of our basic principles was, and continues to be, intended.

69. Many New Deal statutes that were in dramatic derogation of the existing legal fabric when enacted came over time to fit the fabric completely. They were in fact precursors of a new legal order, early tracings of a new map. See Chap. V, text at notes 1-6.

70. See, e.g., Landis, supra note 17.

71. Cf. the legislative reaction to the Wisconsin Supreme Court decision in Vincent v. Pabst Brewing Co., discussed in Chap. IV, notes 16-25 and accompanying text. I am using the word "wrong" here in a rather special way, which I will discuss in Chap. X, esp. at notes 4-5.

72. See Chaps. XI and XII. See also text at notes 78-80, infra.

73. See, e.g., Landis, supra note 17. A problem may arise because of the incremental nature of much common lawmaking. To the extent that a statute can be modified or updated incrementally, all that was said earlier about the safeguards such incrementalism imposes on judicial lawmaking applies here. To the extent, however, that a statute cannot be updated in bits and pieces, application of judicial power to the statute will require the development of other techniques to give us analogous safeguards. See text at notes 78-80, infra, and Chap. X, note 2. I will discuss such techniques in Chaps. XI and XII. There is, moreover, a significant sense in which all judicial adjudication is necessarily incremental. See Chap. X, notes 5-6.

74. Cf. Cutler and Johnson, supra note 40; letter from Clifford S. Fishman (Nov. 15, 1978), note 82, infra. The very qualities that make such a body representative, and able to discern current majoritarian feelings, are also apt to impede any examination of the legal landscape. A body so constituted is not likely to be subservient to principles and is likely to strike down statutes that still fit, but that it deems unsupported by current popular desires. See Chap. V. This is not a problem if we are willing to become less tied to our system of checks and balances. Cf. Chap. VII. It is a fatal objection if instead we wish laws that fit — that have in a sense evolved — to remain in force unless a strong legislative consensus exists against them. If, moreover, we were to decide to solve the problem of dated laws by abandoning checks and balances, it would seem more desirable to do so directly by moving toward a parliamentary system than by giving "unchecked power" to a new semirepresentative body. See Chap. V. For this reason it is little wonder that so perceptive a writer as Lloyd Cutler has moved from the proposal described in his article with Johnson, recommending greater presidential direction of administrative agencies, to a position advocating more fundamental change of our high-friction system of checks and balances, notably adoption by constitutional amendment of elements of a parliamentary system. See Chap. VII, note 2.

75. See text at notes 58-60, supra. If one assumes instead that courts are good at discerning the popular will or what is right for the country, or both, and that these capacities are what justifies judicial common law power, then the problem does not arise.

76. The increasing use of subterfuges or of dangerously ill-suited doc-

trines by courts to attack the problem suggests that living with statutes that do not fit and seem to have lost popular support is not available to us. Courts are already undermining these laws in ways that are either less than candid or, because they are based on constitutional adjudication, deprive legislatures of the chance to reverse an ill-advised judicial decision. See Chaps. II-IV.

77. See note 74, supra.

78. See text at notes 1-16, 38-52, supra.

79. This is in fact what happened in Illinois where the legislature did not react to a judicial threat to reconsider the common law doctrine of contributory negligence. While a lower court subsequently sought to impose comparative negligence judicially, the supreme court of the state retreated from its "suggestion" and stayed with the old rule. See Maki v. Frelk, 40 Ill. 2d 193, 239 N.E. 2d 445 (1968), *reversing* 85 Ill. App. 2d 439, 229 N.E.2d 284 (1967).

80. See Chap. XI; also note 73, supra, and Chap. X, notes 2-4.

81. Given that they do this now by subterfuges, see note 76, supra, it seems obvious that they would do it under the doctrine proposed since the other possibilities are either unavailable or worse.

82. Cf. H. Hart and A. Sacks, supra note 17, esp. at 162-170 ("The Problems Appropriate for Adjudication"). Doubts about the appropriateness of assigning this sort of task to ordinary law courts may be seen in some of the various proposals for noncourt bodies to undertake the necessary scrutiny of statutes. Cf., e.g., letter from Clifford S. Fishman of Catholic University Law School (Nov. 15, 1978) (on file in Yale Law School Library). Fishman proposes two alternative noncourt bodies that could undertake the review of statutes for reconsideration: first, a statutory review commission, to be created by Congress for the purpose, and, second, a special congressional committee. See also Cutler and Johnson, supra note 40 (discussing merit of President's intervention in regulatory review); and Friendly, "A Look at the Federal Administrative Agencies," 60 *Colum. L. Rev.* 429, 435 (1960) (discussing pressures to make regulatory agencies adjudicate more like courts).

Suggestions of this sort are on point insofar as they recognize that the bodies that undertake review of statutes do not necessarily need to be the same courts we turn to for other judicial activity. Historically, the trend in this country has been to meld all courts into one system. But that melding is not foreordained, as is evidenced by the experience in other countries. For example, in France the Conseil d'Etat, a judicial review body composed largely of career officials, is the highest administative law court, see Lagrange, "The French Council of State (Conseil d'Etat)," 18 *Tulane L. Rev.* 46 (1968), but is not part of the ordinary law trial or appeal tribunals. Similarly, in many countries, constitutional court judges are appointed in ways very different from ordinary judges, and the constitutional court is not part of the ordinary trial or appeal court system. It remains a judicial body nonetheless because its functions are judicial. See M. Cappelletti, *Judicial Review in the Contemporary World* (1971). Thus it would appear that it is at least possible to maintain a separate court or court system for the purpose of statutory review without necessarily integrating those courts into the ordinary system of courts. However, each one of these suggestions is misleading if it reflects the assumption that a review body would not be a judicial body were it not part of the traditional court system. What is at issue is not the place of the review body in our current court system, but rather whether or not the job to be done is sufficiently of a judicial nature so that whatever the origin of the reviewing body, it comes in time to act like a court. What is ironic about some of these suggestions for noncourt reviewing bodies is that the suggestions then try to make the body function more like a court (i.e., more judicially) in order to perform the reviewing function well. In short, this sort of suggestion ends up seeking a body that is fundamentally judicial in function if not in description.

If assigning the burden of inertia is basically a judicial task involving skills similar to those we have long expected from courts, then we would expect that asking noncourt bodies to exercise that power would create pressures for those noncourt bodies to become more and more like courts. We have already seen one example of this kind of dynamic: the pressures on agency adjudicatory bodies to act more like courts. See Chap. V, note 12. Another example of the same dynamic may be seen in the development of the Court of Claims. Before the creation of the Court of Claims, recourse of a claimant for money from the United States government was had only by legislative act: the claimant petitioned Congress to redress his grievances through a private bill. The burden on Congress of this procedure, and its inequities to claimants, led to the Act of Feb. 24, 1855, 10 Stat. 612, which established the Court of Claims. Even as it was first established, however, it was less a court than a screening board: though the court could make findings of fact and conclusions of law, its decisions were simply a report to Congress. The congressional committees to which the decisions were referred were free, and apparently willing, to examine the question *de novo.* Not until Gordon v. United States, 69 U.S. (2 Wall.) 561 (1865), was the court able to enter judgment. The final stage of the Court of Claims' development from legislative body into full-fledged court came about when it was congressionally declared to be a court established under Article III. Act of July 28, 1953, ch. 253 §1, 67 Stat. 226, codified at 28 U.S.C. §171. See P. Bator et al., *Hart and Wechsler's The Federal Courts and the Federal System* 375-418 (2d ed. 1973).

83. Cf., e.g., M. Horwitz, *The Transformation of American Law, 1780-1860* (1977).

84. Cf. Clardy v. Levi, 545 F.2d 1241 (9th Cir. 1976), discussed at Chap. X, note 10, for an example of a court that explicitly refused to adopt a more than plausible interpretation of a statute because it believed that such an interpretation would have been immediately overturned by Congress.

85. The requirement that courts in such instances be aware of majoritarian feelings, however, is in practice no more destructive than the need for judges to behave as if they were economists or philosophers. See note 40, supra. For my own "conservative" bias in such situations, see Chap. X, text at note 7. With that bias compare Freund's more activist bias, Chap. X, note 34.

86. Cf. Davies, supra note 44.

87. This point was argued forcefully in A. Bickel, supra note 9, at 156-169 (1962). Cf., e.g., United States v. Rock Royal Cooperative, 307 U.S. 533 (1939) (upholding the Agricultural Marketing Act of 1932, which authorized the Secretary of Agriculture to set parity prices for agricultural products), and Yakus v. United States, 326 U.S. 414 (1944) (upholding delegation of power to the Office of Price Administration to set "fair and equitable" maximum prices under the Emergency Price Control Act of 1942), with Watkins v. United States, 354 U.S. 178 (1957) (striking down a criminal contempt conviction for refusing to answer questions of the House Un-American Activities Committee), and Kent v. Dulles, 357 U.S. 116 (1958) (denying the Secretary of State discretionary power over passports). Bickel argued that the distinction between valid and invalid delegations "must lie in the importance of the decision left to the administrator or other official. And this is a judgment that will naturally be affected by the proximity of the area of delegated discretion to a constitutional issue. The more fundamental the issue, the nearer it is to principle, the more important it is that it be decided in the first instance by the legislature." A. Bickel, supra, at 161.

88. The situation is more problematic, however, when we ask if the Supreme Court could strike down an exercise by a state court of the power, even if the result of the exercise was to keep a state legislature from facing issues which, on Bickellian delegation grounds, were to be faced by legislatures. Our sense of federalism rebels at the prospect of the Supreme Court's striking down a state court's decision that one of its statutes was out of date and in need of revision, just as our sense of federalism causes us to hesitate before allowing the Supreme Court to review delegation by state legislatures even when an analogous delegation would be impermissible at the federal level. But it may be that in Sweezy v. New Hampshire, 354 U.S. 234 (1957), the Court effected just that kind of control of state delegation. The situation in *Sweezy* closely paralleled the situation in Watkins v. United States, 354 U.S. 178 (1957) which was decided on the same day. In *Sweezy,* appellant was held guilty of contempt when he refused to answer questions posed to him by the state attorney general, acting on behalf of the state legislature under a very broad investigative resolution. Although the majority regarded the two cases in a similar manner, 354 U.S. at 235, Justice Frankfurter's concurrence called attention to the federalism question: "It would make the deepest inroads upon our federal system for this Court now to hold that it can determine the appropriate distribution of powers and their delegation within the forty-eight States." 354 U.S. at 256.

In Frankfurter's view, the validity of the delegation was a question for the state supreme court only, but since he found that the state's intrusion into the citizen's right to political privacy violated the Fourteenth Amendment, he concurred in the result.

An analogous undue state-delegation ground might have permitted the Supreme Court to avoid facing the obviously troublesome questions of reverse discrimination posed in Regents of Univ. of Calif. v. Bakke, 438 U.S. 265 (1978). For here too one might have argued that decisions in favor of affirmative action were sufficiently "important" (to use Bickel's word) to demand legislative consideration. The Supreme Court, perhaps mindful of Frankfurter's warning in Sweezy, did not use the delegation-of-powers approach, however, and found other ways of ducking the hardest issues at stake. See Calabresi, *"Bakke* as Pseudo-Tragedy," 28 *Cath. U. L. Rev.* 427 (1979), esp. n.35.

89. Even if it is the case that on occasion the legislature is able to duck an issue because of judicial exercise of the doctrine, it does not follow that the doctrine is therefore infirm. For if the doctrine is infirm because it leads occasionally to legislative avoidance, then the subterfuges employed by the courts in the past to achieve the same result would be constitutionally improper as well. A legislature is just as able, if not more so, to avoid a troublesome question when the courts act under the guise of interpretation, of equal protection or due process, or by exercise of one of the passive virtues. If anything, these less candid techniques are likely to lead to more legislative avoidance because they are less obvious.

90. Cf. note 82, supra.

91. See, e.g., Chap. VIII, note 6.

92. Unfortunately, it is not always the case that adding new functions to governmental or societal organs merely increases their capabilities. Sometimes, instead, the addition of the new function interferes with the other functions already expected of that body.

Juries, for example, are societal organs whose essential functions preclude certain other functions. We expect, in this society, that juries will serve as "aresponsible" representatives of community attitudes and values. See G. Calabresi and P. Bobbitt, supra note 41, at 57-62. If juries are to function adequately in representing community values, then we must take great care to ensure that they are free of pressures that undercut their credibility as unbiased givers of results without explanation. One way to make sense of the Supreme Court case of Witherspoon v. Illinois, 391 U.S. 510 (1968), is to read the decision as a rejection of the state's attempt to pervert the jury's representative function. Illinois at that time permitted the prosecution to exclude from juries in capital criminal trials jurors who had "conscientious scruples against capital punishment." 391 U.S. at 512. The Court held that a defendant cannot constitutionally be put to death at the hands of a jury from which potential jurors who express general objections to the death penalty were systematically excluded. Now the problem with Illinois' system was not that juries so selected reached *results* that were constitutionally unacceptable. The Court had not yet held and did not hold in *Witherspoon* that the legislature could not decree an *automatic* death penalty for certain crimes, 391 U.S. at 540 (White, J., dissenting). I would suggest the problem was that Illinois was attempting to bias the *jury* in order to secure such "valid" results. This attempt was deemed invalid because it perverted a societal organ whose primary function is to be representative and unbiased. For a contrasting view of *Witherspoon,* see A. Bickel, supra note 21, at 70-75.

93. Unless this power led to an overburdening of legislatures so that they could no longer perform their other tasks. I will argue later that an appropriately limited doctrine would not do so. The same question and the same answer would apply with respect to overburdening of courts. See Chap. X.

94. See C. Black, *Structure and Relationship in Constitutional Law* (1969).

95. Cf. Traynor, supra note 1, at 426: "We have seen that history has given the lie to the preachments of such separation . . . The real problem is not whether judges should make use of statutes, but how they can make optimum use of them."

96. See Chaps. XIII and XIV.

97. See Chaps. XIII-XV.

98. See letter from Jack Davies (Oct. 18, 1978) (on file in Yale Law School Library).

99. There is a separate question of whether in some situations courts may be required by the Constitution to force the updating of statutes. This ingenious idea was suggested to me by Charles Black, see Chap. III, note 44. The notion is that there may be some issues as to which the very structure of our government, or the requirement of a republican form of government, or concepts of due process and equal protection, demand a *current* answer by a relatively majoritarian body although there may be no constitutional requirement as to what that answer must be. The constitutional right, which courts would be bound to enforce, is only to obtain a current legislative, or otherwise majoritarian, reconsideration. Thus, by analogy, a one-man-one-vote rule for legislative apportionment might not be required, but any deviations from that rule must frequently be reconsidered and approved in an election where a one-man-one-vote rule obtains. The Supreme Court did not, of course, take that position in reapportionment cases and affirmed instead the constitutional right to equal representation itself. See L. Tribe, *American Constitutional Law* 738-761 (1978). Such a constitutional right to a majoritarian reconsideration but not to a substantive result may be what Justice Stevens had in mind in Califano v. Goldfarb, 430 U.S. 199, 217 (1977). See Chap. II, text at notes 6-13; Chap. II, note 10; and Chap. X, note 29. It is closely linked to Bickel's whole approach to doctrines of vagueness, delegation, and desuetude. See Chap. III and note 87, supra. If it did exist, one presumes that it would apply only to those out-of-phase laws that present issues whose current majoritarian resolution is fundamental to our system of government. As to these, judicial use of the

doctrine we have been discussing would clearly be legitimate, apart from any legislative delegation, for the power would derive from the Constitution itself.

100. See Chap. VI, text at notes 1-11.

101. See note 82, supra.

X. The Doctrine: Limits and Guidelines

1. Cf. Chap. I, text at notes 7-8.

2. It can only be comfortable when that support is demonstrated by changes in the fabric of the law. To say that courts are not good at gauging current support is only to say that they are neither trained nor positioned to discern it directly with any special skill. The same can be said of decisions that require courts to take into account economic or other social science concepts. By and large they do that best when these concepts have come to be filtered, as it were, and presented to the courts in legal language as part of the legal topography. Cf. Calabresi, "Concerning Cause and the Law of Torts: An Essay for Harry Kalven, Jr.," 43 *U. Chi. L. Rev.* 69 (1975). At times, however, they must take these concepts directly into account. That others, trained in economics, say, could deal with these occasional situations better than courts is irrelevant, since most of the time the issues before courts, including filtered economic ones, are ones that courts are best positioned and trained to handle. Courts will do the best they can to consider the relevant social science directly but will, understandably and properly, be skeptical when that consideration leads them too far away from the more filtered wisdom they are trained and enjoined to follow. The same is true for situations in which courts must consider and gauge current majority sentiments or legislative feelings. See also Chap. IX, note 40. Actually the judicial role in such cases is somewhat easier, for if courts have employed appropriate techniques, legislatures will be able to respond by giving them some of the needed data. See note 3, infra.

3. The analogy to bank loans and bridge players may still be helpful. A banker will refuse to make some loans on a hunch, even though good banking practices might suggest that the loans were all right. Similarly, a bridge player will fail to double when the cards seem to call for it, on a hunch. If the player or banker is good, that hunch will turn out right most of the time. One can ask the same of judges. But just as a banker who, on a hunch, makes a loan that violates banking rules will be severely censured, so should a court that strikes down a statute (that fits the legal fabric) on a hunch that its legislative support had waned.

In fact courts have an advantage over bankers and bridge players. They do not need to commit themselves so completely and all at once. They can in cases of doubt use those techniques that encourage legislatures, scholars, and even the public to engage them in dialogue and give back data stronger than hunches. Case-by-case adjudication encourages this kind of dialogue because individual decisions can always be modified by other courts, or even by the same court, after legislative and other reaction. The same is true even when the case-by-case adjudication involves statutes, especially if the techniques used are the ones that encourage legislative reaction before final action is taken. See Chap. IX, text at notes 78-80, and Chaps. XI and XII. Indeed, Alexander Bickel argued forcefully that it was in a sense true even of constitutional adjudication. Constitutional decisions can be and are overruled; they also are at times ignored. As a result, a constitutional decision by the Supreme Court lies in the middle of the process of making constitutional law. See A. Bickel, *The Least Dangerous Branch: The Supreme Court at the Bar of Politics* 244-278 (1962), esp. at 244, 258-259. See also authorities cited in Chap. IX, note 9. In this sense all judicial adjudication is necessarily incremental.

4. The ease with which this kind of criticism can be made, together with the fact that other courts can ignore the "wrong" judicial decision in analogous situations, lend to such court decisions the same types of safeguards that the incremental nature of common law adjudication gave to judicial lawmaking in that area. Cf. Chap. IX, note 73 and Chap. IX, text at notes 78-80.

5. It may seem paradoxical to call something "wrong" if you expect people to do it and will criticize them if they don't. Yet, if the availability of the term serves to control the behavior and to limit it to the extent desirable, then we would be foolish to deprive ourselves of it. Cf. Chap. XIII. This fact explains the use of the term in both the bank loan and bridge examples and its applicability to judicial decisions that go beyond the boundaries of legislative inertia.

6. This assumes that one does not accept as a justification for judicial power to make common law either the courts' disinterested sense of values or the courts' capacity to respond directly to current majoritarian desires. If one does accept those justifications, then any judicial actions based on them, within the range of legislative inertia, are also justified.

7. This kind of statute, which I said posed the hardest problem of legitimacy if subjected to judicial review, see Chap. IX, would be subject to legitimate sunset if one instead accepted a general revisionist bias, because its majoritarian basis would be "unproven." See esp. Chap. IX, text at notes 84-85. The same might be true if one accepted a justification of judicial power based on the courts' capacity "to review old laws to see if they still comport with current political beliefs and values," as Paul Freund has suggested. See note 34, infra.

8. See Calabresi, "Transaction Costs, Resource Allocation and Liability Rules—A Comment," 11 *J. L. & Econ.* 67 (1968); G. Calabresi, *The Costs of Accidents: A Legal and Economic Analysis* (1970); and Demsetz, "When Does the Rule of Liability Matter?" 1 *J. Legal Stud.* 13 (1972). See also Union Oil Co. v. Oppen, 501 F.2d 558 (9th Cir. 1974) (Sneed, J.), for a judicial use of this approach.

9. If one believes, for example, that in certain transactions a party is not likely to know what is best for him or her, one may seek an allocation of

costs that protects the party and makes it difficult for a free-market negotiation to reverse the protection. Cf. G. Calabresi, supra note 8, at 51-54.

10. Clardy v. Levi, 545 F.2d 1241, 1246 (9th Cir. 1976). Here Judge Sneed, after admitting that a good case could be made for application of the Administrative Procedure Act to prison disciplinary proceedings, noted that such application "would induce Congress to act quickly to overturn our decision and perhaps to write into law rules pertaining to disciplinary hearings in federal prisons. On the other hand, to fail to hold the APA applicable . . . will permit the continuation of the evolution that currently is taking place in the federal courts. This course perhaps will not be as an effective spur to Congressional action as would be its opposite. We grasp this nettle . . . Our desire to avoid confusion . . . and to permit continuation of the judicial evolution in this area overcomes our desire to invoke the assistance of Congress."

11. There are, however, dangers in the judicial use of blackmail, for the legislature may not react as the court expects. See Chap. IX, text at notes 24-27. A failed blackmail attempt may explain the Supreme Court decision in Reid v. Covert, 354 U.S. 1 (1957). The wives of two military men stationed overseas argued that their convictions in trials by courts-martial for murdering their husbands were invalid because they had been denied a jury trial. The Court held that Article 2(11) of the Uniform Code of Military Justice, 50 U.S.C. §552(11), providing for the trial by court-martial of "all persons . . . accompanying the armed forces" of the United States in foreign countries, could not constitutionally be applied in capital cases to the trial of civilian dependents accompanying members of the armed forces overseas in times of peace. The decision left such murders without criminal penalties under United States law. The opinion of the Court, written by Justice Black, denounced the extension of military justice over civilians in rather broad terms, but had the support of only three other members of the Court. Justices Clark and Burton dissented, Justices Frankfurter and Harlan concurred very narrowly in the result, on the particular set of facts before them, and Justice Whittaker took no part in the decision. On the basis of this voting and of the separate opinions, Congress might well have thought itself encouraged to draft a new statute dealing with jurisdiction over military dependents, especially since the alternative was either to let the murderers go unpunished or to allow them to be subject to the vagaries of the law of the particular foreign country in which the murders occurred. Each of the separate opinions also emphasized the strong disciplinary interest that the commander of an overseas base had in maintaining control over all persons attached to the base, civilian or military, and Justice Frankfurter may have even pointed a way out for Congress: "If Congress had established consular courts or some other non-military procedure for trial that did not contain all of the protections afforded by Article III and the Fifth and Sixth Amendments for the trial of civilian dependents of military personnel abroad, we would be forced to a detailed analysis of the civilian dependent population abroad in deciding

whether the *Ross* case [In re Ross, 140 U.S. 453 (1891) (upholding the constitutionality of a conviction for murder in a consular court in Yokohama)] should be extended to cover such a case." 354 U.S. at 64. If this was a hint, Congress did not pick it up. It took no advantage of the latitude left by the narrowness of the decision to provide for an alternative trial procedure. Thus, if the decision represented an attempt to force a congressional reconsideration of the statutes, it was a failure and one that resulted in a loss of American jurisdiction over military dependents abroad in such cases.

12. This interpretation of the power of the executive is the one that has been adopted by the Carter administration, and it has recently found some judicial sanction. See Goldwater v. Carter, 444 U.S. 996, 100 S.Ct. 533 (1979). But, as Justice Powell explains in his concurring Supreme Court opinion, that interpretation is not necessarily constitutionally correct: "No constitutional provision explicitly confers upon the President the power to terminate treaties. Further, Art. II, §2 of the Constitution authorizes the President to make treaties with the advice and consent of the Senate. Article VI provides that treaties shall be a part of the supreme law of the land. These provisions add support to the view that the text of the Constitution does not unquestionably commit the power to terminate treaties to the President alone." 444 U.S. at 999. Nevertheless, when faced with a challenge to the constitutionality of President Carter's action in single-handedly abrogating the defense treaty with Taiwan, the Court ordered that the complaint be dismissed, thus letting the President's action stand. Two separate rationales were relied upon in forming a majority. Justice Powell believed that, since Congress as a whole had not chosen to confront the President, the complaint was not ripe for judicial review. 444 U.S. at 997. Justice Rehnquist, writing for four justices, took the view that the basic question presented was political and therefore nonjusticiable. 444 U.S. at 1002-06.

13. In Eck v. United Arab Airlines, 15 N.Y.2d 53, 203 N.E.2d 640, 255 N.Y.S.2d 249 (1964), a California resident brought an action (to recover for injuries sustained in a crash in the Sudan) in the courts of New York where the defendant airline had a ticket office. Jurisdictional problems arose because the Warsaw Convention, under which the suit was brought, limited authorized venue to the jurisdiction of the domicile of the carrier, to that of the destination of the flight, and to that of the carrier's place of business through which the contract had been made. Following modern ticketing procedures, the plaintiff had booked her flight in California through a different airline, and thus, under a strict reading of the Warsaw Convention, there was no forum in the United States with jurisdiction over her suit. The Court of Appeals of New York, however, eschewed a literal interpretation of the treaty and instead applied a canon that, "when a treaty is invoked, *what is to be applied are its principles if its purposes are to be observed presently as in the past.*" 15 N.Y.2d at 59. The Court then noted that ticket-routing methods had changed since the negotiation of the Convention in 1926, that the goal of the Convention was to provide a constant remedy for similarly situated passengers, and that therefore the plaintiff

would not be denied a right to sue in New York. Thus in one tour de force, the New York Court of Appeals—a state court—single-handedly updated this treaty. Such an active judicial scrutiny may be a device of some usefulness in dealing with treaties, although its dangers are also clear. See also Calabresi, "Incentives, Regulation and the Problem of Legal Obsolescence," in *New Perspectives for a Common Law of Europe* 291 (Cappelletti, ed. 1978), which discusses how problems analogous to those considered here may arise under treaties providing for the unification of European laws.

14. Prior to 1970, the United States Court of Appeals for the District of Columbia Circuit acted as the highest court of the jurisdiction, hearing appeals from the District of Columbia Court of Appeals. Act of Dec. 23, 1963, Pub. L. 88-241, §1, 77 Stat. 478; see *D.C. Code Encyclopedia* §11-321 (West & Equity 1966). This situation was altered by the District of Columbia Court Reform and Criminal Procedure Act of 1970, Pub. L. 91-358, 84 Stat. 473.

15. From 1956 until 1970 the chairman of the Standing House Committee on the District of Columbia was John L. McMillan (D.-South Carolina). The regional composition of the remainder of the committee during those years was consistently and disproportionately weighted in favor of the South. These southern congressmen were frequently from rural districts and almost exclusively white. The District of Columbia was of course an important urban center and, according to the 1970 Census, predominantly black. See *U.S. Code Cong. and Admin. News,* listing congressmen and their congressional committee membership (West 1956-1970).

16. See H. Hart and A. Sacks, *The Legal Process: Basic Problems in the Making and Application of Law* (MS 1958).

17. Some of Judge Bazelon's opinions indicate that the United States Court of Appeals was trying to prompt congressional revision of old laws. In Shioutakon v. District of Columbia, 236 F.2d 666 (D.C. Cir. 1956), the court had to determine whether the 1938 revision of the Juvenile Court Act, 52 Stat. 596 (1938), D.C. Code §11-901 (1951), required the court to advise juveniles of their right to engage counsel or have counsel named in their behalf. The court noted that the aim of the statute was to create an informal, social means of disposition of cases, but then went on to state that nonetheless Congress must have intended that counsel be present: "The serious nature and effect of this adjudication suggests that Congress could not have been unaware of the need for effective assistance of counsel. Although the Act in terms neither recognizes nor withholds such assistance, the legislative history reflects congressional understanding that alleged delinquents would be represented by counsel. That there is a need for such representation to protect the child's interests is apparent, for example, from a realistic view of §11-915's provision for 'hearing.' The 'right to be heard' when personal liberty is at stake requires the effective assistance of counsel in a juvenile court quite as much as it does in a criminal court." 236 F.2d at 669 (footnotes omitted). However realistic this view of the need for counsel may have been, the Court well knew that Congress, when it passed the statute,

was attempting to create a nonadversarial forum for the reformation of juvenile offenders. The Court of Appeals, however, having witnessed the operation of the juvenile courts and noted their deficiencies over eighteen years, could be realistic and believe that counsel was needed. It could also believe that congressional consideration of the issue was unlikely, given the District of Columbia committee. Accordingly it sought to supply that need through interpretation or, alternatively, to induce the whole Congress into reexamining the question.

Similarly, in Leach v. United States, 334 F.2d 945 (D.C. Cir. 1964), the court may have been trying to force reconsideration of the procedures established for court referral of a prisoner for mental examination. Under D.C. Code §§24-106 and 24-301(a), courts were authorized to refer prisoners for such examination at their discretion. Furthermore, it appears that the clear intent of Congress in providing this procedure was that it would be invoked only in those few cases where a defendant desired to enter a pretrial plea of guilty and the judge entertained some doubt that the defendant was mentally competent to do so. 334 F.2d at 956-957 (Bastian, J., dissenting). Yet Judge Bazelon held that a judge's decision not to refer a prisoner for mental examination was an abuse of discretion, evidently finding that the congressional provision which permitted trial courts to engage psychiatrists required their use, the clear discretionary language of the statute and the legislative history notwithstanding. 334 F.2d at 948-951.

18. A spectacular example of a determined Court of Appeals refusing to recognize congressional intent is the case of the Three Sisters Bridge. Congress had authorized several highway projects in the metropolitan Washington area, including the Three Sisters Bridge. Hearings on the location for the bridge were held in 1964. There was substantial local opposition to the bridge, and in 1967 an action was brought to halt construction. D.C. Fed'n of Civic Ass'ns v. Airis, 275 F. Supp. 540 (D.D.C. 1967). The District Court refused to halt construction, and an appeal was taken to the United States Court of Appeals for the District of Columbia Circuit. That court granted an injunction, finding that there was no compliance with the guidelines of the D.C. Code, Title 7, on planning and construction. It rejected the defendant's contentions that Congress, by appropriating the money, had approved the project and intended to override the provisions of Title 7, in view of the fact that Congress had not mentioned the bridge project by name (while it had mentioned others). D.C. Fed'n of Civic Ass'ns v. Airis, 391 F.2d 478 (D.C. Cir. 1968). Shortly thereafter, Congress passed the Federal-Aid Highway Act of 1968, Pub. L. 90-495, 82 Stat. 815 (1968), §23 of which directed that all construction should begin as soon as possible on all interstate routes within the District described in certain reports, and should be carried out in accordance with all applicable provisions of Title 23 of the United States Code. The Act specifically directed work on the Three Sisters Bridge to begin within thirty days of enactment. An action to halt construction was once again brought. Judge Sirica in the District Court held that Congress' passage of the Federal-Aid Highway Act of 1968

exempted the Three Sisters Bridge from the requirements of the D.C. Code, Title 7. D.C. Fed'n of Civic Ass'ns v. Volpe, 308 F. Supp. 423 (D.D.C. 1970). On appeal, the Court of Appeals (Skelly Wright, J.) vacated and remanded, finding that the Act required compliance with the provisions in Title 23 of the United States Code and finding no basis on record for determining whether the Secretary of Transportation had made certain findings. D.C. Fed'n of Civic Ass'ns v. Volpe. 434 F.2d 436 (1970).

Such an interpretation of congressional intent was strained at best and clearly did not accord with the interpretation of intent given by the House Committee on Appropriations' Subcommittee on the District of Columbia. Congressman Natcher, the chairman of that subcommittee, was incensed by the delay in construction, and during the course of this litigation he had announced that funds for the metropolitan rapid transit system and other appropriations would be held hostage until the 1968 Act was complied with. The Senate Committee on the District of Columbia and the President also urged the District of Columbia to resolve the impasse. The City Council bowed to this pressure on Aug. 9, 1969, and approved the bridge by a margin of six to two; three members who voted in favor of the project stated that their votes were the direct result of congressional pressure. On remand, then, Judge Sirica not only had to judge compliance with the provisions of Title 23, but also had to deal with new contentions that the City Council and the Secretary of Transportation had based their decisions on political pressures rather than the merits of the proposal. Sirica found that the motives of the council were irrelevant and that the Secretary of Transportation had indeed based his determinations on the merits, but that there had not been full compliance with Title 23. D.C. Fed'n of Civic Ass'ns v. Volpe, 316 F. Supp. 754 (D.D.C. 1970). On appeal, once again, the Court of Appeals found that there was still no compliance with Title 23. Furthermore, Judge Bazelon, in what may have been intended as a warning, stated that Congressman Natcher's use of pressure to speed the construction of the bridge would have been cause in itself to invalidate all actions taken by the Secretary of Transportation; Judge Fahy suggested that those actions would be invalid only if based wholly or in part on pressure from Natcher, but he found no evidence to that effect in the record. The case was remanded to the District Court with instructions to return the case to the Secretary for performance of his statutory function as delineated by the Court of Appeals. Construction was enjoined until there was compliance. D.C. Fed'n of Civic Ass'ns v. Volpe, 459 F.2d 1231 (1971), *cert. denied* 405 U.S. 1030 (1972).

19. I am by no means suggesting that this factor fully explains the Bazelon court. I do suggest, however, that an actively inclined judge finding himself in the United States Court of Appeals for the District of Columbia Circuit before 1970 would react to the unique situation there and carry others with him because, consciously or not, they too had to confront the problem of the blatantly unmajoritarian laws of that jurisdiction.

20. The District of Columbia Court Reform and Criminal Procedure

Act of 1970, supra note 14, reorganized the courts of the District of Columbia so that its Court of Appeals is now the highest court of the jurisdiction. The District of Columbia Self-Government and Governmental Reorganization Act of Dec. 24, 1973, Pub. L. 93-198, 87 Stat. 774, lessened the direct power of Congress over the District.

21. For a discussion of how common law adjudication dealing with issues in the specific context of a case can affect how issues look, and hence be desirable on grounds other than the need for continuity and change, see Chap. IX, note 23.

22. E.g., Baker v. Texas & Pacific Ry. Co., 359 U.S. 227 (1959), Dick v. New York Life Ins. Co., 359 U.S. 437 (1959), and Rogers v. Missouri Pacific Ry. Co., 352 U.S. 500 (1957) (FELA-Jones Act cases); Brown v. Merlo, 8 Cal. 3d 855, 506 P.2d 212, 106 Cal. Rptr. 388 (1973), Schwalbe v. Jones (I), 14 Cal.3d 1, 534 P.2d 73, 120 Cal. Rptr. 585 (1975), Schwalbe v. Jones (II), 16 Cal. 3d 514, 546 P.2d 1033, 128 Cal. Rptr. 321 (1976), and Cooper v. Bray, 21 Cal.3d 841, 582 P.2d 604, 148 Cal. Rptr. 148 (1978) (California guest statute decisions); Li v. Yellow Cab Co., 13 Cal.3d 804, 532 P.2d 1226, 119 Cal. Rptr. 858 (1975) (comparative negligence in California); and Vincent v. Pabst Brewing Co., 47 Wis.2d 120, 177 N.W.2d 513 (1970) (comparative negligence in Wisconsin).

23. Landis, "Statutes and the Sources of Law," in *Harvard Legal Essays* 213, 222 (1934).

24. Moragne v. State Marine Lines, 398 U.S. 375 (1970).

25. Vincent v. Pabst Brewing Co., 47 Wis. 2d 120, 177 N.W.2d 513 (1970).

26. Cf. *Conn. Gen. Stat. Ann.* §53-30 (West 1960) (held void in Abele v. Markle, 342 F. Supp. 800 (D. Conn. 1972)), and *Conn. Gen. Stat. Ann.* §53-32 (West 1960) (held void in Griswold v. Connecticut, 381 U.S. 479 (1965)). See also Chap. II, note 3.

27. See *Conn. Gen. Stat.* §10-63 (1979).

28. Hadley v. Junior College Dist. of Metro. Kansas City, Missouri, 397 U.S. 50 (1970). In this case the Court invalidated a Missouri apportionment plan, pursuant to which 50 percent of the defendant's trustees were elected from a district containing approximately 60 percent of the college district's total school-age population. Because the college district possessed important governmental powers that had a significant impact throughout the district, the Court determined that the one-man-one-vote principle must be applied. Relying on the rule laid down in *Hadley,* the Second Circuit, in Baker v. Regional High School Dist. No. 5, 520 F.2d 799 (2d Cir. 1975), invalidated the apportionment plan of two regional school districts. Each was composed of towns with substantial population differences but had a school board on which each town was equally represented. The court required the application of one-man-one-vote principles.

29. I believe this approach to be the thrust of Justice Stevens' decisive opinion in Califano v. Goldfarb, 430 U.S. 199, 217 (1977) (Stevens, J., concurring). See Chap. II, notes 6-11.

30. Pub. L. 94-553, Title I, §107, Oct. 19, 1976, 90 Stat. 2541, codified at 17 U.S.C.A. §107 (West 1980 Supp.), was enacted to deal with the problems of fair use and the reproduction, mostly by photocopying, of copyrighted materials for educational and scholarly purposes. This act came many years after the development of photocopiers and at least nine years after the problems posed by that development were brought to the attention of Congress. See H.R. Rep. No. 83, *Copyright Law Revision, House Judiciary Committee*, 90th Cong., 1st Sess. (1967). See also Chap. VII, note 19.

31. Landis, supra note 23, at 222.

32. See H. L. A. Hart, *Law, Liberty, and Morality* 68-73 (1963), suggesting that morality changes but only through a gradual evolutionary process.

33. Nonprimacy of Statutes Act, Minn. Senate File 557, House File 1437 (1979). See also Davies, "A Response to Statutory Obsolescence: The Nonprimacy of Statutes Act," 4 *Vermont L. Rev.* 203 (1979).

34. Cf. Paul Freund's comment differentiating the Warren Court from the old New Deal Court on the ground that "the Warren Court struck down old laws which may or may not have reflected current political values, whereas the Court in the 1930s struck down recently passed laws . . . [The] Court should feel freer to review old laws to see if they still comport with current political beliefs and values." Cooper, "Freund: 40 Years of Supreme Court History Recalled," 64 *Harv. L. Record* 1 (Mar. 18, 1977).

35. See Wellington, "Common Law Rules and Constitutional Double Standards: Some Notes on Adjudication," 83 *Yale L. J.* 221 (1973); Wellington and Albert, "Statutory Interpretation and the Political Process: A Comment on Sinclair v. Atkinson," 72 *Yale L. J.* 1547 (1963); and Bickel and Wellington, "Legislative Purpose and Judicial Process: The Lincoln Mills Case," 71 *Harv. L. Rev.* 1 (1957).

36. E. Levi, *An Introduction to Legal Reasoning* (1949), discussed in Chap. IV, note 29.

37. See text at notes 49-51, infra.

38. Thus Rupert Cross, in commenting on the House of Lords decision to permit the overruling of precedents, see Chap. I, note 12, wrote: "The House will probably act on the Statement . . . perhaps more readily when the decision to be overruled is a recent one." He also noted that it would "probably act on [it] less readily in cases of statutory interpretation than in those involving points of common law." Cross, "The House of Lords and the Rules of Precedent," in *Law, Morality and Society: Essays In Honour of H. L. A. Hart* 145, 160 (Hacker and Raz eds. 1977). This last comment reflects the point of view frequently associated in this country with Edward Levi. See Chap. IV, note 29.

39. See Chap. VII, text at note 25.

40. The Miller-Tydings Act of 1937, permitting individual states to enact fair trade laws under which manufacturers might contractually bind retailers to honor fixed sales prices, was enacted during the Depression. At

that time, "the economic atmosphere was quite unlike that which prevails today. Prices, rather than rising rapidly across the board, were actually falling in some sectors of the economy. Real income, and with it demand, fell precipitously with the consequence that price competition was extraordinarily intense. Under this pressure, and in the face of growing competition from large retail outlets with the advantages of scale economies, small retail outlets foundered annually by the thousand . . . Against this backdrop, many argued that the high rates of business failures, though due to many factors, was too high a price to pay for price competition." Engman, "The Case for Repealing 'Fair Trade,' " 7 *Antitrust L. & Econ. Rev.* 79, 80 (no. 4, 1975).

41. Rent controls are typically enacted in the face of a particular housing crisis. Willis, "A Short History of Rent Control Laws," 36 *Cornell L. Q.* 54 (1950). After the crisis passes, they are difficult to repeal. "If the history of rent control teaches any lesson, it is that once such controls have been imposed they are difficult to remove. Country after country found this to be true in the 1920s. Rent control in almost every instance had been adopted as an avowedly temporary measure, under laws of short duration, but in few cases did the legislators find it possible to dispense with controls as early as had been hoped." Id. at 71. See also Note, "Residential Rent Control in New York City," 3 *Colum. J. L. & Soc. Prob.* 30 (1967), which criticizes New York rent control laws dating from World War II as obsolete.

42. Several states have enacted laws to mitigate what has been described as a deluge of medical malpractice claims. See Chap. VII, note 31. Illinois is one state that has passed such laws. Medical Malpractice, Ill. Pub. Act 79-1434 (1976); Medical Malpractice Arbitration, Ill. Pub. Act 79-1435 (1976). See Rathnau, "The Illinois Medical Malpractice Acts: Response to Crisis," 65 *Ill. B. J.* 716 (1977). Such laws have already been criticized as anomalous in the context of the bulk of tort law and have been, in more than one case, invalidated on constitutional grounds. See Chap. VII, note 31.

43. Thus many of the laws, programs, and agencies of the New Deal may be seen as harbingers of a new consistency in the legal landscape. Federal regulation of banks, federal support of home mortgages, the development of a more extensive welfare system, and other innovations marked the path of the future and survive to this day in the extensive administrative structure of the federal government. Other New Deal laws, however, did not foreshadow a new consistency. The National Recovery Act, seeking to promote cooperative action among trade groups and to eliminate certain competitive practices, had strong elements of the syndicalism then in vogue in Fascist Italy. Cf. M. Oakeshott, *The Social and Political Doctrines of Contemporary Europe* 184-186 (2d ed. 1941) (setting forth the Italian Charter of Labor of 1927). These never took hold in the United States and, after the National Recovery Act was struck down in Panama Refining Co. v. Ryan, 293 U.S. 388 (1935), and Schechter Poultry Corp. v. United States, 295 U.S. 495 (1935), it was not repassed in any form.

44. See Chap. IX for an extended discussion of this problem.

45. Grant Gilmore, for example, has argued that the Uniform Commercial Code was written by legal conservatives and traditionalists seeking to protect a position which was on its way out. "These lawyers had perhaps become uneasily aware of the mounting indications of a new style of judicial activism. At all events they insisted on a tightly drawn statute, designed to control the courts and compel decision. To a considerable degree, they got what they wanted." Grant Gilmore, *The Ages of American Law* 85 (1977) (footnote omitted). Some codifications of law he concluded may thus represent the last gasp of a dying majority, building a dangerous bulwark against the new tide of law. The same presumably is true of more specific laws.

46. See Chap. VII on the reasons for the proliferation of statutes and the irreversibility of the process.

47. Cf. Note, "The Legitimacy of Civil Law Reasoning in the Common Law: Justice Harlan's Contribution," 82 *Yale L. J.* 258, 265-266 (1972).

48. See note 45, supra, for Gilmore's view that one such code represented the successful efforts of a dying majority.

49. See note 43, supra.

50. See A. Bickel, supra note 3; Bickel, "The Supreme Court, 1960 Term — Foreword: The Passive Virtues," 75 *Harv. L. Rev.* 40 (1961); Bickel and Wellington, supra note 35; Wellington & Albert, supra note 35; Wellington, supra note 35; Sorrells v. United States, 287 U.S. 435 (1932) (discussed in Chap. VIII, text at notes 34-38).

51. See, e.g., The National Labor Relations Act of July 5, 1935, 49 Stat. 449, codified at 29 U.S.C. §151 et seq. (1976); the Agricultural Adjustment Act of May 12, 1933, 48 Stat. 31, codified at 7 U.S.C. §601 et seq. (1976); the Fair Labor Standards Act of June 25, 1938, 52 Stat. 1060, codified at 29 U.S.C. §201 et seq. (1976); and the Securities Exchange Act of 1934, 48 Stat. 881, codified at 15 U.S.C. §789 et seq. (1976). For a discussion of New Deal legislation and the development of the Commerce Clause, see Stern, "The Commerce Clause and the National Economy, 1933–1946," 59 *Harv. L. Rev.* 645, 883 (1946).

52. The Smith Act of June 28, 1940, 54 Stat. 671, codified at 18 U.S.C. §2385 (1976), makes it a crime for anyone to advocate or teach the overthrow of the United States government or to organize societies to teach, advocate, or encourage such an overthrow. The Act clearly came close to the constitutional line. The Supreme Court, however, in Dennis v. United States, 341 U.S. 494 (1951), *rehearing denied,* 355 U.S. 936 (1958), held that the Act was constitutional, though with many ifs, ands, and buts. The passage of time has not improved the constitutional standing of the statute.

53. See Chap. II, notes 2-10; and notes 26, 29, supra. Cf. Bank of Marin v. England, 385 U.S. 99, 102 (1966) in which the Court openly used newly evolving constitutional principles to change the interpretation of a bankruptcy statute.

54. Alexander Bickel believed that courts should, by using passive virtues, avoid making many constitutional decisions. See A. Bickel, supra note 3; Bickel, "The Passive Virtues," supra note 50. Other writers disagreed, believing that avoiding the use of the constitutional power would cause it to wither away. See, e.g., C. Black, *The People and the Court: Judicial Review in a Democracy* (1960); Emerson, "Toward a General Theory of the First Amendment," 72 *Yale L. J.* 877, 893-908 (1963).

55. See also Chap. III, on the use of constitutional rhetoric. It is in this context, of laws which infringe on the penumbra of constitutional values, that Charles Black's suggestion, that at times the courts may be required by the Constitution to demand a legislative reconsideration, has its greatest impact. In this area it may indeed be the case that there exists a constitutional right to an up-to-date majoritarian review of a law, even though there is no clear constitutional right to what that law must say once reviewed. See Chap. IX, note 99.

56. See Chap. VI on indexing.

57. An administrative agency may be especially useful in performing all three of these functions: stabilizing governmental flows of money, maintaining a general compromise between major interest groups, and achieving uniformity. But judicial action may be needed to spur and frame such agency performance. See Chap. V on administrative agencies.

58. See 1931 *Wis. Laws*, Ch. 242, codified at *Wis. Stat.* §895.045 (the law was changed in 1971) (Wisconsin comparative negligence statute); Federal Employers' Liability Act of June 11, 1906, Ch. 3073, 34 Stat. 232; 1956 Pa. Laws, Act of Feb. 28, 1956, P. L. 1120, §1 (one of many state workmen's compensation laws which were undermined by inflation); 1959 *Cal. Stats.*, Ch. 3, p. 1655, codified at *Cal. Vehicle Code* §17158 (declared unconstitutional in Brown v. Merlo, 8 Cal.3d 855 (1973)) (California guest statute).

59. 1931 *Wis. Laws*, supra note 58.

60. This problem of premature court action is obviously the one posed by Vincent v. Pabst Brewing Co., 47 Wis.2d 120, 177 N.W.2d 513 (1977). After the Wisconsin Supreme Court's decision in that case, the legislature basically reenacted the old comparative negligence law, altering the negligence bar to recovery by 1 percent only. 1971 *Wis. Laws*, Ch. 47. See Chap. IV, text at notes 18-25.

61. Landis, supra note 23, at 222. See also Traynor, "Statutes Revolving in Common Law Orbits," 17 *Cath. U. L. Rev.* 401 (1968), discussing what kinds of statutes should exert gravitational force.

62. Harry Wellington has reminded me that the common law needs backwaters, areas of inconsistencies, if it is to have any future growth. His point is well taken; in any system that depends on treating like cases alike to effect change in the law, a fully consistent legal structure would tend to be a static one in which courts could not advance the law. Yet in a system of fifty-one jurisdictions, the danger that we may not have any backwaters or new eddies from which new law can grow is negligible. We can expect that

conflicts between jurisdictions will exist, and these will ensure the continued growth of the common law. The danger of being without a backwater is further reduced if we allow statutes to have a gravitational effect upon the development of the common law; legislatures will thus constantly be creating new sources of growth.

63. See Chap. VIII, note 13 and accompanying text.

64. See Chaps. XIII and XIV.

65. See, e.g., Calabresi, "Product Liability: Curse or Bulwark of Free Enterprise?" 27 *Cleveland State L. Rev.* 313 (1978). See also Chap. VII, note 30. Such suits not only overburden the courts, but create precedents for litigation in areas where it would not be justified by outdated legislation. These other suits, of course, add to the overburdening.

66. See Chap. IV, note 14.

67. See, e.g., Chap. VII, note 30.

68. See Chap. II.

69. The example used in this and the next several sentences is discussed in more detail, supra, at Chap. III, note 17.

70. See Chaps. II-IV.

XI. The Doctrine: Techniques and Feasibility

1. R. Keeton, *Venturing To Do Justice* (1969); Chayes, "The Role of the Judge in Public Law Litigation," 89 *Harv. L. Rev.* 1281 (1976). Keeton, as we have seen, advocates that courts take an active role in law reform, aggressively overruling or interpreting away out-of-date precedents, whether common law or statutory. He would make full use of techniques of prospective overruling. See note 2, infra. Keeton would not, however, have a court overrule all prior decisions that are no longer in tune with the times. For example, Keeton favors a system of first-party liability for automobile accidents, with recovery limited to economic losses, but has serious reservations about whether a court could overturn the common law rule of negligence as the basis of recovery. It is not clear whether this is because of concern for *stare decisis* or doubts about the technical competence of courts. See R. Keeton, supra, at 43-44. Chayes's article describes sympathetically the new trend of public law litigation, which, he asserts, is ever more popular in the areas of prison reform, housing, employment discrimination, and school desegregation. Chayes, supra, at 1284. This type of litigation, a historical novelty, is characterized by broad rules of standing, participation by unconventional parties, such as public interest groups, fact finding largely in the nature of empirical prediction, and continual judicial oversight after the suit has been concluded. Id. at 1288-1302.

2. Historically, statutes were prospective in their application, while judicial decisions, which only purported to find preexisting law, were generally retroactive. See Levy, "Realist Jurisprudence and Prospective Overruling," 109 *U. Pa. L. Rev.* 1, 2 (1960). With the fading of the idea that courts only discovered preexisting law, argument arose for the forthright

use of prospective overruling techniques so that the expectations of those who had relied on the old rule would not be frustrated. As Cardozo, one of the device's most respectable early proponents in this country, predicted, much of the evasion would disappear from our law forever if there were a statute allowing prospective overruling on the books. "Address of Chief Judge Cardozo," 55 *Report of N. Y.S.B.A.* 263, 297 (1932). It is perhaps no coincidence that Cardozo wrote the Supreme Court opinion holding prospective overruling to be constitutional against Fourteenth Amendment objections. Great Northern Ry. Co. v. Sunburst Oil & Refining Co., 287 U.S. 358 (1932). It is not surprising that advocates of an important judicial role in law reform, such as R. Keeton, supra note 1, and the California Supreme Court, have been partisans of prospective overruling techniques. Since the 1960s, at least six techniques of prospective overruling have emerged: (1) purely prospective relief, (2) prospective-prospective relief, (3) prospective overruling and retrospective application to litigant only, (4) prospective overruling and application to all cases that have not reached final judgment, (5) retroactivity only to those cases that have not reached final judgment in which the issue decided was properly raised, and (6) prospective retroactive overruling.

(1) Relief can be purely prospective, as in Westbrook v. Mihaly, 2 Cal. 3d 765, 87 Cal. Rptr. 839, 471 P.2d 487 (1970). In this sort of case, the party attempting to change the law wins on principle but loses the case.

(2) Prospective-prospective relief, or judicial sunsetting, is one of the most creative techniques employed. See, e.g., Spanel v. Mounds View School Dist. No. 621, 264 Minn. 279, 118 N.W.2d 795 (1962), and In re Jeruzal's Estate, 269 Minn. 183, 130 N.W.2d 473 (1966). These cases overruled sovereign immunity and old precedents exempting Totten trusts from the spouse's indefeasible share, but the decisions were not to be effective until the adjournment of the next legislative session. This technique at once gave the legislature time to reconsider the court-made rule and gave municipalities time to purchase liability insurance, or spiteful husbands and wives the opportunity to replan their estates to cut off their spouses. Although its application in the latter case seems questionable, this approach is desirable where giving affected parties a chance to plan in accordance with the new law is important, or where there are special reasons for encouraging legislative action. See Note, "Prospective-Prospective Overruling," 51 *Minn. L. Rev.* 79 (1966).

(3) Neither of the first two techniques, however, provides a benefit to the parties who brought the law reform litigation. The third approach thus makes an exception to the otherwise purely prospective application of the rule for the litigants who actually brought the case in which the change is made. For them the new rule is applied retroactively. Courts applying this approach such as Stovall v. Denno, 388 U.S. 293 (1967), and Li v. Yellow Cab, 13 Cal. 3d 804, 119 Cal. Rptr. 858, 523 P.2d 1226 (1975), speak of the importance of giving rewards and incentives for litigants who would reform the law, and are notably devoid of sympathy for the losing party in

the action even though that party alone among all potential reliants feels the brunt of retroactive application. See notes 11-14, 25, infra.

(4) The different treatment given by this approach to the single winning litigant has been sharply criticized. E.g., Traynor, "Quo Vadis: Prospective Overruling: A Question of Judicial Responsibility," 28 *Hastings L. J.* 533 (1977). Traynor advocates a fourth technique: permitting all cases that have not reached final judgment to have the benefit of the new rule of law.

Traynor's suggested technique appears to be best suited to cases like Miranda v. Arizona, 384 U.S. 436 (1966), in which only a few of many defendants who raised the same legal issue were arbitrarily selected as parties. The Court, applying the third technique, gave retroactive relief to those selected parties alone, while other equally avid and deserving potential "law reformers" remained in prison. In other situations, however, Traynor's broader application of retroactivity might not be appropriate. For example, in a case where a court is changing the contributory negligence rule to one of comparative negligence, it might be a matter of indifference to the insurance company if the plaintiff in the law reform action received the benefit of retroactive relief, but the insurance company could have just grounds for complaint if the new rule were applied retroactively—and unexpectedly—to a whole series of cases that had not reached final judgment. See note 14, infra, and accompanying text.

(5) A fifth technique, a bit narrower than Traynor's, was employed by the Florida Supreme Court in Hoffman v. Jones, 280 So.2d 431 (Fla. 1973). Relief was granted to the litigating parties and also to controversies that had not reached final judgment, but only if the issue decided in the case had been properly raised. Under this technique, then, retroactivity is limited to those who have guessed or calculated that the precedent overruled was moribund.

(6) Finally, a technique, dubbed prospective retroactive overruling by a writer critical of the approach, was applied in Whitney v. City of Worcester, 373 Mass. 208, 366 N.E.2d 1210 (1977). See Note, "Prospective Retroactive Overruling: Remanding Cases Pending Legislative Determinations of Law," 58 *Boston U. L. Rev.* 818 (1978). In *Whitney,* the Supreme Judicial Court of Massachusetts continued the trial of the case "at least until definitive legislation as to governmental [tort] immunity is enacted, or until the January, 1978, legislative session ends without enactment of such legislation. Similar cases involving other litigants . . . shall be entitled to similar treatment, on any motion of any party." 373 Mass. at 226, 336 N.E.2d at 1220. In effect, the court threatened to abolish municipal tort immunity and to do so retroactively to the date of the *Whitney* decision. (In fact, in this case the retroactivity would reach back to an earlier decision, which had recounted the stupidities of the doctrine in a somewhat more subtle plea to the legislature.) Soon after, the legislature did act. The statute passed, however, abrogated governmental immunity, but explicitly denied retroactive application so that neither the *Whitney*

plaintiff nor others in similar cases would recover. "Prospective Retroactive Overruling," supra, at 833-836. The apparent aim of this sixth technique is to obtain the benefits of the prospective-prospective technique, while giving to litigating parties the benefits of the new rule they helped to bring about. Ironically, the action of the legislature in denying the benefit of the reform to the litigating parties stripped the court's action of its calculated effect.

The third technique (allowing retroactivity for the single winning litigant) could perhaps be profitably replaced by the first or second techniques (allowing prospective relief only), coupled with a statutory reward for inventive litigating parties who brought about law reform, with responsibility vested in the discretion of the supreme court of the jurisdiction to make the award. This system would be much like the discretionary award of attorney's fees, except that the award would have to come from a special state fund created for the purpose. Such a system would directly reward those litigants responsible for reform and so provide incentives for future law reform. The system would also protect the losing party, who reasonably relied upon the now overturned statute from being the sole bearer of the cost of the losing litigation. Cf. R. Keeton, supra note 1, at 35-36.

Others would argue for the application of one or the other approaches without seeing the necessity for the statutory incentive for law reform. It could be argued that, even apart from institutional litigants whose incentive lies in the prospective effect of their victory, see notes 14, 26-30, infra, litigants will find sufficient incentive to try for law reform on the chance that the law will be changed retroactively in their case. For this quasi-system to work, however, courts must resist clarifying the factors upon which the decision on prospective or retroactive application is made.

3. See Vincent v. Pabst Brewing Co., 47 Wis.2d 120, 177 N.W.2d 513 (1970), discussed in Chap. IV, notes 16-25, and esp. note 21, supra. If the justices had revealed their view of what negligence law should exist in Wisconsin, interest groups who wished the law to conform with the judicial position might have tried to prevent action by the legislature. In so doing, they might well have been able to block legislative action, even if a majority of the legislature disagreed with the judicial position. Thus stating a judicial position may be dangerous, although often it is neither possible nor desirable for a court to hide the position it would take on the merits of an issue.

4. Indeed, the examples go further and indicate to a surprising extent (given the lack of a formal doctrine and the need, therefore, to rely on subterfuges) that the decision on whether or not to update itself depends more on the substantive issues and technical problems involved than on the presence or absence of a statute.

5. Maki v. Frelk, 40 Ill.2d 193, 239 N.E.2d 445 (1968), *reversing* 85 Ill. App. 2d 439, 229 N.E. 2d 284 (1967). "The General Assembly has incorporated the present doctrine of contributory negligence as an integral part of statutes dealing with a number of particular subjects . . . and the legislative branch is manifestly in a better position than is this court to con-

sider the numerous problems involved." 40 Ill.2d at 197, 239 N.E.2d at 447.

6. In the torts field, the Illinois Supreme Court had recently overruled at least two longstanding common law precedents. Suvada v. White Motor Co., 32 Ill.2d 612, 210 N.E.2d 182 (1965) (discarding privity as a prerequisite to product liability suit); Molitor v. Kaneland Community Unit Dist., 18 Ill.2d 11, 163 N.E.2d 89 (1959) (eliminating school tort immunity). In those cases, the court noted, "We closed our courtroom doors without legislative help and we can likewise open them." Suvada v. White Motor Co., 32 Ill.2d at 623, 210 N.E.2d at 188, quoting with approval Molitor v. Kaneland Community Unit Dist., 18 Ill.2d at 25, 163 N.E.2d at 96.

7. Wisconsin's experience has already been discussed; see Vincent v. Pabst Brewing Co., supra note 3. The California case adopting comparative negligence was Li v. Yellow Cab Co., 13 Cal.2d 804, 119 Cal. Rptr. 858, 532 P.2d 1226 (1975). The California situation was somewhat different in that the court was dealing with a more malleable statute since its Code was historically subject to more flexible interpretation than is common with other types of statutes. See Chap. VIII, notes 4-9, and Gilmore, "Putting Senator Davies in Context," 4 *Vermont L. Rev.* 233, 242-244 (1979).

8. Loui v. Oakley, 50 Haw. 260, 438 P.2d 393 (1968), did not explicitly call for legislative reconsideration but, relying on the intermediate court decision in Maki v. Frelk (which had not been reversed), intimated that "It may be time to reconsider the applicability of the doctrine of contributory negligence, a judge-made rule, in light of the mores of the day. Perhaps it should be judicially replaced by a comparative negligence standard, as an Illinois court has done after concluding that the doctrine of contributory negligence is 'unsound and unjust under present conditions,' and that courts have 'not only the right, but the duty to abolish the defense.' " 50 Haw. at 265 n.5, 438 P.2d at 397 n.5, quoting Maki v. Frelk, 85 Ill. App. 439, 452, 229 N.E.2d 284, 291 (1967), *reversed,* 40 Ill.2d 193, 239 N.E.2d 445 (1968). It should be noted that the footnote quoted above was purest dictum, since contributory negligence was not even an issue in the case, which concerned apportionment of damages among tortfeasors. Nevertheless, the legislature took the hint and changed the law even before a case that raised the question the Court so clearly was urging could reach it.

9. Hoffman v. Jones, 280 So.2d 431 (Fla. 1973), discussed at note 2, supra and notes 11, 13, infra. The Florida Supreme Court felt compelled to argue that the rule of contributory negligence was not clear in the English common law at the time of the Declaration of Independence and hence was not codified by a catchall Florida statute. 280 So.2d at 434-35. See also note 11, infra.

10. See note 8, supra.

11. See notes 7, 9, supra. The Florida court relied on the fact that "the rule that contributory negligence is an absolute bar to recovery was—as

most tort law—a judicial creation." Hoffman v. Jones, 280 So.2d at 434. The California court felt few pangs of regret in discarding a codification of the common law contributory negligence principle. The Code section "was not intended to and does not preclude present judicial action in furtherance of the purposes underlying it." Li v. Yellow Cab Co., 13 Cal.3d at 823, 119 Cal. Rptr. at 871, 532 P.2d at 1239.

12. See Moragne v. States Marine Lines, 398 U.S. 375 (1970), discussed in text at note 15, infra.

13. The Florida Supreme Court's decision, see note 9, supra, was complicated by the fact that the District Court of Appeal, 4th District, an intermediate court in the state, had improperly overruled the rule of contributory negligence as laid down by precedents of the Florida Supreme Court. The supreme court sternly rebuked the court of appeal, but apparently in "deference" to those who had "relied" on its "overruling" decision in planning their suits, allowed a fairly wide scope of retroactivity to the comparative negligence rule. Comparative negligence would apply to all cases in which trial had not begun and to all cases in which the issue of comparative negligence had been raised. Hoffman v. Jones, 280 So.2d at 439-440.

In contrast, the California court refused to apply its holding to other litigants who had raised the comparative negligence issue. "Upon mature reflection, in view of the very substantial number of cases involving the matter here at issue which are now pending in the trial and appellate courts of this state, and with particular attention to considerations of reliance applicable to individual cases according to the stage of litigation which they have reached, we have concluded that a rule of limited retroactivity should obtain here. Accordingly we hold that the present opinion shall be applicable to all cases in which trial has not begun before the date this decision becomes final in this court, but that it shall not be applicable to any case in which trial began before that date (other than the instant case)—except that if any judgment be reversed on appeal for other reasons, this opinion shall be applicable to any retrial." Li v. Yellow Cab Co., 13 Cal.3d at 829, 119 Cal. Rptr. at 876, 532 P.2d at 1244. The special concern for plaintiff Li was concededly inequitable—"the parties involved are chance beneficiaries"—but was viewed "as an insignificant cost for adherence to sound principles of decision-making,"—namely, "to provide incentives in future cases for parties . . . to raise 'issues involving renovation of unsound or outmoded legal doctrines.' " 13 Cal. 3d at 830, 119 Cal. Rptr. at 876, 532 P.2d at 1244, quoting Mishkin, "The Supreme Court 1964 Term—Foreword: The High Court, the Great Writ, and Due Process of Time and Law," 79 *Harv. L. Rev.* 56, 60-62 (1965).

14. See note 2, supra. See also text at notes 21-22, infra. Justice Mosk concurred with the holding in *Li*, but dissented from the majority's "cavalier treatment of the recurring problem of the manner of applying a new court-made rule." Instead he would have made it clear that at least the litigants who succeed in law reform litigation would always be rewarded through retroactive application. 13 Cal.3d at 831-32, 119 Cal. Rptr. at

877, 532 P.2d at 1245. On the issues of "institutional" litigants, who care more about the principle than the case, and retroactivity, see "Prospective Overruling and Retroactive Application," 71 *Yale L. J.* 907, 945 n.192 (1962). See also notes 26-30, infra, and accompanying text.

15. Moragne v. States Marine Lines, 398 U.S. 375 (1970) (discussed in Chap. IV, note 26); the FELA-Jones Act cases: e.g., Baker v. Texas & Pac. Ry. Co., 359 U.S. 227 (1959), Dick v. New York Life Insurance Co., 359 U.S. 437 (1959), Ferguson v. Moore-McCormack Lines, 352 U.S. 521 (1957) (discussed in Chap. IV, notes 5-14); Eck v. United Arab Airlines, 15 N.Y.2d 53, 203 N.E.2d 640 (1964) (discussed in Chap. X, notes 12-13).

16. See Justus v. Atchison, 19 Cal.3d 564, 139 Cal. Rptr. 97, 565 P.2d 122 (1977) (holding that the intent of the legislature in adopting the wrongful death action was to preempt and replace any cause of action for wrongful death which might have existed at common law).

17. See Vincent v. Pabst Brewing Co., supra note 3 (discussed in Chap. IV, notes 16-25).

18. "These distinctions are so lacking in any apparent justification that we should not, in the absence of compelling evidence, presume that Congress affirmatively intended to freeze them into maritime law." 398 U.S. at 396. "The void that existed in maritime law up until 1920 was the absence of any remedy for wrongful death on the high seas. Congress, in acting to fill that void, legislated only to the three-mile limit because that was the extent of the problem. The beneficiaries of persons meeting death on territorial waters did not suffer at the time from being excluded from the coverage of the Act. To the contrary, the state remedies that were left undisturbed not only were familiar but may actually have been more generous than the remedy provided by the new Act." Id. at 398.

19. On the issue of limitation of actions, Harlan noted that the doctrine of laches was typically applied to maritime claims and said that courts in applying that doctrine "should give consideration to the two-year statute of limitations in the Death on the High Seas Act, just as they have always looked for analogy to appropriate state or foreign statutes of limitations . . . the difficulties should be slight in applying accepted maritime law to actions for wrongful death." 398 U.S. at 406. Although Harlan gave no clear instructions to lower courts as to how they were to resolve problems concerning beneficiaries and the measure of damages in future cases, the opinion strongly implies that in constructing a remedy they should borrow from the Death on the High Seas Act. The Court noted that the very expansion of the Death on the High Seas Act to include deaths in state territorial waters (accomplished in *Moragne*) was being considered by Congress, but decided this was not an argument against the Court's wise use of its inherent admiralty power. Id. at 405, n.17. Cf. Vincent v. Pabst Brewing Co., supra note 3 (the Wisconsin Supreme Court delayed acting because the legislature was considering the proposed reform).

20. See note 15, supra.

21. See text at notes 4-5, supra.

22. Cf. note 2, supra.

23. Such a rule of jury supremacy was thought not only to fit but necessarily to imply the kind of incremental decision making traditional to justifications of court power to evolve the common law. See Chap IX; Chap. X, notes 2-3; and text at notes 78-80, supra.

24. See Chap. IV, note 14.

25. Justice Frankfurter apparently believed that the Court's willingness to correct the occasional ill success of injured workers was in substantial part responsible for the failure of Congress to enact a workmen's compensation law. See Chap. IV, note 14. The individual losing litigants would not likely press for such law reform, but the union to which they belonged might very well. See text at notes 27-30, infra.

26. Cf., e.g., Reid v. Covert, 354 U.S. 1 (1957), discussed in Chap. X, note 11, which left military dependents (American civilians accompanying U.S. military forces abroad) who were accused of murder subject to no criminal penalties under United States law. The Court held that civilian defendants facing capital charges in peacetime could not constitutionally be convicted by a court-martial.

27. Congress did not, in fact, act after Reid v. Covert, see Chap. X, note 26, with the result that American military dependents in Saudi Arabia, for example, would either be subject to that jurisdiction's murder laws or be free to kill their spouses without fear of criminal law.

28. To go from the dramatic facts of Reid v. Covert to more prosaic ones, one may question whether hostile takeover firms would have succeeded in obtaining statutory reversal had the Supreme Court adhered to its rigid §16b jurisprudence rather than deciding to limit the bite of that section as it did in Kern County Land Co. v. Occidental Petroleum Corp., 411 U.S. 582 (1973). In that case hostile takeover bidder (A) purchased more than 10 percent of the stock of a target company (C), but the incumbent management of C succeeded in forming a defensive merger with company (B) in which C stockholders were to receive B stock. A was then forced to take stock of B in exchange for the stock of C it had purchased and, being blocked in its takeover bid, negotiated a binding option to sell B its stock in B. In so doing, A made a considerable profit which the newly merged company B-C sought to recover as a prohibited short-swing profit made by statutory insiders. Section 16b of the Securities Exchange Act, 15 U.S.C. §78p(b), seemed to compel a disgorging of the profits, although the legislative purpose in enacting §16b had been only to discourage trading in a company's stock by stockholders who had inside information. The Supreme Court held that in these circumstances the "involuntary" exchange of stock was not a sale under §16b. Had A lost the case it would have had little incentive to seek a legislative amendment of §16b, because such an amendment would almost certainly have been prospective only and hence no help to A.

29. Davies, "A Response to Statutory Obsolescence: The Nonprimacy of Statutes Act," 4 *Vermont L. Rev.* 203, 214-218 (1979).

30. For an example of a perhaps successful use of the blackmail techni-

que, see Teleprompter Corp. v. CBS, 415 U.S. 394 (1974). The Court staked out a rather harsh position on copyrights and suggested, 415 U.S. at 414, that the problems should be solved by Congress. A bill dealing with the issue was enacted some two years later.

31. See American Bankers Ass'n v. Connell (1978-1979 Transfer Binder), *Fed. Banking L. Rep. (CCH)* para. 97,785 (D.C. Cir. Apr. 20, 1979), *disposition noted* 595 F.2d 887. (Copy on file at Yale Law School Library.)

32. See Chap. IX, text at notes 78-80.

33. Sorrells v. United States, 287 U.S. 435 (1932). In this case, the Supreme Court, in an opinion by Chief Justice Hughes, interpreted the National Prohibition Act as silently allowing for the defense of entrapment. Permission of the defense would, of course, force acquittal, even though the listed elements of the statutory crime were met. To reach this result the Court employed a version of a clear-statement principle of interpretation, see Chap. IV, note 30, and refused to "conclude that it was the intention of the Congress in enacting this statute that its processes of detection and enforcement should be abused by the instigation of government officials of an act on the part of persons otherwise innocent in order to lure them to its commission and to punish them." Id. at 448. Three justices, Roberts, Stone, and Brandeis, would have avoided the majority's "strained and unwarranted construction," which "amounts, in fact, to judicial amendment," id. at 456, and would instead have founded the defense of entrapment on a court's inherent power over the purity of its own processes; they would in effect refuse to enforce an unfair, though constitutional, law. To this eloquent plea the majority answered, "To construe statutes so as to avoid absurd or glaringly unjust results [is] a traditional and appropriate function of the courts. Judicial nullification of statutes, admittedly valid and applicable, has, happily, no place in our system." Id. at 450.

The Hughes reading of congressional intent no longer seems very daring. After all, common law defenses of duress, necessity, and self-defense (which were not mentioned by the Supreme Court) are routinely allowed against federal criminal prosecutions without explicit statutory basis. Nevertheless, at the time of the *Sorrells* case, this interpretation apparently was a bold one; nor did any justice see a constitutional compulsion to recognize the defense of entrapment. If a principle had been available which allowed a court to nullify, pending legislative reconsideration, applications of a statute which were grossly inconsistent with the whole tenor of the law (a standard all the justices but one believed to be met in the case before them), then all but the one justice could have agreed to apply it here, even if the Hughes interpretation had been absolutely untenable because of the statute's language or history. The justices could then have faced separately the other issues that divided them: what the scope of the entrapment defense should be, and whether the judge or the jury should decide upon it. See also Chap. VIII, text at notes 34-38.

34. In Poe v. Ullman, 367 U.S. 497 (1961), a constitutional challenge

to the Connecticut birth control statute brought by a Connecticut doctor was dismissed for nonjusticiability. The plurality opinion argued that the statute's low likelihood of enforcement made discretionary refusal of jurisdiction appropriate. Bickel would have decided the case on the grounds of desuetude. The statute, in his analysis, was nullified by disuse. "The question is whether a statute that has never been enforced and that has not been obeyed for three quarters of a century may suddenly be resurrected and applied." A. Bickel, *The Least Dangerous Branch: The Supreme Court at the Bar of Politics* 148 (1962). As we saw in Chap. III, this rather aggressive use of desuetude will resolve such cases as *Poe* in the same way as the new doctrine we are discussing (if reenactment rather than mere notice is needed before an unused statute can be resurrected), but the new doctrine would also apply if the anachronistic rule of law has been consistently invoked by litigants.

Such a broader type of nullification, pending legislative reconsideration, was advocated by Bickel and Wellington as the course the Supreme Court should have taken in Textile Workers Union v. Lincoln Mills, 353 U.S. 448 (1957). The Court held there that specific performance was obtainable under §301 of the Taft-Hartley Act, that is, under federal substantive law. In the analysis of Bickel and Wellington, this may have been the (ill-considered) intent of Congress, but the Court should have ignored the legislative will even if it was unmistakable, so long as statutory language could bear such a construction, on the ground that courts lacked the institutional capacity to create a federal common law of labor contracts, case by case. Bickel and Wellington, "Legislative Purpose and Judicial Process: The Lincoln Mills Case," 71 *Harv. L. Rev.* 1, 30 (1957). Such a holding would remand the issue to Congress for a more careful reconsideration. Their analysis did not suggest that such nullification of legislative intent would operate far beyond cases of doubtful constitutionality or institutional incapacity: the remanding function's "extension should be undertaken only with great care." Id. at 39.

35. See Abele v. Markle, 342 F. Supp. 800, 805 (1972) (Newman, J., concurring). Had a stay been granted in the case, a mutually beneficial court-legislative colloquy, such as occurred in Wisconsin and Hawaii on comparative negligence (see notes 3, 8, supra), would have been more likely. See Chap. II, text at notes 40-47.

36. See note 15, supra.

37. See Chap. II, text at notes 43-47.

38. See note 8, supra.

39. See note 3, supra, and accompanying text.

40. It is, of course, almost identical to the prospective-prospective relief, or judicial sunsetting, described as the second approach to overruling of past cases in note 2, supra.

41. See notes 7, 9, supra.

42. See Chap. IX, text at notes 78-80. See also Chap. IX, note 73, and Chap. X, notes 3-5.

43. Without more, however, the use of blackmail techniques may reduce incentives to litigate in order to achieve the updating of timeworn laws. If the court issues a stay or merely threatens the legislature, the "winner" in principle may lose in the actual case. Cf. notes 29-36, supra, and accompanying text. That is why courts have worked so hard—in cases overruling common law precedents—at providing incentives to bring such suits. See note 2, supra. It may be that if the doctrine discussed in this book leads to more judicial sunsetting or prospective-prospective overruling, something like the fund discussed in note 2 will become necessary.

44. The rule against perpetuities seeks to minimize the extent to which dead-hand control can delay possession, enjoyment, and use of property. It invalidates transfers that may fail to vest (roughly, to be certain of ownership by a particular person) within "lives in being (at the time of transfer) plus 21 years." Thus, a *devise* "to be held in trust for my grandchildren who live to be 21" would be valid (because my children must necessarily be "lives in being" at my death, and my grandchildren must reach twenty-one within twenty-one years of the death of their parents—a child *en ventre sa mere* being treated as "in being"). A will bequeathing the property to grandchildren who live to be twenty-five would be void under the traditional rule. Leake v. Robinson, Chancery, 1817, 2 Mer. 363, 35 Eng. Rep. 979, is a famous old case involving a will of the latter sort. The court refused to alter the will by permitting the grandchildren to take the property at age twenty-one and so save it from the Rule, much to the Chancellor's regret: "If I could at all alter the will, I should be inclined to alter it in the way in which it seems to be probable that the testator himself would have altered it . . . It is much more than probable that he would have said, 'I do mean to include all my grandchildren, but as you tell me that I cannot do so, and at the same time postpone the vesting till twenty-five, I will postpone it only till twenty-one.' " Id. at 989.

Another notorious example of rigidity in application of the rule against perpetuities' seemingly precise commands is Jee v. Audley, 29 Eng. Rep. 1186 (Chancery, 1787). In this case a devise to "the daughters *then* living of my kinsman John Jee and his wife Elizabeth Jee" was held invalid because of the chance that the Jees would be fertile octogenarians and have an additional child after the death of the person making the will. The Chancellor felt moved to say, "I am desired to do in this case something which I do not feel myself at liberty to do, namely to suppose it impossible for persons in so advanced an age as John and Elizabeth Jee to have children, but if this can be done in one case it may in another, and it is a very dangerous experiment, and introductive of the greatest inconvenience to give a latitude to such sort of conjecture." Id at 1187. Apparently courts, in thrall to the precise numbers of the Rule, did not feel free to apply it only when its purpose would be served.

It is ironic, in view of these functionally absurd applications of the common law rule, to note the origin of the rule of perpetuities in The Duke of Norfolk's Case, 22 Eng. Rep. 931 (Chancery, 1682). The Chancellor in that case, Lord Nottingham, rested his decision on a desire to avoid "such a Chicanery of Law as will be laughed at all over the Christian World." His plea to the judiciary apparently fell on deaf ears: "Pray let us so resolve Cases here, that they may stand with the Reason of Mankind, when they are debated abroad. Shall that be Reason here that is not Reason in any Part of the World besides?" Id. at 951 (Nottingham's first argument). Nottingham was nevertheless unhappy with the substance of the decision, although he felt bound by the logic of it: "I have made several Decrees since I have had the Honour to sit in this Place, which have been reversed in another Place, and yet I was not ashamed to make them, nor sorry to be reversed by others. And I assure you, I shall not be sorry if this Decree, which I do make in this Case, be reversed too; yet I am obliged to pronounce it, by my Oath and by my Conscience." Id. at 962 (final opinion).

45. E.g., if a court were adopting a wrongful-death remedy as part of the common law, it is extremely unlikely that any precise money limit would be imposed. This sort of quantification is left to the legislature. In normal circumstances, courts will use a general rule to be applied by subsequent courts in the light of particular facts. See, e.g., Helvering v. Clifford, 309 U.S. 331, 336-337 (1940). As we saw in Chap. VII, public welfare and taxing activities of the sort frequently found in the modern state, the prime source of numerology in the law, are preeminently legislative.

46. In re Leverhulme, 169 L.T.R. 294, 298 (Ch. 1943): "I hope that no draftsman will think that because of my decision to-day he will necessarily be following a sound course if he adopts the well-known formula referring to descendants living at the death of the testator of her late Majesty Queen Victoria. When that formula was first adopted there was, no doubt, little difficulty in ascertaining when the last one of them died. As a result of my decision the clause in question can still be validly employed in the case of a testator dying in 1925, but I do not at all encourage anyone to use the formula in the case of a testator who dies in the year 1943 or at any later date." The court was referring to the great administrative problem that would be required in searching for the whereabouts of the hundreds of descendants of the queen's line, particularly since the existence of an entire branch, that associated with one daughter of Tsar Nicholas, Anastasia, was unclear.

47. See notes 15, 18-19, sura.

48. Helvering v. Clifford, 309 U.S. 331 (1940).

49. *Clifford* involved a high-bracket taxpayer who established a five-year trust for his wife, appointing himself as trustee and giving himself broad management powers, including power to control distribution and accumulation. Clifford also retained the reversionary interest. The Internal Revenue Code, read literally, would have taxed the income to the wife, who actually received the trust income in the years in question and occupied a much lower tax bracket than did her husband. The Supreme Court, however, held that in view of Clifford's extensive control, he rather than his wife was to be deemed the recipient of the trust income. The Court

noted "that no one fact is normally decisive but that all the considerations and circumstances of the kind we have mentioned are relevant to the question of ownership." Id. at 336. Although the Supreme Court did not explicitly invite regulatory or statutory clarification of the issue, both came in relatively short order, making more mechanical, easily applicable rules of thumb out of the Court's multifaceted analysis. In 1945, T.D. 54881, the famous "Clifford Regulations," were issued; their essence was codified in 1954 at 26 U.S.C. §§673-75.

50. It is not merely fortuitous that an agency — the Internal Revenue Service — was available in *Clifford.* Where a statute is found, as we saw in Chap. V, an agency to enforce it is seldom far behind. Such agencies are especially useful where statutes employ numbers. See note 45, supra.

51. Three cases were consolidated in the D.C. Circuit: American Bankers Ass'n and Tigoa State Bank v. Connell, No. 78-1337; Independent Bankers Ass'n v. Fed. Home Loan Bank Bd., No. 78-1849; and United League of Savings Ass'ns v. Board of Governors of Fed. Reserve System, No. 78-2206. Decision in all three was rendered *sub nom.* American Bankers Ass'n v. Connell, [1978-1979 Transfer Binder] *Fed. Banking L. Rep.* (CCH) para. 97,785 (D.C. Cir. Apr. 20, 1979), *disposition noted* 595 F.2d 887. (Copy on file at Yale Law School Library.)

52. See Note, "Challenging the Scope of Agency Authority in Issuing Banking Regulations: The Validity of Automatic Funds Transfer for Commercial Banks," 59 *Boston U.L. Rev.* 372 (1979).

53. American Bankers Ass'n v. Connell, supra note 51.

54. See text at notes 24-30, supra.

55. American Bankers Ass'n v. Connell, supra note 51.

56. The House Banking Committee almost immediately drafted a bill which would give financial institutions permanent authority to establish and maintain these accounts. "From the time of the Court decision [in American Bankers Ass'n v. Connell] last April 20, we on the Banking Committee have felt it was essential to move as expeditiously as possible to assure consumers throughout this Nation that these accounts could continue and that they could, in a time of inflation, have the right to earn interest on their accounts." 125 *Cong. Rec.* H12,114 (daily ed. Dec. 17, 1979) (remarks of Rep. St. Germain). Senate attempts to tie the House bill to other banking regulation made final resolution of the problem before the expiration of the court's stay on Jan. 1, 1980, impossible, but "a Christmas present to our constitutents," id., a separate bill, Pub. L. 96-161, 93 Stat. 1233 (1979), was amended and passed shortly before the court's stay was to expire on Jan. 1, 1980. The amendments to that bill authorized all the new transfer systems for ninety days, in which time it was hoped that the two chambers of the legislature would be able to agree on a more comprehensive bill. Such a bill was in fact passed on March 31, 1980: The Depository Institutions Deregulation and Monetary Control Act of 1980, Pub. L. 96-221, 94 Stat. 145 (1980). See also American Bankers Ass'n v. Connell, supra note 51.

57. Lockard v. Commissioner, 166 F.2d 409 (1st Cir. 1948), dealt with a situation analogous to *Clifford,* in which the taxpayer established a six-year trust for her husband, retaining a reversionary interest for herself. When *Clifford* was decided after the creation of the trust, the taxpayer was also required to pay tax on the income of the trust under the *Clifford* doctrine. Nevertheless, the Court of Appeals found that she was also liable for gift tax on the value of the income interest at the time of the trust's creation and rejected her claim that the taxable gifts reported before the formulation of the *Clifford* doctrine were errors: "[the taxpayer's] suggested mode of treatment may be appropriate and reasonable: the only trouble with it is that it is not sanctioned by the statutory scheme." Id. at 412. The reason for the court's refusal creatively to remodel the statutory scheme in this case was not just a desire to maximize federal tax revenue. Taxpayers themselves had relied on the statutory scheme and might in analogous circumstances wish the gift to be treated as completed. Such a case was Commissioner v. Hogle, 165 F.2d 352 (10th Cir. 1947). Since estate planning is done further in advance than income tax planning and is much more likely to be done on a one-shot basis, there is a tendency for courts to give taxpayer reliance on the statutory scheme more importance in the estate and gift tax field than to analogous problems of income taxation. See, e.g., Helvering v. Safe Deposit & Trust Co., 316 U.S. 56 (1942) (refusing to read "gross estate" for the estate tax as expansively as "income" was being read for income tax purposes).

58. Chayes, supra note 1, at 1288–1302.

59. Cf. notes 45, 50, supra. The complexity of modern law may indeed make judicial updating harder as to *all* rules, for some of the same reasons that led to the orgy of statutes in the first place — see Chap. VII. This is a different issue from the main argument of this essay and in any case cannot serve an an argument against judicial updating where, as frequently occurs, (a) a court can see what the proper replacement rule should be; or (b) parts of the new rule can be developed slowly and over time. Those states that adopted comparative negligence judicially, Chap. IV, note 19, were often quite content to let the fine points of implementation of the change await decision in proper cases. Justice Sneed's highly sophisticated opinion in Clardy v. Levi, 545 F.2d 1241, 1246 (9th Cir. 1977), pointed out that such an approach avoids the dangers of precipitate action by either courts or legislatures. Chap X, note 10, and accompanying text. Nor can it be justified where (c) the court, by finding the old rule to be out of date but staying its decree, can induce legislative or administrative reconsideration of the rule.

XII. The Role of Courts in an Age of Statutes

1. See Wellington, "Common Law Rules and Constitutional Double Standards: Some Notes on Adjudication," 83 *Yale L. J.* 221, 255 (1973); R. Dworkin, *Taking Rights Seriously* 82-86 (1977). Principles are what is viewed

as right; policies, what is useful. The former thus tend to be more stable over time and can be dealt with by courts — a body without empirical information other than that provided by common experience, but insulated from much low-level politics and with special institutional duties of fairness and even-handedness.

2. Cf. Raz, "Professor Dworkin's Theory of Rights," 26 *Pol. Stud.* 123, 135 (1980) (arguing that the principle of treating like cases alike is based on a fallacious conception of fairness).

3. See discussion of techniques in Chap. XI. Such a dialogue is of a piece and performs the same function in legitimating judicial power as the incremental nature of case-by-case adjudication performed at common law. See Chap. IX, text at notes 78-80. See also Chap. IX, note 73, and Chap. X, notes 2-4.

4. One reason why it may be appropriate that the court exert pressure on legislatures to update statutory rules is that, as Davies has emphasized: "The fundamental fact about any legislature is that it responds rather than leads." Davies, "A Response to Statutory Obsolescence: The Nonprimacy of Statutes Act," 4 *Vermont L. Rev.* 203, 228-229 (1979). There may often be no reason for individuals to believe they can obtain success by asking legislators for help, and there is frequently no self-starting legislative mechanism for law reform in controversial areas. It may thus be appropriate that a court, when confronted by concrete problems arising out of a statute, should bring them forcefully to the attention of the legislature. This does not, of course, derogate from the role of other institutions, such as law revision commissions, in bringing some anachronisms to the attention of legislatures. It simply enlarges the capacity of the system to update itself by raising for legislative review those problems that are best seen as a result of real cases or controversies, and those that are too controversial for advisory bodies to raise. See Chap. VI, notes 15-17, and accompanying text.

XIII. The Dangers of the Doctrine

1. See Chap. X on the danger of overburdening as one of three grounds for caution in employing the doctrine, but concluding that the doctrine can, properly used, lessen the burden on courts and legislatures.

2. A. Bickel, *The Supreme Court and the Idea of Progress,* 22-42 (1970).

3. Cf. J. Ely, *Democracy and Distrust* 4-5, 66-69 (1980).

4. See Chap. IX. Willfulness is entailed, since I am here assuming abuse of the doctrine by the judiciary.

5. See Chap. II, note 23. For a converse proposition, see C. Black, *The People and the Court: Judicial Review in a Democracy* 52-55 (1960), which points out that when the Supreme Court holds that a law is constitutional, such a holding carries greater impact than the narrow assertion that the law avoids constitutional infirmity. The Court's ruling conveys an aura of legitimacy to the statute. This aura is heightened when newspapers inflate a holding

that a statute is constitutionally permissible with a holding that it is constitutionally mandated. Black argues that legitimating a statute is sometimes properly part of the Court's task, but that we cannot treat every ruling of constitutionality as legitimating the law in question.

6. With the definition that *ex cathedra* papal pronouncements on faith and morals were infallible came an understandable reluctance to use such irreversible statements. (Pronouncements of this kind have been rare and have dealt with issues not susceptible to proof.) The practical unavailability of such papal statements created a demand that greater protection and authority be given to less ultimate forms of papal teachings. But as these have come to be given an aura of unchallengeable authority, they too have come to be used more sparingly, and still less formal ways of settling issues have been developed. Once again, however, the greater the use of alternative techniques to resolve controversies, the greater has been the need to regard one or more of them as beyond question. Anything else would mean that the techniques would not resolve many controversies. And so it has gone, with continuous pressure for more, and for less, authoritative means to end disputes. The analogy to the problems of adjudication we have been discussing is not, I think, too distant.

7. See Gunther, "The Subtle Vices of the 'Passive Virtues'—A Comment on Principle and Expediency in Judicial Review," 64 *Colum. L. Rev.* 1, 25 (1964). See also Chap. II (use of equal protection doctrine), Chap. IV (use of interpretation), and Chap. III (use of passive virtues).

8. While legislatures may not acknowledge that any particular law is out of phase, they nonetheless recognize the general problem of obsolescence, as indicated by the growing pressure for sunset laws (discussed in Chap. VI).

XIV. The Uses and Abuses of Subterfuge

1. See, e.g., Posner, "Some Uses and Abuses of Economics in Law," 46 *U. Chi. L. Rev.* 281 (1979); Posner, "Utilitarianism, Economics and Legal Theory," 8 *J. Legal Stud.* 103 (1979); England, "The System Builders: A Critical Appraisal of Modern Tort Theory," 9 *J. Legal Stud.* 27 (1980); Dworkin, "Is Wealth a Value?" 9 *J. Legal Stud.* 191 (1980); Calabresi, "About Law and Economics: A Letter to Ronald Dworkin," 8 *Hofstra L. Rev.* 553 (1980); Kronman, "Wealth Maximization as a Normative Principle," 9 *J. Legal Stud.* 227 (1980); Posner, "The Value of Wealth," 9 *J. Legal Stud.* 243 (1980); Coleman, "Efficiency, Utility, and Wealth Maximization," 8 *Hofstra L. Rev.* 509 (1980); Rizzo, "The Mirage of Efficiency," 8 *Hofstra L. Rev.* 641 (1980). These articles, together with articles by Epstein, Williams, Rizzo, Rubin, Fried, O'Driscoll, Landes and Posner, Komesar, and Priest, in 9 *J. Legal Stud.* 189 (1980) (Symposium on Change in the Common Law, Legal and Economic Perspectives), and articles by Dworkin, Kennedy and Michelman, Kornhauser, Posner, and Tullock in 8 *Hofstra L. Rev.* 485 (1980) (Symposium on Efficiency as a Legal

Concern), are but the latest in a long, long debate. For some earlier views, see, e.g., Fletcher, "Fairness and Utility in Tort Theory," 85 *Harv. L. Rev.* 537 (1972); Calabresi, "Concerning Cause and the Law of Torts: An Essay for Harry Kalven, Jr.," 43 *U. Chi. L. Rev.* 69 (1975); Tribe, "Ways Not To Think About Plastic Trees: New Foundations for Environmental Law," 83 *Yale L. J.* 1315 (1974); and Calabresi, "On the General State of Law and Economics Research," 28 *Acta Societatis Juridicae Lundenensis* 9 (1977). In the Thomas M. Cooley Lectures, which I delivered at the University of Michigan Law School in October 1979 under the title "Nonsense on Stilts? The New Law and Economics Twenty Years Later" and which I am in the course of writing up, I tried to summarize the current state of the debate and to give my own most recent views in far greater detail than I can here.

2. Justices Frankfurter and Black between them framed the question of constitutional balancing versus constitutional absolutes in their respective opinions and writings. Cf. Kovacs v. Cooper, 336 U.S. 77, 89 (1949), "Wise accommodation between liberty and order always has been, and ever will be, indispensable for a democratic society" (Frankfurter, J., concurring), and id., 336 U.S. at 102, "The basic premise of the First Amendment is that all present instruments of communication . . . shall be free from governmental censorship or prohibition" (Black, J., dissenting). Cf. also Feiner v. New York, 340 U.S. 315, 275 (1951), "Adjustment of the inevitable conflict between free speech and other interests is a problem as persistent as it is perplexing" (Frankfurter, J., concurring), and Konigsberg v. State Bar, 366 U.S. 36, 61 (1961), "The men who drafted the Bill of Rights did the 'balancing' that was to be done in this field" (Black, J., dissenting); cf. Frankfurter, "John Marshall and the Judicial Function" in *Of Law and Men: Papers and Addresses of Felix Frankfurter, 1939-1956* 3-30 (Elman ed. 1956), and Black, "The Bill of Rights," 35 *N.Y.U. L. Rev.* 865 (1960). Cf. also J. Ely, *Democracy and Distrust* (1980); and L. Tribe, *American Constitutional Law* (1978).

3. See G. Calabresi and P. Bobbitt, *Tragic Choices* (1977). Cf. Calabresi, "*Bakke* as Pseudo-Tragedy," 28 *Cath. U. L. Rev.* 427 (1979), where I discuss possible abuses of the tragic-choices approach.

4. See G. Calabresi and P. Bobbitt, supra note 3. See also Burt, "Why We Should Keep Prisoners from the Doctors," 5 *Hastings Center Report* 25 (Feb. 1975), where the author argues that prisoners can in some circumstances provide "free, informed consent" to psychosurgery.

5. In Reynolds v. Sims, 98 U.S. 145 (1878), the Supreme Court upheld a Mormon defendant's conviction under a Utah territorial law that made polygamy a crime. Relying on a distinction between religious beliefs, which the Court took to be beyond legislative interference, and religious practices, which might properly be regulated by the legislature, the Court found no error in the trial court's refusal to instruct the jury to consider the dictates of the defendant's faith. The distinction is more apparent than real: Would legislative prohibition of consecrating the host be a regulation of belief or of practice? A similar problem with the belief-practice distinction

was raised in Golden Eagle v. Johnson, 493 F.2d 1179 (9th Cir. 1974), *cert. denied* 419 U.S. 1105 (1975). Plaintiff in that case had been arrested for possessing peyote, which he claimed was used in the sacraments of the Native American Church of which he was a member. The Circuit Court of Appeals explicitly refused to decide the question of First Amendment protection for the sacramental use of peyote but held that, in any event, state police were not required to determine if plaintiff's possession of the drug was in bona fide pursuit of a religious belief before arresting him and seizing the drug. See also Church of Scientology of California v. Richardson, 437 F.2d 214 (9th Cir. 1971) (FDA did not infringe on church's First Amendment rights by examining publications advertising devices claimed to be therapeutic); Theriault v. Carlson, 495 F.2d 390 (5th Cir. 1974), *cert. denied* 419 U.S. 1003 (1974) (remand to District Court to hear government's expert witnesses testify that "Church of the New Song" was only a disruptive political movement), *on remand* 391 F. Supp. 578 (W.D. Texas 1975) (church held not a religion but a "sham," a "masquerade," and an "absurdity").

6. C. Black, "Mr. Justice Black, The Supreme Court, and the Bill of Rights," *Harper's Magazine* 63 (Feb. 1961).

7. See G. Calabresi and P. Bobbitt, supra note 3.

8. Id., at 24, 78-79, 195-199.

9. Cf. J. Ely, supra note 2, and Brest, "The Misconceived Quest for the Original Understanding," 60 *Boston U.L. Rev.* 204 (1980).

10. Cf. Chap. III for an account of how doctrines like delegation and vagueness have been corrupted, and Chap. IV in which the same type of corruption is discussed with respect to interpretation.

11. Justice Hugo Black held an absolutist position on freedom of speech, see note 2 supra, and he was sometimes forced to twist the notion of speech in order to square absolute protection with his opinion that certain speech-related activities could be regulated. In his dissent from the Court's opinion in Barenblatt v. United States, 360 U.S. 109, 134 (1959), he stated: "I do not agree that laws directly abridging First Amendment freedoms can be justified by a congressional or judicial balancing process. There are, of course, cases suggesting that a law which primarily regulates conduct but which might also indirectly affect speech can be upheld if the effect on speech is minor in relation to the need for control of the conduct. With these cases I agree. Typical of them are Cantwell v. Connecticut, 310 U.S. 296 [(1940)] and Schneider v. Irvington, 308 U.S. 147 [(1939)]." Id. at 141. Black joined the Court in *Cantwell* and in *Schneider* despite the presence in those opinions of language that apparently balanced interests to decide on an appropriate regulation of speech-related conduct. See Cantwell v. Connecticut, 310 U.S. at 303-304 (state may not act "unduly to infringe the protected freedom"); Schneider v. Irvington, 308 U.S. at 165. He relied on the same dichotomy in later opinions as well. See, e.g., Street v. New York, 394 U.S. 576, 609-10 (1969) (Black, J., dissenting) (flag-burning case): "If I could agree with the Court's interpretation of the record

as to the possibility of the conviction's resting on [appellant's] spoken words, I would firmly and automatically agree that the law is unconstitutional. I would not feel constrained, as the Court seems to be, to search my imagination to see if I could think of interests the State might have in suppressing this freedom of speech. I would not balance away the First Amendment mandate that speech not be abridged in any fashion whatsoever. But I accept the unanimous opinion of the New York Court of Appeals that the conviction does not and could not have rested merely on the spoken words but that it rested entirely on the fact that the defendant had publicly burned the American flag— against the law of the State of New York." See also Cox v. Louisiana, 379 U.S. 559, 575 (1965) (Black, J., dissenting and concurring).

12. It might be possible, however, to argue that judicial tricks and fictions are justified here by a desire to preserve the value of direct majoritarianism, the myth that ours is a truly democratic, majoritarian system. It seems unlikely that such a proposed justification would be tenable, for there are so many obvious antimajoritarian elements in our legislative institutions that the tension of values seems beyond hiding behind judicial fictions. Cf. Chap. XV.

13. Alexander Bickel was an absolutist on the issue of whether universities should take political stands. See A. Bickel, *The Morality of Consent* 127-142 (1975). When he was pressed, he admitted that his position was designed to prevent the taking of stands because, as is almost always the case with universities, that would be unlikely to do any good and would destroy the credibility of the school as a place open to all sections of truth. If there ever were a case where a university's political stand would demonstrably save many lives, he would, I am certain, have been willing to consider sacrificing the "integrity" of the institution and vote to take a stand. Like Justice Black, in some speech-action cases, however, he might well have denied that he was doing so. See note 11, supra.

14. The social use of our language should preclude one from responding literally to language that is used only conventionally. As Charles Black noted in his *Harper's* article, supra note 6, at 99: "Dr. Johnson, who was addicted both to accuracy and to veracity, said in substance that if one stood before a great orchard and remarked, 'There is no fruit in that orchard,' and there came 'a poring man' who found two apples and three pears, the first speaker would be right in dismissing the objection with laughter." Johnson's colleague, Bishop Berkeley, was able to make philosophical hay with this feature of language. Berkeley was able to argue that the habit in our "common discourse" to refer to things was not inconsistent with his full-blown theory of idealism and its denial of the notion of material substance. See "The Principles of Human Knowledge," in G. Berkeley, *Berkeley's Philosophical Writings* 75 (Armstrong, ed. 1965).

15. See e.g., Traynor, "Statutes Revolving in Common Law Orbits," 17 *Cath. U. L. Rev.* 401, 402 (1968). See also Chap. IV, note 28.

16. Cf. Calabresi, "*Bakke* as Pseudo-Tragedy," supra note 3, at

428-434, and Calabresi, "Concerning Cause and the Law of Torts," supra note 1, at 105-108.

17. Cf., e.g., J. Ely, supra note 2, and L. Tribe, supra note 2. I am not, of course, questioning the propriety of judicial review of statutes for constitutionality (which I accept), but only its appropriate scope.

18. See Davies, "A Response to Statutory Obsolescence: The Non-primacy of Statutes Act," 4 *Vermont L. Rev.* 203 (1979).

19. Cf. Calabresi, supra note 3, esp. at 432-434.

XV. The Choice for Candor

1. The common tendency in tort law to give conflicting signals to a jury in defining intentional wrongs is but one such trivial example. The jury may be instructed to find for the plaintiff if the defendant knew *or ought to have known* of great and probable danger — and then, despite the logical irrelevance under this "objective" standard, is permitted to hear testimony as to the defendant's state of mind and as to his or her good faith and lack of actual knowledge of the risk. Cf. Cope v. Davison, 30 Cal. 2d 193, 180 P.2d 873 (1947).

2. In his essay on Bentham, John Stuart Mill offered this appraisal of the man and his method: "Bentham's mind, as we have already said, was eminently synthetical. He begins all his inquiries by supposing nothing to be known on the subject, and reconstructs all philosophy *ab initio,* without reference to the opinions of his predecessors. He had a phrase, expressive of the view he took of all moral speculations to which his method had not been applied, or (which he considered as the same thing) not founded on a recognition of utility as the moral standard; this phrase was 'vague generalities.' Whatever presented itself to him in such a shape he dismissed as unworthy of notice, or dwelt upon only to denounce as absurd. He did not heed, or rather the nature of his mind prevented it from occurring to him, that these generalities contained the whole unanalysed experience of the human race." J. Mill, *Utilitarianism, On Liberty, Essays on Bentham* 93-94 (Warnock ed. 1969).

3. See e.g., P. Kurland, *Politics, the Constitution, and the Warren Court* 180 (1970): "Is it worse for the Court to read commands inhibitory of government from amorphous phrases that were put there by the Constitution's authors, as Harlan would do, than for it to read the same commands into specific language that can accommodate them only with difficulty, as Black would do?" See also A. Bickel, *The Least Dangerous Branch: The Supreme Court at the Bar of Politics* 85-110 (1962), and Freund, "Mr. Justice Black and the Judicial Function," 14 *U.C.L.A. L. Rev.* 467, 471 (1967) ("Some Metatextual standards are inescapable").

4. Cf., e.g., Gunther, "The Subtle Vices of the 'Passive Virtues' — A Comment on Principle and Expediency in Judicial Review," 64 *Colum. L. Rev.* 1, 25 (1964).

5. See Bickel and Wellington, "Legislative Purpose and Judicial Process: The Lincoln Mills Case," 71 *Harv. L. Rev.* 1, 39 (1957).

6. Cf. C. Black, "Mr. Justice Black, the Supreme Court, and the Bill of Rights," *Harper's Magazine* 63 (Feb. 1961); G. Calabresi and P. Bobbitt, *Tragic Choices* (1978).

7. H. Black, Jr., *My Father: A Remembrance* 143 (1970).

8. Obviously I am not here saying that his Benthamite answer is the correct one.

9. See G. Calabresi, *The Costs of Accidents: A Legal and Economic Analysis* (1970), esp. at pp. 68-94.

WORKS CITED

Ackerman and Hassler, Beyond the New Deal: Coal and the Clean Air Act, 89 Yale L. J. 1466 (1980) (5-30, 5-35).

Adams, Sunset: A Proposal for Accountable Government, 28 Admin. L. Rev. 511 (1976) (6-5).

Alderman, What the New Supreme Court Has Done to the Old Law of Negligence, 18 Law & Contemp. Prob. 110 (1953) (4-10).

Alfange, On Judicial Policymaking and Constitutional Change: Another Look at the "Original Intent" Theory of Constitutional Interpretation, 5 Hastings Const. L. Q. 603 (1978) (1-28).

American Law Institute, Proceedings, vol. I, part I (1923) (1-22, 8-10, 8-11, 8-12, 8-13).

American Political Science Association, Committee on Political Parties, Toward a More Responsible Two-Party System, 44 Am. Pol. Sci. Rev. [Supp. No. 3, Part 2] (1950) (7-8).

P. Bator et al., Hart and Wechsler's The Federal Courts and the Federal System (2d ed. 1973) (9-82).

Bell, The Referendum: Democracy's Barrier to Racial Equality, 54 Wash. L. Rev. 1 (1978) (7-7)

R. Berger, Government by Judiciary (1977) (1-28).

G. Berkeley, The Principles of Human Knowledge, in D. Armstrong, ed., Berkeley's Philosophical Writings 75 (1965) (14-14).

M. Bernstein, Regulating Business by Independent Commission (1955) (5-21, 5-26).

A. Bickel, The Least Dangerous Branch: The Supreme Court at the Bar of Politics (1962) (2-24, 3-1, 3-5, 3-7, 4-30, 8-25, 8-29, 9-9, 9-21, 9-87, 10-3, 10-50, 10-54, 11-34, 15-3).

———— The Morality of Consent (1975) (9-24, 14-13).

———— Politics and the Warren Court (1965) (2-23).

———— The Supreme Court and the Idea of Progress (1970) (8-26, 9-21, 9-92, 13-2).

_____ The Supreme Court, 1960 Term — Foreword: The Passive Virtues, 75 Harv. L. Rev. 40 (1961) (3-1, 10-50, 10-54).

_____ and Wellington, Legislative Purpose and Judicial Process: The Lincoln Mills Case, 71 Harv. L. Rev. 1 (1957) (3-1, 3-6, 3-9, 3-12, 3-21, 3-28, 3-31, 3-35, 3-37, 4-28, 8-25, 10-35, 10-50, 11-34, 15-5).

C. Black, Amending the Constitution: A Letter to a Congressman, 82 Yale L. J. 189 (1972) (7-10).

_____ Decision According to Law (1981) (2-22, 2-25, 9-9).

_____ Mr. Justice Black, The Supreme Court, and the Bill of Rights, Harper's Magazine 63 (Feb. 1961) (14-6, 14-14, 15-6).

_____ National Lawmaking by Initiative? Let's Think Twice, 8 Human Rights 28 (Fall 1979) (7-7, 7-8).

_____ The People and the Court: Judicial Review in a Democracy (1960) (10-54, 13-5).

_____ Structure and Relationship in Constitutional Law (1969) (9-94).

D. Black, The Theory of Committees and Elections (1971) (9-51).

H. Black, Handbook on the Constitution and Interpretation of the Laws (1896) (8-9).

H. L. Black, The Bill of Rights, 35 N.Y.U.L. Rev. 865 (1960) (14-2).

H. L. Black, Jr., My Father: A Remembrance (1970) (15-7).

W. Blackstone, Commentaries (Sharswood ed. 1868) (9-24).

D. Boorstin, The Americans: The National Experience (1965) (7-37).

Breitel, The Lawmakers, 65 Colum. L. Rev. 749 (1965) (9-18).

Brest, The Misconceived Quest for the Original Understanding, 60 Boston U. L. Rev. 204 (1980) (14-9).

J. Buchanan and G. Tullock, The Calculus of Consent (1974 ed.) (9-51).

E. Burke, Appeal from the New to the Old Whigs, 4 Collected Works (1865-67) (9-24).

_____ Reflections on the Revolution in France (1907 ed.) (9-24).

Burt, Why We Should Keep Prisoners from the Doctors, 5 Hastings Center Report 25 (Feb. 1975) (14-4).

Calabresi, About Law and Economics: A Letter to Ronald Dworkin, 8 Hofstra L. Rev. 553 (1980) (14-1).

_____ Bakke as Pseudo-Tragedy, 28 Cath. U. L. Rev. 427 (1979) (5-42, 9-88, 14-3, 14-16, 14-19).

_____ Concerning Cause and the Law of Torts: An Essay for Harry Kalven, Jr., 43 U. Chi. L. Rev. 69 (1975) (10-2, 14-1, 14-16).

_____ The Costs of Accidents (1970) (10-9, 15-9).

_____ Incentives, Regulation and the Problem of Legal Obsolescence, in M. Cappelletti, ed., New Perspectives for a Common Law of Europe 291 (1978) (10-13).

_____ The Nonprimacy of Statutes Act: A Comment, 4 Vermont L. Rev. 247 (1979) (1-5, 4-5, 8-3).

_____ Nonsense on Stilts? The New Law and Economics Twenty Years Later (The Thomas M. Cooley Lectures) (forthcoming) (14-1).

_____ On the General State of Law and Economics Research, 28 Acta Societatis Juridicae Lundenensis 9 (1977) (14-1).

———— The Problem of Malpractice, Trying to Round Out the Circle, 27 U. Toronto L. J. 131 (1977) (5-19, 7-31).

———— Product Liability: Curse or Bulwark of Free Enterprise?, 27 Cleveland State L. Rev. 313 (1978) (3-16, 7-31, 10-65).

———— Transaction Costs, Resource Allocation and Liability Rules — A Comment, 11 J. L. & Econ. 67 (1968) (9-7, 9-8, 10-8).

———— and Bass, Right Approach, Wrong Implications, 38 U. Chi. L. Rev. 74 (1970) (7-31).

———— and P. Bobbitt, Tragic Choices (1978) (5-42, 8-32, 9-41, 9-92, 14-3, 14-4, 14-7, 14-8, 15-6).

M. Cappelletti, ed., Judicial Review in the Contemporary World (1971) (9-82, 10-13).

Cardozo, A Ministry of Justice, 35 Harv. L. Rev. 113 (1921) (6-16, 7-20, 8-15).

———— Address, 55 Report of N.Y.S.B.A 263 (1932) (11-2).

Chayes, The Role of the Judge in Public Law Litigation, 89 Harv. L. Rev. 1281 (1976) (11-1, 11-58).

Coase, The Problem of Social Cost, 1 J. L. & Econ. 3 (1960) (9-7).

Coleman, Efficiency, Utility, and Wealth Maximization, 8 Hofstra L. Rev. 509 (1980) (14-1).

Comment, Recent Medical Malpractice Legislation — A First Checkup, 50 Tul. L. Rev. 655 (1976) (7-29).

Cooper, Freund: 40 Years of Supreme Court History Recalled, 64 Harv. L. Record 6 (March 18, 1977) (10-34).

Cross, The House of Lords and the Rules of Precedent, in Law, Morality and Society: Essays in Honor of H. L. A. Hart, (P. Hacker & J. Raz, eds., (1977) (10-38).

L. Cutler, To Form a Government, Speech (1980) (on file in Yale Law School Library) (7-2, 7-8).

———— and Johnson, Regulation and the Political Process, 84 Yale L. J. 1395 (1975) (5-11, 5-43, 6-4, 6-11, 7-11, 8-2, 9-40, 9-61, 9-74, 9-82).

R. Dahl, Pluralist Democracy in the United States: Conflict and Consent (1967) (1-9).

———— A Preface to Democratic Theory (1956) (9-51).

———— On Removing Certain Impediments to Democracy in the United States, 92 Pol. Sci. Q. 1 (1977) (7-3, 7-8).

Dahlman, The Problem of Externality, 22 J. L. & Econ. 141 (1979) (9-7).

Dahrendorf, A Confusion of Powers: Politics and the Rule of Law, 40 Mod. L. Rev. 1 (1977) (1-28).

David, The Civil Code in France Today, 34 La. L. Rev. 907 (1974) (7-14).

Davies, A Response to Statutory Obsolescence: The Nonprimacy of Statutes Act, 4 Vermont L. Rev. 203 (1979) (1-5, 4-5, 5-41, 6-21, 7-13, 8-3, 9-44, 9-58, 9-59, 9-86, 10-33, 11-29, 12-4, 14-18).

K. Davis, Administrative Law: Cases — Text — Problems (6th ed. 1977) (5-5).

_____ Administrative Law Treatise (2d ed. 1978) (9-2).

_____ Discretionary Justice (1969) (5-31, 5-35).

Demsetz, When Does the Rule of Liability Matter?, 1 J. Legal Stud. 223 (1972) (9-8, 10-8).

Destro, Abortion and the Constitution: The Need for a Life-Protective Amendment, 63 Cal. L. Rev. 1250 (1975) (3-45).

Deutsch, Neutrality, Legitimacy and the Supreme Court: Some Intersections Between Law and Political Science, 20 Stan. L. Rev. 169 (1968) (1-28).

P. Devlin, Samples of Lawmaking (1962) (7-5).

W. O. Douglas, Go East, Young Man (1974) (6-5).

A. Downs, Inside Bureaucracy (1967) (5-19, 5-20, 5-26).

Dworkin, Is Wealth a Value?, 9 J. Legal Stud. 191 (1980) (14-1).

_____ Review of Cover, Justice Accused: Anti-Slavery and the Judicial Process, Times Literary Supp. (London), Dec. 5, 1979, at 1437 (9-34).

_____ Taking Rights Seriously (1977) (3-17, 3-29, 5-15, 5-27, 5-38, 8-16, 8-18, 8-19, 9-17, 9-19, 9-29, 9-34, 9-38, 9-54, 9-56, 12-1).

Ehrlich and Posner, An Economic Analysis of Legal Rulemaking, 3 J. Legal Stud. 257 (1974) (9-40).

J. Ely, Democracy and Distrust (1980) (9-1, 9-2, 9-4, 9-6, 9-9, 9-11, 9-15, 9-22, 9-33, 9-59, 9-60, 13-3, 14-2, 14-9, 14-17).

_____ The Wages of Crying Wolf: A Comment on Roe v. Wade, 82 Yale L. J. 920 (1973) (3-45).

Emerson, Toward a General Theory of the First Amendment, 72 Yale L. J. 877 (1963) (10-54).

Englard, The System Builders: A Critical Appraisal of Modern Torts Theory, 9 J. Legal Stud. 27 (1980) (14-1).

Engman, The Case for Repealing "Fair Trade," 7 Antitrust L. & Econ. Rev. 79 (No. 4, 1975) (10-40).

H. Finer, The Future of Government (1946) (5-3).

_____ The Theory and Practice of Modern Government (1932) (5-3).

Fleming, The Impact of Inflation on Tort Compensation, 26 Am. J. Comp. L. 51 (1978) (6-23).

Fletcher, Fairness and Utility in Tort Theory, 85 Harv. L. Rev. 537 (1972) (14-1).

_____ The Metamorphosis of Larceny, 89 Harv. L. Rev. 469 (1976) (7-39).

F. Frankfurter, John Marshall and the Judicial Function, in P. Elman, ed., Of Law and Men 3 (1956) (14-2).

_____ Some Reflections on the Reading of Statutes, 47 Colum. L. Rev. 527 (1947) (1-1).

Freedman, Crisis and Legitimacy in the Administrative Process, 27 Stan. L. Rev. 1041 (1975) (5-7, 5-22, 5-45).

Freund, Mr. Justice Black and the Judicial Function, 14 U.C.L.A. L. Rev. 467 (1967) (15-3).

L. Friedman, A History of American Law (1973) (1-1, 1-14, 1-17,

7-36, 7-37).

H. Friendly, The Federal Administrative Agencies: The Need for Better Definition of Standards (1962) (5-5, 5-9, 5-13, 5-16, 5-23, 5-35).

_____ The Gap in Lawmaking—Judges Who Can't and Legislators Who Won't, 63 Colum. L. Rev. 787 (1963) (6-15, 8-15).

_____ A Look at the Federal Administrative Agencies, 60 Colum. L. Rev. 429 (1960) (5-5, 5-6, 5-23, 9-82).

Gardner, The Administrative Process, in W. Gellhorn and C. Byse, Administrative Law: Cases and Comments 24 (6th ed. 1974) (5-13).

F. Gény, Méthode d'interpretation (1899) (9-16).

G. Gilmore, The Ages of American Law (1977) (1-1, 1-10, 1-19, 1-21, 1-22, 1-23, 3-32, 4-6, 7-1, 7-4, 7-20, 7-21, 7-25, 7-30, 7-40, 8-38, 10-45).

_____ The Death of Contract (1974) (7-4).

_____ On Statutory Obsolescence, 39 U. Colo. L. Rev. 461 (1967) (1-22).

_____ Putting Senator Davies in Context, 4 Vermont L. Rev. 233 (1979) (1-5, 8-38, 11-7).

_____ and C. Black, The Law of Admiralty (2d ed. 1975) (1-5).

G. Gunther, Constitutional Law: Cases and Materials (10th ed. 1980) (2-25, 3-23).

_____ The Supreme Court, 1971 Term—Foreword: In Search of Evolving Doctrine on a Changing Court: A Model for a Newer Equal Protection, 86 Harv. L. Rev. 1 (1972) (2-25).

_____ The Subtle Vices of the "Passive Virtues"—A Comment on Principle and Expediency in Judicial Review, 64 Colum. L. Rev. 1 (1964) (3-13, 3-15, 4-31, 4-40, 13-7, 15-4).

F. Harper and F. James, The Law of Torts (1956) (4-9, 4-30).

G. Harris, Equal Protection Nullification in Washington State: A Case Study (1981) (unpublished paper, on file in Yale Law School Library) (2-25).

Harrison, The First Half-Century of the California Civil Code, 10 Cal. L. Rev. 185 (1922) (8-4, 8-9).

H. Hart and A. Sacks, The Legal Process: Basic Problems in the Making and Application of Law (MS 1958) (1-14, 1-22, 3-33, 4-1, 4-2, 4-3, 4-28, 4-30, 6-9, 6-17, 7-8, 8-9, 8-19, 8-20, 8-21, 8-23, 8-24, 8-28, 9-17, 9-19, 9-48, 9-82, 10-16).

H. C. Hart, Crisis, Community and Consent in Water Politics, 22 Law & Contemp. Prob. 510 (1957) (6-8).

H. L. A. Hart, Changing Conceptions of Responsibility, in Punishment and Responsibility: Essays in the Philosophy of Law 186 (1968) (9-53).

_____ Law in the Perspective of Philosophy, 1776–1976, 51 N. Y. U. L. Rev. 538 (1976) (9-34, 9-35, 9-36, 9-53).

_____ Law, Liberty and Morality (1963) (9-53, 10-32).

Hector, Problems of the CAB and the Independent Regulatory Commissions, 69 Yale L. J. 931 (1960) (5-16).

Hellner, Indexing of Tort Awards in Sweden, 26 Am. J. Comp. L. 71 (1978) (6-23).

R. Hofstadter, The Age of Reform (1955) (6-8).

O.W. Holmes, Collected Legal Papers (1921) (9-14).

Holt, The New Deal and the American Anti-Statist Tradition, in J. Braeman, ed., The New Deal (1975) (5-2).

M. Horwitz, The Transformation of American Law, 1780–1860 (1977) (1-1, 7-20, 7-37, 7-39, 9-83).

H. Humphrey, The Political Philosophy of the New Deal (1970) (5-2).

Jaffe, Administrative Process Re-examined: The Benjamin Report, 56 Harv. L. Rev. 704 (1943) (5-5).

—————— The Effective Limits of the Administrative Process: A Reevaluation, 67 Harv. L. Rev. 1105 (1954) (5-22).

—————— An Essay on Delegation of Power, Part I, 47 Colum. L. Rev. 359 (1947) (5-5).

T. Jefferson, The Writings of Thomas Jefferson (Paul Ford, ed., 1895) (6-2).

R. Kagan, Regulatory Justice (1978) (5-17).

R. Keeton, Venturing To Do Justice (1969) (1-30, 4-2, 4-3, 4-4, 4-30, 7-21, 8-17, 8-30, 11-1, 11-2).

Kirkpatrick, Toward a More Responsible Two-Party System: Political Science, Policy Science, or Pseudo-Science?, 65 Am. Pol. Sci. Rev. 965 (1971) (7-8).

J. Krier and E. Ursin, Pollution and Policy (1977) (6-8).

Kronman, Wealth Maximization as a Normative Principle, 9 J. Legal Stud. 227 (1980) (14-1).

P. Kurland, Politics, the Constitution and the Warren Court (1970) (15-3).

W. LaFave and A. Scott, Handbook of Criminal Law (1972) (7-39).

Lagrange, The French Council of State (Conseil d'Etat), 18 Tulane L. Rev. 46 (1968) (9-82).

Landes and Posner, The Independent Judiciary in an Interest-Group Perspective, 18 J. L. & Econ. 875 (1975) (9-40).

J. Landis, The Administrative Process (1938) (5-1, 5-5, 5-16, 5-19, 5-20, 5-23, 5-30).

—————— Statutes and the Sources of Law, in Harvard Legal Essays 213 (1934) (1-15, 3-37, 5-4, 7-20, 8-15, 8-17, 9-17, 9-26, 9-27, 9-28, 9-43, 9-56, 9-70, 9-73, 10-23, 10-31, 10-61).

Leach, Revisionism in the House of Lords: The Bastion of Rigid Stare Decisis Falls, 80 Harv. L. Rev. 797 (1967) (1-12).

E. Levi, An Introduction to Legal Reasoning (1949) (1-27, 3-34, 4-29, 10-36).

Levy, Realist Jurisprudence and Prospective Overruling, 109 U. Pa. L. Rev. 1 (1960) (11-2).

L. Levy, The Law of the Commonwealth and Chief Justice Shaw (1975) (7-37).

T. Lowi, The End of Liberalism (1969) (5-11, 5-16, 6-5).

MacDonald, The New York Law Review Commission, 28 Mod. L. Rev. 1 (1965) (6-17).

McKean, Product Liability: Trends and Implications, 38 U. Chi. L. Rev. 3 (1970) (7-31).

D. Mayhew, Congress: The Electoral Connection (1975) (9-51).

_____ Party Loyalty Among Congressmen (1966) (1-9).

Merryman, The Italian Style, II: Law, 18 Stan. L. Rev. 396 (1966) (7-14).

Michelman, The Supreme Court and Litigation Access Fees: The Right to Protect One's Rights, Part II, 1974 Duke U. L. Rev. 527 (1974) (3-17).

J. S. Mill, Utilitarianism, On Liberty, Essays on Bentham, M. Warnock, ed., (1969) (15-27).

Mishkin, The High Court, The Great Writ, and the Due Process of Time and Law, 89 Harv. L. Rev. 56 (1965) (11-13).

Monaghan, The Supreme Court, 1974 Term—Foreword: Constitutional Common Law, 89 Harv. L. Rev. 1 (1975) (3-3).

Morse, Theories of Legislation, 14 DePaul L. Rev. 51 (1964) (7-25).

Murphy, Review of Berger, Government by Judiciary, 87 Yale L. J. 1752 (1978) (1-28).

R. Nader, Unsafe At Any Speed: The designed-in defects of the American automobile (1965) (5-16, 6-8).

_____ and Page, Automobile Design and the Judicial Process, 55 Cal. L. Rev. 645 (1967) (6-8).

W. Nelson, The Americanization of the Common Law: The Impact of Legal Change on Massachusetts Society, 1760-1830 (1975) (1-1, 8-6).

_____ Changing Conceptions of Judicial Review: The Evolution of Constitutional Theory in the States, 1790-1860, 120 U. Pa. L. Rev. 1166 (1972) (1-16, 1-17).

_____ The Eighteenth-Century Background of John Marshall's Constitutional Jurisprudence, 76 Mich. L. Rev. 893 (1978) (8-5).

M. Nimmer, Nimmer on Copyright (1980) (7-28).

Note, California's Medical Injury Compensation Reform Act: An Equal Protection Challenge, 52 So. Cal. L. Rev. 829 (1979) (7-31).

Note, The Supreme Court of California 1975-76, 65 Cal. L. Rev. 231 (1977) (2-18).

Note, Challenging the Scope of Agency Authority in Issuing Banking Regulations: The Validity of Automatic Funds Transfers for Commercial Banks, 59 Boston U. L. Rev. 372 (1979) (11-52).

Note, Furman v. Georgia: Will the Death of Capital Punishment Mean a New Life for Bail?, 2 Hofstra L. Rev. 432 (1974) (3-41).

Note, Indexing the Principal: The Usury Laws Hang Tough, 37 U. Pitt. L. Rev. 755 (1976) (6-22).

Note, Is the Death Penalty Dead?, 26 Baylor L. Rev. 114 (1974) (3-41).

Note, The Legitimacy of Civil Law Reasoning in the Common Law: Justice Harlan's Contribution, 82 Yale L. J. 258 (1972) (4-26, 10-47).

Note, A Model Federal Sunset Act, 14 Harv. J. Legis. 742 (1977) (6-5, 6-6).

Note, Prospective Overruling and Retroactive Application in the Federal Courts, 71 Yale L. J. 907 (1962) (11-14).

Note, Prospective-Prospective Overruling, 51 Minn. L. Rev. 79 (1966) (11-2).

Note, Prospective Retroactive Overruling: Remanding Cases Pending Legislative Determinations of Law, 58 Boston U. L. Rev. 818 (1978) (11-2, 11-14).

Note, Residential Rent Control in New York City, 3 Colum. J. L. & Soc. Prob. 30 (1967) (10-41).

Note, Supreme Court Certiorari Policy in Cases Arising Under the FELA, 69 Harv. L. Rev. 1441 (1956) (4-10).

Note, Zero-Base Sunset Review, 14 Harv. J. Legis. 505 (1977) (6-4, 6-5, 6-10).

M. Oakeshott, The Social and Political Doctrines of Contemporary Europe (2d ed. 1941) (10-43).

O'Connor, Legal Reform in the Early Republic: The New Jersey Experience, 22 Am. J. Leg. Hist. 95 (1978) (8-6).

Padway, Comparative Negligence, 16 Marquette L. Rev. 3 (1931) (4-27).

Page, Statutes as Common Law Principles, 1944 Wisc. L. Rev. 175 (1944) (9-26).

Peltzman, The Benefits and Costs of New Drug Regulation, in R. Landau, ed., Regulating New Drugs 113 (1973) (5-19, 5-20).

Perry, The Abortion Funding Cases: A Comment on the Supreme Court's Role in American Government, 66 Geo. L. J. 1191 (1978) (9-32).

_____ Modern Equal Protection: A Conceptualization and Appraisal, 79 Colum. L. Rev. 1023 (1979) (2-25).

Pomeroy, The True Method of Interpreting the Civil Code, 4 West Coast Rptr. 109 (1884) (8-4).

Posner, Some Uses and Abuses of Economics in Law, 46 U. Chi. L. Rev. 281 (1979) (14-1).

_____ Utilitarianism, Economics and Legal Theory, 8 J. Legal Stud. 103 (1979) (14-1).

_____ The Value of Wealth, 9 J. Legal Stud. 243 (1980) (14-1).

Pound, Common Law and Legislation, 21 Harv. L. Rev. 383 (1908) (1-15, 2-30, 3-30, 7-20, 9-26, 9-43).

_____ Spurious Interpretation, 7 Colum. L. Rev. 379 (1907) (9-43).

W. Prosser, The Law of Torts (1971) (4-32, 4-36).

Rathnau, The Illinois Medical Malpractice Acts: Response to Crisis, 65 Ill. B. J. 716 (1977) (10-42).

Raz, Professor Dworkin's Theory of Rights, 26 Pol. Stud. 123 (1978) (2-26, 12-2).

M. Reagan, The New Federalism (1972) (7-8).

Rizzo, The Mirage of Efficiency, 8 Hofstra L. Rev. 641 (1980) (14-1).

Rostow, The Japanese American Cases—A Disaster, 54 Yale L. J. 489 (1945) (9-55).

S. Rottenberg, ed., The Economics of Medical Malpractice (1978) (7-31).

Rubin, The Abortion Cases: A Study in Law and Social Change, 5 N.C. Central L. J. 215 (1974) (3-45).

Schlesinger, Sources of the New Deal, in A. Schlesinger, Jr., and M. White, eds., Paths of American Thought 372 (1963) (5-1).

Schrock and Welsh, Reconsidering the Constitutional Common Law, 91 Harv. L. Rev. 1117 (1978) (3-3).

J. Schumpeter, Capitalism, Socialism, and Democracy (1950) (5-37).

B. Schwartz, The Reins of Power: A Constitutional History of the United States (1963) (4-29).

W. Schwartz, Comparative Negligence (1974 and 1978 Supp.) (4-18).

Segal, You Can Fight City Hall: Take the Initiative, 133 Read. Dig. 106 (October, 1978) (7-3).

Shapiro, Judicial Modesty, Political Reality and Preferred Position, 47 Cornell L. Q. 175 (1961) (9-9, 9-11).

S. Speiser, Recovery for Wrongful Death (2d ed. 1975) (4-32, 4-33).

L. Steffens, The Shame of the Cities (1904) (6-8).

Stern, The Commerce Clause and the National Economy, 1933-46, 59 Harv. L. Rev. 645 (1946) (5-1, 5-5, 10-51).

Stewart, The Reformation of American Administrative Law, 88 Harv. L. Rev. 1667 (1975) (5-7).

Stone, The Common Law in the United States, 50 Harv. L. Rev. 4 (1936) (1-15, 5-41, 7-20, 8-15, 8-17, 9-17, 9-24, 9-40, 9-43).

J. Stone, The Province and Function of Law (1946) (9-16).

J. Sundquist, Politics and Policy (1968) (7-8).

Sutton, The English Law Reform Commission: A New Philosophy of Law Reform, 20 Vanderbilt L. Rev. 1009 (1967) (6-17).

Symposium, Change in the Common Law: Legal and Economic Perspectives, 9 J. Legal Stud. 189 (1980) (14-1).

Symposium, Efficiency as a Legal Concern, 8 Hofstra L. Rev. 487 (1980) (14-1).

Symposium, Product Liability Law: The Need for Statutory Reform, 56 N.C.L. Rev. 623 (1978) (7-31).

Traynor, Quo Vadis: Prospective Overruling: A Question of Judicial Responsibility, 28 Hastings L. J. 533 (1977) (11-2).

_____ Statutes Revolving in Common-Law Orbits, 17 Cath. U. L. Rev. 401 (1968) (1-1, 1-14, 7-9, 8-15, 8-17, 8-18, 9-1, 9-17, 9-18, 9-19, 9-21, 9-26, 9-28, 9-31, 9-39, 9-43, 9-56, 9-67, 9-95, 10-61, 14-15).

L. Tribe, American Constitutional Law (1978) (2-1, 9-99, 14-2, 14-17).

_____ Ways Not To Think About Plastic Trees, 83 Yale L. J. 1315 (1974) (14-1).

D. Truman, The Governmental Process (1951) (7-34).

Twerski, Rebuilding the Citadel: The Legislative Assault on the Common Law, 15 Trial 55 (Nov. 1979) (7-31).

Tyler, Court Versus Legislature: The Sociopolitics of Malapportionment, 27 Law & Contemp. Prob. 390 (1962) (9-10, 9-11).

W. Webb, The Great Plains (1931) (7-37, 9-64).

Wellington, Common Law Rules and Constitutional Double Standards: Some Notes on Adjudication, 83 Yale L. J. 221 (1973) (3-1, 3-17,

3-28, 3-31, 4-2, 4-28, 4-30, 5-15, 5-27, 5-38, 7-37, 8-19, 9-17, 9-19, 9-29, 9-35, 9-41, 10-35, 10-50).

_____ and Albert, Statutory Interpretation and the Political Process: A Comment on Sinclair v. Atkinson, 72 Yale L. J. 1547 (1963) (3-1, 3-11, 3-28, 4-28, 8-27, 8-31, 10-35, 12-1).

Willis, A Short History of Rent Control Laws, 36 Cornell L. Q. 54 (1950) (10-41).

W. Wilson, Congressional Government: A Study in American Politics (1885) (7-8, 7-38).

Wise, The Doctrine of Stare Decisis, 21 Wayne L. Rev. 1043 (1975) (1-12).

Table of Cases

Index